1995

West African societies were transformed by the slave trade, even in regions where few slaves were exported. While many books have been written on the import and export trade and on warrior predation, Dr. Searing's concern is with the effects of the Atlantic slave trade on the societies of the Senegal River valley in the eighteenth century. He shows that the growth of the Atlantic trade stimulated the development of slavery within West Africa. Slaves worked as seamen in the river and coasting trades, produced surplus grain to feed slaves in transit, and sometimes came to hold pivotal positions in the political structure of the coastal kingdoms of Senegambia. This local slave system had far-reaching consequences, leading to religious protest and slave rebellions. The interaction of ecological crisis, warfare, and famine shaped the history of slave exports.

WEST AFRICAN SLAVERY AND ATLANTIC COMMERCE

AFRICAN STUDIES SERIES 77

GENERAL EDITOR
J. M. Lonsdale, *Lecturer in History and Fellow of Trinity College, Cambridge*

ADVISORY EDITORS
J. D. Y. Peel, *Professor of Anthropology and Sociology, with special reference to Africa, School of Oriental and African Studies, University of London*

Published in collaboration with
THE AFRICAN STUDIES CENTRE, CAMBRIDGE

A list of books in this series will be found at the end of this volume

WEST AFRICAN SLAVERY AND ATLANTIC COMMERCE

The Senegal River valley, 1700–1860

JAMES F. SEARING
University of Illinois at Chicago

Published by the Press Syndicate of the University of Cambridge
The Pitt Building, Trumpington Street, Cambridge CB2 1RP
40 West 20th Street, New York, NY 10011-4211, USA
10 Stamford Road, Oakleigh, Victoria 3166, Australia

First published 1993

Printed in Great Britain at the University Press, Cambridge

A catalogue record for this book is available from the British Library

Library of Congress cataloguing in publication data

Searing, James F.
    West African slavery and Atlantic commerce : the Senegal River valley,
1700–1860 / James F. Searing.
       p.   cm. – (African studies series; 78)
    ISBN 0 521 44083 1
    1. Slave trade – Senegal – History.   2. Slavery – Senegal – History.
3. Senegal – Commerce – History.   I. Title.   II. Series.
HT 1399.S4S43   1993
306.3′62′09663 – dc20   92-27508   CIP
ISBN 0 521 44083 1 hardback

CC

Contents

Maps

Preface

On the north-east side of Gorée island, facing the southern shore of the Cap Vert peninsula, a row of eighteenth-century merchant houses stand as reminders of the era of the Atlantic slave trade. One of the houses is now a museum known as the Maison des Esclaves, and receives a steady stream of visitors who disembark from the ferry that shuttles between Dakar and Gorée. Visitors can observe the spacious quarters of the merchant house on the upper level of the museum, and the dark, cramped dungeons and storehouses below, the *captiveries* or slave pens where slaves were held.

Merchant houses like the slave museum temporarily harbored slaves purchased by individual merchants, who were later transferred to the prison-like fortress across the harbor where the Senegal Company held slaves before they embarked on the middle passage to slavery in the Americas. At the back of the house a doorway looks out on the open sea. Once used to receive small craft ferrying slaves and provisions from the mainland, the doorway is locally known as the "door of no return," a passageway that separated departing slaves from Africa forever. The soft, rose pastel of the stuccoed houses, their crumbling tile roofs, and the beauty of the bougainvillea that hangs over the walls of the enclosed courtyards and shades the narrow streets, contrasts sharply with the images of terror and heartbreak evoked by the narrow dungeons that echo with the sounds of the Atlantic.

On the same side of the island, a visitor might note that one of the narrow streets nestled below the steep hill covered with the ruins of ancient and modern fortifications is called the "rue des Bambaras." The name is one of the few reminders of another side of the island's history. For much of the eighteenth and nineteenth centuries slaves made up the majority of the island's permanent population. In the eighteenth century slaves were referred to euphemistically as "Bambara," because many of them came from distant regions of the middle and upper Niger valley. The slaves of Gorée labored to sustain the maritime trade between the Atlantic world and the African mainland. Gorée's visible reminders of the past have made it the symbol of an entire historical period. In the eighteenth century another island city, Saint Louis, in the mouth of the Senegal River, played an even more important role as a link in the maritime trade between the Atlantic world and West Africa. There too slaves formed the majority of the population in the eighteenth and early nineteenth century.

The slaves of Gorée and Saint Louis were the most visible manifestation of broader historical processes that linked the slave trade and the development of slave societies in the Americas to the expansion of slavery in West Africa. This book is a study of the interconnections between Atlantic commerce and the historical development of slavery on the Atlantic islands of Saint Louis and Gorée and in the adjacent mainland kingdoms of Waalo, Kajoor, and Bawol, a distinct historical region referred to in this book as the Lower Senegal.[1] It focuses on historical processes within West Africa, and is only secondarily a reexamination of the import-export trade between Senegambia and the Atlantic world.

The "door of no return" is an apt metaphor for the passageway that carried slaves across the Atlantic. Historians of the slave trade have focused their gaze in the same direction, on the slaves and commodities that left the continent. This book looks back into Africa through the same passageway, using Atlantic commerce as a window for studying change within Africa. Atlantic commerce transformed West Africa, creating a divide in its history.

Previous historical studies of Atlantic commerce from Senegambia made the measurement of the export trade the primary object of investigation. This book shifts the emphasis to the ways Atlantic commerce transformed African societies, to the emergence and transformation of slave systems in the Lower Senegal, and to broader currents of economic and social change associated with the export trade in slaves and gum arabic. This reordering of priorities gives a new centrality to the trade in grain and other foodstuffs that nourished slaves in transit, which was particularly important in the Lower Senegal. Many of the men and women held in slavery in the Lower Senegal performed labors crucial to the sustenance of the export trade.

Chapter 1 introduces the region and its history in the period before the Atlantic era, setting the stage for the changes that began in the late seventeenth century. Chapter 2 examines the connections between the export trade in slaves and the expansion of slavery in the Lower Senegal, presenting in broad outline some of the arguments that are fleshed out in the rest of the book. Chapter 3 places the Lower Senegal in the wider commercial system of the Senegal River valley, and discusses its emer-

[1] I have used capital letters to distinguish my usage from the narrower geographic reference usually given to the term "lower Senegal", or *le bas Sénégal* in French, referring to the lower river valley, and thus only to Waalo, northern Kajoor, and the island of Saint Louis. The justification for treating the larger region of the Lower Senegal as a single *historical* region is implicit in the arguments presented throughout this book.

gence as a grain-exporting region in the first half of the eighteenth century. Chapter 4 presents the history of the Atlantic islands as slave societies which developed at the interface between the Atlantic world and Senegambia. Chapter 5 examines the crises and conflicts generated by Atlantic commerce, from the great famine of the 1750s to the decline of slave exports in the second half of the eighteenth century, showing the relationship between changes in the export trade and internal developments in the Lower Senegal. Chapter 6 traces the interconnections between the demise of the eighteenth-century commercial system, the emergence of a new export economy, and the beginnings of colonial expansion in the Lower Senegal.

One of my main goals throughout the work is to highlight the historical importance of the eighteenth century and the era of Atlantic commerce as the fountainhead of many developments more commonly associated with the nineteenth and twentieth centuries. The century and a half discussed in this book is treated as a single historical period, but care has been taken throughout to periodize major historical developments and to differentiate three lesser cycles of approximately fifty years each. The book is based in nearly equal measure on oral traditions and European sources. Wolof oral traditions, particularly dynastic traditions, were essential for an understanding of the internal dynamics of political change and social structure. European commercial sources were critical in establishing the economic dynamics of Atlantic commerce and its impact on African society.

Any work of this kind owes a critical debt to previous scholarship. My debts are many, and I have tried to indicate them in my notes. But the work of three historians played a particularly important role in laying the groundwork for the present work and posing the questions that permitted me to build on an established historical edifice. Philip Curtin's work on the economic history of Senegambia is a model of careful, thorough scholarship. Martin Klein, through numerous articles and papers which will soon be followed by a major book, has demonstrated the critical importance of slavery to the history of the societies of the western Sudan. Boubacar Barry, through his history of the kingdom of Waalo and his more recent history of Senegambia, has emphasized the impact of the Atlantic slave trade on the internal development of Senegambian societies. All three provided inspiration and guideposts for my own research.

My personal and scholarly debts to members of the history department at Université Cheikh Anta Diop in Dakar are great. The first draft of this work was written during two very enjoyable years I spent as Fulbright Lecturer in history in Dakar. My greatest debts are to Mamadou Diouf and to Mohamed Mbodj, who welcomed me, shared their office with me, patiently explained the rules and rigors of francophone education to a novice, and delighted me with hours of conversation and repartee. Ibnou Diagne, the chairman of the department during my stay in Dakar, welcomed me as a colleague and imparted wise advice in a sometimes

unfamiliar academic setting. Abdoulaye Bathily, Oumar Kane, and Rokhaya Fall Gning generously made their works available to me. I would
also like to thank my Dakar colleagues Mustapha Kane and Mamadou
Fall for their conversations and encouragement.

I owe a special debt to Ibou Sarr, who was my tutor in Wolof for two
years. Apart from his skills as a language teacher, he served as a cultural
informant, and made special efforts to dig up materials that interested me
and answer my questions. Without his diligence, some of the Wolof texts
used would have escaped my notice. My thanks also go to Babacar Faye,
who introduced me to the world of the Sereer-Saafen, and facilitated my
field research (only partly utilized in this work) in Bandia. My thanks also
to my informants in Bandia, particularly Farba Siis, whose account of the
foundation of Bandia and its early history helped me conceptualize the
role of the Sereer minorities in the history of the Lower Senegal.[2]

A great number of people and organizations provided the financial and
material support that made this work possible. My first debt is to the
history department at Princeton University, which provided a research
grant in the summer of 1988 for travel to France, and which offered me
support and encouragement in difficult times. Robert Tignor and Daniel
Rogers deserve special thanks for the support they offered. My thanks go
to Linda Rhoad of the Council for the International Exchange of Scholars
in Washington and to Helen Picard of USIS in Dakar for their role in
managing the Fulbright program which allowed me to spend two years in
Dakar from 1988 to 1990. I also would like to thank Robert Palmeri,
Jerome Faye, and El Hadj Sarr of USIS-Dakar for the support and aid
granted at various times while I was in Dakar. My Fulbright colleagues
Kenneth Brown, Philip Burnham, Ken Harrow, and Craig Harris deserve
mention as friends and neighbors in Dakar. My thanks also to Leo and
Fiona Villalon for shared experiences and insights in Dakar. Patricia
Hickling and Andrew Leon prepared the maps for the book.

Many of my colleagues are particularly to be thanked for their role as
readers of previous drafts of this work and for the comments and criticisms
they offered. Reid Mitchell read early drafts of several chapters while
visiting Dakar. In Senegal Mamadou Diouf and Mohamed Mbodj relieved
my worst anxieties with their encouraging comments on the first finished
draft. Chris Harrison played a key role in convincing me to send the
manuscript to Cambridge University Press without delay. Martin Klein
offered detailed comments on the entire manuscript, and deserves credit
for some of the improvements in the finished product. Paul Lovejoy was
kind enough to take time out from other work to read the manuscript, and
gave insightful and pointed suggestions when I was making final revisions.

---

[2] Most of my fieldwork produced information relating to developments after 1860, and will
be used in a later work. I have taken care to base this work, as much as possible, on
sources prior to 1860.

Richard Rathbone generously read the entire manuscript while at Princeton as a Davis Fellow, and offered encouragement and advice. In Princeton, Robert Tignor and Stanley Stein read this work, continuing efforts of constructive criticism and support that began when I was a graduate student.

My greatest personal debt is to my wife, Trish, and my daughter Allison. Their lives were affected in many ways by this project. Their contribution went far beyond intellectual criticism and emotional support. Without them, this work could never have been written.

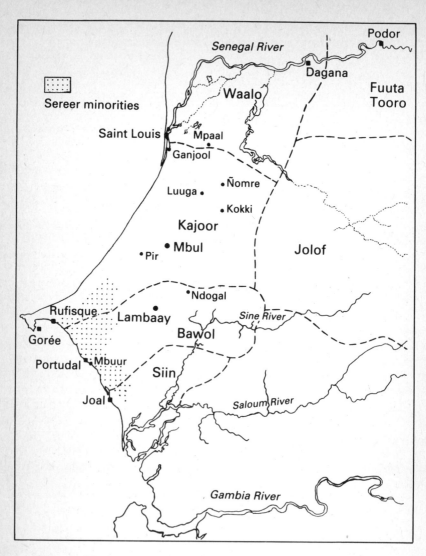

Map 1   The Lower Senegal in the eighteenth century

1

Cosaan: "the origins"

The period from 1700 to 1860 brought dramatic changes to the societies of the Lower Senegal. Much of the impetus for change resulted from the development of Atlantic commerce, driven forward by the demand for slaves in the Atlantic world and for the products they produced: sugar, tobacco, indigo, coffee, and rice. In Senegambia, one of the first regions of West Africa to export slaves across the Atlantic, the first half of the eighteenth century was the apogee of the slave trade. The development of the slave trade set in motion far-reaching changes in the economies and societies of the Lower Senegal, whose history forms the subject of this book.[1] The changes that accompanied the development of Atlantic commerce can only be understood by placing them in the context of the region and its history. Two fundamental factors which shaped the history of the region were its ecology and the historical patterns of human settlement, both of which crystallized in their historical forms long before the arrival of the first merchants from the Atlantic world. Oral traditions, archaeological data, and early European documents permit an understanding of the most important trends in the centuries that preceded the Atlantic trade.

Ecology and history are inseparable in the Lower Senegal, where the historical patterns of settlement and the identity of communities reflect ecological systems and their use and management by human communities. Oral traditions describe the encounters of people with the land. The origin myths of Wolof, Sereer, and Lebu communities fix these communities in the landscape, often describing their arrival from earlier ancestral lands. But each people found a different niche in the ecology, which in turn influenced their historical identity. The Wolof, whose origin myths point to a settlement of the lower river valley after migration from the north and the east, occupy the driest savanna ecology in the region, where wells had to be sunk to depths of over 200 feet to find water. The Lebu, a fishing people who emerged historically in the Cap Vert peninsula, came to the sea after migrations from the interior, and their origin myths focus on their encounter with the ocean. The Sereer, also migrants from the middle

1

valley of the Senegal, occupied the most heavily forested and well-watered regions of the Lower Senegal south of Cap Vert. Sereer origin myths stress that the forest they colonized was not only a homeland to exploit but a place of refuge.[2]

Lebu origin myths provide the most striking example of the fusion of ecology and ethnic identity. The Lebu discovered a landscape of forest and sea after a long migration, leaving behind a homeland of sands and desert in search of water. The encounter of an inland people with the ocean, described through the story of a pact formed with the gods of the sea, provides the mythic framework for describing the sometimes tragic relations of a fishing people with the sea. While the ocean provided its bounty, it reaped an annual harvest in lives lost at sea. In ethnographic terms Lebu myths suggest the fusion of Wolof speakers from the interior with a Sereer fishing culture on the Atlantic coast.[3] Lebu myths speak of their meetings and intermarriage with the people of the south, who taught them techniques for harvesting the riches of the sea. But in times of crisis, as when madness struck one of their community, the Lebu still invoked the memory of the ancestors and the ancestral homeland they left behind.[4]

The origin myths of the Sereer, who inhabited the most heavily forested ecological zone of the region, emphasize the congruence of forest ecology with the search for a land of refuge. The Sereer occupied the forests which ran from the Cees escarpment to the Cap de Naze on the Atlantic coast. Regarded by the neighboring Wolof as peoples without god, laws, or king, the Sereer saw their forest habitat as a refuge from oppression and slavery. Abbé Boilat, a *métis* from Saint Louis, described the "Nones" in the mid-nineteenth century as people whose reputation for ferocity and cruelty was based on their hatred of slavery. "Fearing to be captured and sold into slavery, they resolved to close off their territory to all strangers. This is why they assassinate anyone who dares to enter their villages."[5] On the southern border of the Lower Senegal, in the forest of Jegem, on the borders of the kingdoms of Bawol and Siin, another Sereer group used the forest as a refuge from slavery. Abbé Boilat, eager to pursue missionary work among this small people and worried about their evil reputation as thieves and murderers, took pains to record what he claimed were the words spoken by one of their elders.

> Their greatest crime was to fight for their liberty and independence, for the defense of their fields and forests, for the free possession of their herds, but above all for the inviolable liberty of their wives and children, who were hunted like wild beasts in order to reduce them to servitude and slavery. Alone in the midst of the nations that surrounded them, the little republic of Ndieghem regarded slavery as a crime.[6]

The flight from slavery is a theme that appears in the foundation myths of Sereer villages further to the south, in the Sine valley. The foundation myth of Fatick tells the story of the founder, Waal Paal, who spent part of his life as a slave of warriors from the east before he escaped and set fire to the forest in order to stake his claim to the lands of Fatick.[7]

All these myths contrast sharply with the oral traditions of the Wolof, the dominant ethnic group of the Lower Senegal, which focus on the emergence of the Wolof kingdoms and social order. The Wolof, who inhabit the harshest, driest environment in the region, developed a social order with a dominant aristocratic class, free commoners, specialized "caste" or client groups, and slaves. This hierarchical society was able to mobilize the labor required to exploit the dry savanna environment, particularly for digging wells. It also provided the military specialists required to defend the savanna from attack by mobile desert warriors who periodically erupted into the region, especially during periods of ecological crisis.[8] The ecological transition between the forest and the savanna, which historically formed the frontier between the Wolof and the Sereer, also marked the divide between Islam and traditional religion and the border between the centralized military kingdoms of the northern savanna and the small-scale societies to the south. In the north, savanna society was strongly marked by its location on the desert edge and by the commerce that exchanged desert livestock for grain and slaves from the savanna. Horses, which could be bred and raised in the northern savanna, were inseparable from the historic role of the warrior aristocracy in the Wolof states. Wolof origins therefore fuse with the history of the Wolof social order in the Lower Senegal.

The vanishing landscape: ecological change in the Lower Senegal

The history of the Lower Senegal has been shaped by the geography and ecology of the western Sudan. The Lower Senegal occupies the northern half of a flat plain, with little relief, which stretches from the Senegal River to the Gambia. The south-eastern border of the region is formed by the Sine valley, marking the historic border between the Wolof kingdom of Bawol and the Sereer kingdom of Siin. The flat coastal plain is broken only by the Cees escarpment, a hilly, once heavily forested highland to the east of the Cap Vert peninsula. The northern portion of the region is more arid than its southern limits, but the entire region has the same general climatic pattern, with one rainy season that begins in June or July and ends in October. The rainfall sustains an ecology of lightly wooded savanna where rainy season cereal cultivation of millet and sorghum have provided the agricultural base for human settlement. The absence of tsetse fly in the semi-arid savanna environment has made animal husbandry an important supplement to agriculture and milk products an important supplement to cereal in the diet.[9]

These broad characteristics of the entire region were overlaid with patterns of regional specialization based on the comparative advantage of smaller sub-regions in the production of certain commodities. The pattern

3

of trade and production that resulted was based on exchange between ecological zones of production with different strengths and weaknesses. The flood plain of the Senegal River created certain areas where millet and rice could be produced intensively and where surplus grains could be exchanged for the animal products produced in more arid zones to the north and the south of the river. Fishing villages on the Atlantic coast specialized in the production of dried fish for export to the interior, along with salt collected in deposits near the coast. Almost all agricultural regions produced some surplus grain or cotton for exchange, because of demand for products from the Atlantic coast, the desert edge, or the Guinea forest to the south. Desert merchants provided the animal transport which carried surplus commodities from one region to another and supplied the needs of desert society in grain, cotton cloth and slaves, purchased with horses, cattle, sheep, and other desert animals.

The ecology and geography of the Lower Senegal corresponded closely to the linguistic and ethnic pattern of settlement. Wolof speakers occupied most of the open savanna where rainy season cereal cultivation is the primary economic activity. Agricultural villages are located in sites where water can be obtained and where the soil is richer and moister, often in low-lying valleys in the rolling savanna. In marginal agricultural zones the Wolof have shared the occupation of the region with Pulaar-speaking cattle herders, who build seasonal cattle camps and care for herds which include animals owned by Wolof villagers. Moor pastoralists and merchants also lived within the region, permanent migrants from the western Sahara. Lebu fishing villages were concentrated in the region around the Cap Vert peninsula, while Sereer speakers inhabited the more heavily wooded savanna south of Cap Vert. Most of the rest of the linguistic and ethnic differentiation in the region can be traced to migration within the Senegambian region along commercial corridors, which have also overlapped with channels for the propagation of Islam and Islamic learning.[10]

The Lower Senegal of 1700 was very different than the same region today, because European descriptions of the region evoke a forested landscape, full of wild animals and not completely domesticated by humans. In the 1750s Michel Adanson, a naturalist working for the Compagnie du Sénégal, made careful observations of the landscape, vegetation, animal life, and climate of the Lower Senegal, based on excursions up the Senegal River from Saint Louis, or down the coast to Gorée and trading ports further south. Adanson described herds of elephants in the region near Dagana in the lower river valley and Adanson and other travellers sighted elephants on the Cap Vert peninsula and in the kingdoms of Kajoor and Bawol.[11] Adanson described forests covering much of Cap Vert, and to him it appeared that the millet fields surrounding the village of Sali-Portudal had been freshly cut from the surrounding forest.[12] On Adanson's map of Senegal (1756), the entire region extending east from Cap Vert is labeled the forest of Krampsane.[13] As late as the

4

1850s Boilat described most of the region between Rufisque and Joal as covered by forest and inhabited by abundant wild game, particularly several species of gazelle and antelope.[14] At that time the forest still marked the limit of Islam and the cultural frontier between predominantly Wolof and predominantly Sereer regions. All these areas are today deforested, with the exception of protected areas or trees maintained by humans. The baobab trees that remain today are the sole reminders of the forests of the past, left because they are useful neither for charcoal production or construction.

The climate in 1700 differed much less from that of today than one might expect from the changes in the landscape that have occurred. A recent survey of historical climatic change in the western Sudan places most of the period discussed in this book in a dry period that lasted from 1630 to 1860. European sources chronicle a series of droughts and famines in the eighteenth century but suggest rainfall patterns not significantly different from those of today. In the longer view, the last significant wet period occurred between the years 700 and 1100, so climatic change in the narrow sense has been less dramatic than change in the ecology.[15] In the Lower Senegal climatic change probably played a direct role in setting in motion the last great period of migrations which occurred after the twelfth century. Oral traditions which recall that period describe migrations out of the Senegal River valley, the historic cradle of most of the peoples now living in the regions between the Senegal and the Gambia, and particularly of the Wolof and Sereer.[16] Whether the immediate causes of those migrations were dessication, overpopulation of the river valley, or political troubles, long-term climatic change played a major role in the southward movement of the Wolof and the Sereer.

Although it is impossible to describe the landscape of the Lower Senegal as seen by these early migrants, it is likely that stands of old forest remained, and that this more heavily forested ecology was gradually transformed by human activity.[17] Archaeological research has discovered an important zone of metallurgical activity dating from *c.*AD 600 to 800 in the Senegal River valley. Iron smelting with charcoal fires consumed enormous quantities of hardwood, and it has been estimated that a single smelting forge could level a kilometer of forest in slightly over a month.[18] It is suggestive that by the fifteenth century iron smelting had almost disappeared from the region between the Senegal and the Gambia, as smiths specializing in smelting as opposed to forging iron migrated elsewhere in search of new stands of forest.[19] Iron bars became one of the first important imports from the Atlantic world, replacing iron imported from more distant regions of West Africa. This sequence suggests that the park-like savanna mixed with forest which was described by Europeans resulted to a large degree from the human activity of agriculturalists with iron tools and herds of cattle and other animals, who progressively occupied the region in the period from AD 800 to 1200.[20] The combination

5

of extensive cereal cultivation and livestock grazing gradually transformed the landscape. This process would be vastly accelerated in the eighteenth and nineteenth centuries as the savanna produced more and more surplus grain to feed the demands of the Atlantic and desert trades.

Oral traditions suggest that in the earliest period of historical settlement the land south of the Senegal River was thinly settled and still largely covered with forest. When migrating agriculturalists moved into the forest they claimed land by setting fires. The founder-ancestors of village communities became *laman* ("landowners") because they were the masters of the fire (Wolof, *boroom daay*), and their descendants became the guardians of the land and the harvests. The community that settled on the lands of the *laman* claimed as property the land they cleared, as masters of the ax (Wolof, *boroom ngajj*).[21] Some traditions suggest that the *laman* only arose as leaders when the population increased enough to create disputes over land between village communities and within villages.[22] In much of the Lower Senegal, the *laman* is the putative descendant of the first founder and represents the first figure in the creation of a structured village community. Most founder ancestors claimed lands from the forest. In the foundation myth of the Lebu village of Tengeej or Rufisque, the founder hero Ndooy Njiram finds a forest thick as night "where no human has ever set foot."[23] Bawol is described in the earliest times as nearly uninhabited, full of wild animals, until the first settlers came, seeking refuge from quarrels and conflicts in their homelands.[24]

The creation of village communities in the Lower Senegal, claiming land from the forest, preceded the emergence of monarchy (Wolof, *nguur*) and aristocratic rule. Oral traditions tracing the foundation of village communities suggest that over a long period of time groups of migrants seeking new territories of their own were able to claim territories from the forest and that these foundations preceded the arrival of organized government. The founder hero of Rufisque negotiated only with the *jinne* ("spirit") of the forest, and the *laman* in Bawol, Waalo, and Kajoor long managed their affairs without reference to any higher authority.[25] The village communities of the Lower Senegal have a long history, and constitute the fundamental social units of the region. Most of the villages described by Europeans in the eighteenth century still exist today, although many of them have undergone dramatic growth or decline in the last 300 years.

The permanence of village sites reflected in part the difficulty of finding sources of water. Wolof villages often had to dig wells to depths of nearly 300 feet to find permanent sources of water, and the digging and maintenance of wells represented a significant investment of labor.[26] European observers were impressed with the depth of wells, particularly in Kajoor where one visitor in the first decade of the nineteenth century "halted at several villages, where the wells were of immense depth. One he had the curiosity to measure, and found it to be two hundred and forty feet."[27] Wolof villages tended to be fairly large agglomerations of house-

6

holds, grouped together in a central residential "town," with fields and pasture area scattered fairly widely in the surrounding countryside. The village community was a structured society, with an internal hierarchy based in principle on the history of the occupation of the site. With the development of aristocratic rule in the region, the village hierarchy assumed responsibility for protecting the community through diplomacy, the payment of tribute, and organizing its self-defense.

The historical geography of the Lower Senegal comprised two distinct sub-regions. In Waalo, northern Kajoor, and parts of central Bawol, Wolof peasantries were fully integrated into states which articulated a Wolof version of the hierarchical societies of the western Sudan. Apart from being more anciently settled, these provinces were also the first regions to become entirely converted to Islam. The historic rights of local notables (free, but not belonging to the aristocracy) were preserved and given representation, first in the person of the *laman* and later through the emergence of Muslim leaders or "marabouts."[28] This Wolof core area continuously expanded its influence to the south and the east, particularly in the open savanna where the Wolof cavalry aristocracy found optimal conditions for political expansion. A second zone, located in the wooded savanna south of Cap Vert, remained recalcitrant to state rule and harbored village communities which remained more or less autonomous of state rule and maintained a cultural identity that set them apart from the Wolof. Taxes and tribute, when collected, were seized by force and the Wolof rulers of Kajoor and Bawol regarded the small Sereer groups as "pagans" and "barbarians." The southern and western marches of Kajoor and Bawol were frequently raided for slaves. In response the peoples of the region developed defensive techniques which made their territories places of refuge, much like maroon backlands in the slave societies of the New World.[29]

Founders and dynasties: Wolof history in oral tradition

Cultural ecology provides clues for understanding the relationship between different peoples and the landscapes they inhabit. But it is necessary to examine oral traditions to see the role played by human choice in establishing the patterns of settlement in the region. The oral traditions of the Wolof and the Sereer portray the emergence of the state of Takrur as the central event in the transformation of the Senegal River valley and its peoples. The relationship between the Takrur of oral traditions and the historic state of Takrur, known to us from Arabic sources, is problematic. In all likelihood, the Takrur of oral traditions telescopes the influence of several distinct centralized states into one tradition.

The myths which center on Takrur emphasize the central role of the Senegal River valley in the history of the peoples now dispersed in the region south of the river. In earlier centuries most of Senegambia was a peripheral region, absorbing influences from political and economic centers in the western Sudan, but at the same time receiving refugees and migrants fleeing the same power centers.[30] The main historical influences on the Senegambian region emanated from the Mande world to the east and from the Muslim Saharan societies to the north.[31] After the tenth century, with the emergence of the state of Takrur in the Senegal valley, groups of people moved south and west, creating new centers of population in lands distant from the Senegal River valley, but often bordering directly on the Atlantic coast.[32]

The oral traditions of the Wolof and the Sereer suggest that the current inhabitants of the Lower Senegal gradually came under the influence of centralized warrior states modeled after those of the Mande some time around the tenth century. The Mande political order, dominated by a cavalry aristocracy, divided society into three orders: free persons, occupational castes with specialized functions, and slaves. In the eleventh century this eastern influence was redoubled by the emergence of an Islamic state, Takrur, on the Senegal River. The combined influence of these events set in motion the last great period of migrations, which oral traditions associate with the state of Takrur. Sereer oral traditions chronicle the southward migrations of the Sereer from the Senegal River valley, as the ancestors of the Sereer separated themselves from the centralized Islamic political order of Takrur.[33] Wolof oral traditions center on the legendary founder figure of Njaajaan Njaay, creator of the Wolof political order, who is associated both with the Senegal River and with the state of Takrur.[34]

The ancestors of today's Wolof and Sereer populations responded quite differently to the period of crisis and migration that followed the eleventh century. The Wolof adopted the tripartite social order of the stratified societies of the western Sudan: free persons, occupational castes, and slaves, the whole capped by a warrior aristocracy. The Sereer migrations occurred during the formative period of the Jolof empire and were motivated by rejection of the emerging aristocratic social order.[35] The Sereer exodus from the Senegal valley was motivated by the search for lands free from the claims of centralized states and warrior aristocrats. Nevertheless in the course of their migration southwards and settlement of the Sine valley, the Sereer came under the influence of an axis of Mande expansion from east to west, leading to the creation of the monarchies of Siin and Saalum. By accepting the Gelwaar aristocracy the Sereer of Siin and Saalum adopted a non-Muslim form of aristocratic rule. Although marked by the tripartite Mande social model, Sereer society did not incorporate castes and slaves as fully as the Wolof, since these social groups were linked closely to the Gelwaar courts and their client networks.

The Sereer monarchies of Siin and Saalum fall outside of the region studied here, but their history provides a useful model for interpreting the Sereer groups settled in the border regions of southern Kajoor and Bawol.

The independent Sereer groupings around the Cees (Thies) escarpment (Ndut, Noon, Saafen), politically autonomous, without state structures, and with a history of fierce resistance to incorporation into the Wolof states which surround them, may represent groups isolated during the period of Sereer migrations. Their social structure, acephalous, egalitarian, and without aristocrats, castes, or slaves, represents a conscious rejection of the social order that emerged in the Wolof and Sereer monarchies.[36] The foundation myths of Sereer villages, based on field research in the Saafen region, suggests that these communities were created by populations seeking autonomy from centralized states by taking refuge in geographically isolated and marginal regions.[37] The Sereer populations of Bawol represented a third outcome: incorporated into a Wolof state, much of the population gradually adopted a Muslim Wolof identity, so that Bawol today is considered a typically Wolof region.[38]

Founding myths of Lebu villages, Saafen villages, and Sereer-Siin villages often recount in some detail both the political oppression and war that led to migrations and the discovery of new lands free of domination and covered with forest.[39] Zones of refuge in the wooded savanna from Cap Vert to the valley of the Sine remained peripheral to the centers of political power located near the Senegal River valley and in the open savanna from Jolof to northern Bawol. These regions continued to assert their autonomy from the Wolof states of the Lower Senegal long after the opening of the Atlantic frontier gave new strategic importance to the entire Atlantic coastal region.

The history of the Lower Senegal in the eighteenth century was dominated by the gradual economic integration of the region into the wider Atlantic world. For the Wolof monarchies of Kajoor and Bawol this process was mediated by the political order established by Latsukaabe Faal, who founded the Geej dynasty in Kajoor-Bawol in 1695. Atlantic commerce interacted with longer-term historical trends in the Senegambian region. The development of the Wolof political and social order provides the essential background for understanding the transformations of the eighteenth and nineteenth century. That process began with the emergence of a Wolof warrior aristocracy. From the beginning the new aristocratic social order associated itself with Islam. The Wolof social order was Muslim, even if this Islam was superficial by the standards of later centuries.[40]

Wolof dynastic traditions provide the essential source for understanding the emergence and transformation of the Wolof kingdoms. The dynastic traditions combine myth, historic chronicle, and praise poem in a form shaped by oral performance and organized into dynastic cycles. Compared to the better known Mande epic traditions, Wolof dynastic traditions are more prosaic and secular, with a preponderance of royal chronicle.[41] But each dynastic cycle begins with a more mythic treatment of the royal founder, because the foundation of a new dynasty poses problems of

9

usurpation and legitimacy. Dynastic traditions have to be understood as products of particular reflections about the past. Wolof dynastic traditions were preserved by the *gewel*, a hereditary caste of bards who served as clients of aristocratic families. They explain and justify the passage of political power from one king to another and more rarely the events that led to the creation of new dynasties. The chronicles treat in detail princely rivalries, succession struggles, and civil wars, but always with the object of explaining and justifying the subsequent course of Wolof political history. Conceived as praise poems celebrating the ancestors of ruling dynasties, dynastic traditions were intended as performances directed to the court. "In the Senegalese kingdoms in the past the *griots* [bards] of the king gathered each Friday evening before the king, the prince and the assembled courtiers, and the head *griot* sang the praises of the kings beginning with the legendary founder of the dynasty."[42] Wolof dynastic traditions establish a periodization of Wolof political history, each period defined by a founder hero who stands at the beginning of a period of dynastic rule.

Any discussion of Wolof dynastic traditions must acknowledge the lack of attention to the subject, despite an abundance of sources.[43] The complexity of the problem is daunting. Since Faidherbe published Yoro Jaw's investigations into Wolof oral traditions anonymously in 1864 as the "Histoire des Damels," an "authoritative" version in French has existed.[44] A fuller version of Yoro Jaw's research was published in the 1930s. The tradition of research and publication in French continued, with new contributions by prominent aristocrats and bards (Wolof, *gewel*). At the same time performance in Wolof continued. Today versions of the dynastic traditions can be heard on the national radio. Wolof versions of the traditions have been recorded and published in various forms. The following discussion is based on a study of all of these forms of the traditions. There are many different genres and kinds of performance, which combine recitation and music in different ways. These range from recitations of texts, to discussions (Wolof, *waxtaan*), to musical compositions that sing the exploits (Wolof, *woy jalloore*) of heroic figures from the past. Most performances incorporate the participation of senior *gewel*, accompanied by their juniors and disciples. For the purposes of this discussion, these diverse sources are treated as a body of tradition.

The Jolof empire (1200–1550)

The legendary founder of the Jolof empire, Njaajaan Njaay, is the central, mythic character in Wolof oral traditions. The myth operates on three different levels: it provides a "royal" genealogy for the hero, tells the story of his rite of passage from royal outcast to king, and gives an account of his achievements as king. All three levels inform us about the meaning of kingship in Wolof society.[45] Most of the traditions now available incorporate past revisions that integrate Islamic themes and have been influenced by Yoro Jaw's published texts.

Njaajaan Njaay was the first and only son of a noble and saintly "Arab" father Abdu Darday and a "Tukuler" woman, Fatamatu Sall. Pulaar speakers of the middle valley are referred to as *Tukuler* in Wolof, a linguistic memory of Takrur. The father, given a genealogy linking him to the Almoravids, establishes an Islamic foundation for the Njaay dynasty. The mother links the Njaay dynasty to the state of Takrur. Since the Wolof, who later receive Njaajaan Njaay, are described in the myth as having no real dynasties or princely clans at this time, this part of the myth can be interpreted as giving a Takrurian origin to the Njaay dynasty. This reading of the myth aligns the origins of the Jolof empire with influences from the Almoravids and Takrur.[46]

The myth of Njaajaan Njaay continues by explaining how the founder hero abandons his family when his mother remarries after his father's death and gives birth to a second son. In some versions of the story the mother remarries a slave of her first husband, in others she disobeys her first husband's counsel to marry only a good Muslim. In all versions the first son feels betrayed and throws himself into the river, where he is able to live miraculously for a period of years. During his exile in the water, Njaajaan Njaay descends the river from the region near Podor in the middle valley and reappears as a miraculous being in Waalo in the lower Senegal River valley. In his first reappearance to human society Njaajaan Njaay emerges from the river, human in form, but with extraordinary long hair, and settles a dispute between women quarreling over the division of a catch of fish, all without saying a word.

The last phase of the myth of Njaajaan Njaay describes how the people of Waalo, recognizing the extraordinary character of the being who emerged from the river, conspire to make him speak, integrate him into their society, and proclaim him king because of his wisdom and justice. In all versions of the myth, Njaajaan Njaay speaks his first words in Pulaar rather than Wolof, emphasizing once again his character as a stranger of noble origins. In the myth his extraordinary character is revealed by the founder of the Siin monarchy, whose cry of surprise in Sereer gives the hero his adopted name.[47] After ruling in Waalo for a period of time, Njaajaan Njaay moves his court to Jolof, the historic center of the Njaay dynasty and subsequent base for the expansion of the Jolof empire, leaving behind a brother or half-brother to rule as Barak in Waalo.

As a statement about kingship, the myth of Njaajaan Njaay emphasizes the role of the king as wise peacemaker and arbitrator of disputes, voluntarily acclaimed king by his subjects. Traditions attribute the military expansion of Jolof and the creation of state institutions to later kings. Hidden beneath an Islamic revision of the myth, there is a story which suggests a connection between a miraculous river spirit, the king, and the fertility of the kingdom.[48] These associations were preserved in the rituals

11

of enthronement practiced in the Wolof kingdoms. The prospective king was given a sacred bath commemorating Njaajaan's passage in the river. He then climbed to the top of an artificial hill, symbolizing the high ground where Njaajaan first reappeared to humans. When the king descended the hill he was showered with the fruits of the land by court dignitaries and invited to plant a garden, which was observed for eight days as an augury for the fertility of his reign.[49]

As a mythic figure whose career telescopes the early history of the Njaay dynasty and the Jolof empire, Njaajaan Njaay's life indicates the historic influences claimed by the Wolof dynasties. The Islamic heritage of the kingdoms of the Senegal River valley becomes royal genealogy in the myth. The new dynasty established itself first in Waalo and then in Jolof, taking on quickly the Wolof identity of the inhabitants of the lower Senegal valley. The court of Njaajaan Njaay then served as a vehicle for the expansion of the Wolof language and culture. Most versions of the myth explain how the new dynasty superimposed itself upon a preexisting social structure dominated by the *laman*, Wolof elders who claimed "ownership" of the land as the descendants of the founders of village communities. The *laman* retained many of their functions under the new monarchical order, becoming a kind of lesser nobility within the new state, and serving as electors when the time came to choose a new king from the Njaay dynasty.[50]

The myth of Njaajaan Njaay "explains" the hegemony of the Jolof empire over much of the Senegambian region in the thirteenth and fourteenth centuries. At the point of its greatest expansion the Jolof empire dominated the entire region between the Senegal and the Gambia rivers, and received tribute from Kajoor, Bawol, Waalo, Siin, and Saalum, which existed as tributary kingdoms within the empire. In this period the Wolof language was spoken in courts throughout Senegambia and Wolof aristocracies established their hegemony in Waalo, Kajoor, Jolof, and Bawol, while leaving their mark on the courts of Siin and Saluum.[51]

The monarchy, 1549–1695

The period of the monarchy began with the rebellions against the Jolof empire which led to the independence of the Wolof kingdoms of Kajoor and Bawol. The new founder hero was Amari Ngoone Sobel, the young prince of Kajoor who led the rebellion against the Jolof empire, defeating the Burba Jolof at the battle of Danki, dated 1549 by Yoro Jaw. Recent research, checking dynastic traditions against European sources, has tended to confirm this date.[52] Dynastic traditions are much richer for this period than for the Jolof empire, treating both personalities and events in some detail.

Oral traditions present a consistent view of the leadership and motivations for the rebellion that led to the independence of Kajoor and Bawol.

During the period of the Jolof empire the *laman* became the local agents of imperial authority, and in Kajoor one family, the *laman* Paleen-Dedd had achieved a preeminence which prefigured the role of the Dammel (king) under the monarchy. Among their other functions, the *laman* Paleen-Dedd were responsible for the annual payment of tribute to the king of Jolof, consisting of cattle, slaves, horses, cloth, various agricultural products, and white sand of Kajoor to decorate the court of the king.[53] Portuguese sources, describing the same period, noted the annual payment of tribute to the Jolof empire: "Each year the lords of the country, in order to stand well with him, present him with horses, which are much esteemed owing to their scarcity, forage, beasts such as cows and goats, vegetables, millet and the like."[54] The payment of this tribute, and the humiliations inflicted on the *laman* of Kajoor by the king of Jolof are presented as the grievances which led to rebellion and independence.

The *laman* Paleen-Dedd had already assumed a quasi-monarchical status when they led the struggle for independence from Jolof. During their subordination to the Jolof empire an important group of *laman* had been assimilated into the military aristocracy of the empire. The war of liberation from Jolof did not destroy the aristocratic order to the advantage of the *laman*, but transformed the *laman* Paleen-Dedd into the founders of a new dynasty in the now independent kingdom of Kajoor. Oral traditions focus on the military exploits and strategies of the hero-founder Amari Ngoone, the prince of Kajoor who led his army to victory, with help from his uncle, the Teeñ (king) of Bawol, who aided Kajoor in its bid for independence. After his triumph, Amari Ngoone returned to a hero's welcome in Kajoor and quickly succeeded his father to the new title of Dammel of Kajoor, due to the accidental death of his father only six days after his enthronement as the first Dammel.

The immediate contrast between Amari Ngoone and Njaajaan Njaay is warrior-king versus peacemaker. Amari is a rebel and a conqueror, and the most colorful details in traditions about him focus on the ruses and the magic used to defeat the Jolof emperor. The traditions also focus on the emergence of maternal succession in the Wolof monarchies. The Njaay dynasty of Jolof traced descent in the male line, a principle that gave equality to maternal lines and led to some rotation of the kingship. In the Wolof monarchies succession resulted from the armed competition for power between royal matrilineages. Amari is aided in his rebellion by his maternal uncle, the Teeñ of Bawol. By the logic of maternal succession, Amari was heir to the throne of Bawol. Amari leads the warriors of Kajoor to victory over Jolof with help provided by his uncle and then he inherits the kingdom of Kajoor from his father, who is gored by a bull when visiting his herds. The story poses the important conflict between paternal and maternal descent in the Wolof monarchies.

The story of Amari treats the kingdoms of Kajoor and Bawol as established entities within the Jolof empire. The same impression is given by European sources. Portuguese seamen and merchants treated Kajoor and Bawol as quasi-independent monarchies before the destruction of the Jolof empire. Almost a century before Kajoor's war for independence Cadamosto described being received by "Budomel," a king owing allegiance to the Jolof empire, but who nevertheless ruled Kajoor.[55] It is probable that a Dammel of Kajoor and a Teeñ of Bawol already ruled as monarchs before they achieved complete independence from Jolof in the wars commemorated in oral tradition. European sources suggest that the breakup of the Jolof empire was accompanied by widespread social turmoil and violence. Early documents on the American origins of slaves in the New World from 1526 to 1550 show the Wolof in higher proportions than at any other period of the slave trade from Senegambia.[56]

Historians have focused on the probable role of Atlantic commerce in enriching Kajoor and Bawol, with their outlets on the Atlantic coast, at the expense of Jolof, an inland state with few contacts with the coast. The presumption is that a century of trade which exchanged slaves, ivory, gold, wax, hides, and provisions, for Portuguese horses, iron, swords, and other manufactured goods, benefited Kajoor and Bawol more than it did the Jolof empire. The assumptions are reasonable, especially since the Portuguese had more developed ports of trade in the region south of Cap Vert than in the area around the mouth of the Senegal. Horses had a clear military function and oral traditions specifically mention the production of numerous iron weapons.[57] The Atlantic connection in the revolt against Jolof was real, although not necessarily decisive.[58]

While the historic heartland of the Wolof social order was in the Senegal River valley, Amari Ngoone's new kingdom had its center of gravity further to the south. Since Amari quickly established himself as the ruler of a dual kingdom of Kajoor-Bawol, by inheriting from his maternal uncle the title of Teeñ, the new state represented an important shift of Wolof aristocratic power to the south and south-east. From a Wolof core area in the lower Senegal valley, Wolof power was being extended to the south at the expense of Wolof and Sereer *laman* and the Lebu, as new village communities were brought under the authority of the kingdom and local notables and nobles were forced to recognize the preeminence of the monarchy. This movement of Wolof power to the south preceded the breakup of the Jolof empire and continued thereafter. On the basis of Portuguese sources Boulègue dates Kajoor's incorporation of the Lebu of Cap Vert between 1482 and 1515.[59] Other southern and eastern provinces like Jander, Ndut, Lexaar, and Geet were incorporated into the kingdom of Kajoor after its independence.[60]

Amari Ngoone, of the patrilineage Faal, and of the matrilineage Wagadu, set the pattern for the inheritance of power in Kajoor and Bawol for the entire subsequent history of the monarchy. The Faal patrilineage established its hegemony in Kajool and Bawol, with the result that political competition centered almost entirely on rivalries between matrilineal clans. The matrilineal focus of Wolof aristocratic families is usually explained as "archaic," reflecting a matrilineal organization more ancient than the bilateral kinship system described by ethnographers, now giving way to a patrilineal system under the influence of Islam. Alternatively, the creation of the matrilineal clans can be explained as a differentiation of maternal lines within the dominant royal patrilineage, which then played a central role in elevating a new branch of the patrilineage to power.[61] This system of competition and inheritance led to frequent dynastic conflicts.

The most important theme of the dynastic traditions about Amari is the emergence of matrilineal descent. One descendant of the royal family interpreted the traditions about Amari by noting that Wolof nobles always trusted their maternal relatives and made plans with them, only informing their paternal rivals at the last moment.[62] In the traditions Amari plans his rebellion with his uncle, while leading his father to believe he will pay tribute to Jolof. The same theme appears in the story of how Amari tricked his son into sleeping with his maternal aunt, so his nephew could inherit the kingship.[63] Although this ruse ultimately failed, Amari's actions outlined the logic of maternal descent.

Whatever its origins, the identification of royal princes with their maternal families emerged naturally from competition between children with different mothers in the polygamous royal household. Since princely *garmi* status was granted to all legitimate sons of the king who could claim a noble maternal clan, the sons of different mothers were in direct competition. Historically successful upstarts were sons of the king who imposed themselves by force and intrigue and then elevated their maternal family to royal status. During succession disputes, bloody conflicts between sons of different mothers and between sons and nephews of the king were common and form one of the main subjects of dynastic traditions. In Wolof folktales such as "Biram Njeeme Koo-Njaay," the hero is the sole son from a maternal line rejected by the father, and both the son and the mother are abused, mistreated, and betrayed by the king and his favored sons. Biram Njeeme, educated by his maternal uncle, eventually proves his valor and honor, and the folktale ends in a bloody revenge massacre of his father and brothers, followed by Biram Njeeme's enthronement as king and the restoration of his mother's family to a place of honor.[64] Some of the themes of this folktale reappear in dynastic traditions treating the history of the upstart king Latsukaabe Faal, who created a new royal matrilineage in the seventeenth century. In both cases the future king is revealed when he eats the head and feet of a lamb specially slaughtered by a marabout, who then reveals that the son who ate the "slave's meat," the head and the feet, will become the next king.[65]

The competition for power between royal matrilineages stemmed from the important role of the maternal family as the "owner" of property, particularly slaves and cattle.[66] Since slaves were the most important form

15

of wealth and played an important political role as warriors, their connection to the maternal family greatly increased its importance for the aristocracy. Slaves were not the only client group attached primarily to the maternal family. Many families from the caste groups were considered the clients and the allies of the maternal rather than the paternal family.[67] These factors reinforced the importance of maternal families in the competition for power, because slaves and other clients added dependable political and military clout in a succession struggle.

The royal matrilineages were dominated by men, but women played a significant role in the political system and in the management of aristocratic wealth. The queen or *lingeer* from the matrilineage, usually the king's mother, sister, or aunt, played a more important role than the king's first wife, the *awo*. Both received the revenues of particular provinces, usually administered for them by royal slaves. Aristocratic women managed the work of slaves who worked as domestic servants or as field slaves, this being considered an aspect of the aristocratic household that fell under the authority of the mistress. The political and domestic role of aristocratic women reflected their importance in the maternal clans that princes struggled to place or maintain in power.[68]

The dynastic traditions about Amari also explain the changing relationship between the king and the *laman* and the monarchy and Islam. The traditions explain that Amari created a new capital, Mbul, and appointed a new *laman* or landowner with the title *jawrin Mbul*. This new dignitary, appointed by the king, was raised to a preeminent position above the other *laman*, and particularly above the *laman jawatil*, the traditional head of the council of electors.[69] By making the *jawrin Mbul* the head of the council, and dependent on the king for his appointment, the independence of the electors and the *laman* was considerably reduced. Parallel with this attack on the independence of the *laman* Amari Ngoone granted important ritual functions and land grants to marabouts who accepted a client status. The Moors of Kajoor (Wolof, *Naaru Kajoor*) descend in part from marabouts given a land grant and gifts in exchange for their role in giving the monarch the sacred bath (Wolof, *xuli-xuli*) which ritually recalled the time passed by Njaajaan Njaay in the Senegal River.[70] Subsequent monarchs continued this dual policy of reducing the power of the *laman* and granting special status and autonomy to marabouts who associated themselves with the monarchy.

The period of the monarchy was marked by a number of important developments. Kajoor emerged as the most powerful state in the region. This was partly the result of Atlantic commerce, and partly a result of the extension of Wolof state structures to the south and the east. The Faal patrilineage became the dominant royal clan, splitting into competing royal matrilineages which struggled for power by mobilizing kinsmen, slaves, and clients. The monarchy centralized power at the expense of the *laman*, who tended to become agents of the state at the local level with

16

little independent power. At the same time by granting marabouts special ritual roles and privileges as the leaders of communities of Muslims, the monarchy indirectly contributed to the rise of a new class of leaders with an independent base of power.

Two important episodes illustrated the changing balance of power in Kajoor in the seventeenth century. In 1647 the council of electors, led by Kocc Barma, succeeded in deposing and banishing the Dammel Daawda Demba, replacing him on the throne by a king of their own choosing. This was the last time the council of electors peacefully deposed the king. In the dynastic traditions the triumph of the electors over the tyrannical king was the personal victory of Kocc Barma, who embodies the wisdom of tradition. As a *laman* Kocc Barma was a member of the notables, a *jambur*, free and of noble birth, but not a member of the aristocracy.[71] Kocc Barma is described as the childhood friend and companion of the king Daawda Demba, implying that they were circumcised together. In folk tales Kocc Barma always outsmarts the king who plots to kill him and to trick him into dishonorable acts, and one of his most famous proverbs, *buur du mbokk*, "the king is not a kinsman," expresses Wolof criticism of the arbitrary power of kings, whose behavior violated norms of respect shown kinsmen and allies.[72] According to dynastic traditions Kocc succeeded because he had the support both of the *laman* and the royal slaves (Wolof, *jaami-buur*). The royal slaves had been alienated by the arbitrary execution of their commander and they agreed to support the deposition of the monarch, announced by the *laman* on the Muslim holiday of Tabaski in 1647.[73]

Kocc Barma's triumph over the king gives us one of the few portraits of Wolof opposition to the monarchy in a secular form, based on the role of the *laman* as guardians of tradition. The apparent resurgence of the *laman* under Kocc's leadership had no sequel, and the next challenge to the monarchy came from Islam, in the period of troubles known as the War of the Marabouts. In Kajoor a rare split in a ruling matrilineage provided the opening for Islam, when a new king deposed the *lingeer*, his aunt, in favor of his own mother. The deposed *lingeer* offered her daughter in marriage to a marabout of Kajoor, Njaay Sall, and formed an army of her slaves, allies of the former king, and followers of the marabout. This coalition succeeded in defeating and deposing the king and naming his successor, but broke into warring factions when the disciples of the marabout executed the new king after he was caught drinking alcohol. After an interim of Muslim rule the monarchy was restored by a new dynasty from the kingdom of Saalum, but in many ways disorder and civil war continued until 1695, when Latsukaabe Faal united the two kingdoms of Kajoor and Bawol under his authority.[74]

Events during the War of the Marabouts revealed the substantial power of Islam in the period of the monarchy. The deposed *lingeer* would never have contracted a military and matrimonial alliance with a marabout without being convinced of the force he would add to her coalition of slaves and clients. Although dynastic traditions ignore the regional context of this conflict, which formed part of a wider Islamic rebellion against aristocratic rule, they confirm that the entire period of the monarchy was marked by the emergence of Islamic leaders as the most powerful counterforce to the aristocracy in the Wolof states.

The old regime, 1695–1860

A new period began with the unification of the monarchies of Kajoor and Bawol under a new royal matrilineage, the Geej, which ruled almost without interruption until French military intervention under Faidherbe. Dynastic traditions focus on the founder monarch, Latsukaabe Faal, whose rise to power from obscurity and humble origins is given a legendary character. With the reign of the monarch the historic figure of Latsukaabe emerges from legend, both in dynastic traditions and through the testimony of Europeans who traded and negotiated with Latsukaabe during the early period of the French slave trade. This period can be described as the Wolof old regime, because it represents the last period of the monarchy before the opening of the contemporary period with French military intervention and Muslim jihad and reform in the 1860s, and because the monarchy became a despotic, military regime dominated by aristocrats and their slave warriors.[75] It can also be described as the time of slavery (Wolof, *jamanoo njaam*) because the expansion of slavery coincided with the reinforcement of aristocratic despotism.

Latsukaabe Faal refounded the dual monarchy of Kajoor-Bawol, an unrealized ambition for most of the kings who tried to follow the path traced by Amari Ngoone. Latsukaabe's restoration stands roughly at the mid-point in the history of the kingdoms of Kajoor and Bawol, between their foundation and subsequent unification as independent but linked kingdoms by Amari Ngoone around 1550, and the beginnings of colonial conquest in the 1860s. The main factor behind the restoration of 1695 was military force, rather than any claim to legitimacy. When Kajoor accepted its new ruler in 1695, its institutions and ruling families had been weakened or destroyed by decades of civil war, famine, and chaos. If nothing else, Latsukaabe's army, which surrounded the electors of Kajoor when they chose him as king, was able to monopolize the use of force by driving all rivals from the field, replacing the oppression of many by many, by the oppression of many by few.

The new order that emerged in 1695 came from the frontier rather than the heartland of the Lower Senegal. Latsukaabe and his army came from Bawol, where a Wolof nobility based in the central provinces struggled throughout the seventeenth century to establish its hegemony over a predominantly Sereer population by military force, aided by the iron, weapons, and wealth that moved along a corridor of trade from the

Atlantic coast. By gradually dispossessing the Sereer *laman* of their landholdings in the central provinces, a peasantry with tributary relations to their Wolof warlords was created.[76] The central provinces then served as a base for raids of plunder, slaving, and cattle rustling in the frontier provinces which dominated the approaches to the Atlantic coast. Cattle, hides, and slaves purchased European iron, and later firearms, which could be turned on the independent Sereer populations who formed the majority of the inhabitants of the territory claimed by the monarchy of Bawol. In the 1690s, the army formed in Bawol's wars of conquest and plunder was able to fill the vacuum of power left by the War of the Marabouts in the Lower Senegal.[77]

Dynastic traditions about Latsukaabe focus on his rise to power, addressing the extraordinary conditions that led to the emergence of a new royal matrilineage. Latsukaabe's maternal family, the Geej, had never ruled in Bawol or Kajoor before his reign, and the traditions guard the memory of his mother's non-aristocratic *jambur* origins.[78] In the dynastic traditions the problem of Latsukaabe's humble origins and lack of legitimacy is addressed through the story of his extraordinary youth. The historic Latsukaabe is remade by myth into an archetypal founder king. Latsukaabe was born a cripple, with an infirmity that prevented him from walking without crutches, and his name, Latsukaabe, is explained as derived from a Wolof verb which describes the limping walk of a cripple.[79] His brothers, disturbed by the dishonor brought on the royal house by this infirmity, convinced the king to drive his son out of the house, forcing the boy to live with his maternal uncle, a Fulbe shepherd. While sharing the life of the shepherds, Latsukaabe was healed and regained his strength and health.[80]

After the recovery of his health Latsukaabe went into exile, and traveled alone through Bawol, Siin, Saluum, and Kajoor. Although details vary in different versions of the traditions, this is invariably a period of trials and adventure in which Latsukaabe wanders alone, disguised as a humble shepherd or a *lawbe* ("woodworker"). Two episodes from this period appear in all the versions of the traditions. One is Latsukaabe's visit to Mbuur, a port on the coast of Bawol, where he sees European firearms used for the first time. In some accounts Latsukaabe works as a guide for European hunting expeditions organized by merchants from the Compagnie des Indes at or near Mbuur.[81] During his period of wandering in exile Latsukaabe visits a marabout in Naani, south of Saluum in the Mandinka country. There he recounts his story, recalling his royal origins. The marabout, describing his difficult youth as a series of tests, predicts a great future for him as king and gives him various talismans to aid him in his efforts to seek his destiny. The talismans include either gris-gris (Wolof, *teere*) or seeds (Wolof, *doom yi*) that Latsukaabe buries in the countries over which he wishes to rule, and magical powders (Wolof, *sunguf*) which he will be able to utilize in his struggle against his brothers.

19

Before he leaves the marabout, he is told to return to Bawol to participate in the wars that would follow the death of his father.[82]

The traditions about Latsukaabe's youth use myth to explain his rise from obscurity to power. His crippled childhood results in his being driven from his father's house to the house of his maternal uncle, the archetypical fate of the disfavored son in a polygamous household and a folkloric justification of the primacy of the maternal family.[83] His various trials and adventures may have historic reference, as in the trip to Mbuur where he sees the use of firearms, but it is more likely that these details were added to the story because Latsukaabe was the first Wolof monarch to employ firearms systematically. The legendary youth of Latsukaabe was invented from folk motifs to explain his success in imposing his mother's family as a new royal matrilineage.

During the succession struggle that followed the death of his father, Latsukaabe fought alongside his brothers to preserve the power of his father's patrilineage and he emerged after the wars as the only royal son who escaped serious wounds. Because Wolof traditions required the king to be in perfect physical health, Latsukaabe was chosen to serve as king of Bawol during an interregnum that was to last only until his brothers' wounds were healed. Latsukaabe used his magic powder to prevent his brothers' wounds from healing. During the interregnum Latsukaabe cleverly won over the notables, nobles, and royal slaves of Bawol by giving gifts, by renouncing the king's share of the war booty seized by the royal slaves, and by cultivating alliances with important families. On successive nights he visited the most powerful nobles of the court, challenging them to play *wure*, a game like chess. After winning the game, Latsukaabe offered his opponents the forty-eight pieces of silver they had used in the game, telling them to make jewelry for their wives. In sum, he acted in every way as a just and generous king. By the time his brothers' wounds were healed, Latsukaabe was able to persuade the council of electors to bypass his brothers and maintain his rule as king.[84]

Latsukaabe's diplomacy succeeded in winning over the notables, but he still had to confront his brothers when their wounds were healed. When asked by his brothers to give up the kingship in their favor and to choose for himself a provincial command, Latsukaabe replied that only force of arms would persuade him to give up the kingship (Wolof, *doole rekk a ko mena jele ci man*).[85] Latsukaabe challenged his brothers to combat: "Kingship is force. Let us brothers make war, and the one who kills the others will become king."[86] Latsukaabe then killed his brothers and established his mother's family as the ruling dynasty of Bawol. The most famous usurper in Wolof dynastic history, Latsukaabe expressed in brutal simplicity the rules that would govern the enthronement of kings throughout the succeeding history of the monarchy. Latsukaabe's enthronement in Bawol probably occurred in 1692, and within three years the new king extended his rule into Kajoor.[87]

20

Europeans who met Latsukaabe shortly after he imposed his rule on Kajoor, provide information about his seizure of power which complements that from dynastic traditions. European sources agree with traditions that Latsukaabe was called into Kajoor by the nobles to provide protection and stability in a country weakened by civil war, dynastic instability, and foreign invasion. Having defeated the invading armies of Jolof, Latsukaabe was chosen as king. According to André Brüe, then the director of the French Company, Latsukaabe pursued a dual policy of humiliating the nobility of Kajoor, putting to death or forcing into exile those who refused to accept his rule, and trying to win over "the people by protecting them from the oppression of the nobles."[88] The combination of force and diplomacy used in Bawol was repeated in Kajoor.

Europeans noted the devotion of Latsukaabe to his mother, the *lingeer*, described as the one person with a real ascendancy over the king. European sources present a flattering portrait of the queen mother, described as interceding on several occasions to restore peaceful relations between European traders and her son. The *lingeer* sent a young relative to Gorée to be trained as her interpreter in correspondence with the Europeans, and on at least one occasion convoked an assembly of the council of electors in order to persuade her son to end a trade boycott against the French.[89] The details provided by European sources reinforce the portrait of the disfavored son who rose to power and elevated his mother's family to power over the mothers of other sons. They also confirm the important role of aristocratic women in the Wolof old regime, particularly queen mothers who personified the ruling dynasty.

European sources shed light on the most important innovation of Latsukaabe, described by dynastic traditions as the first monarch in Senegambia to purchase large quantities of firearms.[90] Oral traditions recall that Latsukaabe purchased 300 guns at Mbuur by selling slaves, cattle, and other products. André Brüe described a corps of 200 musketeers in the army of the Dammel-Teeñ, and noted Latsukaabe's efforts to borrow "advisors" from the Company who could train his men in the use of the weapons.[91] The creation of a corps of musketeers involved a second innovation just as important as the use of firearms. The guns were placed in the hands of royal slaves (Wolof, *jaami buur*). Latsukaabe's corps of musketeers was the first real slave army in the Lower Senegal. Throughout the subsequent history of the Geej dynasty, the monarchy depended on the armed force provided by the royal guard, an infantry corps of 200–500 musketeers whose slave status was the best guarantee of their loyalty to the king and the reigning dynasty.[92]

The creation of an army of slaves was accompanied by an expansion of the role of slaves in administration and government. Brüe said that Latsukaabe secluded himself "with a small number of officers and slaves in whom he placed his trust." He described Latsukaabe as the "master" of his chief general, who dismounted before his lord and covered himself

21

three times on the head with dust.[93] The use of slave officials as regional commanders, officials in charge of administering ports of trade and warriors was a characteristic practice of the Geej dynasty. It arose from the need to buttress the power of a new dynasty against the dissidence of aristocratic rivals, but it quickly became a permanent feature of Geej rule. In popular memory and in much recent historiography the rule of the Geej is synonymous with the era of the *ceddo*, slave warriors and courtiers who were the chosen henchmen of the old regime.[94]

The use of slaves in the military and government was not an outright innovation. The real innovation was the creation of a permanent army of slaves armed with muskets. The connection between aristocratic power and slavery was not new. The earliest Portuguese accounts emphasize the integration of slavery and polygamy in the households of the Wolof nobility. Each "seigneur" had several wives, each of whom controlled a separate household of female slave attendants, while other slaves worked in agriculture or tended herds of domestic animals. The great lords and kings differed from the lesser nobility primarily in the number of wives and slaves under their control. In this system aristocratic women were responsible for the management of the household and production, while aristocratic men devoted themselves to the arts of war and government.

> This is his [the king's] manner of living with his wives: he has certain villages and places, in some of which he keeps eight or ten of them. Each has a house of her own, with young servants to attend her, and slaves to cultivate the possessions and land assigned by the lord. They also have a certain number of beasts, such as cows and goats, for their use; in this way the wives have the land sown and the beasts tended, and so gain a living.[95]

Portuguese sources give only a rudimentary description of slavery, but they emphasize the use of slaves in agriculture and the links between slave holding and the existence of a slave-raiding, slave-trading nexus linking Senegambia with North Africa and Portuguese Atlantic trade. One of the few comments on the labor regime of the slaves is contained in Valentim Fernandes' early sixteenth-century account of the Senegambian coast. "The slaves of this country work and earn for their master during six days and the seventh day they earn what they need to live the other six."[96] Although not as detailed as later descriptions of slavery, this passage indicates that the granting of subsistance plots to slaves along with fixed times to work on them was one of the fundamental characteristics of slavery.

None of the early Portuguese texts describe the military use of slaves by the aristocracy. Portuguese descriptions of Wolof warfare stress the important role of provincial nobles in providing armed contingents and the use of levies from ordinary commoners to fill out the infantry. Portuguese sources suggest that military slavery had not developed as a significant institution. The centralized monarchy of the seventeenth and eighteenth centuries contrasts with the more diffuse and "feudal" system of power described by the Portuguese in the fifteenth century. "This kingdom does not descend by inheritance, but in this land there are diverse lords, who through jealousy, at times agree among themselves, and set up a King of their own, if he is in truth of noble parentage. The King rules as long as he is pleasing to the said lords. Frequently they banish him by force and as frequently the King makes himself so powerful that he can defend against them."[97]

Oral traditions suggest that royal slaves played an important role at court as early as the mid-seventeenth century. They appear in Yoro Jaw's account of the struggle between the monarch Daawda Demba and the notables of Kajoor, led by Kocc Barma. It seems safe to conclude that no full-blown system of military slavery existed prior to the expansion of the Atlantic slave trade at the end of the seventeenth century. However, it is also clear that the use of slaves as trusted advisors and administrators in the court preceded their systematic use as warriors, and that the use of slaves in the court constituted the kernel from which military slavery developed under the pressures of an expanding Atlantic trade.[98] Latsukaabe created the first army of slaves, but he drew on the precedent of slave retinues at court and in noble households who served their masters as guards and warriors.

Two aspects of Latsukaabe's reign were particularly significant in defining the attitude of the new dynasty. The era of Geej rule was defined by the Atlantic slave trade and by the new demand for government in conformity with Islam. Latsukaabe initiated policies in diplomatic relations with Europeans and in domestic relations with Muslim communities which would have long-lasting effects on the history of Geej rule. Latsukaabe's diplomacy is known primarily from European sources, his Islamic policy primarily from dynastic traditions and from the traditions of Muslim communities.

Latsukaabe's reign coincided with the establishment of an effective partition of the Senegambian coast into exclusive commercial zones by European mercantilist companies. The entire region of the Lower Senegal was claimed by the French Compagnie des Indes Occidentales, based on the island settlements of Saint Louis and Gorée. The partition of the coast was opposed by Latsukaabe, who claimed the right to trade freely with all nations. Latsukaabe's efforts to preserve free trade in his ports led to several confrontations with the French, culminating with the arrest of André Brüe and all French personnel on the mainland of Cap Vert in the port of Rufisque on June 6, 1701. The director of the French Company was held prisoner by the Dammel for twelve days. The Company lost an estimated 6,000 livres worth of trade goods seized on the mainland and the French paid an additional ransom for the release of Brüe. Latsukaabe's action was in retaliation for French seizures of English ships trading on the coast of Kajoor-Bawol. Although Latsukaabe was unable to force the

23

French to abandon their exclusive trade zone, Brüe's successor, Louis le Maître, was obliged to increase the customs paid to the Dammel for the right to purchase water, food, and wood on the mainland. These concessions were wrung from the French by an eight-month trade boycott following Brüe's arrest, followed by a shorter boycott under his successor.[99]

The logic of Latsukaabe's action was to secure the maximum benefit for the monarchy out of trade relations with the French. Failing to break the French monopoly, he nevertheless succeeded in forcing the French to pay higher duties to secure their right to trade. This limited success was achieved by utilizing Kajoor-Bawol's strategic position in the wider trade region claimed by the French. As the dominant power in the mainland regions immediately adjacent to the French commercial settlements of Saint Louis and Gorée, Kajoor-Bawol could cut off the supplies of food and water that sustained the life of the French ports. Latsukaabe clearly perceived the strategic importance of Kajoor to French trade, warning the French that "they should consider upon whom their trading posts in Senegal [Saint Louis] and Gorée depended; he could expel them or starve them to death by forbidding his subjects to provide them with provisions."[100] Throughout the eighteenth century, boycotts of the provision trade between the mainland and the islands were Kajoor's most effective weapon in disputes with the French. Latsukaabe traced a path that would be frequently followed by his successors.[101]

Latsukaabe's policies toward Islam cannot be understood without presenting the historic context of his rise to power and its place in the modern history of Senegambia. The War of the Marabouts is often seen as the first Muslim revolution of the modern era. Consequently Latsukaabe becomes the founder of a regressive and oppressive political system which plundered and enslaved the Wolof in defiance of Islam. The assocation of his reign with the *ceddo*, plundering warriors who drank alcohol, cements the identification of the regime he founded with "paganism" in the popular memory of the old regime. This interpretation reflects the historic vision of the marabouts, the founder heroes of the most recent period of Wolof history.[102] Although there were continuities in the development of a Muslim anti-aristocratic ideology in the Wolof states, it would be an error not to differentiate as carefully as possible between the phases in the development of Muslim resistance to aristocratic rule. The first Muslim uprising predated the establishment of Geej rule in Kajoor and Bawol. From 1673 to 1678 a series of religious wars engulfed the Lower Senegal, leading briefly to the overthrow of the established political order in the Wolof kingdoms of Kajoor, Waalo, and Jolof, in the neighboring state of Fuuta Tooro, and in the Moor principalities on the north bank of the Senegal River.

The progress of these religious wars was observed with interest by the director general of the Senegal Company, who was astonished that a

24

simple preacher would lead an "uprising of the people and make them kill or chase their kings into exile under the pretext of religion and divine revelation in order to seize and govern them."[103] Louis Moreau de Chambonneau reported crucial elements of the ideology of the first reformist jihad in West Africa. After warning the kings of the region to practice Islam, limit themselves to four wives, and dismiss their courtiers, Nasir ad-Din warned them not to pillage their subjects or to enslave them. When his warnings were ignored, Nasir ad-Din and his lieutenants took the message directly to the people, preaching reform in the villages. According to Chambonneau, the propagandists described themselves as the messengers of God, and said that "God did not permit kings to pillage, kill, or enslave their peoples, that on the contrary, kings were required to sustain their peoples and protect them from their enemies, and that peoples were not made for kings, but kings for peoples."[104]

The condemnation of pillaging kings, who unjustly enslaved Muslims, was one of the central themes in the Muslim critique of aristocratic rule. Nasir ad-Din and his followers did not condemn that institution of slavery, but the enslavement of Muslims, particularly when they belonged to the same ethnic groups and historical communities of Senegambian Islam as the ruling warrior aristocracy.[105] The jihad was not a movement of conversion, as most previous jihads in West Africa had been, but a reformist movement. The religious wars of the seventeenth century had long-lasting effects on the Senegambian region, even though aristocratic rule was reestablished in their wake on both banks of the Senegal River. The War of the Marabouts began as an isolated movement of religious revolt with charismatic and messianic inspiration, but the vehicles for its subsequent expansion and impact were the Muslim communities of scholars and disciples spread throughout the region.

In its Mauritanian birthplace the religious revolt of Nasir ad-Din has been interpreted as an expression of the tension between warriors and scholar-merchants and as an effort by the Moors to destroy the growing commercial hegemony of the European Atlantic trade in the region, which was displacing the trans-Saharan trade.[106] As the religious wars spread into the Lower Senegal, they were transformed into a drive to place a Muslim king (Wolof, *buur juulit*) in power. Although initially successful in Waalo and Kajoor the new order was never stable, and by 1676 European slave traders were purchasing the refugees of war and famine created by the upheaval as aristocratic order reemerged from the debris of the revolution.[107] In spite of the defeat of the movement in its political phase, its significance did not end with the restoration of the Wolof monarchies.

In recent research emphasis has been placed on the participation of local centers of Muslim learning in the revolt and their subsequent role in preserving and developing the ideology of dissidence and contestation that was first expressed in the War of the Marabouts. Jean Boulègue has suggested that the Islamic centers of scholarship in the villages of Pir in

25

Kajoor, and Ndogal in Bawol, played a role in the mobilization of Muslims in the War of the Marabouts.[108] More importantly, those villages, along with Kokki, Luuga, and Ñomre in northern Kajoor, became centers of Muslim learning and Muslim political power in the aftermath of the War of the Marabouts. Oral traditions from those communities recall the political pact established between the monarchy and the marabouts which granted Islam an official political status in Kajoor under the reign of Latsukaabe.[109] In the northern border provinces of Kajoor Latsukaabe recognized the power of the marabouts, granting them titles as *seriñu lamb* ("marabouts of the drum"), which gave them a quasi-noble status and an official position within the state. In times of war the titled marabouts were required to bear arms and provide military contingents, like provincial governors, and in times of peace they served as the administrative links between their communities and the state.

Latsukaabe's decision stemmed from purely political considerations, as part of his broader efforts to create a series of political alliances to secure the power of his new dynasty. European observers described him as personally indifferent to religion. He ignored religious criticism of his marriage to two sisters chosen from a branch of his own maternal family in order to perpetuate the rule of his maternal clan. He reportedly said that he "did not doubt the existence of paradise; but he told Brüe matter-of-factly that he did not expect to go there, having been extremely cruel, and not feeling any inclination to become any better."[110] However, Brüe also noted that only the marabouts were allowed to speak before the king without prostrating themselves and removing their head covers.[111] Whatever his personal beliefs, Latsukaabe recognized the power of Islam within his kingdoms. In addition to creating titled marabouts in northern Kajoor, he granted land to marabouts and restored the land and status of Muslim villages like Pir, which had been nearly destroyed in the War of the Marabouts.[112]

Latsukaabe's recognition of Islam was a double-edged policy. By granting marabouts titles and requiring them to bear arms and participate in the taxation and administration of their kingdoms, the titled marabouts were partially assimilated into the nobility of Kajoor. In the long run the titled marabouts acquired a distinct status, closer to the nobility than to the scholars who remained loyal to the traditional separation between secular power and religious scholarship, between the ways of the warrior and the path of religious learning. During the subsequent history of the old regime the titled marabouts played an important political and religious role, but in the long run their political and religious authority was undermined by their role in the state, and religious leadership passed into the hands of the scholars of Islam.

2

Slavery and the slave trade in the Lower Senegal

In the late seventeenth century a new era began in the Lower Senegal. For the first time in the history of the region, the driving force of change came from outside of the region, from beyond the sea, as the Lower Senegal became a gateway to Africa for expanding colonial empires of the Atlantic world. The Atlantic economy literally reached into Senegambia, and became a dynamic force which put people and goods into motion, transforming the economy and reshaping the geography of wealth and power to suit its own needs and its own logic. The era of the Atlantic slave trade in Africa began in the sugar plantations of America. The sugar revolution drove the wheels of mercantilist capitalism like a mighty wind, propelling ships and cargoes of trade goods to the shores of West Africa, where the Atlantic world purchased the slaves whose sweat and blood fed the engines of economic growth.[1] Ships from the Atlantic poured manufactures from Europe, Asia, and America into the ports and rivers that carried them further inland and gathered the harvest of men, women, and children that flowed with the floodwaters of the rivers towards the sea.

It was the scale of the force exerted by the Atlantic trade which changed in the late seventeenth century. The great Atlantic powers, Britain and France, competed directly for the slaves of Senegambia for most of the eighteenth century, throwing not only their economic might, but also the power of their naval fleets into the balance. The result was the partition and repartition of the Senegambian coast into exclusive commercial spheres of influence, which were periodically redrawn in accordance with the fortunes of war. The struggles of France and Great Britain for hegemony in the Atlantic world had an important impact on Senegambian history, but far more important was the sheer volume of the eighteenth-century slave trade, whose demand for African labor was insatiable. The export of slaves was the final cause of the system of trade which emerged in Senegambia, but the system reached widely into the economy and society, and the flow of slaves to the coast was only the end result of far wider transformations.

Historians of the Atlantic slave trade and its era have often limited their vision of the Atlantic trade to the flood of slaves who embarked on ships to the New World, and to the few export commodities that left with them; in Senegambia essentially gum arabic, gold, and ivory. Philip Curtin centered his interpretation of this period around a systematic attempt to measure the import–export trade, and to evaluate it by economic criteria.[2] More recent research has stressed the ways that the Atlantic slave trade reshaped African labor systems and the economic geography of trade and production.[3] But very little attention has been given to the important trade in grains and other agricultural products that accompanied the slave trade. In the Lower Senegal the expansion of slavery in key sectors of the economy, in commerce and agriculture, and in the military forces mobilized by the monarchy and nobles, was driven by the same Atlantic trade that carried slave laborers across the ocean.

Throughout the eighteenth century the history of slavery in the Lower Senegal was inextricably bound together with the history of the Atlantic trade. Slavery developed in three distinct spheres of activity, all linked to the Atlantic trade, but each with its own logic and systems of slave use and management. The old regime employed slaves in its military forces and in government, as the trusted henchmen of the dynasty in power. Atlantic merchants, primarily concerned with exporting slaves across the Atlantic, turned to slaves to fill their needs for labor and protection in the maritime economy. Finally, slaves farmed and wove cotton cloth for their masters, forming the most important group of dependent laborers in the economy of the Lower Senegal. In all these spheres slavery was powerfully shaped by the integration of the Lower Senegal into the wider Atlantic world.

Slavery and the old regime

After the turmoil of the War of the Marabouts, the Lower Senegal fell under the rule of slave-owning warrior kings, who systematically integrated firearms into their armies, which now relied more than ever on the loyalty of slave warriors. Kajoor-Bawol was the dominant military power of the coast. Although European traders resented the power of the monarch, because he commanded two kingdoms and could assert considerable leverage over the coastal trade, they also described his regime as a predatory warrior state which supplied them with slaves. After a raid which allowed Latsukaabe Faal to deliver 300 slaves to liquidate his debts to the Company, André Brüe noted: "Negro princes always have a ready resource which allows them to procure more slaves; they sell their own subjects. They never lack pretexts to justify their violence and rapine. The Damel used this method because he was already deeply in debt to the Company, and he knew that his credit would not be extended."[4] European traders also described wars between African states as slave raids. When Latsukaabe Faal fought a war with the Burba Jolof in 1701, Brüe perceived the conflict as a series of slave raids by each opponent. "This is the way negro kings ordinarily make war. Decisive battles between opponents rarely occur; the campaigns consist of incursions and pillages. Each side seizes from the other a large number of their subjects, which they then sell as slaves to the merchants who visit their coasts."[5]

Recent research on the slave trade has shed new light on the historical forces that swept slave laborers out of the continent and sent them to the slave ports of the Atlantic. In West Africa historians have devoted considerable research to the mechanisms of enslavement, focusing on the military predation of warlords and states. In Senegambia, where regimes ruled by warrior aristocracies were widespread in the eighteenth century, and where slave warriors played an important role, the whole eighteenth century has been characterized as the era of the *ceddo*.[6] As summarized by Barry, the thesis implies historical regression: "Predatory activity reduced the producer to a simple export commodity, and this was the origin of the regression of Senegambian societies whose history was now dominated by violence."[7] The slave trade reduced the productive population, its wars devastated the economy and provoked famine, while the commodities imported by the aristocratic state and its slave henchmen served primarily to perpetuate state violence and provide luxury goods to the warriors. As a description of a historical period, this analysis sums up certain trends in the Senegambian region. This framework presents more problems when it comes to describing regional variation and the overall development of the economy.

In fact the new military regime created by Latsukaabe devoted little of its energy to wars of conquest or enslavement and the Lower Senegal was remarkable for the stability of its frontiers and dynasties, and the relatively small scale of its export slave trade during the eighteenth century. The Lower Senegal was not unique in this regard, but shared these characteristics with the states of the middle and upper Senegal, particularly Fuuta Tooro and Gajaaga. Those states also sold off relatively few slaves, even in periods of turmoil like the 1720s when they were pressured by invasion by Moroccan and Moor armies based in the western Sahara. At the height of the turmoil of the 1720s, French slave traders noted that the riverine states "only make slaves of other nations who are employed to work for them," demonstrating the vitality of a slave-using and slave-importing economy linked to the transit trade in slaves, an important grain trade, and the "legitimate" trade in gold, ivory, and gum.[8]

The frontier of violent enslavement linked to the slave trade had its center further to the east, in the Bambara states of Segu and Kaarta, which are constantly cited in the archives of the Compagnie des Indes between 1700 and 1750 as the major sources of the export trade. Philip Curtin has estimated that the slave trade from the middle Niger supplied approximately two-thirds of Senegambian exports over the entire course of the eighteenth century, with variations over time ranging from 45 per cent to 85 per cent.[9] Knowledge of slave origins was common on the Senegambian coast in the eighteenth century. Lieutenant Henry Dalrymple testified to the House of Commons about his experience in the 1770s: "I was informed by the mulatto merchants of Gorée, and by the natives of the continent opposite to the island, that the great droves (called Cassilas or Caravans) of Slaves which are brought from the interior parts of Africa, by way of Galam, to Senegal and Gambia, were prisoners of war."[10] The warriors to the east supplied the trade, but they probably received little of the profit associated with the sale of people, which went to the merchants who carried slaves to the riverine ports, to the riverine and coastal rulers who taxed the transit trade in slaves and received customs payments, and to those who profited from the trade in grain and other commodities.[11]

The Atlantic trade created important regional differentiation with regard to the export and use of slaves for production. In areas where grain, cattle, gum, and other products could be sold to Europeans to obtain desired imports, fewer slaves were exported and more were retained within Africa for productive use. In northern Senegambia these trends were evident in the Lower Senegal, in the middle valley, in Gajaaga, and in gum-producing regions north of the Senegal River. Slave holding produced important constraints on slave exports in all these regions, which supplied fewer slaves to the export trade than more distant regions like the middle Niger valley.[12] In the Lower Senegal, where the export trade in slaves was modest in scale, it is likely that the net import of slaves exceeded the export of slaves over the course of the eighteenth century.

The relatively small scale of slave exports from the Lower Senegal was a result of the economic geography of the Senegambian region. It in no way implies that slave exports had little impact on the political and social history of the Wolof old regime. It is difficult to judge the social and demographic impact of internal slave raiding on the population of the Lower Senegal without making some effort to analyze its scope, and if possible to estimate the number of enslaved persons who left the region. This is more difficult than one might expect, because the records of the slave-trading companies often give only estimates of trade from regions, which at best reflected an annual average, but which sometimes reflected wishful thinking. Less frequently there are precise indications of slave purchases, with the origins of the slaves noted. For some years the records only give global figures for the slave trade from the entire colony of Senegal, with no indications of the regional origins of slaves exported. New World data, although it has been useful in allowing a more precise counting of the global slave trade, with indications of origins by major regions, is much less useful for determining the precise origins of slaves.[13] For this reason, the records of the slave-trading companies provide the best sources for estimating the slave trade from a region like the Lower Senegal.[14]

The most striking aspect of the data is the relatively stable size of the slave trade from the Lower Senegal. The most common form of this estimate was a figure which indicated the number of slaves purchased in the vicinity of Saint Louis, and another figure for Gorée. At times these figures indicated the expected size of the trade, rather than a count. For example in 1705 La Courbe estimated the slave trade of Saint Louis as 50 slaves, the slave trade of Gorée as 100 to 150 slaves.[15] In the early eighteenth century the slave factors on the coast advanced goods to the monarchs of the region, as loans repayable in slaves. The debt figures give some indication of the size of the trade of a particular kingdom. The combined debt of the Dammel and Teeñ rarely exceeded the value of 100 slaves, and when it did in the 1720s, it was a sign of trouble that led Europeans to abandon the advance payment system.[16] During the period of debt-driven slave sales, the records of precise purchases or repayments of slaves from Kajoor and Bawol rarely exceeded 150 slaves. This cannot be taken as a full estimate of the slave trade, because debts to the Compagnie des Indes probably encouraged some slave sales to interlopers and English traders.

Sources from later in the century, which are more abundant, indicate a slave trade of roughly the same order, with precise exceptions that can be related to specific historical events. In 1752 Pruneau estimated the slave trade to Saint Louis from Kajoor, Waalo, and Fuuta Tooro, to be "130 to 150 slaves" a year. A further comment indicated that the great majority of these slaves were Wolof. "We hardly buy anything in the Senegal river[17] except blacks from the Wolof nations [*de nations yolofs*]; their women are highly valued in our colonies, where they are all employed as nannies [*nourrices*] or as servants. These negroes are very nimble, and hard-working, and have attractive features and are tall."[18] Later, Pruneau noted that "Gorée yearly draws out 220 to 250 slaves from the kingdoms of Cayor, Baol, and Sin."[19] More specific sales of slaves in this same period, but before the famine of 1753, indicated a relatively small-scale trade. In June 1751 the Dammel sold fifty slaves at Gorée.[20] A letter dated February 24, 1752 reported that the Dammel sold "42 slaves."[21] A year later the Dammel sold "50 slaves" to the English for twelve rifles apiece, a transaction that attracted notice because the price was over twice what the French were paying in the same period.[22]

The great exception to a range of slave sales around 200 or 300 was the period of famine and civil war from 1753 to 1755. The Dammel sold almost 400 slaves in June 1753 to the French. In July 1754 the French reported purchasing 400 slaves at Saint Louis and 350 slaves at Gorée. In 1755 the French traded 600 slaves at Gorée and 500 at Saint Louis.[23] These dramatic sales began with the arrival of famine conditions. Famine was prolonged by civil war, which was blamed for destroying a promising harvest in 1754. With the end of the famine slave exports returned to their previous levels. There is some indication that slave exports declined in the 1760s, when they were generally reported as about 100 from Bawol, and less from Kajoor. In 1765 the French on Gorée reported that they had no trade at Rufisque, and traded 100 slaves, along with cattle, rice, butter, and millet in Bawol.[24] In 1766 the French were only able to buy eighty slaves on the coast during a period of six months.[25] This pattern continued into the early 1770s, when reported slave sales rarely reached 200. One of the reasons was British possession of Saint Louis from 1758 to 1779, which attracted at least some of Kajoor's slave trade to the north.[26]

The period from 1764 to 1778 has a particular interest for estimating slave exports from the Lower Senegal. During this period, French slaving operations in Senegambia were confined to Gorée, which purchased slaves from Kajoor, Bawol, Siin, and the French trading post at Albreda in the Gambia. Because of the more restricted source area for French slave exports, French shipping data can be compared with French records from Gorée, in an effort to pinpoint the number of slaves exported from the Lower Senegal. Mettas' study of the shipping data shows that the French exported 1,820 slaves from Gorée in the decade from 1760 to 1769, and 8,210 slaves in the decade from 1770 to 1779.[27] For the first period, 1760 to 1769, the ten-year total actually represents five years of slave exports, because the French only reoccupied Gorée in 1764, and slave exports were insignificant until 1765. The yearly average for this decade was therefore 364, compared to 821 for the 1770s.

French sources from Gorée give higher figures of slave purchases, but provide important information on the distribution of regional purchases. In 1765 a French study of the coast described the slave trade at Rufisque as non-existent, the trade of Bawol as 100 slaves a year plus cattle, millet, and butter, and the trade of Siin as providing 50 slaves a year plus various provisions.[28] A study compiled in 1776 noted that the French could buy 300 slaves from the ports of Dakar, Rufisque, Portudal and Joal (Kajoor, Bawol, and Siin), 100 to 200 from Saalum, and 800 to 900 from Albreda in the Gambia.[29] A more general description of trade in 1771 cited Kajoor, Bawol, and Siin as kingdoms "that produced few slaves, but abundant provisions" and cited the Gambia as the main source of slave exports.[30] All these studies suggest that the French slave trade from the Lower Senegal averaged 200 slaves a year throughout this period. At least some slaves were sold north to Saint Louis "by Moors who come to Cayor and Baol, the two kingdoms neighboring our island."[31] However, the sources from this period confirm a general range of slave exports from the Lower Senegal of between 200 and 300 slaves a year.

This review of slave exports from the Lower Senegal suggests that the region supplied 300 to 400 slaves to the export trade in the first half of the eighteenth century, and 200 to 300 slaves a year in the period from 1760 to 1790. Even allowing for an undercount of 100 slaves a year in each period, the slave exports of the Lower Senegal represented only about 10 per cent of the total exports of Senegambia, based on the revised estimates of David Richardson for the Senegambian slave trade. From year to year there were important variations in the contribution of the Lower Senegal to the overall trade. In many years the region supplied less than 5 per cent of the export trade, while during the height of the famine of 1750–6 the Lower Senegal contributed nearly 30 per cent of total Senegambian exports.[32] In 1753, 1754, and 1755, the French purchased 900–1100 slaves in the immediate vicinity of Saint Louis and Gorée.[33] Although estimates based on shipping data provide the best overall counts of the Senegambian slave trade, Company records from the eighteenth century suggest that they undercount the slave trade. Pruneau listed Company exports from Senegal and the Gambia as 1,985 for 1736, 1,995 for 1737, 2,352 for 1738, and 2,207 for 1739, figures suggesting higher exports than Richardson's annual average of 1,233 for French exports from the same decade.[34] Again Company records show that the French exported 1,586 slaves in 1786, 1,722 slaves in 1787, and 1,911 slaves in 1788, higher exports than would be expected from the annual average for the same decade of 1,189 derived from shipping data.[35] The fragmentary data from Company records indicates an upward revision of the slave trade from Senegambia, but at the same time would require a downward revision of the estimated share of slave exports from the Lower Senegal. Table 1 gives three different estimates.

The export commerce of the Lower Senegal had other specific characteristics. In Kajoor and Bawol slaves were usually traded for "guns, gunpowder, lead shot, flints, and rum." In the early 1750s this produced the following prices: a slave was purchased with 5 guns worth 35 livres in France, with 100 pints of rum worth 50 livres, with 3,500 flints worth 14 livres, and for 50 pounds of gunpowder worth 25 livres.[36] All of these trade items were goods valued by and necessary to the aristocracy and their slave warriors. The limited selection of commodities used to purchase slaves contrasted strongly with the rich selection of trade items needed to trade for provisions: silver, jewelry and ornaments of various kinds, brass basins, silk stockings, shirts, shoes, hats, knives, iron, paper, cloth, and various other items, including carding combs for cotton.[37] These items were traded primarily for cattle, goats, poultry, millet, palm oil, rice, and butter. It is also striking that the food exports of a region that sold about 200 slaves could feed 2,000 slaves for a year, in addition to supplying many items to the European garrison. Although the slaves were worth far more than any of the other commodities traded, there is a clear suggestion of two distinct trade sectors. The slave trade was monopolized by specialists in violence who preyed on peasant society and used slave sales to finance part of the costs of maintaining themselves in power. Food sales, on the other hand, generated trade in a much wider variety of commodities, some of which had a productive value.

Eighteenth-century European traders have left important accounts of the slave raids that normally produced an export trade of several hundred

Table 1: *Slave exports from Senegambia*

	Estimates[a]		
	Curtin	Lovejoy	Richardson
1700–10	[18,400][b]	18,400	22,230[c]
1711–20	30,900	30,900	36,260
1721–30	22,500	22,500	52,530
1731–40	26,200	26,200	57,210
1741–50	25,000	25,000	35,000
1751–60	22,500	22,500	30,100
1761–70	14,100	14,400	27,590
1771–80	12,100	12,400	24,400
1781–90	20,300	22,100	15,240
1791–1800	6,200	7,000	18,320
Totals	198,200	201,400	336,880

[a] Sources for the table are Philip Curtin, *Economic Change in Precolonial Africa: Senegambia in the Era of the Slave Trade* (Madison, 1975), I, 164; Paul E. Lovejoy, *Transformations in Slavery: A History of Slavery in Africa* (Cambridge, 1983) 50; and David Richardson, "Slave Exports from West and West-Central Africa, 1700–1810: New Estimates of Volume and Distribution," *Journal of African History*, 30 (1989) Table 7, 17.
[b] Curtin's table (Table 4.3, *Economic Change*, I, 164) begins in 1711 and continues to 1810. To make his tabulation conform to the others I have inserted Lovejoy's figure for the first decade in brackets and changed Curtin's total correspondingly.
[c] Richardson uses a different chronology to establish his decades: 1700–9, 1710–19, etc. I have ignored this in establishing the table, because it does not significantly affect the comparison.

slaves a year. These raids, directed "against parts of the kingdom that it was necessary to weaken" began with the posting of sentinels around the village, who lay in wait for fugitives, while the main body of the war party attacked at dawn. Captives were seized by the warriors and the village was burned. In a royal expedition all the captives belonged to the king, according to Doumet, but he described the private banditry that accompanied the royal expedition. "Each dignitary has his trained followers, his domestic [slaves] who pillage for him in secret. When they want to keep one of the captives who should all go to the king, the horseman charged with this kidnapping leads his captive into the woods and ties him to a tree, where he is left until he can be recovered and presented to his master."[38] Doumet also noted that these attacks rarely led to the capture of the entire population: the main victims were women, slaves, and children. "The young men and all those who can bear arms and defend themselves are killed or escape into the forest, where they know little-frequented paths impassable for the cavalry."[39] The defensive techniques of villages included preventive flight into the bush, whenever a village had advance warning of the approach of the king or his governors. "Whenever the king or his governors go on the march, the inhabitants of the villages in his path and its vicinity carry their millet into the forest, where they hide it, and then they hide themselves in remote areas with their animals until calm has returned and they can return home without fear."[40]

Henry Dalrymple, an Englishman who spent time on Gorée in the 1770s, offered a similar portrait of slave raiding in Kajoor, based on information received from "the mulatto merchants of Gorée, and by the natives of the continent opposite to the island." He distinguished between *grande pillage*, lesser pillage, and kidnapping. The *grande pillage* was when "the king sends a number of soldiers, sometimes 300 or 400 . . . who attack a village, sometimes by setting fire to it, and seizing as many of the inhabitants as they can, and selling them to the Europeans as slaves." The lesser pillage described banditry by petty nobles and soldiers: "the smaller parties generally lay in wait about the villages . . . and take such people as they can surprize, who are likewise sold as Slaves." Kidnapping was important, because slaves were frequently sold in lots of one, two, or three at Gorée. "Individuals, often two or three men, who do not belong to the king, but are private robbers of men, when they can surprize any man, woman, or child, bring them down to the coast and sell them, where it is well known no questions are asked concerning the means by which they gain possession of them."[41]

State violence served the interests of the monarchy in several ways. Slave sales paid for military expeditions by providing revenues to purchase guns and horses, which were needed to defend dynastic interests, to intimidate villagers enough to ensure tribute payments, and to keep foreign military predators at bay. If slave raids eliminated or weakened independent populations who refused to pay tribute, they also contributed to the state's broader efforts to tax the population. The king's warriors used force and intimidation to collect tribute from subject populations who accepted the system, and pillaged populations that rebelled or remained outside of the system. In spite of its brutality, the state was weak and used naked force to support its authority. These efforts were resisted, by hiding grain stores or simply refusing to pay. Doumet, who described raids, also said that if a king was "too weak to attack and pillage [his subjects] most of them refuse to pay the governors the usual tributes."[42] Communities exposed to the threat of slave raiding were more willing to pay tribute, as a kind of protection money to the state and the mafia of lesser nobles who claimed rights on the local level. Those sold off into slavery could be replaced by slaves purchased from Moors, and in the late eighteenth century from the merchants of Saint Louis.

Eighteenth-century sources suggest that the independent Sereer populations of Kajoor and Bawol were the main victims of slave raiding in the Lower Senegal. If the military might of the Geej dynasty produced few wars of outright conquest, the Geej kings continued the historic effort of the Wolof dynasties to incorporate the Sereer into their kingdoms. In 1455

Cadamosto located the independent Sereer on the coast south of Cap Vert.[43] Although this corresponds with the present location of some small Sereer populations, the continuity is misleading. As late as the 1750s Adanson described the Sereer as the predominant group in the region immediately south of Rufisque.[44] In recent times refuge areas from Wolof political power favored by geographical terrain have persisted only as remnants of larger historical communities. This is particularly true of the Sereer of the north-west (Ndut, Noon, Saafen, Joobas), who today can be counted in the tens of thousands. The interesting feature of these group-ings is the geographic and ideological features they share with maroon communities in the Americas, and the lesser studied maroon communities in Africa.[45] Cadamosto described the ideology of the independent Sereer-Saafen communities of the coast. The two poles of this ideology were a rejection of centralized rule by Wolof kings, and a hatred of slavery, which symbolized the Wolof social order.

> These people have no king or lords, but they honor some people more than others, according to their qualities and conditions. They do not want any seigneur among them, because they do not want their wives and their children to be taken away from them and sold as slaves, as is done by the kings and the seigneurs in all the other countries of the blacks.[46]

Saafen independence from the Wolof kings of Bawol was achieved in spite of their proximity to Portudal, the major port of trade on the coast.

French sources described the independent Sereer as the object of slave raids by the Wolof kings, but they also noted the resistance of those populations, whose territories constituted a land of refuge from the monarchies of Kajoor and Bawol. Thus in 1719, when the Dammel of Kajoor owed slaves to the French, André Brüe reported hopefully, "He assured me that he plans a voyage to Rufisk to surprise the Seraires" even as he noted that the voyage had been postponed.[47] In 1765 the French on Gorée described a large concentration of population on the coast of Bawol, in the country of the Saafen. "The Sereres live in that country [Bawol]. This nation is worse than the first [Wolof], because their king is not in control. There is, among others, a village of 3,000 negroes called Guereau on the Cap de Masse [Cap de Naze], which can hardly be approached. By sea there are reefs, and by land thick forests, so that the king cannot collect the usual tribute. He has tried several times to pillage them but he has always withdrawn with heavy losses, and without ever reaching the village itself."[48] Although the population of Guereau may be exaggerated, a village of that name existed on the coast in the middle of the Saafen country during the eighteenth century.[49]

Oral informants in Saafen villages still insist very strongly on their historical independence from the Wolof until the 1890s. The traditions recounting the foundation of the village of Bandia insist less on the ethnic origins of the original migrants than on their discovery of a land of refuge, where they could settle independently of any political authority and regulate their own affairs.[50] The founding ancestors of Bandia included two cultivators who cleared forest to plant crops, and an elephant hunter whose craft protected the crops of the village. Saafen villages deny having paid any tribute to Wolof kings, and they agree with European sources as describing their relations with the surrounding states as a state of permanent armed defense. Although populations like the Saafen are not maroon communities in the sense that they were formed of runaway slaves, Saafen villages, like other independent Sereer groupings, were formed of populations who sought out geographically defendable refuge areas, in the hills and forest in the frontier regions of Kajoor, Bawol, and Siin.

The successful resistance of frontier areas was counterbalanced by the Wolofization of the central provinces of Bawol, where land tenure was reorganized and where Wolof settlement also occurred. Wolof migration tended to bypass the Sereer groups of southern Kajoor and western Bawol to flow directly into central Bawol and parts of Saalum, following the drier, more open country which skirts the Ferlo. Wolof settlement was encouraged by the rulers of Bawol, who settled Wolof artisan groups in Bawol, particularly blacksmiths, who supplied weapons and hoes for warriors and slaves. The powers of the Sereer "landowners," the *laman*, were reduced and land was seized for royal estates and clients. This process accelerated after Teeñ Ceendela crushed a Sereer revolt in the seventeenth century. It is likely that Sereer refugees from the central provinces fled to the frontier areas, where they could join still independent communities like the Saafen.[51]

The existence of independent and hostile populations within the borders of Kajoor and Bawol provided target groups that could be raided for slaves and cattle, both high value exports in the Atlantic trade. On the other hand the failure of the eighteenth-century monarchy to conquer and subdue these populations provides an important indication of the limited military power of the Wolof kingdoms, whose firearms and horses provided uncertain advantages against determined adversaries whose villages were located in hilly and forested refuge areas impenetrable by cavalry and where eighteenth-century firearms provided little advantage.

The internal frontiers of the Lower Senegal reflected the ecological frontier between the savanna and the forest, which was at the same time the border between Wolof monarchy and independent Sereer communities, between Islam and traditional religion. In the 1750s Adanson described his encounter with a "Serera negro" between Rufisque and Dakar, who "rushing out of the neighbouring woods, shot his poisoned arrows against me and my negro servant." According to Adanson he "was one of these Serera savages, who are united in a petty republic . . . and he was come out of his own country in quest of plunder."[52] Adanson's description of the "Serera savage" echoed Wolof perceptions of the borderland, where Islam provided a justification for slave raiding. As late as the mid-nineteenth century an official of the Wolof court described the independent Sereer of Bawol to Catholic missionaries as "barbarous and unconquerable peoples who know neither God, nor rulers, nor laws."[53]

Slave trading and slave holding in the Lower Senegal need to be conceived in their regional context, even as these were transformed by the new pressures and incentives created by the Atlantic slave trade. The monarchy balanced its interest in the slave trade with its interest in extracting tribute from rural producers. Although there were tensions between the two, they were interrelated rather than opposed results of the political system created by the aristocracy. As long as violence and political power were centralized in the hands of a strong ruling dynasty, the rule of force was compatible with agricultural production. Devastating social crisis occurred not when force ruled the land, but when centralized power failed and an anarchy of violence was unleashed in the vacuum left by the failure of the monarchy.

There is a striking discrepancy between the image of Kajoor, cited again and again in European documents as a slave-raiding kingdom whose king raided his own people, and the relatively modest volume of slave exports from the Lower Senegal. The king who raided his own people became a central metaphor for Europeans describing the Senegambian coast, a trope that explained and justified the presence of European slave traders. Most observers borrowed the image from published accounts of the coast. The unstated implication was that the enslaved victims of such a "barbarous" social order were better off as the slaves of Europeans. The image of the king who raided his own people fell out of favor in the late eighteenth century, when merchants, under pressure from abolitionists, tended to deny that Africans "went to war for the express purpose of making Slaves."[54] The new implication was that warfare, slave raiding, and slavery would continue even if Europeans abandoned the slave trade. Needless to say, neither opinion was based on a serious attempt to understand the power of the monarchy or the actions of the king and the king's people.

The king's people

The expansion of slavery in the Lower Senegal began with the court of the king, which was an assembly of nobles, courtiers, slaves, and clients, the human satellites who revolved about the reigning monarch and served him in various functions. Although slave warriors, courtiers, and servants grew more numerous and powerful over the course of the eighteenth century, they inserted themselves into a world of dependants and clients who inherited their status, and who helped define the relations of dependency that linked the king with his servants. The role of the slaves at court was determined in part by the long-standing relations of dependency which linked the court with client groups, particularly the blacksmiths (Wolof, *tegg*), *griots* (Wolof, *gewel*), leatherworkers (Wolof, *uude*), and other members of Wolof "caste" groups.

The origins of the Wolof "caste" system are unknown, lost in the mists of times predating the formation of the monarchy. The subdivision of Wolof society into free persons, hereditary occupational groups, and slaves, resembles similar hierarchies elsewhere in the western Sudan. Although sometimes described as a caste system, the occupational groups in question form only a small segment of Wolof society; neither nobles, warriors, marabouts, slaves, or peasants belong to "caste" groups, and most social distinctions based on wealth, learning, power, or occupation fall outside the so-called "caste" phenomenon.[55] Artisanal groups and *griot* groups have been described as castes for two reasons. There is a widespread belief in their social inferiority, accompanied by prejudice and superstitions about members of these groups. In addition, there are strictly observed rules of endogamy between *geer* ("non-caste") and *ñeeño* ("caste"), who do not intermarry. Within the various groups of artisans intermarriage does occur, but intermarriage between artisans and *griots* is very rare.[56]

The prejudices and marriage taboos which form the core of the "caste" principle may be based on ancient religious beliefs, which are no longer fully comprehensible. Blacksmiths (*tegg*) are the most respected and feared occupational group, because of their command of fire and iron, their use of incantations (Wolof, *jatt*) and beliefs that they can bring bad luck. Blacksmiths may have once had a religious role, preserved today in the memory of their role in circumcision ceremonies and as keepers of grave sites.[57] Leatherworkers, who form the second artisan group, may also have once wielded some religious or magical power, represented in recent times by their fabrication of protective charms (Wolof, *teere*). But in any case these beliefs appear to be remnants from the past. The Wolof ideology of caste is attenuated, compared to the more elaborate system of beliefs that defines caste in the less islamized Mande world.[58]

Interpretations of "caste" which emphasize social taboos and magico-religious beliefs can neglect the way that the "caste" principle distributes political power, honor, and economic privilege. The social charter of "caste" denies political power and honor to the *ñeeño*, but rewards them with an economic monopoly in their respective professions. The "caste" principle sustains the social division of labor because no *geer* can perform any of the trades reserved to the *ñeeño*. Honor and power are reserved to the *geer*, a social group that includes the peasantry as well as the aristocracy. "Caste" places agricultural communities at the center of the social world, the source of power and honor. Caste groups participate in the world of power and honor only as clients. At the same time the caste principle obscured the class divisions between the aristocracy and the peasantry.

In the period of the monarchy the "caste" groups became hereditary client groups, attached to particular families. Over time the monarchy reshaped these groups into dependants who were attached to the court. The social relations between nobles and clients, based on inequality and the gifts given by the lord to his clients, came to define the caste system. The demand for iron weapons, spears, daggers, and arrows, employed many smiths, who also learned how to repair European trade guns and to fabricate shot. Some blacksmiths specialized in the production of jewelry in gold and silver for aristocratic women, becoming a distinct subgroup in the blacksmith occupational group.[59] Leatherworkers specialized in the production of saddles and harnesses for the horses of the aristocracy and in the production of handbags and decorative goods for aristocratic women.[60] Both blacksmiths and leatherworkers were given titled leaders who resided in royal capitals to assure the organization of production, but also to serve as courtiers with ceremonial functions and leaders who could mobilize blacksmiths and leatherworkers in time of war.[61]

Apart from the artisan groups, most of the specialized client groups of the old regime were specialists in the verbal arts, in music, or were courtiers by profession. The Wolof commonly divide casted persons in two broad groups, the artisans (*jef-lekk*) who live by their crafts, and the courtiers and bards (*sabb-lekk*) who live by entertaining and flattering their patrons with words and music.[62] The courtiers and bards can in turn by subdivided into subgroups, each with a specialized function based on the instruments they played, the specialized knowledge they preserved, and the role they played at court. As a group the bards (*gewel*) and courtiers (*ñoole*) were considered of baser origins than the artisans and subject to more contempt and ridicule. These prejudices are explained in myths attributing "impure" origins to these groups, but also reflected their social role as praise singers, entertainers, flatterers and courtiers, the "dogs of court" (Wolof, *xaju mbooloo*).[63] In social relations, the inferiority of bards and courtiers is expressed in their constant solicitation of gifts from their social superiors, who are obliged to reward their praises and entertainment with payments.

The *gewel* and *ñoole* were client groups of the nobility. Both played important roles in court. Nobles were constantly accompanied by their *gewel*, who provided entertainment, tasted the king's food and drink, carried the war drums and fought alongside their masters.[64] In the eighteenth century they shared some of these functions with royal slaves, who served as the king's guard, but also as his trusted advisors. The *gewel* of the king preserved the history of the dynasty in power. On the night between Thursday and Friday Wolof courts listened to the recitation of genealogies and the epic history of the dynasty, accompanied by music.[65] As masters of the spoken word and dynastic traditions *gewel* often spoke for the king during assemblies or negotiations. The *ñoole* were a courtier group who served the royal households as doormen, spokesmen, messengers, and tax collectors.[66] In the eighteenth century they shared most of these roles with the royal slaves.

Although caste groups developed a special relationship with the monarchy and the nobility, caste groups were also the clients of *jambur* families. Yoro Jaw described the ancient *laman* before the foundation of the Jolof empire as the patrons of woodcutters and *gewel*. "In very ancient times, at a period when the *laman* alone headed all these kingdoms, they had large drums and small drums fabricated by woodcutters as signs of their authority and their *griots* played them in ceremonies on fixed days."[67] Village society, with its *jambur* dignitaries, reproduced the patron–client relations of the court on a more modest scale. Peasants needed the services of blacksmiths, who fabricated iron tools for villagers in exchange for payment. They occasionally needed *gewel* for family ceremonies, just as the village community depended on them to provide entertainment for holidays and public ceremonies. On the village level artisans and *griots* were the clients of local dignitaries, but their services could be purchased by ordinary villagers, who provided them with raw materials and paid them for their labor.

The existence of ancient client groups in the Wolof courts influenced the way slaves were integrated into the royal household. Slaves had two essential functions in the court of kings and nobles. They served as trusted servants in the roles of warrior, administrator, house intendant, in positions which placed them in the inner circle of the king, extensions of his family and his network of clients. These trusted servants were born into slavery (Wolof, *jaam juddu*) and often inherited their relatively privileged position. Other slaves, more numerous, but often less visible in eighteenth-century sources, labored to produce much of the food consumed at court. Many of these slaves were women who pounded millet and cooked for the court. However, the distinction between privileged servants and slaves was never absolute, except in the case of a small number of slaves with long-standing ties to the monarchy, who were crown slaves (Wolof, *fekk bayyeetil*), belonging to the state rather than to the royal family.[68] These slaves "free of all claims from members of the royal family, were only the slaves of and only served the ruling monarchs in their capitals, where they resided, and where they formed by inheritance the regular and perpetual guards of their masters."[69] Other slaves, more numerous, were commonly owned by the maternal family (*jaami-ndey*). In royal matrilineages these slaves formed the backbone of the slaves at court.

Slaves born in noble households were considered *surga* ("dependants") like all unmarried dependants, and owed "their labor to their masters from six in the morning to two in the afternoon." But in noble families the "*surga* formed the armed entourage that each noble formed at his expense and used to maintain his status, and who formed his escort when he was called to the king, when he travelled or made war."[70] These slaves, owned by particular princes and nobles, led the life of privileged warriors when their masters were in power, "but in the contrary case they fed themselves and their masters, in their native country or in exile, with the products of their labor and other resources owned by their families. They practiced all professions, even the lowest one of all, that of a weaver, to feed themselves and their masters."[71] Young slaves thus formed a pool of laborers in noble households, and even those slaves born in noble households to warrior slaves might have to serve an apprenticeship in the fields before they could fight. A reversal in the fortunes of the master and his family could also return the slave warriors to the fields.

The expansion of slavery in the court of the king and nobles did not eliminate other forms of dependency and vassalage. Free military vassals called *dag* served nobles alongside slave warriors.[72] They were primarily soldiers of fortune who attached themselves to nobles and formed part of their entourage. Many lesser nobles, who had weak claims to political office, surrounded themselves with a retinue of slaves and vassals and offered their services to pretenders or reigning monarchs in the hopes of being rewarded with a provincial command. Yoro Jaw attributed much of the violence and slave raiding of the old regime to the exactions of minor nobles and their military vassals, rather than directly to the monarchy.[73] According to a Wolof proverb, "the king is not dangerous, his vassals are" (*Buur bi aayul, dag ya aay*).[74] The proliferation of military slavery and vassalage on the provincial level was a source of instability during the old regime. The king's court was the most important center of dependency and slavery, but the monarchy was unable to monopolize the power provided by the service of slaves and vassals.

The court of Kajoor was essentially a court of slaves and dependants. Some slaves filled important political and military roles, while others labored to provide for the specialists in violence. Although European observers like Doumet certainly erred when they reported that almost all the generals, governors, and dignitaries of Kajoor were slaves of the king, they observed one of the most important trends of the eighteenth century.[75] Dynastic traditions confirm the domination of royal slaves over the royal household and the army through their titled officials.[76] Rather than replacing the older titled nobility and dignitaries representing the estate of free persons, royal slaves formed a parallel administration directly responsible to the monarchy. Many provinces were divided into districts under noble command and districts administered directly by royal slaves. Other provinces were commanded entirely by royal slaves. Wherever royal slaves were posted, they served the king. The network of royal slaves settled in Kajoor served as a police force which gathered information, watched the roads, and collected taxes on trade. In the capital royal slaves ran the household of the king and provisioned the capital. Vast numbers of ordinary slaves, mainly women, prepared food, served it to the court, and did the royal wash.

The *lingeer* or first queen of the kingdom oversaw the work of feeding and caring for the king, his servants, and the parasites who gathered at court. The *lingeer* was seconded by the *awo*, the first wife of the king. Both women had the rights to districts managed for them by royal slaves. Both lived in royal residences where they took charge of receiving guests and providing hospitality to visitors and the court. According to Yoro Jaw, Wolof queens were escorted in public by armed men (probably slaves) and free women courtisans. They commanded the labor of an entourage of slaves: "The male slaves carried the food and served the feast, the women slaves were pounders of millet, cooks, and washers."[77] Most of the slaves who worked for the royal household as servants of this kind were also drawn from those born into slavery. Women cooks and pounders of millet of this class were called *jebere* and worked under the supervision of the intendant of the royal household (Wolof, *Fara Biir Ker*), a titled slave official.

Wolof courts were important centers of consumption, fed by tribute from the provinces and by slave labor. Dynastic traditions often leave the impression that the court of the king was entirely peopled by clients, courtiers, and warriors and that the court was entirely removed from the world of production. Latsukaabe's successor, Mayssa Tende Wejj (1719–48), constructed a royal capital at Maka, on the borders of Kajoor and Bawol, which was entirely populated by nobles, courtiers, clients, and slaves. Royal slaves kept the capital illuminated at night with lamps fueled by oil. No one in the capital worked in the fields and Maka is remembered in traditions as a symbol of good living, abundant food, dance, and music.[78] This divorce between the court and the world of production was not, however, a permanent feature of the regime. In the late eighteenth century Europeans described the Dammel Makodu Kumba Jaring (1766–78), who ruled after a long period of civil war and famine, supervising the agricultural labor of 300 naked slaves.[79] Dynastic traditions describe the same king as "very interested in agriculture. He founded a new capital at Khandane . . . where he cleared and removed the forest from vast fields. There he made all the *laman* work, accompanied by their subjects."[80]

In the Wolof kingdoms, agriculture remained the base of the economy. Although European sources and dynastic traditions sometimes give the impression that the kingdoms of the eighteenth century became centers of warrior predation and consumption, they simply reflect the historic perceptions of praise singers and slave traders, who both tended to ignore the world of work and production. The productive labor of slaves and peasants provided for the consumption of the court and provided an essential base to the Atlantic trade.

43

Slavery and Atlantic commerce

The history of slavery in Africa in the eighteenth century has only gradually emerged from the shadows cast by the history of the Atlantic slave trade. Problems with sources can explain this neglect only in part. The questions asked by historians played an equally important role. As long as historical research focused on measuring and explaining the volume of slave exports from Africa, the history of slavery in Africa appeared to be a secondary problem and one whose logic was opposed to the primary problem of explaining slave exports. Debates about the slave trade focused on models of enslavement and delivery to the coast, and on the activities of warriors and merchants.

Philip Curtin's work on the slave trade in Senegambia gave central weight to the activities of European and African merchants. In analyzing the mechanisms of enslavement and the transport of slaves to the coast, he constructed a political model of enslavement. He argued that the political authorities who captured slaves profited little from enslavement, and did not respond to price incentives in the slaving economy. Enslavement was thus politically determined, and could not be explained by economic factors.[81] The economics of the slave trade was largely shaped by the merchants who transported slaves from the point of capture to the markets where they were resold. Curtin's work contrasted sharply with studies of enslavement in the Bight of Benin, where initial studies stressed the activities of enterprising slave-raiding warriors, and where the merchant sector has only gradually emerged from a model of slave marketing based on royal monopoly and state control.[82] Interpretations of the slave trade tend to emphasize either the predation of warriors or the efficiency of commerce.

Historians of the slave trade have not placed much emphasis on slavery within Africa as a constraining factor. Many early interpretations of the development of slavery in Africa saw the abolition of the slave trade as a causative factor in the development and consolidation of slave systems in Africa. With the end of the slave trade, the slave-raiding, slave-trading economy continued to function, but the slaves were now diverted into the internal market, where their labor filled new demands for export commodities during the era of legitimate commerce. Eighteenth-century Africa was therefore treated primarily as a source of slave supply, where slave raiding and slave trading existed to serve the needs of the wider Atlantic world.[83] Recent research has qualified these views in important ways. Critics of Curtin's political model of enslavement have characterized the eighteenth century as an era of warrior predation, in which slave raiding was a significant activity, carried out to acquire weapons and trade goods. By focusing on warfare and its side effects, particularly destroyed crops, raided food supplies, and periodic famine, Curtin's critics have also tried to bring into focus the high cost of the slave trade for Senegambian societies. Curtin's critics have also emphasized the fact that the typical eighteenth-century warrior was a military slave, creating a structural link between warrior predation and the Atlantic slave trade.[84]

Recent research has also stressed the fact that merchants in the western Sudan based many of their activities on the exploitation of slave labor. Slaves grew the grain that provisioned caravans, worked as transporters and caravan drivers, and spun and wove cotton cloth. From this perspective, warlords and merchants created islands of slave-based production in the eighteenth century that prefigured the massive expansion of slave production in the nineteenth century. The nineteenth-century consolidation of slave production was directly linked with the decline of the export slave trade and the expansion of "legitimate" commerce. Warrior predation continued on an expanded scale, but its victims were now channeled into economies based on production for export. According to this view slavery expanded in the eighteenth century under the direction of warlords and merchants, reshaping labor systems in specific sectors of the economy, but its full development as a system of production was hindered by conflicts between warfare and trade, and by the massive exports of slave labor.[85]

Nevertheless the conflictive relationship between slave exports and slavery within Africa appears very clearly in Senegambia, where slave exports declined in the second half of the eighteenth century, when the Atlantic slave trade as a whole reached the height of its expansion. But this same problem is implicit in the entire history of the slave trade from the western Sudan, where slave raiding and slave trading always existed within a system that included the use of slaves in production. Slavery is usually seen as a way of coercing labor in agricultural societies where economic conditions make it difficult to mobilize free labor in enterprises with large labor demands. In most agricultural societies, slavery is associated with abundant land relative to labor, particularly when there is a demand for some commodity which can be produced and commercialized profitably. In the Americas the existence of abundant land, the favorable conditions for sugar and tobacco production, and the difficulties of recruiting European settlers or the native Indian inhabitants to work in the plantations, led planters to turn to indentured servants and then slaves.[86]

If African slave systems are interpreted as systems for coercing scarce labor in agricultural societies where abundant land made it very difficult to recruit free laborers, because free persons preferred to live in independent peasant households, then the massive export of slaves over a number of centuries appears as an apparent paradox. The indigenous existence of slavery in Africa and demographic patterns of settlement do suggest an interpretation of slavery based on the scarcity of labor. There was no important landless class; free labor could be recruited, but usually only on a seasonal basis; and slaves were in fact used in almost every important

45

sector of production in the western Sudan. Yet the western Sudan exported its scarce human resources in the form of slaves, selling them to the slave merchants of the Islamic and Atlantic worlds.

The apparent irrationality of such a slave trade is more a product of the abstract framework in which it is analyzed than in the historical conditions which produced it. Although it may make sense for contemporary Africans to decry the depopulation of the continent or some of its major regions through the massive export of people, no unified "African" or "West African" labor market existed during the centuries of the Atlantic slave trade. Labor markets in which slaves were purchased or sold were highly segmented, reflecting the small scale of political organization and economic integration. The internal slave trade within Africa transferred laborers from one region to another and a surplus or shortage of labor and slaves existed only within the functional regions of the existing political economy, and only for the warriors, merchants, and notables who exercised power over slaves. In the eighteenth century the same slave-trading routes which delivered slaves to the coast also transferred laborers to regions where the demand for slaves was strong. In Senegambia these regions included Gajaaga, Fuuta Tooro, and the Lower Senegal, whose location in the Atlantic trade system permitted them to employ slaves profitably in grain production and in other activities linked to the Atlantic trade.[87]

Historical analysis of the Atlantic trade has been hampered by the tendency to isolate the import–export trade from the essential base of the economy, which was agriculture. The harvest of slaves and gum arabic, sought by Atlantic merchants, was directly related to the harvest of grain. In the simplest sense, this relationship existed because the ability of Atlantic merchants to export slaves depended directly on their ability to feed them from the moment of purchase until they departed for the Americas. The problem in the Senegal River trade was greater than is suggested by this statement. The majority of slaves exported from Senegal were purchased over 300 miles upriver. They could only be shipped downriver by boat during three months of high waters coinciding with the rainy season. When they arrived on the Atlantic coast, they had to be held for several months because of the wind and weather patterns that regulated the patterns of transatlantic shipping in the eighteenth century. Slave ships typically brought only partial stores and provisioned themselves with food and water for their slave cargoes on the Atlantic coast. All of these factors generated a significant demand for grain.

The commercial demand for grain had an important impact on the political economy of the Lower Senegal. The eighteenth century was marked by two related processes: the expansion of slavery and the reinforcement of tributary relations between peasant communities and local representatives of political power. These developments were related to one another, and it is artificial to oppose them by analyzing one as the creation of a tributary mode of production and the other as the development of a slave mode of production. The theoretical opposition between these two ways of extracting surplus production from rural producers did not prevent them from developing simultaneously, in response to the new economic, social, and political conditions created by the Atlantic trade. The constant threat of enslavement that hung over the heads of independent rural communities made the payment of tribute, which functioned as a kind of protection money, a logical response to the conditions of insecurity created by the Atlantic trade. Slaves, on the other hand, were the property of households, and their accumulation was essential to the strategies of aristocratic families struggling to maintain their political power and to increase their wealth in dependent people. The accumulation of slaves by aristocrats did not reduce their interest in extracting tribute and protection money from their political subjects. Slaves also had a wider economic value in the agricultural economy. Slaves were worked harder than free persons, and their labor produced surplus grain and other commodities.

Dynastic traditions record the creation of new taxes on livestock and grain production in the eighteenth century, where they are clearly described as protection money. The words attributed to Latsukaabe Faal, a monarch who seized power by force, have to be read with irony, but the message is clear.

> You gave me control of your destiny, which I accepted voluntarily. I have lived up to my duty because for ten years your families, your harvests, and your animals have been protected from the pillages which were common before. You owe me a reward, or rather a compensation, because I am the protector of your property.[88]

It is not difficult to perceive the threat behind this statement, even in the form preserved by dynastic tradition. Those who did not pay the new taxes exposed themselves to pillage. Because tribute paid in millet, cattle, and other local products was ultimately convertible into the same commodities purchased through the sale of slaves or the sale of slave-produced commodities, tribute collection, slave exports, and slave production were alternative ways of acquiring valuable trade goods. The dynastic tradition just quoted noted that the proceeds of the tax were used to purchase firearms and horses, two of the most important commodities acquired by the export trade in slaves.[89]

In the Lower Senegal slavery developed to mobilize labor for grain production and the production of cotton cloth. Slaves produced grain during the rainy season from July to October and wove cotton cloth during the dry season. In the eighteenth century slave management was conditioned by the labor demands of these two activities, but also by the particular conditions of slave holding in a region adjacent to major routes of the international slave trade. The condition of slaves in agriculture was

47

not uniform, but varied importantly over the life cycle of slaves and slave families. The differentiation that resulted became a fundamental aspect of slavery. Slavery was not one social status, but many. The clash between the master's desire for management and control, and the slave's resistance and search for autonomy produced different conditions of bondage. Differentiation was part of a broader system of slave management which emerged from a complex interaction between the economic system, the political goals of slave holders, slave resistance, and constraints imposed by the ideological hegemony of Islam in Wolof society.

Slavery was a way to mobilize scarce labor in a land-rich society. The widespread availability of land to free Africans created labor bottlenecks in the expanding eighteenth-century trade-oriented economy. Enslavement functioned in a way parallel to "proletarianization" in early industrial societies: slaves were violently separated from the means of production through enslavement and transferred to a new society where they had no rights in land and could be forced to work under the control of the master. Slaves who originated as war captives were people without rights, with no social identity until they were purchased by a master and integrated into a new society. The Wolof referred to such slaves as *jaam sayoor*, slaves "exposed" for sale, the naked and halfnaked human chattels sold by slave merchants.[90] Because enslaved persons had little value as slaves in the regions of their origin *jaam sayoor* were purchased from slave merchants while locally enslaved persons were sold to European slave ships or Moor slave caravans.[91] These trade slaves had no rights or privileges. They owed all of their labor to their masters, who fed and clothed them in exchange. Such slaves were whipped and beaten to force them to work, held in chains to prevent runaways and could be sold at the master's will. Slaves in the fullest sense of the term, the *jaam sayoor* represented the starting point in a spectrum of relationships between slave and master.[92]

Recent research on slavery in West Africa has focused on labor systems and management. Although much of the research focuses on the production of export commodities by slaves in the nineteenth century, the essential argument is that the expansion of slavery provided labor for commodity production and that slavery was associated with both an extension in the size of agricultural units and intensification of the labor process.[93] This interpretation has influenced the models used to describe the nature of slavery in Africa and the way slave labor was managed. Paul Lovejoy has argued that the expansion of slavery in agriculture led to the development of a plantation sector where slavery became the dominant mode of production and slave management came to resemble harsh transatlantic systems of slave control.[94] If the conception of a plantation sector refers only to the size of the units of production and the way slave labor was supervised, the analogy is useful. On the other hand, the plantation concept seems to undercut the varieties of slave statuses and labor regimes in West Africa and can be misleading if it suggests close

48

parallels with the capitalist slave economies of the Americas.[95] However, its real weakness stems from the fact that the merchants and aristocrats of West Africa cannot be adequately described as planter classes analogous to those in the wider Atlantic world.

After purchase slaves underwent a time of "seasoning" which had several aspects. Death by disease was common in the period after enslavement and purchase, as slaves were exposed to new disease environments. New slaves were worked hard and assigned work that other members of the household disdained. They were fed poorly and had no chance to cultivate for themselves. The threat of sale was real, because the Lower Senegal lay astride major slaving ports. The fear of sale to the Atlantic trade served the master's interest by favoring accommodation to slave status. Only those slaves who survived and won the trust of the master could marry and form families. Their children and descendants formed the second category of slaves, the *jaam juddu*, "born slaves," usually referred to as household slaves.[96] Although conceived by the Wolof essentially as an amelioration of slavery acquired by birth in the household, the transition could occur in the life of a *jaam sayoor* who was permitted to marry, because the payment of the bride price by the slave groom to the woman's master (often the owner of the male) produced an amelioration in the married couple's status. They received a plot of land where they could work for themselves after putting in a work day for the master which lasted from six in the morning to two or three o'clock in the afternoon. They also were freed from labor for the master for one or two entire days. On the other hand, their children repeated in their life cycle the work routine of the *jaam sayoor*, without sharing their legal status. Slave children born in the house were entirely under the control of the master during their childhood and youth. "The boys held in the service of the master could not free themselves from his control until the age of thirty or thirty-five, when they could go and work for themselves, but only after marriage. For the girls the master required the entire payment of the bride price which belonged to him."[97]

The evidence for the expansion of agricultural slavery in the Lower Senegal is indirect. There are few descriptions of slaves at work in the fields in European sources and few descriptions of agricultural labor. None of these sources would permit even an approximate census of the incidence of slavery. Dynastic traditions describe the slaves of the court, but focus on privileged slaves and slaves serving as servants in the royal households, not on field laborers.[98] Occasional comments in European sources affirm the existence of slavery on the mainland in passing. For example, in 1765 a French project to build stockhouses on the mainland of Cap Vert noted that slave laborers could be used "and there will be no deserters to worry about among these blacks who know that a harsher slavery awaits them all along the coast."[99] Other European texts give the general impression that slaveholding was fairly widespread in Senegambian society, since slaves were owned not only by the court, but by village notables. They particularly described women slaves, who served food to guests and provided domestic labor.[100]

Eighteenth-century European observers of slavery, mainly seamen and merchants, emphasized the differences between American plantation slavery and slavery on the Senegambian coast. Captain Thomas Wilson, a royal navy officer who served with the British forces on Gorée in the 1780s said that the inhabitants of the coast had "many" slaves, but noted: "It is not an easy matter to distinguish them from their masters or mistresses; they live all together."[101] Henry Dalrymple was more insistent on this point. "In the island of Gorée, of which the greater part of the inhabitants are Mulattoes, Slaves are common, but on the continent they are in very small numbers indeed among the natives, and treated so well, eating with their masters, working along with them, and being as well clothed (which they generally are, I think) that it is impossible to distinguish them from free men, unless the circumstance of their being slaves is mentioned; I never saw any whip or instrument of torture used on that part of the coast, nor do I believe, from the enquiries I made, that Slaves are treated with severity."[102] These men judged slavery by the harsh conditions of the West Indies where "they were treated very cruelly."[103]

One of the more important, indirect indications of the importance of slave production in the Lower Senegal was the commercialization of grain production. Millet was an important trade item not only in exchanges with European trade settlements on the coast, but also with the western Sahara. Doumet, who described the trade of the Moors in Kajoor in the 1760s, noted that they exchanged horses for slaves "whom they carry back into their country on the other side of the river where they use them to cultivate their land and guard their herds." But he also noted that they "also purchased all the millet of the interior of the country, travelling all the way to the villages of the coast, opposite Gorée, where they trade some of their millet for dried fish, which they resell in regions further removed from the sea."[104] This trade suggests that the Saharan slave system, like the system on the coastal islands, depended on food imports to sustain itself. Demand for grain in the desert encouraged the expansion of agricultural slavery in the grain-growing regions of the Lower Senegal.

The distribution of the slave population within Senegal in the early colonial period provides indirect evidence for the important role of slaves in producing surplus grain. At the beginning of the twentieth century the French estimated that there were 200,000 slaves in Senegal. Although this estimate must be regarded with skepticism and certainly underestimated the number of slaves, it was based on an actual census of more than 150,000 slaves, with adjustments for regions with inadequate data. The striking pattern in the census data was that about half the counted slave population was concentrated in the Wolof states of Waalo, Kajoor, and Bawol, with the other half in the states of the middle and upper Senegal

River valley. There was a marked concentration of slaves along the Senegal River valley and in regions near ports of trade on the Atlantic coast.[105] All of these regions were major suppliers of millet to either Atlantic merchants or desert society or both in the eighteenth century. It is also striking that these regions, which had the largest slave populations in the nineteenth century, exported few slaves in the eighteenth century.

An expansion in the number of agricultural slaves was one way to meet the demand for surplus grain, particularly in a region like the Lower Senegal, where the margin between production and consumption needs could not have been very great. Assuming that slaves and peasants used the same techniques and produced roughly comparable outputs, the slave owed considerable labor time to the master and had no rights to a good deal of what he or she produced. Slaves had to make up for this lost production in the supplementary hours that they devoted to the plots allotted to them for their subsistence needs. As a result of the structure of this labor system, part of the slave's labor appeared as a surplus available to the master and any significant expansion in the number of slaves would have increased the grain surplus available for export. Peasants also produced surpluses which allowed them to sell grain in good years, but they had larger families than slaves, and would presumably have consumed and stored more grain and withdrawn from the market in poor years. The Lower Senegal produced consistent surpluses of grain for sale, even in periods of famine when prices rose and speculation in grain increased. This suggests that part of the surplus was produced by slave owners who could mobilize a commercial surplus under difficult conditions.

The changing trade goods used to purchase millet from 1750 onwards also indicate a dual market and growing speculation in grain over time. An important analysis of French commerce at mid-century described the millet trade before the great upheavals of the 1750s. Millet was purchased from Kajoor, Bawol, and Siin primarily in exchange for iron bars, at the rate of one hogshead of 350 pounds for two iron bars. However Joseph Pruneau noted that a hogshead could be purchased for six pints of rum, an exchange that would have interested few peasants, but may have shown the importance of surplus sales by slave-owning aristocrats. Pruneau deplored the fact that most exchanges involved millet for iron "solely on the basis of an ancient custom," because in the local bar currency millet would have been cheaper if paid for in "dyed cloth" or "gunpowder." Pruneau's substitute commodities also seem to suggest a dual seller's market, one dominated by consumption goods valued by peasants, the other by aristocratic prestige goods.[106] Shortly after the analysis was written the conventional limitations on the trade broke down. During the famine of the 1750s the French used dyed cloth exclusively to purchase grain, along with other commodities, and by the end of the century guns, powder, flints, cutlasses, and glass wares were all used in transactions for millet.

Pruneau also gives an important estimate of the millet trade from

Kajoor, Bawol, and Siin, which could sell enough food "to nourish 2,000 negroes for a year."[107] Using Pruneau's own estimate of two pounds of millet per person per day, which included a margin of safety which allowed for spoilage, this produces a figure of 730 tons of grain.[108] The grain trade, which involved peasants and aristocrats, created conditions which allowed the widespread circulation of European trade goods in the local economy. Doumet, in enumerating the tribute collected by the Dammel from his subjects, listed "slaves, cattle, cotton, millet, butter, honey, *pagnes* or the cotton cloth of the country, and even some merchandise which the negroes received from Europeans in exchange for their goods and their provisions."[109] These sources, along with oral traditions which stress the importance of agriculture to the monarchy, suggest a need to revise oversimplified models of predatory states producing slave exports, famine, warfare, and regression.

The emergence of social differentiation among the slave population should be understood in the context of the system of labor management under which slaves worked. *Jaam sayoor*, household slaves, and slave children could all be mobilized in a kind of gang labor system on the master's fields from six in the morning until mid-afternoon. During this labor time the slaves were fed by the master. In the late afternoon and evenings the master still had his "purchased slaves" and his slave children under his command. But rather than developing a management system which, through overseers and other controls, would have assured maximum work and control, Senegambian masters cut the costs of keeping their slaves by allowing many of them time to work for themselves. The same decision reduced the cost of food, supervision, and policing the slave population. Slaves in the Lower Senegal lived in a peasant world, and their work day closely resembled that of free dependants or *surga* in peasant households, who worked for the head of the household during the same hours that slaves labored for their masters. Slaves were in a sense permanent dependants, and they benefited fully neither from their own labor, nor from that of their children. But the way they worked and the way that they lived did not differ substantially from the peasantry.

Slaves in the Lower Senegal achieved limited rights to land in the form of a household plot and they formed families, which gave them a greater control over their own labor, although not over that of their children. What masters lost in direct control was compensated by lower costs of control, in the form of management and police, for slaves who "accepted" their status. Historians of plantation slavery have often described such concessions as "positive incentives" which functioned with punishment as a means of seeking control over the labor force. At the same time they have noted that these concessions were sought out and defended by slaves, producing a limited version of labor negotiations and wage concessions within slavery.[110] The concessions won by African slaves also emerged in the context of resistance to slavery.

52

The preferences expressed by African slave holders purchasing slaves for their labor value provide important hints about slave resistance and control in the eighteenth century. African purchasers preferred to buy "re-enslaved" Africans, women and children, and strangers to their own societies. All these preferences expressed a concern with slave resistance, particularly with runaways. Mungo Park, who traveled with a slave caravan, reported that the slave merchants preferred "re-enslaved" captives, who were accustomed to hard work and privations, and who were "not so apt to attempt making their escape, as those who have once tasted the blessings of freedom."[111] Park also reported that leaders of war parties frequently retained "such of the domestic slaves as appear to be of mild disposition, and particularly the young women" while the rest of the captives were sold to slave traders.[112] Other eighteenth-century sources confirm a similar African preference for "seasoned slaves", particularly those born in captivity. Saugnier, who traveled up the Senegal River with a slaving convoy in 1785, reported that slaves who had been born in captivity fetched a higher price with African slave owners in Saint Louis, who "readily buy them, and give in exchange slaves of greater value."[113] The preference for slaves born in captivity reflected the difficulties of managing newly enslaved persons, who were most likely to run away or commit suicide rather than accept their bondage.

The demography of the slave trade from Senegambia also provides important indirect evidence for the expansion of domestic slavery. The sex ratios of slaves exported from the Senegambian region, which consistently favored males by 1.7–2.1 or more, plus fairly numerous descriptions of captives taken in wars and raids, in which women and children generally were in the majority, give strong reasons to believe that women and children were retained in slavery in numbers exceeding slave exports.[114] Women and children were regarded as less dangerous captives than young men, and children could be more easily assimilated into a new social setting. Women were valuable for the range of labor they performed, being equally suited for field work and labor-intensive domestic chores, such as processing millet and spinning cotton into thread. In agriculture free women performed labor-intensive tasks such as weeding fields and winnowing grains. Gender structured labor tasks in a way that created a greater demand for female slaves. This was true in spite of the fact that slavery sometimes violated gender norms in assigning labor.

When female slaves bore children, they belonged to the master of the women. This was another incentive for retaining female slaves, especially since second generation slaves were more valuable to owners for a number of reasons. They spoke local languages, had immunities to local diseases, and had no memories of life before slavery. For this reason they had more reason to cultivate ties to the master and fewer reasons to run away.[115] African preferences for women and children reflected a dual concern with control and reproduction. Women were desired for both their labor and

53

their reproductive capacity, because any children born to slave mothers belonged to the master and contributed to the growth of an "acculturated" group of slaves who knew only bondage.[116] Women slaves were in special demand as household servants, where their labor freed wealthy women from manual labor. A final factor that created a stronger demand for female slaves was sexual exploitation and the demand for concubines in wealthy households. Slave women were subject to sexual demands from masters. They were more highly valued than men because they were sexual objects as well as laborers.[117]

Africans buying slaves showed a clear choice for "strangers" far from their native homes, as opposed to persons enslaved locally. This preference was strongest in the case of male slaves, but it was a general phenomenon. Mungo Park reported that "the value of a slave in the eye of an African purchaser increases in proportion to his distance from his native kingdom."[118] This judgement is confirmed by other sources, which tie the preference closely to the resistance and flight of locally enslaved persons. Saugnier, trading on the Senegal River in 1785, did not chain Bambara slaves continuously in the Lower Senegal, but believed that "one, and even two pair of irons is scarce enough for every single captive of the Yolofs [Wolof]."[119] Wolof slaves were separated from one another, watched closely, and feared as a "seditious" influence on the other slaves. The reason was clear. Wolof slaves "were too near the confines of their own country to let any opportunity of recovering their liberty escape them," while the Bambara, "who come from the interior parts of Africa . . . never think of making their escape."[120] Although the data on the origins of domestic slave populations in the Lower Senegal is fragmentary, it points clearly to a high proportion of slaves from the upper Senegal and middle Niger regions.[121]

In the Lower Senegal acculturated and seasoned slaves were granted access to plots, and allowed to form families in an effort to create a hereditary class of bondsmen with ties to local society. They were also generally exempted from resale, particularly if they were "born in the house." Although some historians have tended to dismiss these concessions as norms more honored in the breach than the observance, European observers noted their relation to slave resistance. Francis Moore, who visited the Gambia in the early eighteenth century, wrote:

> If there are many Family-Slaves, and one of them commits a Crime, the Master cannot sell him without the joint Consent of all the rest; for if he does, they will all run away, and be protected by the next kingdom, to which they fly.[122]

John Barnes, a longtime resident of the Senegambian coast, testified that acculturated slaves could only be sold "with the approbation of their fellow-servants." He distinguished between a master's rights and practice: "I believe it to be a practice more of prudence; because, if he were to treat his Slaves in any arbitrary or cruel manner, he would lose them by desertion."[123] Other witnesses related the ban on the sale of slaves born in captivity directly to the fear of slave insurrections. "They never part with their own Slaves if they have any, because it would be dangerous to themselves if they parted with them, on account of the fear of insurrection among the other Slaves."[124]

The balance of power generated by the master's efforts to control the slave's labor and the slave's attempts to appropriate "rights" in his/her new community led to practices which have caused controversy among historians of African slavery.[125] But the practices had their roots in the struggles between masters and slaves. Sources from the eighteenth century to the early twentieth century suggest three related areas where masters and slaves "negotiated" their relationship. The first was the division of the calendar week and the work day into times that belonged to the master and times when the slave was free to labor for him/herself. Slaves generally had one or two days free from labor for the master. The work day was also divided into periods when the slave labored for the master, from sun-up to mid-afternoon, and times when the slave was free to rest or labor on a separate plot. The second area of master–slave accommodation revolved around the granting of a plot to the slave, which occurred when slaves formed separate families. When the number of slaves was large, slaves living in households were settled in separate villages. The third area of accommodation was in the protection of slaves against resale.[126]

The concessions won by slaves from masters were not fixed rights or privileges so much as they were a reflection of the conflicts between master and slave. They were acquired individually or by slave families in a harsh world that combined threats with concessions. Sale to the Atlantic trade was a very real threat to slaves in the Lower Senegal, and these fears were compounded by widespread stories about European cruelty and cannibalism. These stories, which probably originated with the slave-owning class, made African slaves fear the terrifying uncertainties of sale to the "people of the water." European slave traders tried to calm the fears of Africans awaiting shipment by describing the agricultural bondage of the transatlantic plantation economy.[127] Freedom from resale existed because masters desired acculturated slaves whose families tied them to the master.

If master–slave relations can explain some of the particular characteristics of bondage in the Lower Senegal, others derived from the economic conditions of the region. New slaves were managed in a kind of gang labor system, and their low status as persons without rights was symbolized by their nakedness. Sieur de la Courbe, who commanded the French settlement in Saint Louis in the late seventeenth century, wrote a rare first-hand account of a Wolof aristocrat in the fields supervising the labor of his slaves.

> I found him in the middle of his field, with his sword at his side and his spear in his hand, which encouraged his people in their work. They numbered

55

more than sixty, and were completely naked. Each one held a small rounded iron hoe with a cutting blade at the end, which was attached to a handle and which they used to cut down the weeds and work the soil at the same time, working only the top surface of the soil. All of this was accomplished to the energetic music of six *griots*, who played drums and sang. It was a pleasure to watch them move as if they were possessed, quickening or slowing the pace of their work as the beat of the drums rose and fell.[128]

This passage depicts the labor of *jaam sayoor*, new slaves who had been purchased. Their labor was an intensified and unfree variation on labor processes in free village communities. Adanson described many of the same elements in his account of the first breaking of the ground on the island of Sor. "Early in the morning, the 8th of June [1752], all the inhabitants attended the lord of the village into the field, singing and dancing as on a great festival . . . After they had all danced a few minutes on the very spot, the latter, without interrupting the cadence, began to throw up the ground with their spades, in order to root out the weeds. During this operation they accorded so well the sound and measure of the instruments in their motions and singing, that you would have concluded all those husbandmen to be professed dancers and singers. It was pleasing to see how they tossed their arms and legs, and into what contorsions they threw themselves with an air of content, according as the sound of the tabor was more or less quick, and as the *guirots* [*griots*] gave more life to their singing."[129]

Slaves who obtained the confidence of their masters or who were born into slavery and reached the age of maturity were often rewarded by a ceremonial rite of passage that conferred new privileges, the most essential of which were access to a plot of land and marriage in a slave family.[130] The passage was often marked ceremonially by a gift of new clothes to the slave, but could also include payments to the master.[131] At the same time the slave entered into a work world divided into times for the master and times for the slave. The new work regime reflected a new stage in the individual slave life cycle or the life cycle of a slave family. Economically, the plot of land and the free time constituted a "wage" of sorts within the condition of bondage. By transatlantic standards the resulting slave condition appears relatively unregimented. This is particularly true if the reported practice of letting some slaves work for themselves during the long agriculturally idle dry season is accurate.[132] At root the slaves were still landless dependants. They owned no land, only access to land on the sufferance of the master. Unless they undertook a long and dangerous flight to their homeland or a distant country where they could pass as free, a flight in which every stage was accompanied by the threat of re-enslavement and sale, acculturated slaves had to accept the restrictions imposed upon them.

The social and economic conditions of the Lower Senegal contributed to the development of slave management systems which systematically utilized differentiation as a form of accommodation and control. In comparison to transatlantic slave systems, slaves in the Lower Senegal region worked under a variety of labor regimes.[133] While newly enslaved persons labored in gangs under the supervision of the master or an overseer, acculturated slaves lived in separate villages, cultivated their own plots, and produced for their masters under labor regimes that resembled share-cropping and tenancy labor in the Americas or the Russian *barshchina* system of serf management more than they resembled plantation slavery.[134] Some slaves in the Lower Senegal, usually those with many generations of service to the master's household, paid an annual tribute in grain as a substitute for the labor services they owed the master. They were dependent tenants who achieved some control over their labor, even though their status as slaves meant that their hard-won gains were continually at risk.[135]

Economic and cultural factors in the Lower Senegal contributed to the emergence of a slave labor system where slaves possessed more autonomy and greater possibilities for earning independent income than in the more centralized, regimented, and capitalist plantations of the Americas. With no racial caste system or close direct ties to the capitalist world market, there were few incentives for labor systems which maximized the exploitation of labor and no cultural parallels to the sharp divisions of race in the Americas. Like Russian serfs and Latin American tenant laborers, slaves in the Lower Senegal produced food crops and shared a common religious and cultural identity with their lords and masters. Racism and class disdain were not absent, because slaves were considered inferior and impure, but they existed in a more fluid and less rigid system of social relationships. Slaves in the Lower Senegal did not have more "rights," but they exploited the limited possibilities for advancement within bondage that existed within the life cycle of a slave family. The result was an agrarian world in which slaves could achieve a degree of control over their lives that narrowed the gap that separated them from dependent peasant households over time.

Slavery was full of contradictions. In his discussion of slavery, Yoro Jaw, a nineteenth-century Waalo aristocrat, stressed his belief that slavery was an "indelible stain," passed through the mother, and inherited by her children. The descendants of slaves could never be the equals of free-born men and women. But in another passage, when discussing how slavery could be ended, Yoro Jaw argued that "slaves who risked all the dangers to which runaways exposed themselves, escaping from the pursuit of their masters and the political authorities, and reached the foreign countries where they had been captured or purchased, recovered their full liberty."[136] In the mid-nineteenth century Boilat told a story that illustrated how slaves took advantage of the confidence they won from their masters. A shopkeeper in Saint Louis purchased a slave and kept him under surveillance and in rags until the slave convinced him by good behavior that he had accepted his condition. His master bought him a new suit of clothes and entrusted him with the key to his shop. The slave then ran away with the contents of his master's shop.[137]

Slavery was a socially constructed status. It meant different things to aristocrats, urban merchants, and peasants. In the eighteenth century the military aristocracy defined slavery most harshly. In their vision slavery was a mark of inferiority, an inheritable stain of impurity that could be passed on from generation to generation. If slaves were permitted the "freedom" to live like peasants, peasants were little more than potential slaves in the eyes of the aristocracy.[138] At root slavery was a system of forced labor. Slaves worked harder than free persons. Gender norms were violated by slavery; women did men's work, and men did women's work. The creation of large-scale agricultural units and the intensification of labor expanded the production of grain and other commodities, but slaves did not profit from their labor. In the eighteenth century, when slave systems were expanding, and when slavery coexisted with a brutal export trade that reduced slaves to human commodities, slavery was undoubtedly harsher than in later, better documented periods. When environmental crisis threatened food security, slaves were the first victims of famine. The laborers who produced surplus grain in times of plenty were sold off by their masters. If they did not starve to death first in the miserable slave pens on the Atlantic coast, they joined the emaciated human cargoes who set out on the voyage of no return.

3

The Atlantic kingdom: maritime commerce and social change

Throughout the eighteenth century the typical slave began his or her journey to Saint Louis from the middle Niger valley, over 600 miles to the east. The slave caravans first traveled overland under the command of slave merchants, who then directed the caravans either to the French slave markets of the upper Senegal, or to British slave ships waiting in the Gambia River. The slave caravans whose drivers headed for the upper Senegal moved toward the slave markets in the kingdom of Gajaaga, where a French fort marked the outer limits of the Atlantic trade networks under direct European control. By that time many of the slaves who had started the journey over a month before had died from exhaustion and hunger, and others had been sold off to African purchasers.[1] Many of the slaves who survived to catch sight of the French fort had already been marched nearly 400 miles across the West African savanna.

The slaves who reached Gajaaga carried loads on their heads weighing fifty to sixty pounds. Caravans carried their own food and water, along with trade goods like ivory and gold dust. When there was nothing else to carry the slaves bore fifty to sixty pounds of rock, "so that extreme exhaustion would remove all desire to escape or to plot against those who drove them."[2] The largest slave caravans brought 200 slaves from the east, most of them destined to be sold to the French at Fort Saint Joseph, although others were purchased in the market towns by Soninke merchants and nobles, who needed slave labor to cultivate their fields, to weave cotton cloth, to mine gold, or to serve as attendants and household laborers. For the French and for the Soninke merchants the slaves were half-naked chattels whose value as laborers animated the commerce of the Soninke towns. Apart from slaves, the French merchants in Gajaaga hoped to purchase gold dust and ivory from the trade caravans, all valuable commodities which could be shipped downriver to the Atlantic ports.

When slaves were finally purchased by the French after negotiations over the assortment of trade goods, they entered the slave pens of the fort, where they awaited shipment downriver. The height of the slave-

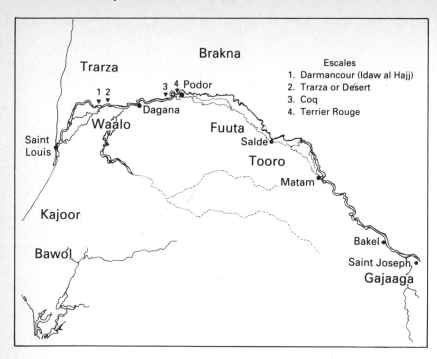

Map 2   The Senegal River valley

trading season in Gajaaga occurred between July and November, when
the waters of the Senegal River, swollen with the rains, rose enough to
permit riverboats to travel upriver.[3] For French slave traders the time
between purchase and shipment was the most dangerous and uncertain
time. Slaves exhausted by the overland march had to be guarded and fed
until they could be loaded onto the fleets of riverboats coming upriver
from Saint Louis. To reduce expenses, French slavers paid less for slaves
brought to them during the dry season, because those slaves would have
to be fed for months before they could be shipped out.[4] The more routine
problems of feeding hundreds of slaves for briefer periods in the rainy
season sometimes led to starvation and slave deaths. Not surprisingly the
slave trade generated a substantial trade in grain, which made Gajaaga
one of the three most important sources of grain for the French in the
eighteenth century.

In Gajaaga (or Galam) slaves made their first contact with the commercial networks of the Lower Senegal. In Fort Saint Joseph they would have
heard for the first time the mixture of French and Wolof which served as
the lingua franca between the French merchants and the Africans who
worked under them as sailors and soldiers. The Africans and mulattoes
who worked for the French were far more visible than the Europeans,

60

since there were rarely more than one or two Frenchmen in the unhealthy ports of the upper Senegal. Closer contact between the newly purchased slaves and the African men and women who guarded and fed them revealed certain affinities. Most of the Africans who worked for the French were slaves themselves, and most of them came from the "Bambara" country to the east.[6] They had been purchased from earlier slave cargoes that went downriver, but instead of continuing their voyage into the middle passage, they had been purchased in Saint Louis, where slave labor was needed to sustain the trade system that sent most of the slaves across the Atlantic.

At times the common ethnic origins of slaves in transit and slave laborers affected the course of the voyage downriver. In 1795 Scipio, a riverboat captain of slave origins, did not hesitate to arm Bambara slaves when the French river fleet was threatened with attack in Fuuta Tooro. "As they were his countrymen, that is, from Baabarn, he found no difficulty in determining them to fight, in case of being attacked on the part of the Poules. [Fulbe]"[7] During the confrontation, Scipio and his crew were taunted from the banks of the river by Fulbe warriors, who threatened them with enslavement. "At day-light he retired into the wardroom from when he heard the Poules crying from shore, Scipio, thou canst no longer escape from our hands, thou shall come among us to plant pistachio nuts."[8] Even if the outright seizure of slave cargoes by Africans was a rare event, the threat reflected the importance of slave holding in all the societies along the river passed by the slave convoys. The slave cargoes traveled downriver through a river system flanked by slave societies. In the voyage downriver slaves in transit passed through regions of grain production and gum extraction where slaves from the east labored to produce commodities for the Atlantic trade. By the time the river fleets reached Saint Louis, their numbers were increased by a smaller number of slaves purchased along the river and in the Lower Senegal.[9]

The Lower Senegal served as an important base for European traders tapping into the trade networks of the Senegambian region. The Atlantic coastal region had a comparative advantage in supplying high-bulk, low-cost provisions such as grain, precisely because of its coastal location. With the development of Gorée and Saint Louis as permanently occupied commercial cities, the Lower Senegal became the "breadbasket" of the islands, which purchased large quantities of grain for the urban market, to feed slaves held in transit, and to supply slave ships preparing to cross the Atlantic. Because of the relative efficiency of river transport, grain was also produced for commercial sale in the Senegal River valley.[10] The trade in grain and other foodstuffs was an essential component of the Atlantic trade, because the traffic in enslaved human beings, their transport within Africa, and to the coastal entrepots of the slave trade, depended on the mobilization of important quantities of food and provisions.[11] In times of famine, or in times of shortages created by trade boycotts and war,

61

eighteenth-century merchants perceived clearly the strategic role of the provision trade. These crises became increasingly frequent over the course of the eighteenth century.[12]

In the Atlantic coastal region the provision trade was broad-based and led to the expansion of maritime transport, production, and labor, as well as an expansion of grain production and other agricultural activities.[13] Ocean fishing was a specialized activity carried out by maritime villages on the Atlantic coast, which sold dried fish to merchants who in turn sold it further inland. During the eighteenth century Atlantic merchants purchased important quantities of fish from coastal villages, which they used to feed slaves.[14] Salt mined in northern Kajoor formed a major component of cargoes shipped upriver because of the high scarcity value of salt in the major slave markets of the Upper Senegal.[15] The provision trade included the supply of water, meat, fish, wood, live cattle, poultry, milk, fresh vegetables, and condiments. Many of these commodities were purchased only from regions close to Saint Louis and Gorée.[16] In addition there was an important trade in manufactured goods between the mainland and the coastal islands. The islands imported leather goods, dyed cloth, clay pots, woven mats, and jewelry from the mainland. Much of this trade was to satisfy the demand of the inhabitants of the islands, but some goods were reexported by merchants who needed assortments of European manufactures and local goods to make purchases on the mainland.[17]

The slave export economy of Senegambia developed during the long dry period from 1630 to 1860, which put new strains on ecological systems.[18] In spite of the common experience of environmental crisis, the historical outcome was different for densely populated regions of the interior, such as the delta of the middle and upper Niger valley, and the more sparsely populated Atlantic coastal region. On the Atlantic coast and along the Senegal River valley the impetus to economic activity produced by maritime trade was reinforced by the desert-side trade. Grain exports from the Senegal River valley to the desert expanded as a result of the stimulus given to the economy of the western Sahara by the development of the export trade in gum arabic. The dual stimulus to agricultural activity helps explain the relatively small scale of slave exports from these regions, in spite of periodic famine and grain shortages.

Environmental factors added a powerful incentive to slave exports from particular regions at particular times, as the ability of African societies to feed their populations was pushed to the breaking point.[19] In the Senegambian slave trade the predominance of slaves from the middle Niger valley in the cargoes departing from the shores of the Lower Senegal and the Gambia resulted in part from the overpopulation of a region experiencing prolonged dessication, accompanied by the decline of commercial cities, and conquests by new military states.[20] William Littleton, who spent eleven years in the Gambia as a merchant, believed that the "greater proportion" of slaves brought by Muslim traders from the interior "become so from famine, which in that part of the world is frequent from the want of a sufficient quantity of rain, and the immense quantity of locusts which spread devastation."[21] If so, the military predation of the Bambara states of Segu and Kaarta needs to be placed in the broader context of ecological stress and food security. The geography of hunger influenced the geography of military predation and slave exports.[22]

The geography of Atlantic commerce led to regional specialization and produced important variations in the economy of slave holding and slave trading in the wider region of the western Sudan. The geography of trade provides a partial explanation for this difference. While regions far removed from the coast participated in the Atlantic trade by exporting high-priced goods such as slaves, gold, and ivory, regions nearer the coast could retain slaves and employ them profitably in grain production. Coastal and riverine states that controlled European access to mainland points of trade had the further advantage of being able to collect tribute from European traders in the form of customs duties, which gave those states access to European trade goods without selling off slaves. In the middle Niger, over 600 miles from the coast, specialized long-distance merchants formed the only link with the Atlantic economy. The merchant logic of purchasing cheap and selling dear encouraged slave exports from the interior to the ports of the Upper Senegal, and a return trade in Atlantic imports.

Although European traders in the eighteenth century tended to see the Senegal River primarily as a conveyor belt which supplied slave laborers to the Americas, the river linked the regions of northern Senegambia together into a trade system. Labor and commodities circulated throughout the entire river valley, which was knitted together into a unified economic system whose parts interacted as parts of a larger whole. The production of export commodities like slaves, gold, and gum, depended on the production of other commodities, particularly grain and salt, which were traded within Senegambia. Salt was highly valued in the interior countries of the east which supplied exports like slaves and gold, and European merchants organized the shipment of salt from the Lower Senegal upriver to supplement the trade goods from Europe and Asia which purchased slaves and gold. Grain supplemented the imported cloth offered to desert peoples in exchange for their gum, but its most important function was to feed slaves in transit from the moment of their purchase upriver until they were embarked on ships for the Atlantic crossing. The production and trade of all these commodities shaped the Senegal River system, and linked the economies of different regions together in the eighteenth century.

The kings of the sea: imported wealth in the Atlantic trade

For the Portuguese, the king of Jolof was poor. Cadamosto, one of the earliest visitors, wrote: "You must know that this King is lord of a very poor people, and has no city in his country, but villages with huts of straw only . . ."[23] Cadamosto identified wealth with the presence of cities, but then he went on to describe the wealth the king did possess: tribute from the lords of the provinces, numerous wives, slaves to work for him, and slaves to trade to the "Azanaghi and Arab merchants in return for horses and other goods, and also to Christians, since they have begun to trade with these blacks." The contrast between Atlantic wealth and African poverty was a perception shared by Europeans and Africans from the beginnings of the Atlantic trade. In the mid-fifteenth century during the first contacts between the Portuguese and Africans of the Lower Senegal, Alvise da Mosta reported that the Dammel of Kajoor defended the superiority of Islam by saying that since the Europeans were so wealthy and enjoyed paradise on earth, Africans would surely be rewarded "with celestial beatitudes."[24]

In spite of Cadamosto's affirmation of European wealth and African poverty, in the first centuries of the Atlantic trade Europeans were in fact not wealthy enough to provoke a massive transfer of slave labor out of Senegambia. The Portuguese trade never totally reoriented existing trade patterns or provoked the cataclysms, wars, and famines that would follow in the seventeenth and eighteenth centuries.[25] It was the northern European nations, France and Britain, and their colonial slave empire of sugar production which would organize large-scale commerce which centered around the exchange of European, American, and Asian manufactures for African slave labor. By the mid-seventeenth century the nations of northern Europe were wealthy enough to fit out large fleets of slavers, and to fill their holds with the guns, Asian cottons, American alcohol, glasswares, iron bars, hardwares, and assorted luxuries which could entice slave labor out of Senegambia. Throughout the eighteenth century Atlantic merchants were described as the "kings of the sea," because of their ocean-sailing ships, but also because of the wealth in their cargoes.[26]

The flood of European, American, and Asian imports into Senegambia was unprecedented in scale, and was offered with credit and bribes which made it difficult to refuse. The Europeans who traded on the Atlantic coast of the Lower Senegal in the eighteenth century were in fact the representatives of a wealthier world, and their essential function was to stockpile and market European trade goods in exchange for slaves and other commodities. For most of the eighteenth century merchants, rather than soldiers or administrators, predominated. The Compagnie des Indes, which ran the French concessions in the Lower Senegal from the beginning of the century until 1758, was aggressive and had more means at its disposal than many of the royal governments which would follow. The directors of the Company and their employees spent most of their time on the islands of Saint Louis and Gorée, although the late seventeenth and early eighteenth centuries were also the period of "heroic" French ventures into the interior. The Compagnie des Indes built and maintained a fortified outpost in the upper Senegal, a feat that was not repeated by Europeans until the nineteenth century.[27]

The slave trade required the supply of stocks of goods from at least three continents; manufactures from Europe, cloth from Asia, and rum from the sugar islands of the Americas. The scale of the eighteenth-century slave trade made it a major branch of the European capitalist economy, because of its role as a strategic source of slave labor, but also because of its contribution to European manufactures and worldwide European trade. Although Europeans and their descendants have liked to imagine the development of the capitalist economy as a moral tale in which the "Protestant work ethic" produced hard-working frugal entrepreneurs, who plowed their profits into savings and investments, the slave trade illustrates other features of the eighteenth-century economy. Sugar, rum, tobacco, slaves, and guns were major items of international trade, and the "heroic" age of European empire and capitalism, dominated by planters, merchants, and bankers, was fueled as much by the desire to consume new foods and drugs, as it was by the frugal accumulation of entrepreneurs.[28]

Slave trading played a strategic role in the international economy, by supplying labor to the centers of slave production in the New World, and that was why it was frequently supported by royal subsidies. The global importance of the slave trade to European empire contrasted sharply with its local organization in Senegambia, where the slave trade was in the hands of a small clique of merchants linked by family and business ties. French slave-trading interests in the first half of the century were concentrated in the hands of the Compagnie des Indes, with trade interests in Asia as well as Africa. The Senegal concession was managed by a small group of merchants, many of whom were related, and who worked for a politically powerful group of Parisian bankers, who participated in the colonial trade through monopoly trading concessions.[29] In Africa, Senegal was the favored preserve of the Company after it had renounced its monopoly on the entire French slave trade in 1725. For most of the rest of the period until the Seven Years War, Senegal was the African preserve of the Compagnie des Indes.

The Company's special ties to Senegal can best be explained with reference to Senegambia's location in the eighteenth-century maritime world and the diversity of its trade. Senegal was astride the major maritime route to the West Indies, via the Madeira, Azores, and Cape Verde islands.[30] This route could be navigated even during the summer months avoided by slave ships that continued down the windward coast. As a result trade entrepots in Senegambia could be easily supplied with trade goods throughout the year, and ships leaving Senegal could continue to the West Indies or return directly to Europe. This gave additional importance to the gum trade, which allowed the Company to reduce the risks associated with a total reliance on the slave trade. The early eighteenth-century gum trade was highly profitable, and it also supplied a ready market for the Indian dyed blue cotton cloths, known as *guinées* in Africa, which were supplied by another concessionary monopoly in India under the control of the Company. In the gum trade the *guinées* served as the main currency, and filled much of the desert demand for cotton cloth which had previously come from the savanna. The gold trade from Galam was also a factor in the Company's decision to maintain its presence in Senegal, especially if smuggling by Company employees and directors was as important as some historians have suggested.[31]

In the eighteenth century the managing directors of the concession in Senegal were a tightly linked group. Some of the most ambitious and successful directors, like André Brüe, returned to Senegal more than once and was followed by other members of his family. The same was true of Sieur de La Courbe, who was the first of several La Courbes to serve in Senegal. The David family had a father who served as a prominent director of the Compagnie des Indes, and a son who had served as the director general in Senegal.[32] By the mid-eighteenth century the names of these merchants appear as the family names of mulatto families, independent of their French progenitor, but still allied with the French, and with their French families. Many of the eighteenth-century French directors spoke Wolof, and maintained complex ties of alliance and patronage with key African families on the islands and on the mainland.

European society on the coast, as far as it can be reconstructed, lived in extravagance and drunkenness, but also in fear of disease, and slave revolts. If we are to believe the reports written by the directors of the Company, employees spent the time not occupied by drinking and womanizing smuggling goods, particularly gold, for their own profit.[33] Many of the seventeenth- and eighteenth-century memoirs of Company officials revealed the atmosphere of back-biting, suspicion, and rivalry that existed within the Company. The directors intercepted each other's correspondence with the Company, and searched each other's baggage.[34] The power exercised by Europeans was largely economic, and it came from the commodities and the credit they controlled. The most common goods were iron bars from Europe, cotton cloth from India in various styles, some African cottons which Europeans transferred from one region to another, European cloths, especially fine linens and silks, brass pans, Flemish sword blades and knives, pewter basins, glass, crystal, paper, rum, guns, gunpowder and lead balls, amber, coral, and jewelry of various kinds. These commodities purchased slaves, but also live cattle, rice, millet, fish, hides, gum arabic, and other products.

Some impressions of the world of the merchants, their jealous management of the Senegal concession, and the ways they related to local society can be gathered from the accounts of European outsiders who tried to break into the merchant society on the coast. When Adanson, a young naturalist eager to make his name and fortune by undertaking the first serious study of a tropical country in Africa, arrived in Saint Louis in 1749, he came with a letter from David, one of the members of the board of the Company, to whom he had been introduced by his father. "As soon as I set foot on shore, I waited upon M. [Estoupan] de la Brüe, the director general, who gave me a most kind reception. I delivered to him the letters of recommendation which I had from his uncle M. David . . . who was pleased to interest him in my favor."[35] When Adanson sought out contact with local Africans, he entered a world of structured relationships, in which he found himself treated with great respect, including being seated alone in a place of honor. "This is a mark of respect they shew the French, whom they look upon as great people; that is, as great lords, and far their superiors."[36] Adanson also discovered that Africans frequently asked him for gifts, for Europeans dispensed wealth freely in an effort to buy good relations with important people. They were also obliged to give gifts to less privileged and dependent classes, in imitation of African nobles. Adanson, however, soon discovered that as a subordinate employee of the Company he enjoyed few of the privileges of the Company directors. He was poorly lodged and paid, and during the food shortages that occurrred on Saint Louis in the 1750s he suffered from hunger and became one of the most bitter critics of Company privilege.[37]

There was a brutal hierarchy of wealth and power in the European world of maritime commerce. While ordinary seamen, the "Jack-tars" of Atlantic fleets, lived in squalor and faced brutal discipline, merchant directors and accountants wore starched linens and fed on imported delicacies. The common leveler was death by disease. European seamen died like flies on the African coast, in numbers rivaling those of emaciated slaves whose traffic fattened the merchant directors.[38] Seamen drank foul water and ate bread baked with spoiled flour, while merchants dined on fish, fowl, and game washed down with imported wines and spirits. While malaria and yellow fever made no class distinctions, well-fed merchants under the care of European surgeons and their African "wives" did their best to sweeten the odds dealt out by the pestilential environment of the African coast.

The power of the merchants, and the honors granted them, were the result of the power they held over things, articles of wealth from beyond the seas. The imported wealth of the merchant adventurers of the eighteenth century permitted them to live and act as great lords. The same imported wealth was the driving force behind the long march of slaves from the interior to the slave ports of the coast. The Atlantic trade was never limited to slaves, even when slaves were the only valuable export. A company agent trading at Bissau for the French in 1718 noted that from July 22 to July 31 his operation had consumed 8,200 pounds of rice, 4,200 pounds of millet, 5 cattle, 77 goats, 204 chickens, 400 pounds of flour, 600 pints of wine, 200 pounds of wax, 10 pints of alcoholic spirits "for the wounded," 10 pounds of gunpowder, 12 pounds of lead, 12 pounds of lead shot, 40 pounds of "butter from Gorée," and an assortment of other goods. These goods, mainly used to feed the slaves, the French merchant, and his employees, were part of the operating costs. The same account books show the purchase of 150 pounds of rice for a brass basin, a sword blade, and an iron bar. A live cow was purchased for three brass basins, one iron bar, and two "yougoulade" cloths. A male slave named Malu, aged twenty-eight years, was purchased for five large brass basins, two small brass basins, three "yougoulade" cloths, two pewter basins, six iron bars, twelve Flemish sword blades, eight "Garas" cloths, and twelve pints of rum. Malu's purchase price was calculated as twenty-four bars in the currency of account used on the Senegambian coast.[39] The trade goods that entered the Lower Senegal through the Atlantic trade reached those with animals and food to sell, as well as slave merchants and political authorities.

The trade was taxed by African rulers, who demanded an annual payment of customs, and collected specific taxes on the volume of the trade. These payments were important, but so too was the credit which was extended freely to African rulers. In 1719 André Brüe could report complacently to the Company that "the king Damel has not yet come to visit the coast and I do not think he will come to pay the eighty slaves that he owes the Company until after the rains." Almost three months later, in late December, well after the end of the rains, Brüe reported that the Dammel had still not appeared, and revealed that the debt went back over a year, but he was still optimistic, or at least pretended to be, in his correspondence with the Company.[40] Brüe had in fact advanced the Dammel of Kajoor European goods whose value he calculated at 1,512 livres. The advance of credit and the use of gifts, was one of the signs of the disparity of wealth between Europe and Africa, and was one of the ways that Europeans increased the flow of slaves.

The slave caravans were driven toward the slave ships by the powerful demand for the trade goods brought by the slave merchants. This factor has received less attention than might be expected, since African demand for imports from beyond the seas was the driving economic force on the African side of the Atlantic trade. Exponents of the thesis of warrior predation have distorted African consumption by focusing almost exclusively on firearms, powder, shot, and alcohol, the weapons of enslavement, and the spirits consumed by warrior groups.[41] These were important, but coexisted with a trade in iron bars, finished metal goods like basins, which were used in cooking and serving food, finished cotton cloth, jewelry for women, clothing of various kinds, fineries, combs, mirrors, and assorted manufactures.[42] In coastal regions, and at important river ports, these trade goods reached Africans selling cattle, grain, fish, poultry, cattle hides, ivory, and gum, as well as warriors and merchants with slaves to sell. The Atlantic trade was broader than the export trade in slaves, or the entire export trade.

Senegambians sold slaves to obtain European merchandise because of the high value of these imports in the African economy. Some goods, like Indian cotton cloth, were valued both for their usefulness and their exchange value. Cloth could be made into clothes, but it could also be saved, serving as a kind of money that could readily be traded. The same was true of iron, valued as a raw material that could be made into tools, utensils, or weapons by blacksmiths, but also for its exchange value. Both goods were substitutes for African products, but strong demand for these imports suggests that they were competitive in price with local products, which may have been relatively scarce in relation to local demand. Cotton cloth and iron, common in most transactions conducted by European merchants, were particularly important in purchases of agricultural products like millet and gum.[43] In the same trade these staples were supplemented by finished metal goods, like basins, amber and trade beads, and paper. Gum, which was sold partly by desert warriors, also traded for gunpowder and shot, and cattle were exchanged for cloth, iron, amber and trade beads, powder and shot, sword blades, and metal basins.[44]

Finished metal goods, paper, powder and shot, trade beads, and other imports, were valuable in Senegambia because they were "high technology" imports, either unavailable locally, or offering higher quality at a lower price than locally produced equivalents. They stood between goods of mass consumption, like iron and cloth, and expensive high technology imports and luxuries, like guns, pistols, finished luxury cloths, clothes, beds and other furnishings, which were usually exchanged only for slaves or paid as part of the customs-tribute offered to ruling monarchs and the court. These goods all had a high scarcity value in Africa, and the value placed on them by Africans gave "windfall" profits to Atlantic merchants on the African coast. The high proportion of manufactured goods traded reflected the fact that European merchants could buy cheaply and sell dear by offering goods which incorporated manufacturing technologies unknown in Africa.

For the most expensive and valuable imports slaves were the currency of "foreign exchange" between West Africa and the Atlantic world. From the African perspective Europeans paid high prices for slaves in scarce imported goods. But Europeans calculated the value of slaves in terms of their price in the slave societies of the New World, deducting the costs of slave mortality and the cost of their transport across the Atlantic. In these terms the African purchase price of slaves was negligible.[45] In spite of local markets for slave labor for the production of grain, cotton cloth, and other goods, and demands for courtiers and warriors, European merchants could buy slaves cheaply and sell them dearly in the Americas, passing onto planters most of the costs and risks of recuperating their investment. For the slave traders the risks came mainly from slave mortality, the need to pay protection money to African rulers and maintain a military and naval presence, losses of cargoes and trade goods at sea and on land, and, as the century progressed, from the growing debt of American planters. The overall profitability of the system was maintained by the higher productivity of the Atlantic economy, which produced cheaper manufactures than Africa, and which squeezed higher profits from slave labor in the form of commodities like sugar and tobacco.

The disparity in wealth between eighteen-century Europe and eighteenth-century Senegambia was great enough for Europeans to exert immense influence and pressure through the sheer volume of the goods they were willing to pour into the region, much of it on credit. Some historians have emphasized African perceptions of their own superiority to Europeans in this period, based on the superiority of Islam, and perceptions of European military weakness and susceptibility to disease. But Senegambians were awed by the wealth of the Atlantic world.[46] Throughout the eighteenth and nineteenth centuries Europeans were perceived as coming from lands that possessed immense wealth.

Sieur de La Courbe, who commanded the French settlement at Saint Louis for the Compagnie des Indies at the end of the seventeenth century, has left an interesting account of Senegambian perceptions of European wealth. La Courbe was returning from a diplomatic and trading mission in Waalo, and was obliged to spend the night in the village of Yemsec, where he was lodged and entertained. While the young people of the village were preparing for a dance that eventually kept La Courbe up most of the night, he got involved in a discussion with the elders of the village about "the natural inclination of negroes to steal." La Courbe provoked a response from the imam of the village.

> The marabout, or curé of the village, wanting to justify them, told us a pleasant story which has some connection with the story of Noah. He said that their first father had three sons, one of whom was white, another Moor, or brown, and a third who was black. The father having died, the sons assembled in his house to prepare for the division of the inheritance, which consisted of gold, silver, ivory, cloth, furniture, horses and other herds. During the night, while the others slept, the white, more vigilant than his brothers, took everything that was most valuable, such as gold, jewels, and other fineries, and fled with them and retired to the countries inhabited by us; the Moor, who awakened second and noticed that his white brother had taken everything that was precious, took the horses, the camels, and all the other beasts and left with them. Finally, the black who was the laziest and who awakened late, did not find anything left but a few cotton cloths, millet, pipes, and tobacco, and so he took that for his share. As he smoked he began to reflect upon the deception that his brothers had carried out, and he resolved to chase after them and to take what he could from them, and that is why blacks take what they can when the chance presents itself.[47]

Although some distortion must be allowed for in this transmission of this story, its form and content give it a ring of authenticity. It is also interesting for its early date (1685). La Courbe's is the earliest version of this story, and he was probably the source of later writers. The story has the general form of a Wolof folktale (*leeb bi*), including a moral presented through a surprising twist or reversal in the auditor's expectations.[48] Instead of directly challenging La Courbe's affirmation of African thievery, which was a common complaint of slave traders on the coast, the story attributes the wealth of Europe and the Arabs to an original act of theft which victimized Africans. At the end of the story, the desire of Africans to profit as much as they could, and by whatever means presented themselves, appeared as a legitimate desire to restore the balance of wealth originally disturbed by the treachery of Europeans.

The kings of the land: tribute and taxation

The maritime commerce of Atlantic merchants was regulated by the mainland kingdoms. As representatives of a wealthier world European merchants were taxed for the right to trade in Senegambia. Atlantic merchants called the annual, but not necessarily the most substantial part of this taxation "customs."[49] Part of the diplomacy of trade, the payment of customs to the king and the court permitted European merchants to set up markets where they could trade. These markets were opened at mutually agreed sites in Atlantic ports or river ports. The markets were supervised and taxed by state officials who set aside a fixed proportion of the exports, one measure of grain for every ten, one cowhide for every ten, so that in most markets the tax equaled 10 per cent of the volume of goods sold. These commodities were then sold by the state. Slaves were taxed differently than other commodities. Market officials, merchants, or both, received a fixed payment for each slave known as the *coupe corde*, which was paid in addition to the agreed-upon price for each slave. In the period from 1695 to 1750 prices of slaves were relatively stable at 30 bars or 120 livres, with an additional tax of 1.5 bars or 6 livres.[50] In Gajaaga the taxes paid on slaves sold were slightly higher: two bars in taxes were paid for each slave purchased, one to the king, and one to the merchants.[51] Although specific practices varied with markets and commodities, the general structure of market taxes was similar in Atlantic and river markets.

The resentment of Company officials about the annual customs and market taxes has obscured the fact that taxes were collected on all trade. Ship captains purchasing provisions from the mainland were regularly taxed. Captain Thomas Wilson saw the taxes as a reflection of the "regular government" exercised by the Dammel. "Alcaides and petty magistrates are distributed in every village, to collect the dues for their kings, and they seem very regular and exact in collecting and demanding them . . . We paid regularly for every boat load of water or wood."[52] Henry Dalrymple also testified that "there was a fixed price for every boat landing" wood and water from the mainland.[53] Ships received from the mainland "everything which they could raise, produce, or with safety catch, whether of beef, pork, fish, fowls, partridges, venison, palm wine."[54] When asked about the punishment for refusing to pay Captain Wilson replied: "As we paid for every thing we received from the continent, I cannot speak of my own knowledge; but I have heard, they had seized the boats and men who have refused paying it."[55]

Along the Senegal River, the payment of customs and the opening of markets followed the seasonal rhythms of the river trade. In the trade of the lower Senegal River, the customs for the gum trade could be paid as early as March, to trade gum at the markets known as Terrier Rouge and the Desert.[56] Customs were paid there to the Barak (king) of Waalo and the leader of the Moor merchant scholar group which dominated the supply of gum. In the gum trade the market tax consisted of five lumps of gum from every 1,000 pounds for the Barak, in addition to one-eighth of the gum traded to the Moor merchant leader. The French paid customs to the warrior states of the desert as well. The Brakna and Trarza Moors both received protection money, similarly to Wolof kings. As the river began to rise in June, French ships began to venture further upriver, paying customs to Fuuta Tooro and to Gajaaga for the right to open markets and trade, and to provide protection for the river fleets. Customs were paid to all states for the right to trade, whether for millet and cattle, gum, or slaves, and all markets were supervised and taxed.

Over the course of the eighteenth century the amount of customs paid tended to rise steadily. In 1701 the Dammel of Kajoor received 100 bars, or 400 livres in customs. In the 1750s Kajoor received about 900 livres, Waalo 600 livres, Fuuta Tooro 1,500 livres, and Gajaaga 600 livres.[57] This pattern reveals the premium paid to transit areas which could interfere with the passage of French riverboats, because Fuuta Tooro's trade with the Company was insignificant by comparison to the trade of Gajaaga or Kajoor.[58] In important transit areas for the slave trade, taxes on transiting caravans or riverboats could become a significant source of state revenue. In the Lower Senegal this was particularly true in the kingdom of Waalo.[59] However, the high customs payment received by transit areas are somewhat misleading. Where trade was active, state authorities collected more revenue from the taxes on the volume of trade than from customs payments.[60] In the eighteenth century high customs payments typically went to political authorities who could disrupt or prevent trade: the ruler of Fuuta Tooro, the emirs of the Trarza and the Brakna Moors. But in all these cases the market taxes were paid not to these political rulers, but the merchant leaders who brought commodities to market. In Kajoor and Gajaaga, by contrast, where customs duties were moderate, the state received taxes on the volume of trade.

Senegambian states placed great importance on the payment of customs duties by European merchants. The annual customs duties had to be paid or trade did not take place. The taxes were collected by port officials known to the Europeans as "alcaides" or "alquiers." The customs consisted mainly of firearms, rum, and European trade goods valued by the court. Although the payment of customs was negotiated by the king, the revenues were not entirely concentrated in the hands of the monarch. In Kajoor and Bawol significant payments were distributed to titled members of the court. The king controlled their distribution indirectly, by his ability to influence or control appointment to these positions.

A French source from 1766 gives an unusually detailed account of how the customs were paid that year, at a time when the French were trying to purchase rights on Cap Vert from the Dammel. The preparations began when the French received notice from the Dammel in February that he would be coming to Rufisque to collect his customs and meet with the French. The actual meeting, which occurred several months later, was prepared with elaborate precautions.[61] Pierre de la Courbe, the French official who met the Dammel, was accompanied by forty *laptots* (sailors) and the principal inhabitants of Gorée, both men and women. The *laptots* who served as guards, were slaves, just like many of the warriors in Kajoor. Before leaving his ship at Rufisque, the French commander verified the arrival of the hostages demanded by the French as a guarantee of their security. The Dammel "sent his brother and four of his great men or principal ministers" and they were embarked on a French ship which was waiting. The French were received by the Alquier of Rufisque, who accompanied them to the compound where the Dammel was waiting. La Courbe was struck by the simplicity of the king's lodging, and found him seated in a courtyard, sitting on a mat under the shade of a large tree, surrounded by "women, seigneurs, and generals." In honor of his guests the Dammel had ordered the preparation of a meal, and table and place settings *à la française* had been readied for 150. However, La Courbe estimated that between 300 and 400 people were present and ate. Nevertheless, the lavish display of European cutlery, plates, and glasses was impressive.[62]

After the meal the Dammel asked to see the French troops exercise. This was almost a ritual request. Latsukaabe, in his meetings with André Brüe, had shown a great interest in European military technology, and had also entertained Brüe with a demonstration of martial exercises by his army. The Dammel in 1766, the young Majoor Yasin Issa, was simply following the precedent of his ancestors.[63] When the exercises by the *laptots* were over the Dammel was given his presents, which included a large bed with two mattresses, two chairs, a table, and candlesticks, in addition to the usual payments of "guns, shot, and powder." La Courbe reported hopefully that the Dammel "has already been responsible for several acts of violence and it is believed that he will prove a warrior." The French had little immediate evidence of these qualities, because they had only been able to purchase eighty slaves on the coast in the last six months. Nevertheless the violent character of the Dammel is amply confirmed by dynastic traditions. The electors of Kajoor took the drastic measure of condemning the Dammel to exile or death at the hands of his own people later in 1766, leading to a brief civil war which placed Makodu Kumba Jaring on the throne of Kajoor-Bawol.[64]

The report of La Courbe is interesting for the portrait it gives of the westernized consumption patterns of the court of Kajoor. Dynastic traditions note that Majoor "devoted himself to numerous amusements with his comrades without worrying about the administration of his kingdom."[65] La Courbe's report on his visit to the Dammel does not indicate the total value of the customs. It is likely that the bed and furnishings were a special gift connected with French efforts to purchase rights to Cap Vert. Other sources allow an estimate of the value of the customs payments in the second half of the eighteenth century. In 1776 the French paid the Dammel of Kajoor customs "presents" whose value was judged to be 1,822 livres.[66] This payment did not include "20 bars" in customs paid for every slave purchased, in addition to the purchase price of 100 bars, which reflected a steep increase from the old Company price of 30 bars.[67] Since the Dammel-Teeñ sold between 100 and 200 slaves at Rufisque and Portudal in this period, the additional customs on the slave trade would have come to between 200 and 400 bars, or 800 to 1,200 livres. If market taxes on cattle, grain, and other commodities were added to these sums, the market taxes would significantly exceed the customs themselves.

Sources from 1785 and 1786 allow a more detailed examination of the composition and complexity of the customs payments. In 1786 the French paid the Dammel-Teeñ customs whose value they calculated at 3,270 livres, a payment which was smaller than that paid to any of the riverine states and powers.[68] These payments were more complicated in practice than on paper, as is indicated by a detailed explanation of the customs from 1785. The Dammel of Kajoor personally received "50 silver dollars [*piastres lourdes*], 14 pieces of *guinée*, 3 ounces of cloves, 3 ells of scarlet cloth, 6 muskets, 400 flints, and 200 lead balls." But these formed only a small part of the whole, as similar payments, but with smaller quantities of goods, were paid to eleven other members of the court. A separate payment was made to the *lingeer* for the right to take salt at Ganjool: one piece of *guinée*, one musket, 4 pounds of gunpowder, 100 lead balls, 100 flints, 16 pints of rum, and 16 pints of wine. In addition the French promised to provide gifts for the major Muslim holidays (Korite, Tabaski, Gamu, Tamxarit), gifts that ironically consisted mainly of alcohol. The Dammel received 100 pints of rum at Saint Louis and 60 pints at Gorée for each major Muslim holiday. The customs also specified specific taxes in rum for every boat that brought food or water to Gorée, payments for the right to cut wood, and specified the amount of food and drink the French would give the king and his messengers each time they made an official visit to Saint Louis, Rufisque, or Gorée.[69]

The Atlantic and the desert: merchant networks in the river trade

The trade of the Senegal River was organized around the specialized activities of merchant groups, whose trade operations shaped the regional economy into zones of trade and production.[70] The division of labor and specialization of merchant groups did not eliminate competition from the system. Atlantic merchants were primarily interested in export commodities like slaves, gum, and gold, but their trade operations put them into direct competition with desert merchants for slaves and grain. The Lower Senegal exported its grain surpluses toward the merchant cities of the Atlantic, Saint Louis and Gorée, but also to the desert societes of the western Sahara. This competition for grain extended to the three main grain-exporting regions, Kajoor-Bawol, Fuuta Tooro, and Gajaaga. The demand for grain on the Atlantic islands and in the desert was related to the expansion of slave-holding merchant societies in both regions. The Atlantic islands produced no grain at all, and were totally dependent on grain imports from the mainland, both to sustain themselves and to feed the slaves held in transit. The merchant societies of the desert produced some grain, but were never able entirely to feed themselves, and depended on grain imports from the agricultural societies of the savanna.[71]

Desert merchant groupings in the Lower Senegal can be divided into two important groups, both subdivisions of the Idaw al Hajj group of merchant-marabouts.[72] One group resided permanently in Waalo and northern Kajoor. They performed the role of landlord-brokers for Moor caravans trading in the Lower Senegal. Over time this grouping adopted the Wolof language, established marriage and kinship ties with the host society, and became known locally as the Moors of Kajoor (Wolof, *Naari Kajoor*). Their kinship ties with other Idaw al Hajj merchant groups living north of the Senegal allowed them to serve as hosts for Moor caravans which sold animals and purchased grain in the Lower Senegal. The Idaw al Hajj sold their gum at the river port known as the Escale du Désert, in the kingdom of Waalo, and also at Serinpate (Darmencour), which was controlled by the Trarza emir.[73] The linking of these two merchant networks permitted the Idaw al Hajj to dominate the desert-side trade between the Lower Senegal and the western Sahara. This trade exchanged animals for slaves, grain, dried fish, and other savanna commodities on the one hand, and gum for Atlantic imports such as cotton cloth, iron, and firearms, on the other.

In the eighteenth century the gum "forests" located on the north bank of the Senegal River were the most important source of gum exports. Most of the gum trees were exploited by desert merchants, although much of the production and transport of gum was carried out by African slaves. Gum extraction and trade required the mobilization of considerable slave labor, brought together several distinct merchant groups, and involved tribute payments by the French to a number of African states and desert warrior groupings, all of whom had to maintain at least an uneasy peace for the trade to take place. The production of gum for export required the organization of a complex interregional trade to supply the gum forests with slave laborers. Many of the slaves who worked in the gum forests were enslaved and then purchased in the middle Niger valley, where desert merchants carried on an important trade which exchanged desert salt for slaves, grain, cloth, and other goods.[74]

At the *escales* ("ports of call") of the Desert and Serinpate, gum markets brought together political representatives of Waalo and Trarza, as well as merchants from the Atlantic and the desert. French Company officials negotiated the purchase price of gum with the chief merchant-marabout of the Idaw al Hajj, the Shems, who collected one-eighth of all the gum marketed, which was later sold to the French for his benefit.[75] At gum markets the desert merchants of the Idaw al Hajj served as cultural brokers between the desert and the savanna as well. When desert people sold gum the Shems or one of his slaves translated Hassaniya into Wolof, the lingua franca of the river markets. The use of slaves as translators and market police sometimes provided them with opportunities for private profit. In 1686 La Courbe noted that the Shems' slave interpreter told him "it was the custom of company officials who traded gum to make a deal with him and trick Chamchy [the Shems], stealing part of his eighth share of the gum."[76] Although La Courbe refused the slave's offer, he promised to say nothing to his master.[77]

The gum caravans were manned by half-naked slaves, dressed according to the French only in goat skins or small cloths that barely covered their hips. These slaves received some gum to sell for their own benefit, because La Courbe described them as fighting over the pieces of cloth they received when they grouped their gum together in order to sell it to the French in bulk. During the period when the market was open, the French Company was required to feed the Moors, distributing a daily ration of millet and meat to every person who came to sell gum.[78] Gum caravans carried no food, and the slaves who crossed the desert with the caravans sucked balls of gum as their sole nourishment until they arrived at the river markets.[79] The gum was brought to market by camel caravans or on oxen, with each merchant owning between twenty and thirty pack animals.

In the ports of the Senegal River desert caravans met maritime fleets from the Atlantic world. One of the distinct features of the Senegal River trade was the construction of a specialized fleet of riverboats under European control. Atlantic merchants conducted their long-distance trade within Senegambia from relatively small river craft, of between thirty and fifty tons. In the early years of Company trade the French relied heavily on European workers, sailors, and soldiers. As late as 1736 there were 185 Europeans in these categories working for the Company in coastal and river ports.[80] From its inception this river commerce called into being a labor force of African sailors, interpreters, and laborers. The African crews of the river fleets were referred to by the French as *laptots*, which in its French form came to refer primarily to the sailors on the river fleets.[81] The Wolof word *lappato bi* pinpoints more clearly the essential function of the Africans who worked for French commerce: interpreters, intermediaries, cultural brokers.[82] The French merchants needed not only laborers to haul their ships upstream, to load and unload cargoes, to guard the merchandise and slaves, and to protect the French from attack, they needed cultural guides and interpreters to help them conduct the sometimes complex and frustrating negotiations that preceded the trade.[83] In the late seventeenth and early eighteenth century the majority of the *laptots* were free laborers from Waalo and northern Kajoor and Fuuta, who worked alongside French sailors and soldiers and Company officials.[84] Over time the Company replaced its European sailors with Africans. In 1738, the Company decided to train skilled workers from the population of Saint Louis so the "Company could discharge part of the white population which it supports here at great expense. We already have apprentices working with our gunsmiths and carpenters."[85]

The new African workers were recruited primarily among Company slaves, and slaves owned by the *signares* (from Portuguese *signora*, "a female merchant") of Saint Louis. The turn to slavery was an "unthinking decision,"[86] nowhere explicitly explained in Company records, and sometimes resented by Company officials in Paris and slave-ship captains, who saw all slaves as laborers destined for export to the Americas.[87] However, the difficulties experienced by the French during the period of free labor help to clarify the turn to slave labor. Free African sailor-interpreters had mixed loyalties, those to their employers and those to their homelands. Since conflicts frequently broke out between the French and neighboring African states, this reduced the military value of the *laptots* in times of crisis. For example, in 1686, a minor conflict between a French trading party purchasing cattle and a village in Waalo escalated into bloody conflict. The conflict began when Company employees set fire to a house while hunting game. The village headmen took one Frenchman and one *laptot* hostage, forcing the French to pay thirty-six cowhides in damages. After leaving the village the French seized an African fisherman as a hostage in retaliation, but their prisoner turned out to be a slave owned by the king of Waalo. While La Courbe was trying to negotiate a settlement in Saint Louis, another French trading party returned to the village and forced the villagers to return the cowhides. While returning to their ship they were ambushed and four French merchants and a number of *laptots* were killed.[88]

These events put the French fort at Saint Louis on alert, and preparations were made to defend the island from possible attack. During this crisis La Courbe sent all of his free Wolof *laptots* back to the mainland, because he clearly did not trust them in the event of a war with Waalo. He did entrust a message to one Fulbe *laptot*, whom the French had hired to watch their cattle, confirming that his decision was based on what he perceived as the ethnic loyalties of the free African sailors. While the French prepared for war, the only Africans permitted to remain with the French garrison were "Christian negroes" who also worked for the French as sailors.[89] When the Company began to replace its free *laptots* with slaves, the conflicts of interest which made free *laptots* untrustworthy disappeared. Company slaves, sometimes referred to simply as "Bambara" were from distant upriver states, and could be molded into a force loyal to the Atlantic merchants.[90]

Over time, European merchants came to resemble their African counterparts, in that they surrounded themselves with a retinue of slave laborers who protected them from attack, transported their goods upriver, and served them as interpreters and guides. Apart from their commercial role as transporters and interpreters, the slaves of the Atlantic merchants had a marked military character. Temporary trading huts were guarded by armed *laptots*, while riverboats provided additional firepower: "The ships of floating warehouses should be moored as close to the land as possible, with their artillery aimed at the market houses, charged, primed, and fuses at the ready. This is the only way to protect the ships from pillage, and to prevent ill designs by the Brack or the Moors."[91]

Although markets were organized, taxed, and supervised by political authorities, merchant groups, and their slaves, they were not exclusively dominated by these groups. Political authorities and merchant leaders set the conditions for markets, established prices and taxes, but once the market was opened anyone with goods to sell was free to trade. In gum markets much of the disorder began when individual merchants and their slaves pressed into the market, eager to be the first to sell their goods, since markets often closed when the French had filled their ships. In the gum trade, the long-distance transport and labor requirements restricted participation to wealthy merchants and their slaves. Grain markets, which were usually opened by one or two river boats of fifty tons, attracted a much more numerous and diverse group of sellers. La Courbe described a grain market which he opened in the kingdom of Waalo at the village of Cayare (Kajaar).[92] After the price of grain and the conditions of trade were agreed on by the village chief, over 500 Africans and Moors arrived to sell millet and beans, mainly in small quantities, in exchange for iron. La Courbe, who watched them struggling to push their way to the front of the line, commented; "I never heard such a charivary or saw such confusion. Nevertheless, there was no serious trouble. It only took us a day and a half to fill our boat, which held only 20 tons, and the whole cargo only cost us one hundred francs. We sent away more than 500 persons without trading, because we had no more storage space."[93]

Grain and slaves: the political economy of the Lower Senegal, 1700–1750

In the eighteenth century the grain trade was an essential accompaniment to the export trade in slaves and gum. Three regions supplied grain regularly to the Atlantic trade: Kajoor, Fuuta Tooro, and Gajaaga. All of them had geographic advantages which permitted them to dominate the trade in grain. French riverboats already stopped at the trade ports of the middle valley and Gajaaga to purchase slaves, gold, and gum, and they could use relatively cheap river transport to bring grain downriver to Saint Louis. Nevertheless, the grain trade on the river was also fueled by French strategic concerns. From the end of the seventeenth century, the French were faced by periodic trade boycotts by the state of Kajoor, which threatened to starve the French settlements of Gorée and Saint Louis into submission. When Kajoor also dominated Bawol, the French presence in the Lower Senegal could be threatened unless the French could secure other sources of supply. This strategic concern, that the French would never be entirely dependent on one source of supply, led the French to place great importance on the development of upriver sources of grain supply in the eighteenth century.

In the period from 1700 to 1750 trade in grain and other provisions from the Lower Senegal created close links between the local economy and the economy of the slave trade. Because the main frontiers of enslavement were located outside the region, alternate periods of prosperity and crisis were linked to the performance of the agricultural economy, which was affected by both natural calamities and political stability. In good years grain was widely traded, and its sale involved the largest number of producers in the Atlantic trade. But the grain trade also occasioned considerable suffering in times of food shortages because the price of grain rose, speculation increased, and European traders purchased as much grain as they could, in order to feed the large numbers of slaves coming onto the export market. Each major famine not only increased the number of slaves exported, but left behind a higher proportion of slaves in the Lower Senegal, as desperate victims of famine sold themselves to masters who possessed grain surpluses. "Your grandmother was purchased with a handful of grain," became a common insult for descendants of slaves in Fuuta.[94]

The dynamic interaction of the slave trade and the provision trade was not unique to the Lower Senegal and other grain-producing regions of the Senegal River valley. Similar developments occurred elsewhere in Africa. In south-eastern Nigeria inland regions supplied yams to the coast and provisioned slave ships, with much of the surplus food being produced by slave labor.[95] In Dahomey the land near the port of Whydah was planted with cassava, which was transformed into flour and sold to provision slave ships.[96] The island of Bioko (Fernando Poo) supplied yams to ships leaving the Gulf of Benin and Central Africa.[97] Perhaps the closest parallel was in East Africa, where the mainland slave plantations at Malindi, Mombasa, and other settlements produced grain for export to Zanzibar, the Arabian peninsula, and the Persian Gulf.[98] In all these examples slave labor played an important role in producing the food surpluses necessary to sustain an expanding commercial economy based on slave labor and slave trading. As in East Africa, the expansion of grain production is Senegambia was based on putting new land in production, importing slave laborers, and intensifying the labor process. New imported crops played a marginal role, compared to other African regions.[99]

During the eighteenth century the strategic link between the slave trade and the provision trade was never far from the minds of European merchants. But the relationship was not perceived as an aspect of commerce, so much as the threat of starvation. In fact the grain trade was poorly organized in the first half of the eighteenth century. Any change in trade patterns or political disturbance could threaten French access to surplus grain. Most of the mentions of "famine" in European documents until the mid-1730s referred to food shortages in the mainland kingdoms, caused by war, drought, or locusts.[100] Mentions of such famines are particularly frequent for the riverine kingdoms in the 1720s, when the invasion of Moroccan and Moorish armies was nearly an annual event in Waalo, Fuuta Tooro, and Gajaaga.

The commerce in foodstuffs was an "invisible" trade, rarely analyzed by European merchants. This curious blindness was connected to the slave trader's habitual denial of Africa's agricultural potential. The harvest of Africa was its people, delivered to the coast by slave-raiding kings. Africans were brought into the world of agricultural production as slaves in the New World.[101] Interruptions in the "invisible" trade were perceived as natural disasters or biblical famines. In the early eighteenth century these "famines" rarely seem to have threatened the survival of the French settlements, which provisioned themselves from the kingdom of Kajoor. However, as early as 1723–5 conditions of drought, invasion of the riverine kingdoms by an alliance of Moroccans and Moors, civil war in Kajoor and Bawol, and locust invasions produced widespread food shortages and famine. The grain famine of 1723–5 coincided with a power struggle in Kajoor-Bawol that followed the death of Latsukaabe and was not resolved until his successor Mayssa Tend Wejj imposed himself in Kajoor.[102] When the French were able to purchase grain, it cost them between five and ten times more than in years of abundance. In 1726 a Company employee estimated that it would take Fuuta, Waalo, and Kajoor three years of peace to recover from the "continuous wars" which had destroyed their prosperity. Kajoor in particular could no longer be relied on as the breadbasket of Saint Louis. "Many things have changed in the last four or five years. The kingdom of Cayor, which was so fertile and prosperous is today so miserable that its population is barely able to feed itself. A hogshead of millet which once only cost four livres in iron now costs between 30 to 35 livres in coral. It seems unbelievable, but it is true."[103]

Slavers saw the critical relation between the slave trade and the grain trade during famines and food shortages. The supply of slaves increased as Africans sold off slaves that became a burden to feed. During serious famines hungry people who wandered in search of food became easy targets for slave raiders. But as food became scarce, the Europeans also faced critical difficulties in feeding their slaves, and high mortality resulted when slavers purchased more slaves than their grain stocks could support. At times the existence of grain shortages on the mainland created favorable conditions for the slave trade, as it did in 1715–16, when the French fitted out five slave ships between August 1715 and February 1716, and shipped out a total of 1,190 slaves. These high exports occurred in spite of severe grain shortages. Brüe's report on the export figures noted: "We have suffered very much from a famine caused by wars and by locusts."[104] One has to assume that in 1715–16 the grain shortage was severe enough to encourage Africans to sell off slaves, but did not totally cripple French ability to feed the slaves they had purchased.

At other times, famine conditions ruined the slave trade, as in 1735–6, when there were serious grain shortages in the Lower Senegal. In June 1736 the Company's director reported providing thirty Wolof slaves to two slave ships, but noted that he had been unable to provide either ship with millet. "The shortage of this grain was so severe last year that we had to use all the means available to us just to provide enough for our own needs." Normally the concession "imported five or six hundred hogsheads [about 150 tons] from this department [Lower Senegal] and for that reason there is currently a shortage."[105] In spite of the famine conditions there were few slaves for sale on the Senegal River, and the French sent slave ships to Gorée to buy provisions, where the shortages were not so severe. In the upriver trading fort in Gajaaga, the famine of 1736 was even more severe than in the Lower Senegal. The French director of Fort Saint Joseph reported "that the whole country is in flames, and the famine has caused everyone to desert the village [near the fort]." In spite of these troubled conditions, which could have stimulated slave exports, the first Company ship returned from the voyage to Gajaaga in September "without a single slave."[106]

By the 1730s there were increasing indications that the trade system was strained to its limits by the European demand for slaves and grain. Grain production became a major bottleneck in the trade system when harvests were reduced by drought or warfare. The response of the slave traders was to expand the grain trade into upriver regions that had previously only supplied locally based trade operations. The grain port of Podor in the middle valley was integrated into the river trade in the 1740s, and grain was purchased more systematically in Gajaaga. Grain shortages in the

81

upper and middle river valley interested the French primarily for the way they affected the slave trade. Shortages in Galam sometimes made it difficult for the French to maintain their trading operations there. Beginning with the famine that followed the disastrous harvest of 1735, which affected the entire Senegambian region, the problem of famine began to assume a more strategic dimension. When the French were no longer able to feed the slaves they purchased with their established sources of supply, they had only two recourses. The first was to have food supplies shipped in from France, and the second was to expand the region from which they purchased grain supplies. Both of these strategies are evident from 1740 on, as the slave-trading settlements were repeatedly faced with food shortages.

The emphasis of French documents on the critical importance of upriver supplies of grain has led many historians to conclude that the middle valley and Gajaaga were the most important source of grain in the eighteenth and nineteenth centuries. Gajaaga developed as an important center of the grain trade to sustain the slave trade, and grain exports continued during the early nineteenth century in connection with the river trade.[107] But at different times Company trade operations in Gajaaga had to import grain, and at others grain was exported downriver. The grain trade from Fuuta also varied in importance.[108] In the 1740s Fuuta was seen as a new supply area, but in the 1750s trade was disappointing. These fluctuations continued until the end of the eighteenth century. In Gajaaga and Fuuta millet was purchased in large quantities just after the harvests which coincided with the large movements of traffic on the river. By contrast, the grain trade of the Lower Senegal was a daily affair, as grain and other foodstuffs trickled in over the course of the entire year, carried by animals overland to trading ports near Saint Louis or Gorée and then shipped by boat.to the islands.

Between 1720 and 1750 upriver supplies of grain became a necessity rather than a hedge against political instability or trade boycotts in Kajoor. The grain markets of the Senegal River valley were linked together by the expansion of Atlantic commerce. The problem of assuring grain supplies was related to the volume of slave exports, which peaked in the period between 1720 and 1740, but it did not disappear when slave exports declined later in the century. Atlantic commerce stimulated commerce between the desert and the savanna, leading to increased desert consumption of savanna grain. At the same time, Atlantic commerce created new urban agglomerations on the coast which depended on imported grain for their survival. In these conditions any crisis could threaten food supplies, in spite of a steady expansion of commercial grain production. Atlantic merchants did not play a dominant role in the grain trade, despite their increased attention to the problem.

In 1743–4 a poor harvest caused food shortages that menaced French trade operations and Company officials worried constantly about the grain trade. Pierre David, the company director, made into an official policy what had already been a French practice: the development of an important new grain trade fromn Fuuta Tooro. In David's instructions to his successor, the imperative of trading grain on the river was the result of changes in the structure of the grain trade from Kajoor, as well as a mediocre harvest in 1743 and a drought in 1744. The French needed to cultivate the friendship of Fuuta Tooro because "the Moors, in taking over the commerce of Kayor and all the states of the Damel have ruined that country. From now on it is the country of the Foules [Fuuta Tooro] that you should count on for the food for all our settlements on the river Senegal and for Senegal itself." Later David specified the reasons for the ruin of Kajoor, at least for the French. "The country of Cayor is now more a charge for Senegal than a useful country. The Moors have taken over its trade, and they import its food in their country, with the result that we no longer receive anything."[109] David's instructions, written in 1746, reflected the lessons of the famine of 1743–4.

One of those lessons was that desert merchants, who controlled much of the bulk trade in grain in the Lower Senegal, were able to shut Atlantic merchants out of grain markets during periods of crisis. Moor donkey caravans purchased grain regularly in the Lower Senegal as far south as Cap Vert, dominating the trade through superior organization and, in times of crisis, because of the lower elasticity of demand for desert animals compared to Atlantic imports. From their dominant position in the grain trade, desert merchants expanded their operations to include the important trade of dried fish for millet which linked the Atlantic coast to interior regions. When environmental factors led to a crisis in food security, desert merchants expanded their trade operations, while Atlantic commerce withered and the islands were haunted by the spectre of starvation.[110]

Company records from 1743–4 give some indication of the progress and consequences of the famine. As early as July 1743, the French reported grain shortages, which they linked to the apprehensions of the local population. "We are threatened with a shortage of millet which has begun to have its effect. The inhabitants of the country [near Saint Louis] don't want to sell the grain they have left because they have the same apprehension." The shortages existed in spite of the arrival of fifty tons of flour and beans from France.[111] Drought conditions in 1743–4 led to more severe food shortages in 1744.[112] The French imported more shipments of food from France, and sent two ships to trade for millet in the middle valley during the high water and earliest harvests, but all of these efforts produced "barely enough for our daily consumption." In Saint Louis sixty slaves awaiting export had died by the end of July, presumably from malnutrition and accompanying diseases. The mortality rate was high; nearly 25 per cent of the slaves held in Saint Louis had died.[113] The famine also had political ramifications. During much of the year the Dammel of Kajoor shut down trade between his kingdom and the French settlements, and only reopened the trade after the satisfactory harvest at the end of the year. The trade boycott occurred in spite of French efforts to maintain good relations, and aggravated the problem of food supplies, particularly at Gorée, which had to be supplied with food and water from Saint Louis for much of the year.[114]

David's journal of his voyage upriver in 1744 reveals a constant preoccupation with the need to supply Saint Louis with grain from the river, because of poor relations with Kajoor and the recent trade boycott.[115] In his negotiations with the riverine states to expand the gold trade, David claimed that the Company was considering abandoning the slave trade from Galam "which was ruinous because of the yearly mortality of the slaves." This mortality was in turn at least partly the result of inadequate food supplies. David could have cited the trade of 1742, when the French purchased 900 slaves in Galam, but lost 200 to starvation and disease.[116] But David was not above using famine conditions to trade grain for gold dust for his own profit while Company slaves were starving in the slave pens. According to one of his subordinates, David transferred surplus Company grain purchased in 1743 in Galam and the lower river to the upriver states at the height of the famine of 1744, where he was able to trade millet for gold dust in very profitable transactions.[117]

There are only scattered indications of the total volume of grain purchased by Atlantic merchants until the 1750s, when documents permit a more global estimate. In 1726 a Company document estimated the annual consumption of Saint Louis in millet to be 600 to 700 hogsheads, or between 150 and 175 tons.[118] In 1736 the Company estimated that it purchased about 150 tons of millet for Saint Louis in the lower river between Saint Louis and Dagana.[119] It is likely that both of these figures underestimate consumption. In 1736 the population of Saint Louis included 48 skilled African workers, both free and slave, and "94 negro slaves" who belonged to the Company and worked in the sea and river trades. This permanent labor force of 142 Africans did not include the "free and seasonal *laptots*" who hired themselves out for the river trade for four or five months of the year, and who were fed by the Company during their employment.[120] In 1734 the Company hired over 230 free *laptots* for four or five months. These numbers include only persons directly hired and fed by the Company.[121] Using the eighteenth-century Company estimate of two pounds of millet per person per day, the African permanent and seasonal labor force on Saint Louis would have consumed eighty tons of millet per year, leaving the Company very little grain to feed the estimated 2,000 to 2,500 slaves exported from Saint Louis and Gorée in the period from 1735 to 1740.[122]

Figures of grain purchases and consumption are more complete for the 1750s, and they show the close link between grain consumption and the slave trade. The most interesting information is provided by Pruneau, who gives the Company's grain needs for the three major settlements, Saint

Louis, Gorée, and Galam (Gajaaga). Pruneau broke millet consumption into two separate categories, the grain consumed by Company employees and slaves, and the grain consumed by slaves in transit toward Atlantic ports. In Galam the Company needed 27 hogsheads of grain for its slaves and employees, and 430 hogsheads of grain to feed the slaves in transit to Saint Louis. For security reasons, the French imported the grain for their *laptots* from the lower river, but relied on local purchases to feed the slaves.[123] In Saint Louis, the French purchased 109 hogsheads for their "Bambaras," 75 hogsheads for their seasonal laborers, and 100 hogsheads for slaves in transit.[124] Gorée, which was the center of an important trade region from Cap Vert to the Gambia, which exported about half of the slaves in this period, purchased 869 hogsheads of grain, 560 for slaves in transit, 109 for Company slaves and employees, and 200 hogsheads to hedge against losses and to use as feed for poultry.[125] These figures reveal two important characteristics of the grain trade in this period. The grain consumed by slaves in transit represented about 68 per cent of all the grain purchased by the Company. And Gorée, which bought grain primarily in Kajoor and Bawol, was the only department with an important surplus. Pruneau believed that Gorée could have purchased 730 tons of grain a year in the kingdoms of Kajoor, Bawol, and Siin, a figure which exceeded the total purchases of the Company in 1752, which Pruneau estimated at 403 tons.[126]

Numbers based on the Company's account books give only a partial picture of the grain needs generated by Atlantic trade. Company accounts only include grain purchased by the Company to feed its own dependants. They do not include the grain consumed by the African inhabitants of Saint Louis and Gorée, who far outnumbered the slaves and free persons directly hired by the Company. There is good reason to believe that the population of Saint Louis numbered 3,000 in the early 1750s, although it dropped to 2,500 in 1754, during the worst famine of the eighteenth century.[127] Using Pruneau's daily ration of two pounds of millet a day per person, Saint Louis would have consumed 1,095 tons of grain a year. The most credible contemporary estimate of Saint Louis' grain imports in the 1750s is 3,000 hogsheads, or about 750 tons.[128] Because Saint Louis had a large proportion of women and children in its population, who would have consumed less grain than the Company ration, 750 tons is a reasonable estimate. The gap between Company grain purchases, only 403 tons in 1750 for all three departments of the Senegal concession, and Saint Louis' consumption needs was filled by an independent grain trade carried on by the African inhabitants of Saint Louis and Gorée. With the profits earned by masters who rented out their slaves to the French, and the earnings of free workers, the inhabitants of the islands purchased much of their own food on the mainland.[129]

There is clear evidence that the food trade continued during most periods of shortage and famine, when high profits attracted merchants to the grain trade. When the grain trade was profitable it affected the export trade in gum and slaves because African merchants satisfied part of the demand for European trade goods through the grain trade. This situation was noted by the French in 1752, at the beginning of a period of famine. One of the first consequences of the famine was a decline in the gum trade, which the French linked to the Moors domination of the grain trade. "The first cause [of the decline] is that the Moors have seized control of the trade in grain for the last ten or twelve years, which they will only sell us in exchange for Indian cloth which has become too common now that this [grain] trade supplies the needs once furnished by the trade in gum."[130] The saturation of the local market with Indian cloth from Kajoor to Galam led the French director to propose that the Company send enough salted beef and food from France to feed the slaves, so that the Company's supply of Indian cloth could be reserved for the trade in slaves and gum.

The Company's problems in 1752 reveal some of the underlying characteristics of Atlantic commerce. It was "import-driven," shaped by African demand for European trade goods, as well as "export-driven." In the crisis African merchants shifted the commodities they were willing to supply, on the basis of their own needs and variations in price and supply of essential commodities. The structure of the export trade allowed some African states and merchants to obtain imports in exchange for grain, salt, and other commodities. Although Europeans tried to limit the circulation of their most valued imports, particularly Indian cloth and guns, to the trade in high-priced exports, this proved impossible, particularly in times of famine. European imports circulated widely in the coastal and riverine kingdoms.

Periods of war and famine often caused temporary shifts in the trade geography of the Senegambian region, as slaves, grain, and gum became scarcer or more abundant in the short run within the wider region. Nevertheless, over the long term there was a clear tendency for the wider region to structure its trade according to comparative advantages of production. Kajoor's location made it a strategic source of grain, wood, fresh water, fish, and other foods, particularly in the dry season when grain transport on the Senegal River was difficult or impossible. In order to make up shortfalls in the grain supply from Kajoor, the French extended the grain trade upriver to Fuuta Tooro and Gajaaga during the high waters. The scale and importance of this upriver grain trade tended to increase over time until it was essential during periods of high-volume slave exports. Although all of the grain-producing regions sold off surplus slaves, none of them were major slave exporters, except in times of serious war or ecological crisis, because grain production encouraged the retention of slaves. This trade geography increased the misery of the slaves who moved over long distance by caravan and riverboat, and contributed to a high mortality rate among undernourished slaves exposed to new disease environments.

The grain trade from the Lower Senegal was generally taken for granted by the French, and as a result it is usually mentioned only during a crisis in trade relations with Kajoor. The documents of the eighteenth century reveal a general uneasiness provoked by the daily dependency on trade with Kajoor. One of the rare documents that gives a rough estimate of the relative importance of Kajoor and Gajaaga in the eighteenth century was written in 1782, when the French occupied Saint Louis, but not Gorée.

> An essential problem for Senegal that the government cannot ignore is famine. Millet is the food staple of the *habitants*, and they can only procure it from the kingdom of the Damel, which extends from the Senegal to the village of Bargny, situated a few leagues south of Gorée . . . Those *habitants* who are rich enough to have their own ships, and the number is very small, purchase small quantities of millet during the Galam voyages, but they never have more than enough for three months, and therefore they are always forced to have recourse to the Damel.[131]

According to this document Kajoor supplied the bulk of Saint Louis' grain supply, while Gajaaga could at most be counted on to provide three months' supply.[132] For this reason French relations with Kajoor, and the frequent conflicts that resulted, were essentially conflicts over the provision trade rather than the slave trade. Kajoor's most effective diplomatic weapon was always a boycott of the grain trade, and the customs payments received by the Dammel and his agents reflected the importance of the provision trade, not the slave trade from Kajoor.

The geography of grain production in the eighteenth century can be reconstructed from commercial records, along with some sense of how the region involved in commercial grain production expanded over time. But European sources only hint at the story of the slaves whose labor produced the grain. Behind the story of the fitful progression of the grain trade, broken by periodic crisis and famine, but expanding after each crisis into new regions, is the story of the slaves who labored in the fields of grain. Although it is impossible to know how many slaves in Kajoor, Fuuta Tooro, and Gajaaga produced grain for commercial sale, there is a striking correspondence between the geography of grain production in the eighteenth century and the geography of slavery in the nineteenth century. Regions which sold grain exported few slaves because they were absorbing slave labour. The expanding exploitation of slave labor explains how commercial expansion continued, in spite of frequent crises and growing consumption of grain in the Atlantic trade and in the desert. The import of slave laborers allowed an extension of the land cultivated; the exploitation of slaves ensured that the slaves themselves would consume little of what they produced, making surplus grain available. The Atlantic coastal region and the Senegal River valley were centers of slave production because of their proximity to major markets, defined by the availability of river transport and the range of pack animals from the desert. Over the course of the first half of the eighteenth century the activities of merchants gradually linked the societies of the Senegal River valley into a single interacting economy linked to the Atlantic world.

The quiet revolution: Islam and commerce

Because the Atlantic trade was broader than the export trade in gum and slaves, it affected the development of Senegambian societies in various ways. Historians have focused on its links with *ceddo* oppression, on the assumption that states controlled and manipulated the Atlantic trade to serve their interests. Less attention has been paid to the way the commercialization of some sectors of the economy tended to place wealth and social authority in the hands of Muslim merchants and Muslim scholars. It is not that the reinforcement of Muslim wealth and power in the eighteenth century has been neglected. There is a rich historical literature on the role of Islam as the main ideological and political expression of resistance to the old regime.[133] Rather, most of these works see jihad and political revolution as the most important expressions of Islamic revival, and tend to see the development of Islam in Senegambia as a series of political revolutions, beginning with the War of the Marabouts, continuing in the eighteenth century with the emergence of Islamic states in Fuuta Tooro and Fuuta Jallon, and continuing into the nineteenth century with the jihads of Al Hajj Umar and Maba.[134]

The emphasis on jihad and political revolution has strongly shaped the way historians have viewed the history of Islam in Senegambia, dividing the region into "successful jihad states" and areas where jihad "failed."[135] This political vision of Islam has led to a relative neglect of the economic and social foundations of Islamic resurgence in the eighteenth century. In contrast to the detailed attention given to Islamic resistance to state power and the enslavement of Muslims by the slave trade, historians have shown little interest in the connections between Islam, commerce, and economic production, except in studies of merchant groups. Popular Islam, with its ties to commercial agriculture, has been seen as a revolutionary new development that emerged during the period of legitimate commerce in the nineteenth century.[136] However, the distinction between the era of the slave trade and the era of legitimate commerce is blurred when one examines more closely the economy of the eighteenth-century Atlantic trade. Long before the development of an agricultural export economy, the trade in grain, cattle, and provisions contributed to the development of economic conditions which favored the expansion of Islam.

Discussions of Islam in Senegambia have often centered on ambiguous terms such as "conversion," "reform," "revival," "charisma," and "jihad," and the way these can be linked to social movements or used to explain relations of domination and subordination in Wolof society. The development of Islam in the eighteenth century reinforced particular social relationships, the relation of desert merchants to savanna cultivators, of teachers to students, and of village communities to Muslim religious leaders. These relationships in turn were linked to economic exchange, to commercial networks, and to the emergence of a scholarly elite whose influence extended into virtually every village in the Lower Senegal. The history of Islam expressed itself in a gradual transformation of society at the grass roots of village society. This history defies analysis as a succession of revivals and jihads. Most villages in the Lower Senegal had an imam (Wolof, *ilimaan*) or marabout as well as a headman-landowner (Wolof, *laman* or *boroom suuf*), although in some villages the fusion of these two offices occurred. This quiet revolution at the village level meant that throughout the eighteenth century most Wolof villages saw their lives as ordered by Islam, by the rituals of the Muslim calendar, and by the conceptions of justice taught by the marabouts. European sources, whatever their weaknesses, amply attest that this quiet revolution occurred well before the political upheavals of the eighteenth and nineteenth centuries.

European comments on Islam in Senegambia in the seventeenth and eighteenth centuries provide a limited vision of Islamic culture, but they do provide important testimony to the importance of Islamic belief and practice. Europeans noted ritual practices, particularly the major religious holidays of the Muslim calendar. La Courbe, describing the religious practices of the free *laptots* who worked for the French in the 1680s, witnessed the scrupulous observation of Ramadan (Wolof, *koor gi*), the month of fasting. "Our negroes observe their fast with such regularity that they never eat or drink before sunset . . . I worked with *laptots* at Gorée who, even when occupied rolling stones, a painful job, never failed to observe Ramadan regularly and pray seven or eight times a day."[137] La Courbe, who witnessed the ceremonies of Korite at the end of Ramadan, also described how the religious ceremonies were closed by dance music led by *griots*, traditional wrestling matches and feasting, followed by a public prayer the next day.[138]

Another seventeenth-century merchant, Chambonneau, described Ramadan and the principal beliefs of the Muslims of the Lower Senegal, and commented that "in reality they make us see that to our great shame we are practically without fear of God when compared to them."[139] Europeans cruelly abused the faith of African workers. Chambonneau said that he sometimes "took pleasure in throwing some lard in the cooking pot of my *laptots*, who would have rather died than taste the dish."[140] When due allowance is made for the cultural bias of Europeans, eager to point out the superstitions and lapses of Senegambian Muslims, European sources document the deep hold of Islam and the coexistence of Islam with cultural practices, like circumcision of youths, which had their roots in Wolof traditions. Ironically, it was the economic activities of

Atlantic merchants which contributed strongly to the dynamism of Islam in the period of Atlantic commerce.

Throughout the eighteenth century the Atlantic trade coexisted with an important desert trade that linked the societies of the Lower Senegal with the desert societies of the western Sahara. Desert merchants occupied an important social niche in the Lower Senegal. The desert merchant diaspora of the Idaw al Hajj occupied a number of permanently settled villages in Kajoor and Waalo, where the Moors of Kajoor filled the dual role of landlord-brokers and hosts for their kinsmen from the desert, and scholar-teachers for the Wolof amongst whom they settled. The combination of the roles of landlord-broker and marabout was not unusual in the western Sudan, as illustrated by the *juula* merchant diaspora that dominated the trade between the middle Niger and the upper Gambia.[141] Settled merchant-scholars whose main role in commerce was to serve as hosts and to maintain positive relations with the political authorities lived as scholars, cultivators, diplomats, and spiritual advisors, and over time tended to become a distinct group, with close ties to the host society and different interests than the long-distance merchants who traveled between the desert and the savanna.[142]

The trade diaspora from the desert brought a distinctive Islamic model. According to oral traditions preserved by the Moors, the Idaw al Hajj were the first maraboutic (*zawaya*) group to renounce warfare and jihad during the struggle for power in the desert. They did so because they saw warfare as contrary to Islam, but also because of the loyalty they felt to their African students, caught up in the conflict, and subjected to the repression of the hassani-warriors from the desert.[143] In the aftermath of the War of the Marabouts, the Idaw al Hajj provided a model of Islamic devotion to scholarship and commerce which was combined with renunciation of war and submission to political authority. This cultural model had an important impact on the development of Muslim society. The desert marabouts served as hosts for traders from the desert, provided education to Wolof students, served as spiritual advisors to the court of Kajoor, and maintained a productive economy of livestock rearing and agriculture, with the labor provided by their students and their slaves.

The contrast between a Muslim way of life based on peaceful economic pursuits, scholarship, and commerce, and an aristocratic warrior culture based on warfare and the collection of tribute was widespread in the western Sudan, and the desert marabouts were only one of several Muslim networks which embodied the way of Islam. *Juula* traders also tended to occupy a role in the Sudan as merchant-scholars whose economic interests and religious traditions favored accommodation with political authorities and a distinct way of life which combined commerce with religious scholarship.[144] In the Lower Senegal the influence of these two religious models produced a sharp distinction between the lifestyle of marabouts and the lifestyle of aristocrats, who tended to define the poles of social authority perceived by the Wolof as the contrast between *ceddo* ("pagan") and *taalibe* ("Muslim"). In its origins, the model of the marabout was influenced by models from the east (Soninke and Mande) and models from the desert, but these cultural influences were assimilated and domesticated over time, producing a particular configuration which made for a distinct Islamic culture, less rooted in the world of commerce than in the world of agriculture.

The typical religious center was at once an educational and agricultural enterprise. Wolof dynastic traditions contrast the political capital of the king with "the villages of marabouts where there are plantations and mosques requiring perpetual surveillance."[145] Agriculture and education were linked by the structure of the Muslim *daara* or school, where the students (*taalibe*) worked for the marabout throughout their educational apprenticeship. Teaching marabouts are known in Wolof as *seriñ-fakk-taal*, marabouts "of the hearth," partly because their students read out their texts at night by firelight, but also because the teaching marabouts were the heads of households.[146] Education began when the parents confided their child to a marabout and from that moment until the completion of the education the *taalibe* worked for his teacher, becoming a dependant (*surga*) within his household. In addition to his labor, the *taalibe*'s parents paid for the education by giving the marabout a gift of a slave or a horse, if they were from wealthy families, or a lesser gift in livestock and grain if they were poor. Until this payment was made, the *taalibe* remained the dependant of the marabout.[147]

In the first half of the eighteenth century Islamic education and enterprise flourished, first under the guidance of desert marabouts and then as an independent and autonomous domain under the leadership of marabouts fully assimilated into local society.[148] Desert marabouts brought the influence of Islamic renewal and reform in the form of a revitalized Sufism, based on brotherhoods that incarnated the spiritual leadership of marabouts and the spiritual submission of their disciples.[149] By the late 1740s Sidi al-Mukhtar al-Kunti was using the Qadiri brotherhood in the western Sahara as a vehicle for expanding commercial enterprise, supported by an ideology which linked the accumulation of wealth with religious piety. Wealth was linked with dignity and status, and was second only to knowledge in the Kunta vision of Islam.[150] Until the 1740s European observers equated Muslim ascendancy in Senegambia with Moor ascendancy, and their perception reflected the importance of desert commerce and desert religious teachings in the Lower and Middle Senegal in the first half of the eighteenth century.[151] The main centers of the desert savanna grain trade were at the same time the main centers of Islamic militancy and reform.[152]

By the mid-eighteenth century the Lower Senegal had emerged as an important center of religious scholarship in its own right. The village of Pir in Kajoor was one of the most important centers of religious scholarship in Senegambia in the period from 1750 to 1790. It was in Pir that many of the future leaders of the revolution of 1776 in Fuuta Tooro received their religious education. According to the oral traditions of the *toorobbe* (religious scholars of Fuuta Tooro), the leaders of the revolution went to Pir to study because its teacher was the most renowned in Senegambia.[153] The leaders of the jihad in Fuuta Tooro combined an Islamic inspiration with a national one: to reduce the dependency of Fuuta on the Moors.[154] This suggests that the transformation of religious education into a fully indigenous enterprise was largely complete by the mid-eighteenth century.

The importance of Kajoor as a center of religious scholarship was only one of the signs of the growing hegemony of Islam. In northern Kajoor the titled marabouts (*seriñu-lamb*) appointed by Latsukaabe became powerful leaders of village communities with close trade links to Saint Louis. In Saint Louis itself free Muslim migrants from Waalo and Kajoor formed one segment of the emerging *habitant* community, bringing the influence of a revitalized Islam into the heart of the merchant community linked to the Atlantic world.[155] On the southern borders of Kajoor a phenomenon more akin to conversion was spreading Islam into the Lebu villages of Cap Vert and neighbouring regions described by Europeans as Sereer and as "pagan" in the first half of the eighteenth century. In the 1750s Adanson described his surprise when, after visiting all the houses in Rufisque, he discovered a "second village" made up of the "mausoleums or tombs erected over the dead bodies . . . according to the custom established among the several clans of the Serera nation."[156] By the end of the eighteenth century Cap Vert, like Northern Kajoor, was a center of Islamic resurgence which joined the rebellions that swept the region in the 1790s. In both regions Atlantic commerce reinforced the wealth and power of social groups who identified their interests with Islam and opposed the way of Islam to the way of the aristocracy, peace to war, and commerce to pillage. Their vision was the foundation of a powerful ideology, a vision of history, which today shapes the way a majority of the Wolof perceive their past.

4

Merchants and slaves: slavery on Saint Louis and Gorée

At the end of the seventeenth century European concessionary companies began to occupy strategic points on the West African coast, and to fortify them as the outposts of trade monopolies granted by a European power. In the Lower Senegal two small islands, Saint Louis in the mouth of the Senegal River, and Gorée off the coast of Cap Vert, were occupied permanently, except in times of war, from the mid-seventeenth century onward. During the eighteenth century slave societies came into existence on both Saint Louis and Gorée. These societies were tributary to the Atlantic trade, whose interests they served. Yet even though they were fully integrated into the maritime economy of the eighteenth century, they maintained a distinct African culture that tied them historically to the mainland.[1]

The history of these island societies is usually introduced through the *signares*, charming and hospitable local women, who welcomed European merchants, married them according to the customs of the country, and gave birth to the mulattoes of Saint Louis, the favored middlemen in the trade between European merchants and the mainland.[2] Eighteenth-century travellers like Adanson described their reaction to the women of Saint Louis, who played such an important role in establishing contacts between European merchants and mainland society, in terms that reflected the world of the merchant directors. "Their skin is surprisingly delicate and soft; their mouth and lips are small; and their features are regular. There are some of them perfect beauties." An English gentleman who had resided in Senegal, and who wrote the notes for the English edition of Adanson's work commented on this passage. "The vast numbers of children, and children's children, the French begat by them, and left there, prove our author is not singular in his opinion."[3] Adanson, a naturalist with a scientific eye for detail, also described his reaction to the women who lived and worked in the vicinity of Saint Louis, showing that the *signares* were simply the privileged beneficiaries of the general attraction exercised by local women over lonely European men. "The women all had a half-paan [*pagne*] round their waist, which served them for a petticoat;

93

but from the waist upwards they were naked. Being generally well made, they have a very good air in this dishabille, especially when a person is used to their colour: those who are not accustomed to them, must be content with admiring their shape, which is extremely fine."[4]

This romantic view of the history of Saint Louis and Gorée neglects the fundamental development of the period: the birth of slave societies which served the interests of the Atlantic slave trade. From the middle of the eighteenth century slaves formed the large majority of the populations of both Saint Louis and Gorée, a demographic position that they would keep for over a century. For the slave traders themselves, this development appeared paradoxical, particularly in the second half of the eighteenth century when slavery expanded on the islands during a period of declining slave exports. Nevertheless, Atlantic merchants generated new demands for slave labor within Africa, increasing the number of slaves in the continent even as they organized the march of slaves to the coastal ports.

Eighteenth-century Saint Louis and Gorée were maritime societies, settled by free Africans and slaves who migrated to the islands. Both islands were nearly uninhabited when they were acquired by European merchants. Small, infertile, and almost totally lacking fresh water, the islands had little value to the Africans who sold their rights to the land. Some features of the islands' history were shaped by geography. At the mouth of the Senegal a treacherous sandbar had to be crossed before a ship could enter the lower reaches of the river. Europeans relied on African canoemen and pilots to cross the bar and this need for local maritime expertise led to the emergence of a migrant labor system in the seventeenth century. Once European ships entered the river they encountered the broad sheltered waters of the lower Senegal. The lower river was navigable year round, but it could accommodate medium-sized craft more easily than ocean-going vessels. In the rainy season the river rose and ships could sail as far as Gajaaga. Gorée was strategically located at the westernmost extension of the African continent, at the beginning of the strip of coastline known to eighteenth-century seamen as the windward coast. It was a landmark, and a natural first stopping point for ships trading on the West African coast, whether they were trying to purchase slaves or simply to load fresh water, meat, fish, and wood.

The geography and ecology of the Senegal River valley had specific implications for Atlantic commerce. The Senegal River fell somewhere between the Gambia, where ocean-going vessels could sail upriver and access markets, and rivers like the Niger or the Zaire, where geography and ecology favored African commercial control over all or part of the river. In the Niger delta, the complexities of the lagoon system and disease ecology allowed African coastal and riverine societies to monopolize commercial traffic on the river.[5] On the Zaire the existence of important cataracts allowed African traders to divide the river into spheres of influence, permitting traders like the Bobangi to exercise monopoly control over portions of the river.[6] On the Senegal River, European maritime technology could be utilized on a seasonal basis, provided that suitable river craft were constructed. This was the option pursued by the Compagnie des Indes Occidentales. The Company built sloops and schooners armed with artillery, negotiated rights of passage, and manned their ships with European crews supplemented by seasonal migrant laborers and African slaves.

The slave labor system that emerged on the Senegal River had distinct features, even though slave labor was common to a number of maritime societies on the West African coast. In the Gambia River European sailing ships could penetrate upriver, where they were met by caravans from the interior. Canoe transport, controlled by riverine villages, linked the caravan traffic to the ocean-sailing ships. Although "canoeboys" in the Gambia were often slaves, the labor system was decentralized, and the slave holdings small in scale.[7] The closest counterparts to the islands of the Lower Senegal were on the coast of Sierra Leone, where African maritime laborers were called *grumettas* (from the Portuguese *grumete*, "ordinary seaman"). In the 1780s the merchant firm of Alexander and John Anderson on Bance Island owned over 200 *grumettas*, slaves whom they employed "in navigating our craft along the Coast, and in supplying our out-factories with goods, and bringing back the returns to Bance Island."[8] South of Sierra Leone, the Kru maritime diaspora, dominated by free migrants, loaded and offloaded ships prevented from landing on the coast by the pounding surf. Similar maritime systems dominated on the Gold Coast and the Slave Coast.[9] In the Niger delta coastal peoples dominated the canoe trade that brought slaves and other goods to the coast. Slavery was essential to the "canoe house" system of the Oil Rivers, but like most of the maritime economies on the leeward coast, maritime labor was supplied by coastal societies or migrant laborers, rather than by new maritime societies which emerged through the colonization of previously uninhabited offshore islands.[10]

The Atlantic islands were inhabited by a very diverse laboring population in the early eighteenth century. The crews of ships that sailed upriver included European sailors and soldiers, Company slaves and free Africans from Saint Louis, and free seasonal laborers from the mainland. Gradually, slaves came to predominate. Most of the slaves of Saint Louis and Gorée were the property of the *habitants*, a group of diverse origins, but dominated by *signares* and the mulatto families they founded. One reason for the relatively slow development of a locally rooted slave population on the islands was the European interest in maximizing the export of slaves. The Compagnie du Sénégal never in fact favored the accumulation of a permanent slave population on the islands. The development of slavery depended on the emergence of a local master class. The key historic role

95

of the *signares* was to set in motion a process of local accumulation which eventually created a distinct class of slave-owning merchants who were tied to the islands.

European merchants and employees formed links with local women in order to conduct trade for their own profit, in defiance of Company regulations and policy. The local women who "married" European merchants "according to the customs of the country" also profited from their alliance. The families they founded became autonomous from their European husbands, and invested most of their wealth in slaves and in boats. But "sex" and "contraband," emphasized in Company documents, provide only a partial explanation of the pioneering role of women in the colonization of the islands. Because Atlantic merchants specialized in the purchase and transport of enslaved persons, they acquired human dependants who had to be fed and cared for. African seasonal workers and slaves hired to load and offload cargoes, man ships, and protect merchants and trade goods, had to be fed and provided for as part of the conditions of employment. The business of purchasing water and provisions, processing and preparing food for slaves in transit and Company workers, washing clothes and keeping house, was undertaken by the *signares*. They were slave owners, and the households they headed were composed primarily of female slaves who labored under their direction.

Over time a successful female-headed merchant household could expand its activities. Women merchants began by selling provisions, prepared food, and domestic labor to European merchants. The purchase of female slaves allowed an expansion of these activities. "Marriage" to a European provided women with important contacts and additional slaves, given as gifts at the time of the marriage. Because European men frequently died and those who survived the "seasoning" were eager to accumulate a fortune and return to Europe, the typical "marriage" only lasted a few years. European fathers often gave their names to their children, but rarely exercised any authority over them. The *signare* household was female-dominated at least until a *signare*'s own sons reached maturity. In this manner the *signares* gave birth to the prominent *habitant* families.

The *habitants* eventually achieved a dominant position in the provision trade which was necessary to the survival of urban, island societies with no agriculture. The commercial role of the *habitants* was to purchase, bulk, and transport locally produced low-cost commodities like grain, salt, hides, and fish. European merchants concentrated on the slave trade, on organizing the nearly constant diplomatic negotiations with the African states of the mainland, and on maintaining correspondence with the metropole. The accumulation of slaves by *signares* and *habitants* began with the profits gathered from the provision trade. The *habitants* turned to slave labor to satisfy the labor needs generated by their commercial activities. Male slaves served as sailors in the ships that ferried goods between the mainland and the islands, while women slaves carried out the labor-intensive job of preparing millet for consumption. From this early role in the provision trade the *habitants* acquired the skills and capital that permitted them to gain a role in the more lucrative export trade in slaves and gum. In the course of the eighteenth century European merchants delegated considerable authority to the *habitants*, who gradually became indispensable middlemen in the trade with the coast and the middle and upper Senegal regions. But the *habitants* only gradually gained enough power and slaves to play a major role in the upriver trade.

The predominance of the *habitants* also resulted from their superior adaptation to the disease environment. The fragility of European society resulted from deadly fevers which cut short the lives of many European traders. Mortality was particularly high in the first year on the coast. A British seaman named William MacIntosh was stationed in a ship with a crew of fifty-seven in the Senegal River from January 1760 to July 1762. "There was a very singular degree of mortality – we were frequently supplied with men by men of war – they sent down the Coast of Africa a few men at a time, sometimes by pressing, and sometimes by men entering, and we buried a great many more than our original complement. – To the best of my recollection there were only two other persons besides myself that ever came off the Coast."[11] Those who survived the first years could still be killed by periodic epidemics, especially of yellow fever. Although there is little reliable statistical data on eighteenth-century European mortality rates, some epidemics killed between 30 and 50 percent of the Europeans. In 1778 an epidemic of yellow fever killed 43 Frenchmen on Gorée out of a total European population of approximately 150.[12] The same yellow fever epidemic reportedly killed one half of the English on Saint Louis in 1778, and reduced the entire population of the island by one-third.[13]

The dangerous environment contributed to the development of a merchant community which focused on quick profits for individual merchants, followed by a return to the metropole or some healthier French colony. As the result the mulatto merchant families that emerged were female-centered, and culturally tied to the Lower Senegal. Local women showed a strong entrepreneurial instinct in their attraction for European men, but they also provided them with slaves and children who could survive the disease environment of the coast and the interior. *Signares* cared for their "husbands" when they were stricken down by fevers, which was often the case. Pruneau de Pommegorge, an employee of the Company who had lived on the islands, described the women of Saint Louis as "strongly attached to the whites, and they give them the best care possible when they are sick."[14] A French memoir from the late eighteenth century attributed the fevers of the coast to the climate, promiscuous sexual contacts with local women, the poor quality of imported food, particularly flour, and the poor quality of water, but also to the abuse of alcohol, which in different forms was one of the major trade items on the coast. The medical treatise described "tertiary fever," "daily fever," "continuous putrid fever," and "violent fever," all attributed to various disruptions of bile in the body, and to the abusive habits of the merchants who lived on the coast. Although "quinina" already figured as one of the remedies, it was usually administered with salts, tartar, and bleedings,[15] and therefore did little to prolong European lives.

African diseases kept would-be European conquerers confined to the coast, and dependent on African intermediaries in their trade with the African hinterland.[16] Whereas in the Americas European diseases, animals, and plants served as agents of colonization as important as the settlers and traders who brought them to the New World, Africa shared most of the disease history of the Eurasian land mass, and in addition harbored many of its own deadly microbes, which killed off large numbers of Europeans, and in some cases followed slave traders and slaves to the New World. The same disease factors that encouraged the replacement of native American inhabitants of the West Indies and the North American mainland by colonists from Europe and Africa, worked in reverse to discourage permanent European settlement in Africa. They undoubtedly also help to explain why even the Euro-African populations produced by contact and colonization in the eighteenth century ultimately were assimilated into the African cultures that surrounded them, rather than maintaining a distinct European or even Euro-African identity.

The development of slavery

The earliest French documents from the island settlements of Saint Louis and Gorée give some information on the contraband trade carried on between Company employees and local women, which served as the starting point for the development of the distinct eighteenth-century population of the islands. Sieur De La Courbe, who served as the Company's director during the late seventeenth century, described his futile efforts to drive local women from the island settlement of Saint Louis.

Company sources shed only a partial light on the emergence of the *signares*, precisely because Company officials in Paris saw them as a class of smugglers and parasites whose sexual charms allowed them to corrupt Company employees and defraud the Company. The so-called debauchery of Company officials was part of a larger pattern, in which local women provided sexual services and domestic labor to European men. La Courbe, who investigated the private lives of Company employees on orders from Paris, reported that each Company employee kept a female servant to cook his food and do his wash.[17] To end this abuse La Courbe created a Company kitchen and a Company laundry. African female servants and companions were ubiquitous in Senegal. When La Courbe traveled to the *escale* of the Desert to trade gum, he was presented "with a young black woman, very pretty and well made, of between seventeen and eighteen years of age." For La Courbe this was another chance to display his high moral standards. "She told me that she came to offer me her services, that she was accustomed to doing the laundry for the directors and merchants who came to trade, to comb their hair, to look them in the eyes and to give them a massage. I could not help myself from laughing at such a compliment, and from admiring the weakness of our merchants, and how much this country exerted a pernicious influence on our young people. I told her that she could wash my laundry, but as for the rest, I had no need."[18]

La Courbe also noted the presence of prostitutes in public houses, women of "ill repute" who entertained and offered companionship to Company officials during their leisure time.[19] This was also an abuse he had orders to end. The concern of Company directors in Paris was based on reports that "the principal merchants, as well as the other inhabitants and the sailors lived as freely and openly with negresses as if they were their legitimate wives." This behavior shocked the Company because the directors believed that Company officials gave away "the most beautiful and most precious merchandise of the Company to please and satisfy the extravagance of these lewd women."[20] The efforts of La Courbe and the Company officials in Paris failed miserably, because European men had no intention of cooking, washing clothes, or foregoing sexual pleasures and companionship while they labored for the Company in Senegal.

Incidentally, as part of his inquisition, La Courbe testified to the important role of women traders at Saint Louis at the end of the seventeenth century.

> Returning to the fort, I entered into the store where we carried on our trade. There I found several women from Bieurt and other neighboring villages, who had brought hides, millet, *pagnes* or cotton cloths, because they are the ones who control almost all the trade of Senegal [Saint Louis]. They own female slaves who they send far away into the country to buy hides which they carry for more than 15 leagues on their heads or on donkeys. They buy them cheaply, and when they have gathered a considerable number they bring them to the fort in boats.[21]

La Courbe's description of the dominant role of women merchants, particularly in the trade in "country goods" such as food, cattle hides, and cotton cloth is confirmed by other seventeenth-century sources.[22] This country trade was already highly developed, as witnessed by the use of slave labor and the ownership of transport animals and possibly riverboats. The same women who came to Saint Louis to sell food and other country goods were accused by La Courbe of debauching "our whites in order to make a profit, because they never make love except for a price."[23]

The *signares* of the eighteenth century were not an entirely new social group. They borrowed their name from a similar group of Afro-Portuguese women entrepreneurs who lived in the coastal ports of Senegambia in the sixteenth and seventeenth centuries, particularly in the regions south of Cap Vert. This earlier merchant group declined when European monopoly traders occupied the coastal islands, and African states in return established direct royal control of trade in the coastal and river ports. But André Brüe, writing of his experiences in Kajoor in 1700, described the role of the "signora Catti," a mulatto woman, who still had an official role in Rufisque alongside an "alcayde" appointed by Latsukaabe. The signora Catti owned lands near the royal capital of Maka "where several of her slaves carried on commerce in her name."[24]

The *signares* of the mainland, merchants, interpreters, and intermediaries, gradually lost their utility in the mainland kingdoms, as they were replaced by royal officials, usually slaves, who filled the roles once held by the Afro-Portuguese. In 1666 Villault reported that at Rufisque "the alcayde spoke French, English, and Dutch," effectively undercutting some of the middleman roles once played by the Afro-Portuguese.[25] However, a new generation of *signares*, based on Saint Louis and Gorée, reproduced the same social functions in the heart of the Atlantic settlements of the eighteenth century. Like their predecessors they were merchants and slave owners who served as key links between Atlantic merchants and the society of the mainland. The origins of the *signares* remain obscure, but it is likely that they were formed by three separate currents of emigration to the islands. Free women traders from the mainland, like those described by La Courbe, expanded their commercial activities by "marrying" Atlantic merchants and establishing themselves as *signares*. Secondly, it is likely that some of the Afro-Portuguese *signares* based on the mainland migrated to the islands and reestablished themselves as intermediaries in the Atlantic trade, and that this group gave its name to the *signares*. Thirdly, European sources suggest that some *signares* were slave women chosen as mistresses by Atlantic merchants from the female slaves that the slave trade brought to Saint Louis and Gorée.

Courtesans and care-givers, the intimacy of the *signares* with European traders offered them lucrative opportunities for private gain, as Europeans accepted the cultural role of male providers and paid for the privilege of marriage like local men. Women had the advantage of monopolizing certain economic functions that were essential to the economy of the islands. Europeans could buy the millet required to feed their slaves and African hired laborers, but only women's labor could transform the millet into food, pounding it into the various flours used in the preparation of couscous and porridge, and only women were able and willing to provide the domestic services of washing clothes and keeping house for European men and their employees. Women merchants provided the female slave labor that filled these essential roles and they eventually transformed this domestic economy into a beachhead that allowed them to become merchant-entrepreneurs who played an essential role in Atlantic commerce.

Even though local marriages with African women developed early in the history of the islands, the relations between this local society and the French merchants of the islands followed no fixed patterns in the first decades of the eighteenth century. Agents of the Company in Senegal worked out their own *modus vivendi* with local women and their children. At times however, new agents of the Company felt obliged to ask the advice of the board of directors in France about the policy they should follow, and their correspondence with Paris permits a partial reconstruction of the process that led to the emergence of the *habitants*. For example, a letter from Gorée dated June 14, 1736 asked the Company for advice on the policy to adopt toward the *signares*, even as it affirmed that local custom dictated nonintervention. The precise problem was the inheritance of property by the *signares*. The interest of the letter is the specific information it contains: the *signares* were already slave owners, and established Company practice on the islands allowed them to pass on wealth that they had acquired or inherited from their European "husbands."

> There is a negress here who is fairly advanced in age who has a number of slaves belonging to her and her daughters. This woman has two daughters, one of whom is the widow of Pierre Le Luc; the other has departed for France with her husband Robert. The latter left all her slaves with her mother when she left; some of the slaves were given to her as part of her marriage contract, and others were acquired later. In fact there are a number of other women here with bastard children and it has been the practice of the Company to let them inherit the property of their mothers.[26]

Women merchants and their female slaves provided sexual services and domestic labor to European men, while selling them the provisions they needed to feed their African workers and slaves in transit. This combination of activities transformed female-headed merchant households into the nucleus of an emerging urban popultion. Female merchants formed one stream of urban migrants; maritime labor provided an equally important second stream. The history of maritime labor on riverboats and coasting vessels can be traced in the bookkeeping of the Company. The recruitment of African sailors and the training of skilled artisans was as essential to commerce as supplying merchants with a proper assortment of trade goods.

In the early eighteenth century the Company employed mixed crews of Europeans and seasonal migrant workers in the river convoys that sailed up the Senegal River during high waters to trade for slaves, gum arabic, ivory and gold. The greatest demand for labor began with the rise of the river in June. The sailing vessels, riverboats, and small ships used by the Company depended ultimately on the physical force of the crews for the difficult voyage up the river. "The ships are pulled upriver with ropes by the negroes, and it usually takes fifty days to travel the 250 leagues between Senegal [Saint Louis] and fort Saint Joseph, unless they are favored by the wind, which is fairly rare."[27] This back-breaking labor was the work of the *laptots*. In the early eighteenth century *laptots* were paid one bar or four livres a month, and throughout the period of their employment they were fed and cared for by the Company. This monthly salary, although considered modest by the Company, would have permitted a *laptot* to purchase 1,600 pounds of millet at current prices in the early eighteenth century for each month of labor. In five months, the common seasonal contract of workers who signed on for the upriver trade, a *laptot* could earn the equivalent of the exchange value of the millet produced by a household of four active adults.[28] Since *laptots* were in fact paid in trade goods, and had ample opportunity to trade during their voyages, free workers received a salary attractive enough to explain free migration to the islands.

However, it is somewhat misleading to describe the *laptots* as wage laborers. *Laptot* is derived from a Wolof word which means "interpreter" or "intermediary."[29] The Wolof meaning gives an indication of how the *laptots* perceived themselves: they were guides, intermediaries, whose skills permitted the French to trade on the river. When this self-perception is combined with what we know of wages, the analysis can be taken one step further. The *laptot* was not just a wage laborer, but a petty trader. Workers received their wages in trade goods and salt. Salt was extremely cheap in the lower river valley, but very valuable in the upper river. The wage was a stock of trade goods available to those who worked in the river trade.

Alongside of the seasonal *laptots*, there was a smaller group of permanently employed workers, who tended to have more specialized skills. These included trained artisans who maintained Company ships, and workers and servants who catered to European tastes. Many of these year-round Company employees required special training. From very early on many of the permanent workers were slaves, owned either by the Company or *signare* households. Mulatto sons of *signares* and free African men attached to *signare* households formed a second group. In 1734 the Company employed mixed crews in its boats, with slaves and free workers laboring side by side under the supervision of Europeans. The European presence was important, because there were 130 Europeans on Saint Louis fulfilling diverse functions: "employees, naval officers, sailors, workers, and soldiers," according to a Company report.[30] Slaves formed a prominent part of the permanent labor force on the island. "The [Company] has in its employ 170 domestic negroes, apprentices, and manual laborers; the apprentices are known as *gourmettes*; the rest are known by the name of Bambara and are in majority slaves."[31] This permanent labor force, made up essentially of slaves from the same upriver regions that supplied most of the export trade, was supplemented by a larger number of free workers. "Independently of the 170 blacks that the Company maintains for the entire year, we hire more than 230 *laptots* for four or five months. They are free blacks from the mainland who are hired for service in the gum trade . . . or who serve on the ships and riverboats that make the voyage to Galam."[32] Even though slave labor was already important on the islands, there were not enough slaves to fulfil the demands for labor during the trading season.

In 1736 the Company employed 231 Europeans in the three permanent settlements of Saint Louis, Gorée, and Galam. There were 43 employees, a term used to describe administrators, bookkeepers, and commercial agents. The majority of Europeans were sailors (71), workers (42), or soldiers (72). The largest number of Europeans were stationed at Saint Louis, where 127 Europeans lived. In addition there were 67 Europeans on Gorée, and 37 at Fort Saint Joseph in Galam.[33] The occupations of the Africans in the service of the Company reveal the commercial and maritime character of the French settlements. There were 48 skilled African workers on the island of Saint Louis. "14 negro and mulatto sailors, 2 cabin boys, 1 carpenter, 2 carpenter's apprentices, 2 sawyers, 4 calkers, 1 apprentice gunsmith, 1 blacksmith, 4 apprentice blacksmiths, 1 cooper, 2 sail makers, 2 apprentice masons, 3 bakers, 1 cook, 3 cook's helpers, 2 gardeners, and 2 butchers." Apart from the cooks, butchers, and bakers, who prepared food for the French on the island, almost all of the workers had skills that were needed for the maintenance or piloting of the Company's trading fleet. These skilled workers, free or slave, had a higher status than the *laptots*: "94 negro slaves who serve as sailors on the sea and in the river and who live on the island." The same report revealed that this permanent work force of 142 blacks and mulattoes was insufficient, because "free and seasonal *laptots*" were still hired by the Company during the peak trading season.[34]

The composition of the African workforce at Gorée and Galam was similar, on a smaller scale. In both cases *laptots* formed the majority of the workforce. The list for Galam included "*laptots* and women" in a single category of twenty-six persons, while the lists of Saint Louis and Gorée do not mention women. On Saint Louis and Gorée women slaves belonging to the *signares* filled the needs for domestic labor on the islands. All later census data from Saint Louis and Gorée document the importance of women's work. The preparation of millet for consumption required considerable labor, and female slaves also worked as domestic servants and as washerwomen. In the second half of the eighteenth century all the census data shows that female slaves formed the majority of the slave population on the islands of the Lower Senegal. Women's work was labor-intensive, and it served needs for which there was a continuous demand. By contrast many of the tasks that men performed were seasonal.

The last census of Saint Louis before the British occupation was taken in 1754. It is incomplete, like all the census data from the first half of the eighteenth century. However, it does give a brief analysis of the total population of the island, unlike earlier documents which focus only on the personnel of the Company. The census of 1754 was taken in the midst of a serious famine which started in 1751 and which lasted until 1756. The document was inspired by the difficulties created by serious food shortages in the Lower Senegal. The context in which the census was taken influenced its content, and the census of 1754 is in a sense a response to the critics of the Company, who blamed the famine on the large-scale purchases of food by French and English slavers, and on the food consumed by the expanding slave populations of Saint Louis and Gorée. The criticisms of the Company's management help explain the defensive tone of the report, and the tortured logic of some of its arguments. The census of 1754 explained that the "useful" population of Saint Louis was 800, and the report goes on to give the occupations of 753 persons, almost all of them men. At the same time the report noted that the actual population of Saint Louis was 2,500: 800 men, and the rest women and children. These facts were followed by the ridiculous suggestion that the number of inhabitants could be limited to 800 if celibacy was enforced.[35]

The analysis of the "useful" population of Saint Louis documented a decline in the number of slaves belonging to the Company, an expansion of mulatto property owners with their own ships or in important positions of authority, and above all a vast expansion of the number of slaves owned by the *habitants*. In 1754 there were fifteen *habitant* ship captains, fifteen first mates, thirty-six sailors or *gourmets*, three chief interpreters, thirty-six apprentices, and ninety-eight "slaves of the Company" who were employed as sailors and who received their food and three francs a month in wages. In addition there were "550 slaves of the *habitants* or free persons employed by us for the voyages to Galam." These figures reveal an important expansion of the population of the island, which also harbored "100 free persons from Oualo and Cayor who are attached to us by their cohabitation with women of the island."[36] The decline in the number of slaves belonging to the Company resulted from the priority given to slave exports. A letter from Gorée illustrated the practices which led to a decline in the number of Company slaves. The letter explained that the Company had "cleaned out our slave pens and shipped out the majority of the negroes in our employ."[37] On the other hand the *habitants* almost never sold the slaves that they had trained as workers in the Atlantic and upriver trade.

The great weakness of the analysis of the population given by the Company in 1754 was to treat women as useless members of the island population. In fact the *signares* played a very important role on the islands as the owners of slaves and boats, and women slaves made up the majority of the slave population. Slave women played a double role: their labor was important and as bearers of children they allowed the reproduction of the slave population. Slaves born on the island were valued more highly by masters because they were less inclined to revolt or to run away.[38]

Once the Company decided in 1738 to begin training skilled Africans to replace European workers, it was inevitable for the Company to turn to slave labor. Training free *laptots* as carpenters, gunsmiths, or sailmakers would have made little sense, because the Company had no way of retaining control over free workers.[39] Although the Company probably began by training its own slaves, the *signares* offered their own slaves for this role. They used their contacts with Company officials to secure training and employment for their own slaves, thus creating the system of hiring out skilled slaves that dominated the labor market of the islands in the second half of the eighteenth century. However, the driving force behind the emergence of slave societies on the islands was subsistence rather than long-distance trade. The seasonal demands for labor in the Galam trade were furnished over a long period of time by free laborers from the mainland. Women slaves labored daily to feed the inhabitants of the islands, and male slaves daily ventured out to the mainland to provide food and water. These activities, first carried out by free emigrants from the mainland, rapidly became the province of slaves.

Although the emergence of a slave-owning merchant class was the most important development in the formative period of the islands, the culture and society of the islands maintained strong links with the mainland. Free emigrants from Waalo and Kajoor gave their imprint to the culture of Saint Louis, so that the urban population was in majority Wolof and Muslim. Michel Adanson, writing about Saint Louis in the 1750s, commented: "As the island of Saint Louis is within the dependence of the kingdom of Oualo, the negroes who live there, especially those who are free are of that nation . . . Those whom the company entertained in my service, were Oualofes, as they call themselves."[40] Adanson also described the celebration of Tabaski, which brought the people of the island together with the inhabitants of Sor for a celebration that included dancing after the prayers, and a display of horsemanship in which "lords and persons of distinction" made their horses dance to the cadence of the music.[41] The majority culture, Wolof and Muslim, was shared by the free emigrants from the mainland and the slaves of the island, by everyone except a small number of mulatto families who were Catholic. But the mother tongue of the Catholics of Saint Louis was Wolof, as the French learned in 1778 when they reoccupied the island after a period of British dominance, and had to use interpreters to confess the *signares* who had retained their Catholic identity.[42]

In the mid-nineteenth century, when the tiny mulatto Catholic elite began to write about their society, they recognized the fragility of French cultural influence and the dominant Wolof and Muslim character of the island's population. Abbé Boilat, a mulatto priest trained as a missionary to his own people, regarded the Catholicism of the islands with dismay, because of the strong influence of Islam on religious belief and practice. Boilat's judgement that the religion of the *signares* was a melange of Christianity and Islam echoed the opinion of French observers in the eighteenth century.[43] Carrère and Holle, while deploring the growing role of Islam on the island, described the culture of the island as an extension of Kajoor. "The South part of the island was inhabited first. It is certain that this part of the island was peopled by emigrants from Cayor, a country whose customs are still very visible here today."[44] In the course of the eighteenth century a distinctive free Muslim quarter developed on the south end of the island, while the center of the island was occupied by the French fort and the Catholic mulatto population, and the north was inhabited by slaves.[45] Although the free Muslim emigrants began their careers as *laptots*, they often succeeded in becoming slave-owning merchants, like the *signares* and the *habitants*. The Catholic *habitants* enjoyed certain political privileges, but the demography and culture of the islands in no way justifies the colonial stereotype of a French or Afro-French society distinct from the mainland.[46]

By 1758, when the Seven Years War brought the British to Saint Louis, they discovered a well-established island society which had formed during the years of Company rule. According to the British "30 to 40 families" dominated the island, and these principal inhabitants were the descendants of the *signares* and the French. When the British arrived they were presented with the "mayor" of Saint Louis, Charles Thevenot, a mulatto who had spent part of his youth in France, and who now took on the task of defending the interests of the inhabitants as the island was occupied by a new European power.[47] Undoubtedly, the change in the island's sovereignty allowed the *signares* and their sons to gain even greater economic power than they had wielded under the rule of the Company, because many of the houses, slaves, and boats of the Company passed into their hands. British preference for using African merchants to carry on trade with the interior, which contrasted with the Company's direct management of the trade, accelerated the process which transformed the inhabitants of Saint Louis into a powerful slave-owning merchant class in the second half of the eighteenth century.

Slavery on Gorée, 1763–1777

The French defeat in the Seven Years War led to a repartition of the Senegambian coast. The French lost possession of Saint Louis and the French presence was reduced to the settlement on Gorée and a trading post at Albreda in the Gambia. Gorée became the major base of the French slave trade. Slavery expanded rapidly on Gorée in the decades between the Seven Years War and the War of the American Revolution. One of the consequences of the French defeat was the reorganization of the French settlements, which were now ruled by a governor appointed directly by the French monarchy. The expansion of royal power was the consequence of French determination to maintain a presence in settlements that were less profitable than the pre-war French possessions. The royal governors of the period left detailed records on the small-scale society of Gorée. Consequently it is possible to examine the process which led to the rapid emergence of a slave society. In an abbreviated process that paralleled what had happened earlier on Saint Louis, Gorée developed from a small society of *signares*, French merchants, and slaves, into an urban slave society dominated by a slave-owning class of *habitants*.

The slave society that developed on Gorée after mid-century was much more independent from Atlantic merchants than in the first half of the century. War between the French and British ended Company rule and the Company monopoly over trade. New relations between Atlantic merchants and *habitants* emerged when the British occupied Saint Louis in 1758 and when the French returned to Gorée after 1763. War permitted the *habitants* to acquire assets in slaves, boats, and houses, which had once belonged to the Company. The disruptions created by war allowed the *habitants* to renegotiate their partnership with Europeans. After 1758 the *habitants* became nearly obligatory intermediaries in the trade between the islands and the mainland. European merchants increasingly remained confined to the coastal islands and relied on the *habitants* to deliver export commodities to them. The fact that this new system emerged on Gorée as well as Saint Louis suggests that it was the result of the new bargaining power of *habitant* merchants, rather than the result of a new strategy by Atlantic traders.[48] The informal practices of the Company now became formalized in privileges acquired by the *habitants*.

Prior to 1763 the population of Gorée rarely exceeded a few hundred, although as early as 1723 the island was divided into a village of "gourmettes" (free blacks and mulattoes) and a village of "Bambaras" or slaves.[49] In 1754, the population of Gorée was minuscule, and the shortage of labor that resulted became a problem during the great famine of the 1750s. In October 1754 Gorée was forced to call on Saint Louis for help in supplying the laborers that were needed for provisioning the island with food, water, and other supplies. Gorée requested three European ship captains for the longboats used in the coasting trade, three African first mates and interpreters, two African or mulatto pilots, and twenty-two "sailors for three or four years, in which time we will train negro crews that will be chosen from the slaves of the inhabitants of our island."[50] In 1763, when the French reoccupied the island the population of Gorée was very small, and had probably declined as a result of the war. The census carried out by Adanson in 1763, which listed all the households of the island, counted 220 inhabitants: 25 mulatto women, 18 mulatto men, 16 African women, 6 African men, and 131 slaves. Adanson noted that the number of slaves "was expanding continuously rather than declining because slaves were the only wealth of the masters who owned them." [51] His judgment turned out to be correct, because in 1776, the population of Gorée would include 1,200 slaves.[52]

In 1763, the *signares* were the dominant group in the population of the island. *Signares* headed nine of the twelve households for which Adanson gave census data. The nine *signare* households contained 152 persons and the majority of the slaves. Poncet de la Rivière, the first royal governor, claimed the *signares* acquired "their fortunes from the commanders and administrators of the Company, to whom they had been attached."[53] Adanson added smuggling as an explanation of the social position of the *signares*: "The abuses went so far that these women, who commanded a number of negro slaves who were employed by the Company, carried on a commerce at the expense of the Company for the profit of the merchants they were united with."[54] The *signares* of Gorée were an established social group in 1763, because the majority were mulattoes, *signares* of the second generation. On the other hand the community on Gorée was less differentiated than that of Saint Louis, because there were very few households headed by a male mulatto. That phenomenon developed rapidly after 1763.

There was a racial hierarchy at Gorée, because all mulattoes were free, regardless of the social status of their mothers. Adanson noted this social distinction, which was already well established. "Mulatto boys have been employed in our service as sailors, but always in positions of command, because they are the children of French men, and never as slaves, even if born to a slave mother."[55] This racial hierarchy reflected European prejudices, but it also served the interests of *signares* and their children, who tried to monopolize their privileged relationship with Atlantic merchants. Color was more important than religion on the islands, because the "regulations for the company of *laptots*" of 1765 noted that "twenty Christian *gourmets* who are slaves will take the rank of corporal." Conversion to Christianity conferred some privileges of rank, and permitted Christian slaves to bear firearms, unlike the Muslim *laptots* who were armed with pikes, but it did not eliminate slave status.[56]

The rapid expansion of the population of *habitants* and slaves on Gorée from 1763 to 1776 reflected the important intermediary role played by the *habitants* in the slave trade and in the provision trade to Gorée. For the French, the rapid accumulation of slaves in the hands of the *habitants* provoked concern and anxiety. From 131 in 1763, the slave population expanded to "about 800" in 1773, and reached a total of between "1,100 and 1,200 creole slaves, including women and children" in 1776.[57] This rapid expansion of the slave population created conditions which favored slave revolts, according to the *mémoire* of Doumet (1773).

> There are on the island about 800 negro men and women who belong in different proportions to a number of mulattoes who rent their labor to the royal government, to vessels on the coast, to our warehouses, trading settlements, and for other work. These mulattoes buy slaves on the coast which they then sell to ships that anchor at Gorée. From time to time there is such a quantity of slaves on the island, and the slaves have such a natural love of liberty, that when they cannot revolt by force they run the risk of drowning in their efforts to swim to the mainland, which is only 1,000 yards

away, or they set fire to the island in order to create a disorder which will permit their escape.[58]

With numerous newly purchased slaves in the hands of the *habitants* and with other slaves on the island awaiting their moment of departure for the Americas and an unknown fate, the conditions on Gorée did favor slave revolts and escapes. Gorée was the site of a number of important rebellions and attempted escapes between 1750 and 1776.

The growing hostility of the French to the rapid accumulation of slaves on Gorée had other motivations than simple considerations of security. French royal officials were obsessed with the crisis of the French slave trade from Senegambia, symbolized by the high costs of occupation and the small volume of slave exports.[59] French slavers preferred to purchase slaves elsewhere, with the result that French governors considered desperate measures to increase slave exports.[60] In 1776 Brasseur wanted to revive a French plan of 1770, which authorized the use of coercion in efforts to force the *habitants* to sell their slaves to French slavers. This plan had originally been abandoned when rumors of the plan leaked to the *habitants*, who threatened to resist. But the French commander did not have complete confidence in the French soldiers on the island, each of whom "had a negro mistress." Nevertheless, Brasseur believed that "twelve years of experience have proved that these negroes will never be of any use for the cultivation of our colonies, or to French commerce, unless the government can convince the *habitants* to sell them."[61] The desire of French governors to satisfy the needs of the French slave trade explained their hostility to the accumulation of slaves on the island.

Nevertheless, the French on Gorée depended on the mulatto traders and their slaves, because "the island continually receives its provisions from the mainland."[62] The slave sailors of Gorée were valued for the low cost of their labor, when compared to French sailors. "They [the *laptots*] carry out zealously all the voyages which they are daily ordered to make, whether it is to go look for food, water, and wood, or in aiding the ships who anchor in the port."[63] French commerce depended on the labor of the slaves of Gorée and therefore also on the good will of their masters, the *habitants*. The provision trade also depended on good relations with the mainland, whose inhabitants "came onto the island daily to sell their food supplies."[64] Because of the difficult position of French commerce in this period, the relationship between the French and the *habitants* was fraught with conflict.

French relations with the *habitants* were conditioned by the dominant position of the British in the region and the new conditions of free trade created by the destruction of the Company monopoly. In 1764 the French governor complained that some of the sailors and workers on the island were leaving for Saint Louis, where they could be paid "in dollars."[65] The French were forced to import specie for the island's trade, and the Spanish dollar or "piastre" became one of the standard trade currencies. The most important consequence of free trade was a dramatic increase in the price of slaves. By 1776 the price of a slave reached 380 to 400 livres, an increase in price from 30 bars to 120 bars in the currency of the coast, counting 20 bars in taxes for each slave. The French attributed the increase "to the great competition between private slavers."[66] Brasseur summed up the situation in 1776 by reporting: "We have no friends on the African coast . . . because the Africans generally believe that France no longer has any money or ships."[67]

The latent hostility between the *habitants* and the French emerged openly in times of crisis. The most serious crisis occurred in 1777–8, when the Dammel-Teeñ Makodu Kumba Jaring cut off trade between the mainland and Gorée for eleven months. This crisis followed a French royal decision to reduce the status of Gorée to a simple trading post, implying a sharp cut in royal subsidies to cover the costs of customs payments to mainland kingdoms and other expenses.[68] The cessation of these payments rapidly ended trade. But although the crisis began as a conflict between the French and Kajoor-Bawol, the boycott had serious consequences for the *habitants*, who in 1776 numbered 120 mulattoes, 110 free blacks, and 1,200 slaves, all dependent on the mainland for their food supplies.[69] The boycott was political as well as economic. The Dammel-Teeñ seized French hostages, and nine "black creoles" from Gorée, and held them as hostages throughout the conflict. In retaliation the French arrested and put in irons thirty-five Africans from Kajoor who happened to be on the island when the crisis broke. These hostages included "interpreters, *jeraffes* [royal officials] and other people belonging to the King, several marabouts of Cayor highly esteemed by the king, and several goldsmiths whom he greatly needs."[70] The French also held prisoner an official they called the "philor of Portudal", but they did not chain him because he was a relative of the king.[71]

The trade boycott severely tested the relations between the French and the *habitants*. On the night of July 31 the French narrowly repressed a revolt by the prisoners from Kajoor, which had been prepared with the help of some of the inhabitants of the island and the village of Dakar. The plot was discovered when a guard noticed that the pins in the prisoners' chains had been removed with tools smuggled in to the prisoners with their food. When the guard intervened, the prisoners revolted. The French killed one of the rebels who had seized a gun, wounded several others, and forced the rest, still improperly chained, back into the prison. "They were forced to return to the prison from where we heard an abominable rattling of chains from people who now demanded nothing but death."[72] Brasseur finally calmed the prisoners by informing them that negotiations for their release were underway with the Dammel.

In the aftermath of the attempted revolt Brasseur described a situation that was catastrophic. He was convinced that the people of Dakar had planned a night attack on the island, with the aid of fires set on the island to spread confusion, and that "a great number of the island's inhabitants, who are our enemies" had conspired with them. French military forces were on constant alert and a ship patrolled the channel separating Gorée from the mainland. Patrols and lookouts were established and the *habitants* were given strict orders to keep their slaves in chains. Brasseur succeeded in getting his prisoners properly chained, binding their legs, arms, and attaching neck collars, by having them removed from the prison under guard one by one. The island lacked everything; food, water, wood, and the few supplies that arrived had to be shipped in from the Gambia and as far south as Casamance. Although Brasseur drew up ambitious plans for a military action against the mainland villages with 600 armed men, he concluded his report by noting that over the last ten years the blacks of Gorée had "worked at becoming our dominators by steps, each one hardly noticeable," and that the French had constantly appeased this process by agreeing to give presents and make concessions in the interest of maintaining their trade.[73]

French fears that the *habitants* might conspire against them, or welcome a British takeover, were rooted in the crisis of French trade in Senegambia in the 1760s and 1770s. As slave-owning merchants, the *habitants* could only prosper if Atlantic commerce provided them with the means to carry on their trade with the mainland. As urban slave owners entirely dependent on the mainland for their subsistence needs and those of their slaves, the *habitants* deeply resented what they regarded as the inept diplomacy of Atlantic merchants when it led, as in 1777–8, to a breakdown of trade relations with the mainland. In the end it was the mutual dependency of the islands and the mainland that led to a resolution, because Brasseur himself reported that his "mediation was not necessary in any way." The Dammel returned his prisoners in exchange for the hostages held on Gorée, because the people of Kajoor were deprived of essential commodities. "It appears that the negroes have suffered from the absence of trade which deprived them of the most essential commodities for almost a year . . . It was finally the pleas of the subjects of the Dammel who convinced him in spite of his obstinacy, greed, and injustice, and he was finally forced to release Sieur Brunel without a ransom."[74] In the restoration of trade the *habitants* played a more active role than the French. But the near defection of the *habitants* during the crisis pointed to the increasingly independent role that they would play on both Saint Louis and Gorée in the second half of the eighteenth century. The emergence of a merchant society on the islands created conditions that led to conflicts with Atlantic merchants, as the *habitants* attempted to protect what they regarded as their essential interests.

The consolidation of *habitant* society was accompanied by the emergence of a distinct identity and political consciousness. The first political protest of the *habitants* of Gorée expressed the interests of a class of slave owners. The "memoire of the *habitants* of Gorée to the Minister of the Navy," dated December 26, 1772, defended the right of the *habitants* to participate freely in the slave trade and accused French merchants of wanting "to seize our property in order to make it theirs." The "precious property" in question, "which is the object of envy and . . . the reason for the memoires written against us" was "some of our skilled slaves who have more knowledge than the others, they were born in our households, we have raised them up, and now they want to take them away from us." This complaint was prefaced by a profession of loyalty to France. "We are French, our fathers were French, and when through the fortunes of war we were forced to accept foreign laws, our hearts never ceased to look forward to the moment when we would be reunited with France."[75] The root of the conflict which provoked this protest was the suspension of the freedom of the slave trade, established since 1763, in favor of a monopoly concession granted to the Compagnie de la Guyane.

The provisory monopoly was supposed to permit the new Company to fix the purchase price of slaves during a period in which slave prices were rising rapidly. The pent-up European demand created by disturbances in the Atlantic trade during the Seven Years War had led European slavers to conduct a kind of price war, in which the British and the French offered price incentives to increase the supply of slaves flowing to ports of trade under their control. African sellers responded aggressively to these price incentives and refused to sell slaves for less than a competitive price based on both British and French offers. Commercial interest groups with political connections like those behind the Company of Guyana pushed for the reestablishment of monopoly, blaming free trade for the steep increases in slave prices. In its negotiations with the French government the Company of Guyana constantly cited the aid it had given the French government during the Seven Years War.

The efforts of the Company of Guyana to establish a monopoly and force prices down immediately provoked resistance from the *habitants* of Gorée. "We are going to be forced to sell our slaves to European merchants. Whom have we been selling them to up until now? We buy them for between three hundred and fifty and four hundred livres and we sell them for five hundred. Is our profit exorbitant? . . . In addition our trade is usually carried out far in the interior and we only really act as the agents of the Europeans." The first protest of the *habitants* of Gorée was essentially a declaration of their right to freely purchase, sell, and own slaves.[76] The *habitants* defined themselves in their protest as slave traders and slave owners, and portrayed themselves as essential links in France's African commerce. These same elements would reappear in later protests from the *habitants* of Gorée and Saint Louis.

The petition of the *habitants* of Gorée was signed by De La Courbe, De Saint Jean, with marks added for Louis Waly, Etienne Jouga, Pierre Waly, and Jean St. Hubert. This fact signaled the emergence of mulatto men as spokesmen for the *habitants*, a development which also occurred at Saint Louis beginning with the British occupation. The political discourse of the *habitants* in the eighteenth century was essentially a defense of both slavery and free trade. The autonomy of the *habitants* was based on their commercial role, but also on the control they exercised over their slaves, the only source of skilled laborers that could serve the interests of French commerce.

The founding era of the *signares* was in some sense over, even though French merchants would continue to form temporary marriages with local women, sometimes forming new mulatto families. In the eighteenth century the French explained the term *signare*, which was Portuguese in origin, as essentially a description of light-skinned mulatto women, the preferred choice of European men.[77] Many French sources emphasize the elegance of the women of Saint Louis and Gorée throughout the eighteenth century, when *signares* dressed in expensive clothes and wore jewelry made from gold purchased in Gajaaga. When *signares* went out into society, they were accompanied by a court of female slaves whose near nakedness was a direct manifestation of their slave condition. *Signares* maintained a kind of court. They were entertained by *griots*, who danced for them and sang their praises.[78] The growing political consciousness of the *habitants* encouraged the existing mulatto families to try and maintain a privileged relationship with the French merchants, including supplying them with local wives. The overall trend was for the consolidation of existing mulatto families, which included the gradual accumulation of property and political power in the hands of men, who acted as political spokesmen and heads of households. The *signares* of the late eighteenth century lived in a different social context than their predecessors.

Between 1763 and 1776 Gorée passed from the age of the *signares* to the age of the *habitants*. This transition repeated the history of Saint Louis, but over a much shorter period of time. Local fortunes began in the contraband trade that was carried out by Frenchmen in alliance with their local "families." These fortunes were invested in slaves, who rented their labor to the French at first, but who later formed the labor force which permitted the *habitants* to expand the trade under their direct control. The trade in slaves and in provisions opened a wide field of activity for *habitant* traders. Gradually mulatto men emerged as the political spokesmen of the *habitants*. They also played an increasingly important role in commerce. The end of the age of the *signares* did not end the important role of women on the islands. They continued to control important fortunes in slaves and boats. Rather, the emergence of the mulatto men was a sign of the demographic maturity of the families founded by the *signares*, which began to resemble African families in the Lower Senegal. The formation of these mulatto families was in a sense a

113

natural byproduct of the Atlantic trade in the eighteenth century, when most businesses, whether in Europe, the Americas, or in Africa, were based on family relations.

The golden age of the habitants, 1763–1790

The golden age of the *habitants* was the period between the end of the Seven Years War and the French Revolution. During this period, divided between the British occupation and the French reconquest, the *habitants* of Saint Louis came of age politically and economically. Although it is clear that European wars and the changing political status of Saint Louis had some influence on the course of history, European interventions only accelerated trends that had their roots in the history of the Lower Senegal. Between 1763 and 1790 the *habitants* affirmed their political and commercial autonomy from the occupying European powers. The formal political autonomy of the population of Saint Louis began with the British occupation, when British authorities were obliged to recognize the economic and military power of the *habitants*. During the occupation the British recognized the mulatto Charles Thevenot as the "mayor" of Saint Louis. The primary goal of the *habitants*, who were at the mercy of developments in the wider Atlantic world, was to protect their property and their commerce. Periodically, the *habitants* combined diplomacy with force, or the threat of force, to achieve these goals.

In 1765 the French Governor of Gorée, who maintained contacts with Thevenot, reported: "There has been a rebellion in Senegal for the last three months, opposing the *habitants* and the English soldiers. The alarm was sounded by both sides, and afterwards a compromise was made."[79] The military force of the *habitants* was the *laptots*, the slave sailors who were already accustomed to fight on the seas and on the river. Although slave *laptots* had originally been owned and trained by the French Company, in the second half of the eighteenth century the majority of the *laptots* were the property of the *habitants*. In 1775 the *habitants* played an important role in the sudden departure of Governor O'Hara from Saint Louis, and in precipitating an official inquiry into his governance. The accusations filed against O'Hara in a petition presented by the *habitants* to the British government are interesting because they closely parallel the conflicts between the French and the *habitants* of Gorée in the same period. O'Hara was accused of interfering with *habitant* commerce, forcing the slaves of the *habitants* to work without pay, confiscating *habitant* property, including their slaves, and using his office to enrich himself. A British inquiry eventually confirmed all these charges.[80]

The next major demonstration of *habitant* autonomy came during the War of the American Revolution, when the *habitants* of Saint Louis, still bitter about O'Hara's despotic governance, decided to cast their lot with a French invasion force. The immediate context of the invasion also played an important role. In 1778 a devastating yellow fever epidemic struck both Saint Louis and Gorée, killing half of the Europeans and a substantial number of *habitants* and slaves.[81] The British governor, John Clark, died in office, and the demoralized remnants of the British garrison turned mutinous, got drunk, and began shooting at the *habitants* from the walls of the fort. Three days before the arrival of the French expeditionary force, the *habitants* and their slaves had killed most of the British soldiers and Saint Louis was delivered to the French without a shot being fired. French military planning took account of the *habitants*, who were described as being capable of mobilizing 1,000 slaves. Instead of confronting the *habitants* the French decided to make a deal with them, counting on the fact that the "established [French speaking] inhabitants" were more numerous than the "young English blacks and mulattoes."[82] The political and military autonomy of the *habitants* worked for the benefit of the slave owners, but it was above all a result of the numerous slaves under their command.

The readiness of the *habitants* to use force was a reaction to their daily experience of the brutality of the slave trade, aggravated by European rivalries on the coast. The *habitants* could easily fall victim to the trade system they served. From 1779 to 1784 the British occupied Gorée in retaliation for the French conquest of Saint Louis. During the British occupation a free Muslim *habitant* from Saint Louis, who was employed by the British as a courier, was kidnapped while delivering dispatches to the Gambia and sold to a French slaver in spite of the fact that "he was a freeman . . . spoke the French language fluently, and had dispatches in his pocket to a British governor."[83] When the French captain, whose name was Rouchan, refused to return his captive, the British commander of Gorée seized stores and trade goods left by the French vessel on the island. To secure the release of Barbousin, the *habitant* held in slavery, Captain Thomas Wilson seized and held the men sent by Captain Rouchan to retrieve his stores. "Near a fortnight from this date, finding my perseverance at least equal to his own obstinacy, he at length sent me the man, but in such a condition as would have forced compassion from a Savage. In an open canoe . . . lay this poor emaciated wretch, who had been near thirty-six hours on the water without food, and both legs in irons, in which state he had been hoisted over the vessel's side, Rouchan declaring, as he was his property and Slave, he should wear the marks of it until he reached Gorée; these he had worn near a month, insomuch that the iron, by the swelling of his legs, had eaten into the flesh."[84] The solidarity of the *habitants* was schooled by the cruelties of the slave trade and its dangers.

The consolidation and coming of age of the *habitants* can be measured in the census of 1779, the most detailed of the eighteenth century, taken at the moment when the French reoccupied the island.[85] The population of Saint Louis, 2,500 in 1754, numbered 3,018 in 1779: 206 *habitants*, men and women, 177 children, 1,858 slaves, who belonged to the *habitants*, and 777 free persons without slaves.[86] Almost all of the demographic growth between 1754 and 1779 took place within the slave population, a clear indication of the prosperity of *habitant* commerce. Almost every household on the island possessed at least some slaves. The census of 1779, which listed the composition of each household, permits a calculation of the distribution of slaves in the population. Out of 209 households, only twenty-seven owned no slaves. Seventy-eight households owned five slaves or less, a category that could be considered more or less typical of the households on the island. Forty-five households owned six to ten slaves; thirty-seven households owned eleven to twenty slaves. These households were larger and more prosperous than average. Finally, sixteen households owned twenty to forty slaves, and six households owned more than forty slaves. The overall distribution of slave holding was important, because over 80 percent of the island's households owned at least some slaves. Even in comparison to the slave societies of the Americas, the absolute number of slaves in the population was substantial, because slaves outnumbered free persons. No slave owner on Saint Louis owned hundreds of slaves, as was the case in large plantations in the Americas. On the other hand the majority of families on Saint Louis owned more than six slaves. In the eighteenth-century Atlantic world only the sugar islands of the West Indies, and a few regions of continental North America, notably South Carolina, were more dominated by the institution of slavery than the islands of the Lower Senegal.

One of the distinctive characteristics of the slave society on Saint Louis was its strictly urban character. None of the slaves of Saint Louis worked in the fields, because the island was entirely dependent on commerce for its subsistence. The slaves of Saint Louis were sailors, artisans carrying out the specialized labor needed in a maritime economy, and women who labored to feed and care for the island's permanent population and slaves being held in transit before embarking on the "middle passage." Even though urban slavery existed in the American colonies of the eighteenth century, it is usually thought of simply as a byproduct of plantation agriculture. In reality, urban slavery in the New World was significant in its own right. Near the end of the eighteenth century Philadelphia alone counted 1,400 slaves, and slaves formed about 15 per cent of the population of New York during the colonial period. Urban slavery existed on a small scale in the cities and towns of New England, and had an important dimension in colonial Charleston and in the cities of Brazil, where slaves dominated the labor market. In the eighteenth-century cities of the Americas slaves performed hard physical labor, when they worked as dockers in the port cities, but many others were highly qualified artisans.[87]

The composition of the slave population of Saint Louis showed a clear preference for women: 979 female slaves compared to 478 men in 1779.

This again was one of the distinctive features of slavery on the islands of the Lower Senegal. The balance between the sexes, by contrast, was almost equal among slave children: 195 boys and 206 girls, a sign that the children, unlike the adults, were born on the island.[88] The strong demand for female slaves reflected economic realities, even though European observers emphasized the demand for concubines and the role played by women slaves in displaying the wealth of a household. French observers tended to regard women slaves as a display of luxury. A nineteenth-century document described "large numbers of young women slaves, living in near indolence within wealthy households, less required for their labor than to form the court and display the extravagance of their mistresses." This same document noted that the sexual "conduct" of the female slaves was rigorously supervised "to prevent them from giving birth to mulatto children who, for that reason, cannot be kept as slaves." The sexual controls included, in extreme cases, forced abortions and infanticide.[89] Eighteenth-century texts, although less detailed, describe the same system of color stratification, and note the way the *signares* used their female slaves to display their social rank.[90] Nevertheless, the number of women slaves reflected the strong demand for female labor, particularly in the labor-intensive preparation of millet for consumption by mortar and pestle.

The number of male slaves in 1779, 478, was not sufficient to fill the demands of the peak trading season during the voyages to Galam. In 1789 the crews employed by the thirty-seven ships who sailed to Galam numbered 784 in all. Even allowing for a number of Frenchmen in the six Company ships, and a larger number of free *laptots*, the seasonal demands of the Galam trade easily account for the number of male slaves on Saint Louis. The majority of male slaves served as *laptots*. During the slack trading season the *laptots* worked in the small ships that purchased millet and other foodstuffs in the creeks and inlets formed by the estuary of the Senegal River. They also purchased the salt of Kajoor from the salt pans near Ganjool, guarded herds of animals belonging to the *habitants* and the Company, rented their labor to the French, and provided the urban work force.[91]

The flowering of *habitant* society, evident from the census that followed the French reoccupation, was above all the result of the important commercial role they played in the second half of the eighteenth century. The prosperity established during the British occupation was menaced by the French desire to reinstate monopoly through concessionary companies granted royal privileges. In 1784, when the *habitants* learned about the French plans, they reacted with a justification of their role as indispensable intermediaries, which was at the same time a threat. "In this case [reinstatement of monopoly] the Company will find itself absolutely deprived of the aid of the *habitants* in conducting its commerce, and the river trade can only be carried out by the *habitants*, who understand better

117

than the Europeans the character of the nations with whom they trade." In the view of the *habitants* a monopoly concession would hardly reward the zeal with which the *habitants* "delivered Senegal into the hands of the French without a shot being fired" in 1779.[92]

The *habitants* were in fact protecting important commercial interests. In 1784 the *habitants* fitted out twenty-one ships for the Galam trade and purchased 214 slaves, 581 "gros d'or," 675 hogsheads of millet, and 6,016 pounds of ivory for a total value of about 167,276 livres.[93] In the trading season of 1786 eleven ships fitted out "by diverse inhabitants of the island" purchased 200 slaves, 1,170 pounds of ivory, and 181 "gros d'or."[94] Finally, in 1788 the *habitants* fitted out thirty-seven ships for Galam, which returned to Saint Louis with 619 slaves, 1,799 pounds of ivory, and 441 "gros d'or." In the trading season of 1788 the proportion of the trade in the hands of the *habitants* was very significant: they purchased two-thirds of the slaves and more than half of the gold traded upriver.[95] The profits of the trade were substantial. The *habitants* resold the slaves they purchased in Galam to French merchants in Saint Louis for twice what they paid for them, according to one estimate.[96] The trade of the *habitants* was carried out in their own ships, built and maintained by their slaves.

This period of *habitant* prosperity was also marked by important conflicts with French commercial interests. From 1784 onwards the new Company of Senegal (ex-Company of Guyana) attempted to reimpose monopoly trading conditions. From 1785 onwards the Company began to outfit its own ships for the Galam trade, a decision that harmed *habitant* commercial interests. In the *cahier de doléances* published by Lamiral in 1789, the *habitants* denounced the disloyal competition of the Company, which fixed the price it would pay *habitants* for slaves and then offered higher prices in the upriver trading ports. This was one of the complaints "of the unhappy inhabitants of Senegal, weighed down by the insupportable yoke of the harsh despotism created by a privileged Company."[97] In addition, the Company was accused of wanting to ship out the slaves of the *habitants* and sell them in the American colonies. The fear that they would be forced to sell their slaves was a long-standing source of friction between the *habitants* and the French. What was new in 1789 was the perception that the incompetent diplomacy of the Company with the mainland kingdoms formed part of a larger conspiracy. Perhaps "the continual millet famine" since 1784 had been organized by the Company to force the *habitants* to sell their slaves. "The Company wishes to reduce us to such a state of misery that we will be forced to sell our slaves, when we can no longer feed them. The Company is wrong to form such a project, because many of our slaves are slaves in name only, whom we regard as our brothers and our children."[98]

The conflict between the *habitants* and the Company led to a major crisis, which lasted from 1788 to 1791. This crisis was aggravated by the rupture in relations between Saint Louis and the mainland states, particularly Fuuta Tooro and Kajoor. The Almaami Abdul Qaadir, who was the most visible leder of a wave of Islamic revival which swept the Senegambian states at the end of the eighteenth century, demanded a considerable augmentation of the customs paid by the French in 1785. He also claimed the right to inspect French slave ships on the Senegal River, in an effort to prevent the sale of Muslims from Fuuta. French negotiations and concessions "provided no guarantee that the fleet would not be pillaged."[99] In addition, between 1788 and 1789, the kingdom of Kajoor imposed a trade boycott against Saint Louis and Gorée, which cut off the normal supplies of grain to the islands. The Company was obliged to ship in rice and flour from Le Havre to feed the slaves being held for export, and to organize an extensive coasting trade for grain on the Atlantic coast between the kingdom of Siin and the Gambia.[100]

Although the *habitants* could not be blamed for these developments, they did encourage their Moor allies to boycott the gum trade as a protest against the Company monopoly. In response to these events the Company of Senegal demanded the aid of Paris in 1788 and 1789 in its efforts "to maintain the subordination of the *habitants*, both blacks and mulattoes, to prevent them from forming plots or unreasonable demands against the Company."[101] In Senegal, Pelletan, the director of the Company, tried to impose a new treaty on the *habitants*, described by the French military commander of the island as "more burdensome, harsher, than the last agreement." The *habitants* would now be required to pay part of the customs owed African states, based on the importance of their commercial activities. At the same time the Company reserved the right to fix the price that it would pay the *habitants* for slaves and other trade goods. Finally, the Company demanded the right to trade for grain freely throughout the Senegambian region, thus eliminating certain restrictions on the grain trade that had favored the *habitants*.[102]

The policies pursued by the Company of Senegal finally led to a total breakdown in relations with the *habitants* in 1790, when the *habitants* declared a strike against the Company's trade operations. The minutes of the negotiations recorded the resolution of the *habitants* which signaled the end of the discussions and the beginning of the strike. "They refuse for the present, and in the future, to provide the Company with the use of their slaves, their real estate, or their ships." The Company perceived the strike as an insurrection and tried to convince the French military commander to suppress the revolt by force. But the commander was more interested in maintaining peace on the island, and was very conscious of the military weakness of the French. In his view the relations between the Company and the *habitants* took the form of a contract freely entered into by both sides. "Is the refusal of the *habitants* to work for the Company really an insurrection? How can the refusal of a free service be a rebellion, when the service is not required by any law, or commanded by any authority? . . ."[103]

119

Boucher, the French commander, recognized that the real power of the *habitants* came from the control they exercised over their slaves, the *laptots* who were essential to French commerce on the river. The Company accused the *habitants* of using force and threats to prevent the *laptots* from working. Boucher saw the strike from another perspective, because he understood it as a strike organized by the masters in a slave society. "There is no question that they did not have to use force to persuade the *laptots*, who belong to them. They are in fact the masters to control and they do control in reality their slaves, without consulting them . . . *Laptots* who are slaves form the vast majority, because there are few who are free."[104] The conflict between the *habitants* and the Company was finally settled by the decision of the revolutionary National Assembly to revoke the Company's charter in 1791. The strike prevented the upriver trade convoy from departing in 1790 and the *habitants* convinced the Brakna Moors to boycott the Company's trade. But in the final analysis the bargaining power of the *habitants* rested on their control of the *laptots*, the slave-workers of the Atlantic trade. Throughout the period of crisis with the Company the *habitants* acted as a self-conscious class of slave owners, well aware of the link which existed between their participation in the Atlantic trade, their commercial autonomy, and their slave property, which was the real base of their autonomy in the commercial system of the Lower Senegal.

Men and women in slavery on the islands

The conditions under which slaves lived and worked on Gorée and Saint Louis have commanded little attention from historians, even though they were the dominant demographic group on the islands. Historians of Saint Louis and Gorée have generally focused on the history of trade, the French presence, and the role of the islands as entrepots in the slave trade. More recently, there has been interest in the history of the *habitants*, particularly their role in commerce and their emergence politically in the period between the British occupation and the French Revolution.[105] The "exotic" aspects of the islands' history, particularly the sex life of the *signares*, has always received some attention.[106] But the *habitants* have rarely been seriously analyzed as a slave-owning class, and the slaves have received little explicit attention.[107] Historians of nineteenth- and twentieth-century Saint Louis and Gorée have rarely cast more than a glance back on the period of slavery, and they have certainly not seen it as an essential phase in the development of an urban culture on the islands.

The influence of commerce in molding interpretations of the islands' history has led to a neglect of the island settlements as crucibles of modern Wolof urban culture. Without calling into question the importance of commerce in the islands' history, more stress needs to be placed on their importance as urban settlements, where a system of labor and an urban culture developed which was important in its own right. Saint Louis was the largest urban settlement in the Lower Senegal from the late eighteenth to the early twentieth century. For much of that period slaves were the dominant demographic group, and from 1848 to 1900 freed slaves and fugitive slaves dominated migrants into the city. In other words, once Saint Louis is considered as an urban center, slavery becomes central to its history.

The most important sources on the life of slaves in Saint Louis in the eighteenth century were written by European merchants and administrators who lived on the islands. Some of these sources tend to portray slave life as easy, and even indolent. For the Europeans of the eighteenth century, who worked essentially for the slave trade, and whose conception of slavery was formed by the labor system of plantation America, these observations may have been sincere efforts to contrast the slaves of the island with those facing the "middle passage" and life on a sugar plantation. Lieutenant-Colonel Maxwell, writing in 1811 during early British abolitionist efforts on the African coast, believed that the "superior condition of African slaves," compared to plantation slaves in America, derived from their occupations as mechanics, sailors, and artisans, in the case of men, and their employment in food preparation, childcare, and spinning thread, in the case of women, "as there is no labour in the field to be performed." He also noted that relations of familiarity existed between masters and slaves which contrasted with the sharp racial hierarchies of plantation America. Thirdly, he pointed to the ease of "escaping from the bondage of a harsh master and returning to their own country, which can be effected at all times without much difficulty."[108]

Eighteenth-century observers give a more realistic portrait of slavery on the islands than later witnesses. Eighteenth-century sources which describe "indolent" "unproductive" slaves all emanate very clearly from slave-trading interests who favored increased exports and who tried unsuccessfully to convince their superiors and the *habitants* that there was an excess slave population on the islands. Once the slaves of the island are conceptualized as an urban labor force, their productive role emerges very clearly from the records of the slave-trading companies. Those records also reveal the threat of slave revolts by slaves being held in transit, and the compelling reasons masters on the island had for granting some rights and privileges to the slaves they wished to keep and employ in the Atlantic trade. When slavery on the islands is treated as a labor system that responded to specific needs and conditions, the relations that developed between masters and slaves can be analyzed with some confidence from the written sources of the eighteenth century.

The work of women was described far less often by European observers than the work of men. The most labor-intensive task fulfilled by women slaves was the pounding of millet and rice by mortar and pestle to remove the husks and prepare the grain for cooking. In the case of millet, the

121

staple grain of the island, the hulled grains needed further preparation before obtaining the different kinds of millet flour used to prepare couscous (Wolof, *cere*) or porridge (Wolof, *laax*). Although the demand of labor for food preparation was probably the most significant factor in explaining the demand for female slaves, it was only a fraction of women's work. Women were responsible for the entire management of the household. They fetched water and wood, tended small gardens, took care of the animals, spun cotton into thread, dyed clothes, cleaned clothes, took care of children, cleaned the houses, and prepared all the food and drink that was served.[109] In the distinct labor market in which women slaves could be rented out to the French, the terms *pileuse* ("pounder of millet") and *blanchisseuse* ("washerwoman") are those most frequently encountered. Women slaves who filled these functions accompanied the convoys that went upriver to Gajaaga, to cook and clean for the men, and they formed an essential part of the ship's crew.[110] As in most other parts of Africa, women slaves were also in demand as concubines and as wives for male slaves who would bear children belonging to the master of the woman. The sources from Saint Louis and Gorée also stress the role of women slaves as the courtesans and servants of the wealthy light-skinned *signares*. The half-naked slave women who escorted their mistresses when they went out into society were a concrete display of wealth.

The *laptots* or slave sailors of Saint Louis and Gorée had a very special place in the labor system that developed on the islands. When the *laptots* rented their labor to French authorities or French merchants, they received a wage in money or trade goods. At the end of the seventeenth century the *laptots* were paid one bar a month in trade goods plus food. By the end of the eighteenth century the wage had risen to three bars a month, or nine livres in French currency, plus three pounds of millet per day. One half of this wage was paid to the slave's master.[111] This relatively privileged position reflected the skills and the dangers of the labor performed by the *laptots*, which was recognized by the French from the beginning of the convoy trade to Galam.

> Without these people it would be impossible to go upriver, for they are the ones who, when the wind is contrary, pull the boat with a rope and sometimes submerge themselves up to the neck in the water when the banks of the river are unsure. They are given a *maître-langue* who is also a negro like them as their commander, because most of them do not understand French. They are the ones who do all the hard labor and they even serve the [French] sailors, as if they were their servants.[112]

Other sources emphasize the hard physical labor of the *laptots* and the dangers of their work. Drownings were not infrequent, and occasionally *laptots* were attacked and killed by crocodiles. A second factor in the relatively privileged status of the *laptots* was their military role, because they were sailors in the full sense of the word. According to Lamiral,

122

"whenever one departs upriver for this [Galam] or any other trade, on the Senegal, the riverboats are armed like ships at war, and the ships are prepared as if they are going into combat."[113] The *laptots* bore arms to protect the river convoys from attack and to protect French merchants when they left the ships to negotiate and trade on the mainland. The skills of the *laptots* as warriors, their difficult work of piloting and hauling the ships upriver, made them the elite of the slave population on the islands. For this reason, they had a position in the society of the islands parallel to that of the *ceddo* slave soldiers of the mainland kingdoms. Like the *ceddo* the *laptots* were slaves by origin, and like the *ceddo* it was partly their role as warriors which allowed the *laptots* to attain a rank that set them apart from ordinary slaves. While most *laptots* were skilled workers who performed the most difficult and dangerous jobs in the river trade, the role of the *laptots* as warriors and salaried workers who could trade for their own profit allowed some of them to accumulate property, to purchase their liberty, and to achieve an important rank in Saint Louis society.

The wages paid to the *laptots* in the upriver trade secured their position as privileged slaves. At the end of the eighteenth century the French paid sixteen bars a month to a ship's captain, eight bars a month to the first mate, five bars a month to the pilots, ship's carpenter, and other skilled crew members, and three bars a month to the ordinary *laptots* and the women who cooked for the crew. In addition to this salary and a daily ration of food, each member of the crew received part of the cargo of salt shipped upriver: four hogsheads for the captain, two hogsheads for his lieutenant and first mate, one and a half hogsheads each for the skilled crew members, one hogshead for the *laptots* and one-half hogshead each for the women on the crew.[114] Although some of these positions were filled by free mulattoes and blacks, slaves were employed in every rank from captain on down in the eighteenth century. The main constraint on slaves was that they paid half of their wages to their master, but even so, slave salaries permitted some slaves to accumulate wealth.

In the off-season for trade, slave sailors and artisans maintained and built the ships used in the river and coasting trade. At least as early as the mid-eighteenth century, the Compagnie des Indes built ships at Saint Louis and Gorée. Pruneau suggested that the Company needed to build one 30–35 ton ship at Saint Louis each year.[115] By training Company slaves and the slaves of the *signares* to build and maintain vessels, the Company bequeathed the skills needed for the *habitants* to build and maintain their own fleets in the second half of the eighteenth century. By 1788 the *habitants* commanded a fleet of at least thirty-seven ships at Saint Louis.[116] However, the *habitant* fleet was probably much larger than this, because when the French surveyed the fleet of Saint Louis in 1825, the *habitants* owned over 250 coasting vessels and riverboats, all of them constructed in Saint Louis.[117] Some of these ships were substantial vessels.

The *Goelette la Coumba*, built by the *signare* Coumba Jean in 1802, was a 50 ton ship, 56 feet long, 17½ feet wide, complete with artillery, and with a value of 13,500 francs, as estimated by the French in 1809.[118]

The *laptots* were the skilled laborers of an active maritime economy. By the late eighteenth century there was a complex maritime labor market on Saint Louis, with its own ranks and hierarchy. According to Saugnier, the ideal ship for the Galam trade was a schooner or flat-bottomed boat of 20 to 30 tons, armed with artillery, with a crew of thirty-five men and women. The crew consisted of a captain, "acquainted with the working of the ship, the river, and the languages of the nations among which it is intended to trade," a first mate with the same qualifications who seconded the captain, five *gourmets* "or negro officers" (two steersmen, one carpenter, one sailmaker, one boatswain or "linguist"), twenty-four *laptots*, four *pileuses* "to pound the millet and dress the victuals," and "as many *rapasses* as offer their services . . . These *rapasses* are negro children, who undertake the voyage gratis, with a view to making themselves acquainted with the river, and the languages of the nations on its banks."[119] Alongside the labor market, there was a specialized commercial market in maritime supplies and building materials needed by the *habitants*. Saugnier recommended that merchants trading in Saint Louis import axes of the first quality, adzes and carpenters' tools, planes and joiners' tools, oak planks for shipping, nails, pitch and tar, canvas, oars, grappling irons and anchors, in short "all the articles necessary to facilitate the means of performing the voyage to Galam, which is, as it were, the harvest of all these countries."[120]

The career of Charles Scipio gives a striking example of the social mobility that was possible for *laptots* to achieve. In all likelihood Charles Scipio began his life at Saint Louis as a slave during the British occupation. His classical name, common for slaves in the English-speaking world of the eighteenth century but little used by the French or the *habitants*, makes it probable that he first belonged to a British master. The best source for his life is the voyage of Saugnier, who traveled upriver with the convoy to Galam in 1785. By that time Scipio was a ship's captain. In the disastrous convoy of 1785 Saugnier was a passenger on the French ship *Furet*, one of four French vessels which departed with twenty-seven ships fitted out by the *habitants*, including one which belonged to Charles Scipio. Even though Thevenot, a *habitant*, was the official leader of the convoy, and carried the customs payments, Scipio was in charge of the defense of the convoy and the rescue of vessels in danger. According to Saugnier, Scipio was a freed slave, who had obtained his freedom and his rank as ship commander because of his military exploits. He had been promoted to captain after his victory over "the great Fouquet of Tuago," in other words the Tunka of Tuabo in Gajaaga. According to the narrative of Saugnier, Scipio, then a slave, had organized the defense of a convoy under attack and had repulsed a force of 12,000 with the aid of 800 *laptots*.

Although the details of the battle are probably exaggerated, there is little doubt that the narrative contains a kernel of truth.[121]

In any case it was Charles Scipio, a freed slave of Bambara origins, who was the real leader of the convoy in 1785. With one ship run aground, another sunk and with the convoy under attack from the forces of the Almaami of Fuuta Tooro, Scipio's skills as a warrior and a sailor were put to the test. The convoy, weakened by its losses and the hostilities with Fuuta Tooro, was then threatened by the Almaami of Bakel and the Tunka of Gajaaga. Originally the captain of the *Furet*, Scipio took command of the entire convoy and assured its defense. In the course of the military operations, Scipio exchanged insults and threats with the Almaami of Bakel, the Tunka, and the Fuutanke, and many of these exchanges centered around the threat of enslavement. In his discussions with the Tunka of Gajaaga, Scipio recognized the power of the Tunka on the mainland, but he described himself as "the monarch on the river . . . he was ready for battle; and that a Senegalian, bearing the title of Frenchmen, could never think of becoming a slave to a negro king."[122]

The name of Charles Scipio or Scipiou appears on several documents from Saint Louis, where he signed as one of the notable *habitants* of the island. He signed the protest against the return of a monopoly concession in 1784, and he signed the document declaring a strike against the French Company in 1790.[123] Scipio had an exceptional career, but not a unique one. A French report from 1836 noted the important role "of freed slaves" in the quarters of Saint Louis. "They used to lead the military expeditions of the blacks of Senegal [Saint Louis], who would not fight except under their command." Without a doubt, the freed slaves in question were military commanders that arose from the ranks of the ordinary *laptots*.[124]

Saugnier's narrative also includes some interesting details about the world of the *laptots*, which had its own rituals and rites of passage, a cultural world created by the slaves. As in slave societies of the New World, music figured prominently in the labor rituals of the *laptots*.

> We had scarcely left Senegal when the whole crew began to pray. Every person, with melancholy visage and tears in his eyes, turned his looks to that barren spot of sand which gave him birth, and where he abandoned his wife and children. They bade their relatives a woeful farewell, as if they had lost all hope of seeing them again. These sad ceremonies, and the lamentations of the negroes, made me form a disagreeable idea of the dangers of the voyage. But scarcely had we lost sight of the colony, when every visage brightened up, and the *laptots* began to sing.[125]

When the ship entered the main course of the river all crew members who had not previously sailed upriver, including Saugnier, were baptized in the waters of the river in a ceremony that was accompanied by cannon salvos. "He sprinkled water of the river on my chin and forehead; a ceremony which was announced by a general discharge of the artillery."

125

The work of hauling the ships upstream was accompanied by song and dance. Each *laptot* took his turn at the head of the hauling line, pulling the rope to the accompaniment of the work song, and then danced back to the end of the line. The work songs and dances formed part of the labor discipline of the crew, and each ship brought along a drummer to maintain a cadence. Saugnier was impressed by the military discipline of the *laptots*, who followed the orders of their captain without question.

Just as the departure from Saint Louis had its rituals, so the return from the long voyage to Gajaaga was the occasion for celebration. Abbé Boilat, writing in the middle of the nineteenth century, described the rituals that accompanied the return of the *laptots* to Saint Louis at the end of the Galam voyage. The return of the ships was an occasion not only for the crew, but for the entire population of Saint Louis. "When the ships came within a dozen leagues of Saint Louis, the entire crew dressed in their finest clothes, putting on fine *ckoussabes*["cloaks"] from Galam and magnificent belts. Cannon salvos announced from afar the return of the voyagers. There is no one on the island whose heart does not beat in that moment, the entire anxious city waits for good news or bad news about their loved ones . . ." As the convoy approached the island of Saint Louis the *laptots* began to perform a joyous music of return that complemented the dirge that accompanied their departure four or five months earlier.

> The drums begin to sound from on board in the midst of rifle fire and the songs of the *laptots*, who, as if they need to reward themselves for all the difficulties of the voyage, leap about and vary their melodies with new accents . . . The *laptots*, who are the enemies of economy and the friends of pleasure, then will plant their flags in the middle of the streets, and invite the women and the girls to dance. Five or six *griots* arrive in haste with their large drums; everyone celebrates, dances, sings, eats and drinks until all that has been earned at the risk of life has been spent. When they are completely broke the *laptots* hire themselves out for the river trade [in provisions] and depart again in January.[126]

Abbé Boilat, who was a religious reformer and an enemy of pleasure, perhaps exaggerated the cult of consumption among the *laptots*. But it is certain that in the eighteenth century the *laptots* returned to Saint Louis from a successful voyage with money to spend. In 1784 the *Bordmane*, a ship belonging to the *habitant* Etienne la Brüe, returned to Saint Louis with a cargo that included "30 gros d'or" for the *laptots*.[127] The *laptots* received part of their salary in merchandise, particularly in salt, which they could then trade profitably in the markets of the Upper Senegal.

The Galam voyage was the most spectacular labor of the *laptots*, but it is likely that they used their salaries to engage in petty trade during their routine labor in the provision trade. Saugnier described the price differentials for salt between Saint Louis and the mainland, which allowed the *habitants* and the *laptots* to make a profit from a trade usually neglected by the French. "This traffic of salt is carried on at the bar of the Senegal, the articles of exchange are swords, gunpowder, balls, flints, and glass ware. The salt cost me this year three livres per cask, and was sold at Senegal [Saint Louis] at the rate of five livres, to those who had not the opportunity or the will to trade for themselves."[128] Similar opportunities for profit existed in the provision trade in grain and other foodstuffs between the islands and the mainland. Women slaves sometimes were able to profit from their position as *pileuses* by trading processed grain. This could lead to a gradual movement into the merchant class and slave ownership.

Saugnier, who engaged in the slave trade as well, warned his readers about the dangers of confusing the slaves of the island with the trade slaves destined for shipment to the Americas. In doing so he described the accommodation between masters and slaves that permitted the development of a slave society in a major entrepot of the international slave trade. "The Tapade's slaves [Wolof, *tapaat bi*, "enclosure," "slaves of the household"] by inheritance are only nominally so; their masters cannot sell them without bringing dishonor upon themselves, according to the customs of the country . . . Brought up with the natives, they are considered as inhabitants, and form a body apart in the colony. They have their friends and relations there, who would become implacable enemies to those who should endeavor to sell them . . ." Saugnier followed this explanation with a warning to any slave trader foolish enough to confuse the slaves of the *habitants* with slaves in transit.

> Whoever should dare, either from a spirit of vengeance, or by way of bravado, to embark the Tapade's captives, would run the greatest risk, nor could he escape being stabbed or poisoned but by miracle: at the best he would be sure to lose his merchandise, and to be reduced to slavery among the negroes or the Moors.[129]

Other observers noted the particular conditions of accommodation between masters and slaves on the islands. Lieutenant-Colonel Maxwell tried to analyze "the superiority of condition of the African slaves" compared to slaves in the American colonies. As noted earlier he attributed it in part to the absence of field labor, and the ease of escape to the mainland for slaves who worked in commerce. At the same time he insisted on the familial relations between masters and slaves on Saint Louis. "There is not that distinction of ranks, that distance betwixt the master and the slave here as there is in the colonies; the latter confesses the former is his master, that he is entitled to the produce of his labor, but in every other respect he considers they are equal. He does not bow or cringe at the door, he enters firmly, takes his seat on the same mat, joins in the conversation with his master, and puts his hand into the same bowl to eat his coos-coos."[130] However, the familiarity of masters and slaves had its limits. Slave punishment could be harsh. On April 16, 1819, Pierre Senegal, a slave born on Saint Louis, aged twenty-nine, the property of

Pierre Valentin, an *habitant* merchant, was condemned for stealing a pair of pants and shoes. He was punished by being publicly branded with the letter V [*voleur*] on his left shoulder, and he was given 200 lashes with a whip, 100 on the day of his sentencing, and 100 two days later.[131]

The relations between masters and slaves on the islands of the Lower Senegal must be understood in the context of the labor system that developed to serve the needs of the Atlantic trade. The concessions by masters to slaves were essential to stabilize a slave population and maintain a skilled labor force in a world surrounded by the miseries of the Atlantic slave trade. But although European sources emphasize the favorable conditions produced by accommodation, the slaves must have thought more frequently of the fate of those who disappeared into the slave ships, entering a portal of no return. A British merchant who lived in Saint Louis in the 1770s was asked whether "Negroes who are sold for Slaves to Europeans . . . consider this sale as a punishment." He replied, "I believe no punishment short of death is so great a one to them," and this fear extended to "those Slaves near the sea coast, who are in the habit of seeing Europeans, and who are acquainted with them."[132] Whatever the social sanctions against the sale of slaves, the threat of sale to the slave merchants was undoubtedly the greatest incentive to accepting the status of a slave on the islands.

5

Famine, civil war, and secession 1750–1800

The second half of the eighteenth century was a period of crisis for Atlantic commerce and for the societies of the region. The crises of the eighteenth century were multifaceted, with their roots in the Atlantic world and in the reactions of Senegambians to the demands of Atlantic commerce. The decline of slave exports was one of the symptoms of change. French and British slaving activities had been growing steadily for decades. Although there is currently no consensus on the scale of the slave trade from Senegambia, a conservative estimate for the peak decades from 1720 to 1750 puts slave exports in the range of 5,500 to 3,500 a year.[1] The nearly continuous expansion of slave exports in the first four decades of the eighteenth century was followed by an almost equally steady decline in the second half of the century.

Although many factors contributed to this decline, it was accelerated by conflicts in the wider Atlantic world. Because Senegambia was partitioned into trading spheres by France and Britain, it was affected by the economic difficulties and frequent wars that convulsed their slave empires in the second half of the century. The early eighteenth-century slave trade was highly profitable, as the boom in sugar production in the Americas fed decades of expansion. After 1750 saturated markets, rising prices of slaves in Africa, the growing debt of the American colonies and frequent wars between France and Britain complicated the balance sheet of the slave trade, and demanded more elaborate financing and a redivision of risks and profits.

Increasing competition between French and British sugar producers created new economic difficulties in the American colonies. The Seven Years War, fought in America, on the continent of Europe, on the seas in the Caribbean, and in Africa, and Asia, disrupted slave exports and economic production.[2] The apparent predominance of Great Britain after 1763, expressed in Senegambia by the British occupation of Saint Louis in 1758, was soon undermined by colonial rebellion on the American mainland. The revolt of the American colonies raised the costs of British sugar producers, by cutting off access to American grain, fish, and raw materials, and allowed France to recoup some of its earlier losses by supporting the American war for independence.[3] In 1778 a French naval fleet reoccupied Saint Louis in an effort to restore the French preponderance on the Senegal River lost during the Seven Years War.

In the 1780s it appeared that the French colonial empire and its slave trade was going to enter a new period of expansion, reflected in Senegambia by the one decade of rising slave exports in the second half of the eighteenth century. But Senegambia was only a minor participant in the massive French slave trade of the 1780s. The expansion of French commerce was cut short by the French revolution and the wars which followed, which reduced French trade in Senegambia to the lowest levels of the century. Although the French Revolution was followed by another period of British ascendancy, the British were no longer interested in slave exports, as anti-slavery replaced the slave trade as the central factor in British commercial policy toward West Africa.[4] These developments in the wider Atlantic world had an impact on Senegambia, but they do not provide a convincing explanation for the decline of slave exports, which began at mid-century.

The decline of slave exports from Senegambia resulted partly from the growing demand for slave labor in the Senegal River valley. This was itself the result of the expansion of Atlantic commerce. Slave labor was absorbed into the maritime economy of the Atlantic islands and into coastal fishing and salt production. Commercial grain production in the Senegal River valley and the Atlantic coastal region for export to the desert and the Atlantic depended on the expansion of the slave population. Gum extraction in the desert demanded imports of slave labor. As the Atlantic economy "matured," the growing demand for slave labor cut into the slaves available for export. European merchants perceived these developments as a conflict between gum exports and slave exports. Atlantic merchants in Senegambia began to see the export trade in gum arabic, a raw material needed in the cloth printing industry, as a branch of the Senegambian trade that rivaled the slave trade in importance. The relationship between gum extraction and slave exports was not perceived directly, but appeared as a dangerous trade-off between warfare and commercial decline, between slave raiding and famine.

The most horrifying aspect of merchant calculations in the second half of the eighteenth century was the growing concern about famine and the slave trade, and the risks of profiting from hunger and starvation. Merchants weighed their grain supplies against the flood of emaciated captives thrown onto the market in times of famine. By encouraging warfare in years of hunger and starvation Atlantic merchants believed that they could procure an abundant harvest of slaves. But when they did so, they risked destroying the gum trade and watching their slaves starve to death. The structural transformations of Atlantic commerce appeared in calculations about the relationships of warfare, famine, and slave exports.

130

In Senegambia the second half of the eighteenth century was marked by a succession of crises, beginning with the great famine of 1750–6. In the Lower Senegal, the crisis of the 1750s began with the simultaneous arrival of drought and dynastic crisis in the state of Kajoor. In 1749 the Geej dynasty was overthrown by rival aristocratic families for the first time since its foundation by Latsukaabe Faal in 1695, creating an interregnum which lasted until 1766, when the Geej were restored after over a decade of civil war. The political crisis in Kajoor coincided with a prolonged period of poor rains and drought, from 1747 to 1754, in which a series of poor harvests culminated in serious famine. These political and ecological factors interacted, as war disrupted agricultural activities and ruined harvests which might have prevented food shortages from leading to general famine. During the crisis slave exports from the Lower Senegal rose dramatically, and Kajoor in particular sold more slaves than it had ever sold. To maintain the flow of emaciated captives to slave pens on the coast, merchants had to extend the geographic range of their food supply area and transfer grain supplies from one region to another on a more massive scale than ever before. In spite of all their efforts, at times the slave merchants had to renounce the purchase of slaves that they could not feed.

The history of the Lower Senegal is often treated in the framework of the grand transformations taking place in the Atlantic world, particularly the new context created by the French Revolution and the emergence of anti-slavery. But the great famine of the 1750s was in many ways the central event in a half century of crisis. Neither the slave-trading economy nor the political order ever quite recovered from the crisis of the 1750s, which was followed by the beginning of a drawn-out challenge to the political order by revolutionaries and reformers inspired by Islam. The mid-eighteenth century crisis was caused by a combination of natural disaster, political revolution, and civil war. But the great famine was only the beginning of a protracted period of social and religious conflict.

The turmoil in Senegambia was fueled by the worst series of ecological disasters of the century, as drought repeatedly struck the region in the 1750s, the 1770s, the 1780s and the 1790s. Although none of the other droughts and famines were as severe as the great famine of the 1750s, this series of disasters fostered warfare on the desert edge and contributed to the explosion of religious revolt which shook Fuuta Tooro in the 1760s and 1770s, and Kajoor in the 1790s. In 1776, as North American colonists were beginning their rebellion against Britain, Muslim revolutionaries seized power in Fuuta Tooro, beginning two decades of religious war and revolution in Senegambia. In the Lower Senegal the religious upheavals led to the creation of a new political entity, when the Cap Vert peninsula achieved its independence from the monarchy of Kajoor around 1795.

The crisis of the 1750s began with the environment, as drought and locust swarms reduced harvests and food supplies. Grain shortages in turn

131

were a stimulus to warfare at the desert edge, the incursion of desert warriors into savanna states, and shifts in the commercial strategies and priorities of desert merchants. Atlantic merchants aggravated the crisis by arming warriors and warrior factions, by purchasing the slaves thrown onto the market in growing numbers by warfare and famine, and by contributing to the soaring prices of surplus grain as the famine progressed and European slavers struggled to corner a share of a diminishing food supply. Environmental crisis, warfare, and famine thinned out the population of the Lower Senegal through starvation, expanding slave exports and violent death, but the crisis did not destroy the movement toward economic specialization and regional differentiation that emerged in the first half of the eighteenth century. In the second half of the eighteenth century slave exports continued to decline, the export trade in gum arabic assumed new importance, and slave-based grain production in the Atlantic coastal region and the Senegal River valley continued to expand.

The great famine, 1750–1756

The famine of 1750–6 occurred in the midst of the worst ecological crisis of the eighteenth century. Beginning with a period of failing rains that started in 1747, compounded by visitations of locusts in 1750, the drought was transformed into the worst famine of the century when prolonged civil war destroyed the few promising harvests of the dry period, and starvation killed uncounted thousands of Senegambians. First and foremost, the great famine was the local manifestation of a much wider crisis, a period of prolonged drought and hunger that struck much of West Africa. The Cape Verde islands suffered drought and famine twice, in 1748–50, and again in 1754–5, when mass starvation occurred.[5] In the Niger bend the worst recorded famine occurred between 1738 and 1756, killing about half of the population of Timbuktu.[6] In Senegambia itself the famine of the 1750s was region-wide, and its importance has been noted by historians.[7] Yet the significance of the famine and its causes have not been fully explored from a historical and ecological perspective.

Philip Curtin argued that the drought of the 1750s was the culmination of a long dry period that spanned most of the half century from 1700 to 1750. However, Curtin's data, which implies a marked improvement in rainfall patterns after 1756 is not entirely convincing.[8] There is evidence for a famine in 1710, another in 1715, and another in 1723, but not for a period of prolonged drought from 1705 to 1721. Famines in 1710 and 1723 were caused by the failure of the rains, but the famine of 1723–5 was aggravated by a succession struggle in Kajoor and by major wars along the Senegal River valley between desert warriors from Morocco and the Sahara and the people of Fuuta Tooro.[9] There were crises again in 1735–6, and 1743–4, but none of these were as severe as the crisis of the 1750s.[10]

In reality the second half of the century was just as subject to drought as the first half, but drought was more frequently accompanied by famine and social crisis. In 1771–5 severe drought struck the Cape Verde Islands, the Niger bend, the western Sahara, and Senegambia. While thousands starved to death in Timbuktu and on the Cape Verde Islands, Senegambia was less afflicted than other regions.[11] Nevertheless, the drought of 1771–5 was linked to the invasion of Waalo by desert warriors in 1775 and the warfare on the desert edge in Fuuta Tooro which contributed to the Islamic revolution of 1776. Throughout the early 1780s Saint Louis had serious difficulties buying grain, because of low rainfall and poor harvests in the surrounding region. A severe famine struck the Gambia in 1786, caused by drought and locust swarms. Littleton reported that the inhabitants of the south-east bank of the Gambia "were reduced to the horrible necessity of selling each other in order to buy what they needed to subsist . . . The Mandingues bought slaves for flour and European goods and sold them to white merchants on the coast, which is how a large number of these slaves came into my possession."[12] From 1788 to 1789 Saint Louis experienced food shortages, which may have been the early signals of a period of drought and famine that struck most of Senegambia in 1793–5, which also overlapped with a period of warfare.[13] It is difficult to distinguish a clear difference between the first and second halves of the eighteenth century on the basis of climatic patterns alone. The cumulative effect of this series of events was to create the conditions for the social, religious, and political conflicts that erupted between 1770 and 1796.

The historic context of this entire period was the increased commercialization of grain surpluses, cattle, and other key foodstuffs to feed the demands of the Atlantic and desert trades. Without taking into account this element in the economy of food security, famine can be misperceived as the direct consequence of climatic "events" or as the direct result of war. The famine of 1750–6 occurred in the midst of expanding grain production and expanding grain sales, and its first victims were vulnerable social groups, dependants in the economy of food production, food consumption, and political predation. The early victims were slaves sold off by their masters, slaves in transit who could not be fed, peasants whose crops were seized by marauding armies and countless others whose surplus grains were devoured by years of successive drought and warfare.

As the crisis in food security deepened, it broadened into a crisis in the human ecology of the Lower Senegal. The warfare that accompanied all the major droughts in the Lower Senegal was driven forward by the contraction of grain supplies. For desert warriors, the invasion of the savanna was a search for booty and tribute from communities that still had food for the taking. Prolonged drought tended to blur the border of desert and savanna ecologies, producing conflicts, tensions, and warfare in frontier areas that separated the two. Each ecological crisis in the Lower Senegal was accompanied by renewed pressure from desert warriors, and by intensified efforts by desert merchants to purchase stocks of grain.

133

Desert merchants began migrating in important numbers into the Lower Senegal during the famine that followed the War of the Marabouts in 1676. In 1722–3 desert warriors attempted to conquer Waalo and Kajoor in the midst of drought and famine. During the Kajoor civil wars of the 1750s Trarza warriors intervened repeatedly in Waalo and Kajoor. The Trarza assault on Waalo in 1775 followed a drought that began in 1771 in the western Sahara.[14] The savanna–desert edge seethed with conflict during ecological crisis. For the most part desert merchants were able to purchase grain by selling animals, and by offering their transport services to move grain supplies and other foods. But desert warriors used war to extract tribute and booty from savanna society.

Although periodic crisis caused by drought was a relatively common occurrence in the Lower Senegal, food security was threatened only by prolonged drought combined with warfare. Droughts often led to an expansion of trade with the desert, and throughout most of the eighteenth-century droughts Atlantic merchants bought slaves and the grain they required to feed them, although they were often forced to pay a premium price for grain during periods of food shortages. Atlantic merchants were directly affected by the famine of 1750–6. Their observations of the famine provide the crucial sources for understanding the development of the crisis, and its intimate links with both the Atlantic trade and the desert trade in grain.

In historical terms this period of crisis has considerable interest, because of the unusually rich documentation on the links between the slave trade and food production. The obsession with food supplies was an obvious reflection on the crisis situation created as early as 1751 by the simultaneous drying up of grain supplies from Kajoor and Fuuta Tooro, the two mainstays of the French trade settlements. The grain trade at Podor, a trade station established in 1744 to supply Saint Louis with millet, failed completely in 1751. Fuuta Tooro was described by the French as entirely at the mercy of the Moors, depopulated by warfare and pillaging, and politically unstable. "The millet trade failed completely at Podor, and a terrible famine exists in the Lower Senegal [le Bas du Pais]. Nevertheless we will be able to survive until the harvest in October with the help we receive from Gorée and by exercising great economy."[15] This note, written in November 1751, described the situation created by the second bad harvest in a row. A few months earlier, in June, the French had noted that a bad harvest threatened to create "a famine worse than the one we have just lived through," and the fear of food shortages forced the French to tolerate the aggressive and hostile behavior of the Dammel of Kajoor-Bawol, who preferred to sell his slaves to the British. The Company decided not to challenge the British incursion in their own trade zone, because they feared that the Dammel would close down the French trade in grain and cattle at Portudal.[16]

One of the first effects of the early food shortages in 1751 was to sensitize the French to the diplomacy of food supply. Company merchants feared boycotts in the provision trade from the Dammel of Kajoor in June and from the Barak of Waalo in July. The concerns were partly a reflection of uncertain relations with the new dynasty in Kajoor, which the French suspected of regional ambitions and pro-British sentiments. Trade boycotts were most effective in times of shortage. In November 1751 the Company requested a shipment of salted beef and beans from France to relieve their dependency on local supplies. The Company also purchased large quantities of millet in Gajaaga, where there were no shortages and transferred them to Saint Louis where grain was in short supply.[17]

French evaluations of their relationships with the neighboring kingdoms in 1751 contrasted their good relations with Waalo, described as poor and dependent, with their poor relations with the new regime in Kajoor. Yet in the crisis the distinction seemed to make little difference. The Barak threatened to cut off the cattle trade which crossed his territory to supply Saint Louis when the French refused him a loan of twenty *guinée* cloths. And when a French ship sunk with a full crew and cargo in the Barak's territory, the French had to pay the Barak 3,000 livres in "gifts" before he renounced his claim to the ship, the cargo, and the crew. Because the ship contained an estimated 30,000 livres worth of "food supplies and merchandise" the French considered the bargain satisfactory. Nevertheless, they feared setting a bad precedent, and requested food supplies from France in November to give themselves greater independence from the neighboring kingdoms.[18]

The slave trade was not directly affected in the early phases of the crisis. In November 1751 the French reported having 425 slaves in their slave pens, 220 men, 134 women, 40 boys, and 31 girls, and of these 380 were considered healthy enough to ship. Neither the numbers nor the mortality rate were exceptional. The sources of supply followed the usual patterns. The upper Senegal was the main source of supply, and the Lower Senegal sold small numbers of slaves. The new Dammel sold fifty slaves to the French in June 1751, and six slaves to the British in July. On the other hand the gum trade declined early in the crisis. The French purchased only 100 hogsheads of gum in 1751. They attributed the decline to the importance of the grain trade to Moor traders, who had abandoned the gum trade. "According to the merchants themselves . . . many of their colleagues have given up the trade to concentrate on the commerce in cattle, salt, millet and other foods, a trade which is attractive because it is much less difficult than the gum trade and at the same time brings them about the same advantages."[19] Although the shifting commercial activities of desert merchants reflected food shortages, surplus grain remained available for most of 1751 and 1752. The French described grain supplies at Gorée, which purchased primarily from Kajoor and Bawol, as abundant in February 1752 and the slave trade from Kajoor remained modest. In February 1752 the Dammel sold the French forty-two slaves.[20]

By February 1753, after another rainy season marked by drought and a third year in a row of deficit harvests, there were signs that the normal patterns of trade were collapsing under the pressures of crisis and famine. In February 1753 the slaver *Le Philippe* purchased 306 slaves at Saint Louis and completed its cargo at Gorée by purchasing 44 slaves. The Company director at Gorée immediately requested a ship with a capacity of not less than 300 slaves because Gorée had 200 slaves on hand and was negotiating with the Dammel for further purchases. Many of the slaves were "sick," but the French believed that the most "dangerous season for them had almost ended." At the same time the letter noted that "famine reigned on the entire coast and we are having the greatest difficulty feeding our slaves." The French reported that the British had purchased fifty slaves from the Dammel at Portudal for twelve guns each. This was a sign that the civil war in Kajoor continued and was the beginning of several years of exceptional slave exports from the Lower Senegal.[21]

By June 1753 famine and war had produced extraordinary patterns of trade in the Lower Senegal. The Dammel had sold almost 400 slaves to the French in the course of the year, and the trade would have been even more abundant if there had not been "a shortage of food supplies." In exchange for his slaves the Dammel "took almost exclusively arms and war munitions," leaving the French trade stock of guns, powder, and shot nearly exhausted. The French recognized the exceptional character of this trade. "None of his predecessors have ever supplied such an abundant slave trade." The famine was also exceptional, because the Company had never seen such a general famine, extending from Galam to Bissau. It was still possible to purchase millet, although it was difficult. At first the Company refused to bow to pressures forcing up the price of millet. The French had almost 600 slaves in their slave pens which they had to feed, so in the end they were faced with the choice of letting the slaves starve to death, or giving in "to the people of the country who know our situation which gives them the hope of making us pay an exorbitant price for their grain." The French paid the higher price.[22] A report from 1754 indicated that the price of millet increased during the famine from 4 livres for a hogshead to thirty livres or more.[23]

By August 1753 the main problem of the slave traders on the coast was finding food to keep alive the large numbers of starving slaves who ended up in European slave pens. Efforts to purchase millet as far south as the Gambia brought no relief. Gorée reported that "misery in the Gambia was so terrible that it was difficult to buy a single hogshead of millet, which would cost ten or twelve guns." By 1753 a hogshead of millet had reached parity value with a slave in the Lower Senegal. The strong demand for guns throughout the famine demonstrated the inextricable links between natural disaster and the political economy of slave trading, because civil war continued in Kajoor throughout 1754 and warlords used guns to seize the refugees of famine and sell them to European traders.

By 1753 even the periodic shipments of food received from France could not replace the loss of local grains, and the food supply began to place limits on the ability of the slave merchants to purchase slaves. The choices facing the slave merchants were clear. "Either we have to renounce this trade, which will considerably harm our commerce, or we will have to run the risk of watching our slaves starve to death."[24]

In October the grim economics of slave mortality began to weigh heavily on the export trade. When the slaver *La Sirenne* arrived at Saint Louis, it took on only 216 slaves and departed for Gorée to complete its cargo of 300. Although Saint Louis and Gorée held over 700 slaves, most of them were sick and starving and unfit to ship. The 700 slaves held in October were the survivors because 121 slaves had died in Saint Louis and 50 in Gorée since June. After the departure of *La Sirenne* Saint Louis had "240 slaves, most of them sick due to malnutrition and the cold which surprises them in their emaciated condition, so that it is to be feared that only a quarter will survive." At Gorée the Company had already been forced to renounce the purchase of 100 slaves offered by the kings of Kajoor and Siin, who were at war. Absolutely no cattle could be purchased at Gorée, which supplied itself from southern Kajoor, Bawol, and Siin, because "the famine has obliged the inhabitants of the country to eat them." Food supplies were totally unavailable at Gorée, where 500 slaves had been purchased in the course of the year.[25]

A year later, in June 1754, the famine reached its height in the months before a relatively good harvest led to some restabilization of the region. The Company requested a slaver with a capacity for at least 500 slaves. "Since the departure of the last ship we have traded here [Saint Louis] and at Gorée many more slaves than we could have hoped for and many more than we have ever purchased in the Lower Senegal [*le bas de la concession*]." This upbeat assessment of the consequences of the famine for the slave trade was followed by a description of starving refugees fleeing Kajoor and Jolof for Waalo, where certain enslavement awaited them. "The famine which continues to reign in the kingdoms of Cayor and Dyolof has forced the poor people of those countries to seek refuge in the country of Brack [the Barak]. That King has seized all those wretches and sold them to us. The certainty they have of being enslaved was not able to deter them from coming to the one place where they can relieve their misery. Since they have no alternative but death or slavery we can presume that the trade will not end until the harvest of little millet, that is, at the end of September." The same letter requested "100 hogsheads of food for negroes, flour, beans, or rice" because the French did not expect to be able to purchase much of the millet from the harvest.[26]

In mid-1754, at the peak of the famine, French traders on the coast began to try and analyze the causes of the famine and its effects on the export trade. The profitable millet trade in the interior, which was dominated by the Moors, had caused a decline in the gum trade. "With this grain they can procure a great quantity of dyed cloth which before they only received in exchange for their gum." Desert merchants purchased millet by selling livestock and desert salt, and resold some of the millet to Europeans in exchange for the imported Indian cloth they had once received primarily in exchange for gum. One French memoir written in 1754 suggested importing more food to Senegal, as a way of reestablishing the gum trade. The memoir also commented on the movement of millet prices during the famine. "When it is abundant millet costs in Saint Louis, four livres [a hogshead], including all expenses. In the shortages that we have experienced for the last several years, it has cost 30 livres and even more." Grain purchases from the Moors required "2,000 *guinées* per year for the food trade." These estimates suggest the importance of grain sales to the general trade economy.[27]

The most dramatic effect of the famine on the slave trade was to reverse the usual patterns of supply. Although the upriver region was affected by the drought of 1753, the upriver areas were spared the misery and starvation which reigned nearer the coast. The French were able to make important millet purchases in Galam in 1751, 1754, 1755, and 1756, years in which grain was in short supply in the Lower Senegal. During the same period the relative share of slave exports from the upper and lower Senegal reversed themselves. A letter from Saint Louis dated July 1754 noted that Galam had "only" exported 454 slaves in 1753, a year when Gorée alone purchased over 500. In 1754, at the beginning of the high water trading season, the same proportions maintained themselves. By June 1754 the French had purchased 400 slaves at Saint Louis, 350 at Gorée, and 94 in Galam. The reversal in slave supply patterns called for comment. "Never before has Senegal [the lower river] produced such a great number. The famine which reigns in the vicinity has given us this good trade." The main problem experienced by the French in the Lower Senegal in 1754 was still the lack of grain, and the shortages of trade goods, particularly rum and trade guns, which were in short supply after the massive purchases of slaves.[28]

The famine in Kajoor was prolonged into 1754–5 by civil war, which continued and intensified. The Dammel was dethroned briefly by a rival, and then returned to power with the aid of the Barak. Although the French only poorly understood this dynastic conflict, which continued until 1756, when the Geej returned to power, it was the beginning of a period of conflict which would last until 1766. The civil wars of Kajoor were not simply dynastic conflicts. The period of warfare in the 1750s was the first phase in a period of extended conflict that would lead to a dramatic shift in the balance of power at the desert edge. In the 1750s Waalo, aided by Trarza desert warriors, appeared to be extending its power and influence southwards into Kajoor.[29] But within less than two decades Waalo would be devastated by conquest by desert warriors and lose most of its territory north of the Senegal River.[30]

If Atlantic merchants failed to understand the deeper roots of dynastic conflict and civil war in the 1750s, they did perceive the consequences of warfare. "The country of Cayor has just received a shock which it will feel for a long time. The reigning king was chased from the throne by his nephew and then returned to power after a month with the aid of the Brack. The war cost little in bloodshed, but ravaged the country, and what is most disastrous destroyed part of the grain which promised an abundant harvest. This war will probably produce many captives, but Gorée will not escape from its current destitution and we will be obliged to supply that department with cattle for the subsistence of the garrison."[31] The director of the Company in Saint Louis showed a new concern for the food production of Kajoor, long taken for granted by the French, and informed the Parisian directors: "This country, *Messieurs*, is the breadbasket of the surrounding area."[32] In October the Company celebrated its good fortune in having already requested a shipment of 100 hogsheads of "negro rations" when locusts "ravaged three-fourths of the crops in our vicinity."[33]

Death reaped its greatest harvest in the slave pens of the coast in 1754. Even though the worst part of the famine was over in much of Senegambia, desperate conditions in the Lower Senegal continued. French analysis of slave mortality in 1755 focused on the "violent periods of cold" and the difficulty experienced by slaves from Galam of adjusting to the climate in the months of October, November, and December, when they were afflicted "with colds and chest lesions." But the famine undoubtedly played a major role, as malnourished slaves succumbed to disease. The slave purchases for 1755 showed the patterns established during the famine. The French purchased almost 500 slaves at Saint Louis, 450 in Galam, and over 600 in Gorée. Of these slaves, 980 had been exported, 445 had died in the course of the year, and 222 remained in French slave pens. [34] Although the arithmetic of the company left about 100 slaves unaccounted for, the figures clearly show the importance of slave purchases in the Lower Senegal and the high rate of mortality. The slaves who starved to death under the eyes of their captors were victims of the general crisis caused by drought, civil war, and famine. But they were also the victims of merchants who celebrated the "good trade" caused by famine, who purchased slaves they could not feed, and then let them starve to death.

The political economy of famine

The sources on the famine of the 1750s suggest three overlapping explanations of the crisis: natural disaster (drought and locusts), war, and the pressures on food supplies created by the grain purchases of the slave merchants, who needed to feed slaves in transit and the growing populations of Saint Louis and Gorée. Two of these explanations were advanced at the time, during a highly political discussion of the reasons for the famine and the resulting high slave mortality. Adanson and independent slave traders criticized Company management and suggested that the growth of a "surplus" population on Saint Louis and Gorée and grain purchases by slave ships had strained the agricultural economy of the region beyond its capacity to produce. In reply, the Company argued that the famine was caused by revolution and civil war in Kajoor. The sudden end of grain exports from Kajoor led to grain shortages and the death of Company slaves. Both arguments deserve closer examination, in the light of a broader historical examination of the crisis.

Strictly speaking, neither the grain purchases of slave ships or the coastal islands caused famine. But the commercialization of millet reduced the surplus grain stored during good years, leaving populations more suscep- tible to the food shortages created by drought or locust invasions. It is impossible to calculate precisely the size of the commercial grain market generated by the Atlantic trade, but broad estimations are possible based on the number of slaves exported and the size of the populations of the Atlantic islands. Using a simplified model which assumes that 1,600 slaves were exported through the Lower Senegal, that they spent four months in transit within Africa after purchase and another two months in the Atlantic crossing, consuming nothing but locally produced grain, slave ships would have consumed 200 tons of grain per year. Saint Louis and Gorée, with a population of 3,000, would have consumed 750 tons of grain in one year.[35] This gives a global estimate of 950 tons of grain per year for the Atlantic trade based in the ports of the Lower Senegal.

The most difficult aspect of the model to verify is the amount of grain purchased by slave ships. However, certain patterns can be discerned. While it is fair to assume that slaves in transit within Africa and in African ports were fed entirely with locally produced grain and foodstuffs, except in cases of dire emergency, the same assumption cannot be made about slave ships crossing the Atlantic. Slave ships trading in Senegambia expected to take on local provisions, but ships also carried food supplies sufficient to feed the slaves for at least part of the crossing, in case local foodstuffs were in short supply.[36] William Littleton, who traded in the Gambia for eleven years, gave a typical description of this strategy. "We carry from hence split and kiln-dried horse beans, and a large quantity of Biscuit and Flour, and in the Country we purchase all the Grain we can, of the Country Corn, and Rice." When asked if ships could procure a "sufficient quantity of Guinea corn" for the slaves crossing the Atlantic he replied, "Seldom a sufficient quantity of that alone."[37] James Kiernan, who described his experiences in Saint Louis in the 1770s, noted that slave preferences played some role in the emphasis on local grains, based on the belief that familiar foods reduced mortality rates in the Atlantic crossing. "Those ships going to the West Indies with Slaves were supplied by the Blacks with large quantities of corn, which the Slaves preferred to any other kind of provisions."[38] Ships that could not purchase enough grain in Senegambia supplemented their supplies with rice purchased on the Windward or Grain Coast. For all these reasons, it is likely that most, but not all of the grain consumed by slaves shipped from the Lower Senegal came from the Senegal River valley and the Atlantic coastal region.[39]

The role of Saint Louis and Gorée in creating famine conditions on the coast was first discussed in Company documents in February 1754, and took the form of a response to questions and speculations formulated in Paris. The response of the Company directors in Senegal had a defensive tone, because critics in Paris believed there was an excess population on the islands, which became a burden to feed in times of famine. The Company offered an analysis of the population of Saint Louis, estimated at 2,500, which accounted for the need for 800 workers, free and slave, necessary as sailors, interpreters, and artisans for the Company's trade operations. The rest of the population, which was made up mainly of women and children, proved more of an embarrassment to the Company. But the essential argument of the Company was that millet had never been in short supply "until the famine."[40] The Company affirmed that millet cultivation had expanded dramatically in the vicinity of the coast to accommodate European demands. "On the other hand the negroes have found a greater market for their grain, have become more attached to the cultivation of the land, and it is certain that they now cultivate four times as much as they did fifteen years ago."[41] For the first time the Company provided rich detail on the mechanisms which supplied the European settlements with provisions. The report noted the dependence of the islands on coastal villages for the supply of fish needed to feed slaves in transit. "There are no negro fishermen on the island of Senegal or the island of Gorée, they are all inhabitants of neighboring villages," but the supply of fish was normally abundant enough "to feed the slaves in chains."[42]

In the view of the Company the real cause of the famine was a combination of natural disaster and war in Kajoor. "It is not the argumentation of the inhabitants [of our settlements] which caused the shortage of grain, but the poor harvests of the last four years, the revolutions which began five or six years ago in the kingdoms of Cayor and Baol and the poor government of a new king which created a general famine. All these causes were accidental, and abundance will return with good harvests."[43] The Company's analysis suggested that an important part of the grain crop of Kajoor was commercialized and that production had expanded in response to European demand. The same was true of the supply of fish from the coast. In normal years the Company only needed to import "bread and wine" to maintain its trade operations. The explanation of the Company directors emphasized the importance of Kajoor in the provision trade, because the political trouble in Kajoor was the major reason why poor harvests were transformed into general famine.

   The idea that the "idle" population of Saint Louis and Gorée had caused the famine seems to have first been proposed by independent slave traders, who resented the Company monopoly in Senegal. Slavers believed that the slaves living on Saint Louis and Gorée served no real function and should be shipped out to the colonies. The same argument appears in the analysis of the famine by Adanson. He described the sufferings of lower-level Company employees on the islands during the famine. Adanson's testimony revealed the class tensions that existed within the European settlements. According to Adanson, the Company directors and their African and mulatto mistresses, the *signares*, lived in luxury at the expense of the Company and the "French who didn't have the means to support women of their class." The *signares* had "double and triple rations, in reality as much bread, meat, fish, wine, and rum as they desired" and even "their slaves were furnished with meat and millet at the expense of the Company." The result was suffering among lower-class Frenchmen and employees like Adanson. "In the end these abuses created shortages of bread, wine, and other supplies for the Frenchmen of the lower estate, the workers, soldiers, sailors, and even lower ranking officers who experienced shortages even before the famine, while provisions were consumed openly in banquets organized by those blood-suckers [the *signares*] and the directors, who fattened them with the provisions intended for their compatriots."[44]

   Although some of Adanson's accusations expressed his anger, he gave an important estimation of the annual grain consumption of Saint Louis. "The island supported at the expense of the Company more than 3,000 negroes and negresses, and mulattoes of both sexes who caused famines not only on the island and in the vicinity, but in all the surrounding country for the distance of 60 leagues, because the negroes, accustomed from time immemorial to only plant the grain needed for their own annual consumption without important stores could hardly furnish the 3,000 hogsheads, each of 500 to 700 pounds required by each inhabitant of the island per year."[45] Adanson's figure, which equaled about 750 tons of millet per year, would have fed not only the population, estimated at 2,500 by the Company and 3,000 by Adanson, but also the slaves in transit. Adanson's figure of one hogshead of 500 to 700 pounds per inhabitant gives an annual consumption of millet higher than the figure calculated by the French in the early nineteenth century, when minimum millet rations were estimated by the French to be 350 grams a day per inhabitant, and one kilo a day for an adult male worker. For a population of 3,000 this would create minimal needs for 400 tons of millet, slightly more than half of Adanson's estimate (using the lower end of Adanson's estimate of the weight of a hogshead). Therefore Adanson's figure appears reasonable, considering that Saint Louis sometimes harbored more than 1,000 slaves in transit in the course of a year and that the city's needs were linked to wider trade operations along the coast and the river, which also demanded millet supplies.[46]

Adanson's estimation of Saint Louis's annual consumption of millet is more credible than his general explanation of the famine or his belief that grain supplies were inelastic. Although 750 tons did not imply a massive commercialization of the grain economy, it indicated a substantial trade that could not have been satisfied by the casual sales of subsistence producers indifferent to marketing grain surpluses. This impression is reinforced when grain sales to the southern Sahara are taken into account, and they were undoubtedly important in an era when the Moors controlled the grain trade in the Lower Senegal. The Company's belief that Africans were producing more grain in response to the demand for their crop is more credible than Adanson's portrait of a tradition-bound subsistence economy. The demand of the coastal cities did not cause the famine, but the growing commercial demand for surplus grain, and the willingness of Europeans to pay high prices for it, put pressure on food supplies. Adanson's figures for the peak price of millet during the famine, 60 to 120 livres per hogshead, are much higher than the Company's, which may have tried to hide some of the expenses of the famine from the Company directors in Paris.

Although Adanson does not mention drought or locusts in his explanation of the famine, Company records clearly show that the famine of the 1750s was in part the result of ecological factors. But what turned natural disaster into human catastrophe was the combination of drought and war. From 1749 until 1756 Kajoor was under the rule of a rival dynasty that had been out of power since the establishment of Geej power by Latsukaabe in 1695. Both European sources and dynastic traditions indicate that the Dorobe dynasty was never able to consolidate its power. The new dynasty faced constant opposition from the Geej in shifting alliances with various outside supporters until 1756, when the Geej were restored. But even after that date Kajoor experienced a period of political instability which lasted until 1766. Although the dynastic traditions of Kajoor do not directly discuss the famine, they portray the rule of the last representative of the Geej before the crisis as a time of prosperity, of abundant food, particularly meat, and of ease, elegance, and pleasure. Mayssa Tend Wejj ruled over a Kajoor at peace with itself and Mayssa's capital Maka became a figure of speech for plenty.[47]

The civil war in Kajoor and Bawol, which frequently pulled in neighboring states, was an important cause of famine in 1751–4. War disrupted agricultural production, destroyed standing crops, encouraged slave sales to finance arms purchases, and civil war made enslavement a covenient punishment for political dissidents. The importance of arms sales, and the exchange by Kajoor of an exceptionally large number of slaves for guns, shot, and powder, are well documented. Nevetheless the war does not

143

easily fit into a model of slave-raiding entrepreneurship, in which warrior kings sold off the producers of their own and neighboring kingdoms in exchange for the quick profits to be made from the sale of war captives.[48] The civil war in Kajoor was a serious struggle for power between two rival dynasties, fighting to control alliances and to build military coalitions. It produced slaves, but it also seriously weakened the country, and it was not driven forward by warriors' interest in producing slaves for the export market. It is therefore difficult to argue that the civil wars were "normal events" in a system of aristocratic slavery in which warriors produced captives for sale, and relied on purchased slaves to provide them with the means of subsistence.[49]

Warfare was recognized in the eighteenth century as the most important source of slaves for the Atlantic trade, along with famine, sale for debt, and enslavement as the punishment of crime.[50] On the other hand, there was less agreement at the time and since among historians on whether these wars were directly provoked by the demand for captives, or developed from indigenous causes independent from or at most indirectly linked to the Atlantic trade.[51] There is no single answer to this question, which has to be approached on a regional and chronological basis. In the Lower Senegal small-scale slave raiding was more common than major military campaigns, and more directly linked to the demands created by the Atlantic trade. Larger scale and more devastating warfare also occurred, particularly in the dynastic civil wars that swept the region between 1749 and 1766. Although these wars and the famines that accompanied them produced an important slave trade, they were the product of a life and death struggle for power between competing royal factions, rather than a direct product of state-sponsored military campaigns designed to produce slaves for export. Internally, these wars did not reinforce the use of slaves in agriculture, but created a crisis in which masters were forced to sell off slaves they could no longer feed or employ productively.

If warfare in the Lower Senegal in 1751–6 cannot be linked directly to the dynamic of slaving for profit, it was tied to the more general conditions created by the Atlantic trade. The militarization of power and the need for rulers to invest in the technology of firearms were byproducts of the Atlantic trade in all the coastal kingdoms, along with a general climate of insecurity and violence. Although state-sponsored warfare against neighboring kingdoms and exposed populations never reached the massive levels attained elsewhere, all the dynastic states of the Lower Senegal placed a priority on military organization and enslaved their domestic enemies and the neighboring populations who fell into their hands. In times of political stability the geographic location of the region favored the provision trade and the collection of transit taxes and customs duties from the European trade community. Together, those factors worked to limit the scale of slave raiding, which swept with greater force and brutality across more distant regions of the Senegambian interior.

144

The politics of slavery

The crisis of the mid-eighteenth century resulted from the civil wars which devastated Kajoor and Bawol from 1749 to 1766. These wars were the first major crisis of the political order created by Latsukaabe Faal at the end of the seventeenth century. The creation of a small, royal army of slaves armed with firearms was the major institutional innovation of the Geej dynasty. Dynastic traditions portray the first two kings of the dynasty as powerful, dynamic rulers who ruled over prosperous kingdoms and maintained control over Kajoor and Bawol.[52] European sources permit a more nuanced portrait: they reveal the devastating crisis that preceded the emergence of the new order, the frequently brutal methods of the kings, their efforts to exploit and control Atlantic commerce and the periodic droughts and famines that struck the region. The succession struggle which followed the death of Latsukaabe was particularly bitter and coincided with the famine conditions during the drought of 1723–5.[53] The new Dammel Mayssa Tend Wejj, a Geej son of Latsukaabe, prolonged warfare into the 1730s when he succeeded in driving a rival Geej prince from Bawol, recreating the dual monarchy ruled by his father. Each succession struggle planted new seeds for future wars. The two rival princes defeated by Mayssa Tend in the 1720s and 1730s went into exile with their slaves and allies and both succeeded in seizing power during the period of drought, famine, and civil war that began in 1748 and lasted until 1766.

The crisis of the 1750s had multiple causes, but it clearly revealed the weak point of the political system. The use of slaves strengthened the monarchy, but it also complicated the problem of succession, because the slaves who reproduced the power of the political system were a form of property which had to be inherited. State investment in slave property was held by the royal matrilineage and passed on within it. In theory this put a standing army of royal slaves at the disposition of the legitimate successor chosen by the council of electors.[54] But there were inherent tensions in the system from the beginning. Although the matrilineal system meant that nephews inherited power, kings often tried to pass on important roles to their sons, who were often members of rival matrilineages. Sons from rival matrilineages inherited military slaves from their patrilineage (*jaami baay*), and this allowed ambitious princes to create the nucleus of a private army, which was supplemented by free vassals (*dag*). Even when the Geej dynasty controlled both Kajoor and Bawol, efforts by kings to place a son on one throne and a nephew on another frequently led to war.

The dynamics of succession struggle and civil war appear most clearly in the career of Mawa Mbatio Sambe (1749–56), who became Dammel-Teeñ during the crisis of the 1750s. He was a son of Latsukaabe, from the matrilineage of the Dorobe. Ousted from the succession by Mayssa Tend, he spent much of his youth in exile, allying himself with states and families willing to help him in his pursuit of the throne of Kajoor. In dynastic

145

traditions his determination to seize the throne was symbolized by an episode that occurred between Mawa's successive efforts to seize the throne of Kajoor. Accepting his defeat by his brother, Mayssa Tend, Mawa returned from exile to Kajoor. One day while resting under the shade of a tree, Mawa watched a thirsty toad struggle for hours before it was able to reach the top of a water jar and quench its thirst. Announcing to his retinue that the toad had taught him a lesson about perserverance, Mawa went into exile once more to rebuild a military coalition capable of ousting the Geej from power.[55] The portrait of Mawa that emerges from oral traditions is that of a tragic founder hero, tested by exile and hardship in his youth. His career was cut short after he succeeded in uniting the crowns of Kajoor and Bawol, in what might have been a successful usurpation of power much like that achieved by his father Latsukaabe. According to dynastic traditions Mawa was assassinated by one of his own slaves. After uniting the dual kingdom Mawa went to Lambaay, the capital of Bawol, to punish a slave who abused his authority by putting the countryside to ransom. The slave, surprised in his residence, killed the Dammel-Teeñ with a thrust of his lance, and then was immediately put to death by Mawa's retinue.[56]

European sources confirm many of the details of dynastic traditions. Pruneau described Mawa as a usurper who had no right to the throne, because he did not belong to the reigning royal matrilineage. He seized power by force, proving that he was "not an ordinary Negro. It took his skillful conduct, his vigilance, and his energy to bring his fortunes that far."[57] For Company officials, Mawa presented a danger to their interests, because he used the dependency of Saint Louis and Gorée on the mainland to force new concessions from the French. Mawa's years in exile and wide travels in Senegambia gave him knowledge which made him a dangerous enemy. "The new Damel traveled all along the course of the Gambia, as well as that of the Senegal and the Atlantic coast, when he was just an individual, and he knows how to distinguish between the high prices paid for slaves by the English in the Gambia, and the modest prices offered on the Senegal River and at Gorée."[58] Like other Dammels, Mawa put pressure on the French by declaring a trade boycott, but unlike most of his predecessors he organized a canoe trade from Portudal to the Gambia so his boycott against the French never cut him off entirely from Atlantic commerce.[59]

Mawa's career showed that it was still possible for an individual prince to seize power with the aid of a private army of slaves and vassals. This suggests that the royal slaves of the Geej dynasty were not yet powerful enough to defeat adventurous pretenders, or that they had not yet identified themselves thoroughly with the Geej dynasty. The royal slaves may have played a critical role in the civil wars that devastated Kajoor in the 1750s. French sources confirm that Mawa was killed by a military slave, as reported in dynastic traditions. In 1756 a French Company agent reported that the Dammel, who had seized power seven years earlier from the Geej, was "assassinated by one of his slaves" in a power struggle that ended with the restoration of Geej power.[60]

Prolonged and bitter civil wars were the main exception to the norms of violent conflict in the region. Unlike small-scale state violence these conflicts led to the enslavement of members of dominant social groups. One example can be documented from the account of a slave revolt that occurred on Gorée and the slave ship *Avrillon*, between 1749 and 1751, near the beginning of the civil wars in Kajoor. Pruneau de Pommegorge described the revolt in a work published in 1789, but Company records and his account indicate that he was on Gorée at the time of the revolt.[61] Pruneau prefaced his narrative by noting that the slave trade at Gorée rarely exceeded two or three hundred slaves a year, the product of raids by the Dammel "on the borders of his kingdom, particularly against the Serrzes [Sereer], his neighbors." Then he described the civil war between the Dorobe and Geej lineages as a circumstance which allowed him to purchase an unusual number of slaves. "I once purchased almost five hundred Yolofs, the product of one of these wars, what one could call a civil war" and then described why this trade almost cost the lives of all the whites on the island.[62]

What was unusual in this case was not only the number of the slaves, but their social status. Pruneau described the slaves as warriors who had fought for the recently deposed Geej king. As warriors, the captives probably included *ceddo* slave soldiers and low-ranking notables and aristocrats. Because of their high status in African society, where slave warriors served the monarchy and were normally exempt from agricultural labor, the prisoners proved to be dangerous captives. The French learned accidentally of a well-planned revolt from a child who had been placed in the slave pens as punishment for petty theft. One-third of the prisoners planned to attack the guard, one-third were to attack the arsenal, and the other third were to disperse on the island and "massacre all the whites." When they had gained control of the island, the captives planned on seizing weapons, trade goods, and boats, and departing for the mainland to join their king in exile.

When the French interrogated the leaders of the planned revolt, "whom we knew were great men in their country," they did not deny the plot, but affirmed

> that they all experienced the greatest shame because they had not died in combat for him [the deposed king]; but now that they had failed in their coup they preferred death to slavery. To this response, truly Roman in spirit, all the other captives cried with one voice [in Wolof] de gue la, de gue la, [*degg la, degg la*] that's the truth, that's the truth.[63]

The next day the French executed the two leaders of the revolt with two small cannons "charged only with powder and wad." This was not the end

147

of the incident, however. In spite of being warned about the danger, the captain of the slaver *Avrillon* took no extra precautions with his dangerous cargo. The same 500 slaves revolted once again at sea, where many of them proved their preference for death over slavery. In their revolt the Kajoor slaves killed seven whites on the ship, including the captain, and they were not subdued until 230 had been killed, after the ship's crew turned the ship's guns on the revolting slaves.[64]

European merchants often came into contact with slave officials, who played important roles in the administration of official ports of trade. Rufisque and Portudal were under the administration of royal officials the Europeans called Alquiers, and many of these were royal slaves.[65] In 1765–6 the French administration on Gorée tried to have the Alquier of Rufisque removed from office. The conflict revealed some of the rules of thumb that governed relations between the king and his slave officials. The French believed they were bargaining from a position of strength, with a young Dammel who had gained power in a kingdom weakened by civil war. When the Geej regained power in 1756 the French argued that the royal family owed them "gratitude" for harboring some family members and aiding them during their long years of exile.[66] In 1764 the French governor of Gorée reported that he had again aided the Geej dynasty "by ransoming from slavery one of the relatives of their king, purchased by the English."[67]

Throughout 1765 and 1766 the French complained to the Dammel that his Alquier was ignoring the treaties signed between Kajoor and themselves, demanding extra presents and customs duties from them, and taxing the trade between Gorée and the mainland. "He collects contributions not only from the inhabitants of Gorée when they visit the mainland to satisfy their needs, but also from the inhabitants of the mainland who want to bring food and other provisions to the island, to the point that he has discouraged them, and the trade which is so useful to the Damel and his subjects is almost completely interrupted."[68] The Alquier had also enslaved "by force or ruse free persons, whom he sold to us, and which honor obliged us to return." The uncharacteristic mention of "honor" concealed other concerns. The enslaved persons were Lebu fishermen from the mainland and the French feared a trade boycott. Lebu fishing vessels supplied the island with fish, and carried provisions from the mainland. A serious conflict with the Lebu villages of Cap Vert would have cut essential links between Gorée and the mainland.

The French believed they had convinced the Dammel to punish his Alquier and sell rights to Cap Vert for 100, then for 200 bars. But the Alquier continued to tax the trade between Gorée and the mainland and threatened to bar Europeans from the mainland entirely. In September 1766 the French arrested a person they described as the "valet" of the Alquier, who was in fact a royal slave, for disorderly conduct on Gorée, where he insulted the French governor and other officers. They asked the

Dammel for permission to ship the man into slavery in the Americas, and offered the Dammel thirty bars, long the standard price for a prime slave. The Dammel refused, firmly, but he also suggested possible punishments for the man that revealed the vulnerability of privileged slaves. "It is impossible for me to sell off a slave [*un valet*] that I have inherited from my ancestors. Let the Governor do what he likes with the man; he can put him in chains for a year or put him to work, or even whip him on top of a cannon. If he is embarked on a ship all relations will be cut off between Gorée and Cayor." On October 23 the French released their prisoner to Farba-Sef, the military commander of the royal slaves, to be punished.[69]

The protection given by the Dammel to his slave reflected the very real dependence of the court on its slave retinue. The impact of the royal slaves was important enough in the eighteenth century to color perceptions of history. In the dynastic traditions recorded by Brasseur in 1778, Amari Ngoone (Amarigonne in Brasseur) was encouraged to revolt by a slave confidant named Manguenoukat.[70] The royal slave upbraided his master and encouraged his revolt: "If your ancestors lived in slavery, it is for you to break the chains that have nearly been destroyed by the hand of time." Afterwards it was again the slave who fought the first battle with the Burba-Jolof, and encouraged Kajoor's wars against the Moors. None of these details are recorded in later versions of the history of Amari Ngoone, but they are interesting because they cast Kajoor's history in the light of eighteenth-century political realities.

Brasseur's account of Amari Ngoone is followed by a description of the rebellion of one of the Dammel's most powerful slave warlords, the Fara-Kaba, who commanded the western provinces of Bawol and the port of Portudal. "Faracaba, Alquier of Portudal and son of a slave belonging to Dammel" was forced into exile after he had committed adultery with one of the Dammel's wives. After the pronunciation of a death sentence in case of his capture, the Fara-Kaba took refuge in Siin "and today he has the reputation of the most intrepid warrior." According to Brasseur the Fara-Kaba had 4,000 men under his command (which seems doubtful) and brought "steel and flames" into the possessions of his former master.[71] But the important information provided by Brasseur was that Fara-Kaba's rebellion was repressed by the Dammel Makodu Kumba Jaring on the prodding of the *lingeer*, his sister, who refused to see the country laid to waste "by a slave of her house."[72] Brasseur's account demonstrates that the slaves of the Geej split into rival factions during the aftermath of the civil war of the 1750s, which helps explain why political instability continued into the 1760s.[73] Although Brasseur may at times have been a gullible transmitter of court gossip, and popular exaggeration, his portrait of the royal slaves reflected the attitudes of his informants, and thus gives us some idea of what people thought about the influence of privileged slaves in the court of the king.

Brasseur's account of Kajoor was written during the reign of Makodu

Kumba Jaring (1766–78), which was marked by the reinforcement of many of the features of the regime established by Latsukaabe. Makodu, who ruled Bawol twice as king before he became Dammel-Teeñ in 1766–7, was a veteran of the civil wars and inter-Geej rivalries that had devasted Kajoor and Bawol for almost two decades. When he became Dammel he was almost sixty years old, with a long experience of political exile. Remembered by dynastic traditions as a king who restored prosperity and had a great love of agriculture, his reign was a disappointment to European slave traders, who complained of the paucity of slave exports.[74] Like Latsukaabe, Makodu was from Bawol and became Dammel-Teeñ on the invitation of notables whose experience of civil war and foreign invasion led them to look for a strong king who could restore peace. European accounts of his reign described the royal slaves as the centerpiece of his army and government. In the decades that followed the reign of Makodu the slaves of the Geej (*jaami geej*) emerged as a cohesive political force in the kingdom of Kajoor.

After 1778 kings were chosen from eligible princes by the council of electors, which often ignored the wishes of the deceased king. In 1790 and in 1809 the council of electors of Kajoor chose princes who had been driven into exile by the previous king, and in all these cases a nephew was chosen from the ruling matrilineage in preference to any of the king's sons.[75] The renewed authority exercised by the council of electors reflected the growing influence of the royal slaves. By the early nineteenth century dynastic traditions attribute major decisions affecting the Geej dynasty to the *jaami geej* rather than to the king.[76] The new influence wielded by the royal slaves emerged gradually in the period from 1766 to 1790, in the aftermath of devastating civil war and famine.

The political crisis that accompanied Kajoor's civil wars was essentially a crisis of the "slave power" that Latsukaabe had placed at the center of the monarchy. By centralizing military power in the hands of the ruling dynasty and their military slaves, violence had been circumscribed within defined limits. In the chaos of civil war, that central force was lost and the military predation of rival aristocratic factions devastated the agricultural economy and plunged the countryside into famine. After the civil wars stability returned as the restored Geej dynasty devoted its energies to agricultural production. But the restabilization under kings like Makodu Kumba Jaring (1766–78), who are remembered in dynastic traditions as rulers devoted to agriculture and friends of Islam, was called into question by bloody revolts and repression in the period of Islamic revival and revolution that marked the last decade of the eighteenth century.

Crisis and conflicts in Atlantic commerce

After the famine of the 1750s Senegambia no longer produced an expanding volume of trade in slaves, gum, and grain, and the latent conflicts between the various branches of the export trade became more and more evident. These changes were dimly perceived by Atlantic merchants, who found themselves forced to make choices that their predecessors had not been required to make. From 1758 to 1800 the essential choice appeared to be between a strategy centered on the slave trade, and a strategy that gave equal weight to the gum trade, even if slave exports leveled off or declined.

These choices are more interesting for what they reveal about the underlying economic constraints on Atlantic commerce than as guides to European economic policy. Commercial policy reflected a compromise between interest groups who favored maximizing slave exports at any cost (the dominant policy in French Atlantic commerce as a whole) and interest groups who saw gum arabic as Senegal's most important export (resident merchants concerned with the cost of trading in Senegambia). The debate was animated by the complicated financial balance sheet of the slave trade. Some of the underlying problems appeared during the 1750s, when the *Compagnie des Indes* retained exclusive trading rights within the concession, but sold its slaves to private slaving vessels flying the French flag. In compensation for selling slaves to private vessels, the Company received a rebate for each slave delivered to the French colonies.[77]

This system worked reasonably well until the crisis of the 1750s, but in 1751 the Company analyzed the factors that clouded the future of Atlantic commerce in Senegambia. Experience proved that the Senegal trade prospered as an exclusive concession, because individual merchant vessels were unable to mine its commerce. The company regarded its exclusive privilege as a mixed blessing. The Company's difficulties were caused by the costs of maintaining its forts and trading posts, by "the frequent wars of the negroes which interrupt our commerce," by the "mortality caused by epidemic diseases," and by the difficulty of making the colonists pay what they owed the Company for the slaves shipped across the Atlantic.[78] The price of slaves in the colonies "was determined less by the purchase price in Africa than by the expenses and mortality inseparable from the transport of blacks."[79] One of the interesting points made was that "the frequent wars of the negroes" could harm Atlantic commerce by disrupting normal channels of trade. Wars, on the other hand, were essential in providing slaves for export.

The gum trade assumed a new importance in the management of the Senegal concession. With French sugar planters increasingly in debt and dependent on credit from the metropole, the profitability of the slave trade depended on complex financial arrangements and profits often could be realized only after considerable delays. By contrast, the gum trade, which generated high profits, could be carried on directly between Senegal and Europe and had certain advantages over the slave trade. The profits of the gum trade helped finance slave trading in Senegambia by providing the cash flows needed to offset the slow returns on slave sales. Gum had special advantages as an export commodity. Gum from Senegal dominated the European market for gum in the eighteenth century, replacing supplies once imported from the Middle East.[80] Whoever controlled trade at the Senegal concession was able to dominate the world supply of gum. During the period of Company rule French and British merchants diffused competition for gum by arranging an exchange of gum for slaves. French merchants in Senegal, who dominated gum supplies, agreed to trade 360,000 pounds of gum for 300 prime slaves from the Gambia.[81] When the British seized Saint Louis in the Seven Years War, their primary goal was to secure supplies of gum for British commerce and manufacturers.

The position of Senegambia in the African slave trade contrasted sharply with its dominant position in the world gum market. After 1750 Senegambia's trade on all carriers never exceeded 5 per cent of the total slave trade from Africa, and this weak comparative position reinforced itself over time, as total slave exports from Senegambia declined absolutely in every decade but one in the second half of the eighteenth century.[82] Declining slave exports were combined with increasing prices for slaves, so that Senegambia looked less and less attractive to merchants primarily interested in slaves. The clearest indication of this came during the period from 1763 to 1778 when the French held only Gorée and the British controlled the gum trade from Saint Louis. French slave merchants from Nantes could see no reason for the French government and French commerce to spend money maintaining forts and posts in Senegambia when French planters and French slavers preferred to buy slaves in the Bight of Benin and West Central Africa.[83] The French government eventually agreed with this assessment. Gorée was downgraded to a simple trading post in 1776. But as it turned out this decision was simply a prelude to the preparation of a war plan to seize Saint Louis from the British, restoring the lucrative gum trade to the French.[84]

For most of the eighteenth century slave exports and gum exports from Senegambia complemented one another, with gum exports tending to offset cash flow problems and compensating for the decline in slave exports. Nevertheless, conflicts did emerge, and Atlantic merchants perceived these conflicts primarily in terms of the contrary effects of war on the trade in slaves and on the trade in gum. During the civil wars in the Lower Senegal in the 1750s European traders began to argue that a judicious policy of distributing rifles, powder, and shot to rival political factions would prevent the emergence of a dominant regional power and increase slave exports.[85] At the same time frequent wars disrupted trade, threatened grain supplies, and often led to a decline in gum exports. Competition and conflicts were particularly important at the desert edge, where the Atlantic economy intersected with desert–savanna exchanges of livestock for grain and slaves. The gum trade poured textiles, firearms, and other Atlantic imports into desert society, upsetting the balance of power and wealth between the desert and the savanna.

One of the indirect results of the gum trade was to increase the military strength of desert warriors, particularly the Trarza and Brakna desert states. During a period of drought from 1771–6 Trarza warriors increased their pressures on the river valley, virtually conquering the state of Waalo in 1775. The devastation of Waalo was accompanied by the massive sale of slaves to the British in 1775 and 1776. A French document from 1783 said that the British received 8,000 slaves from the Moors, and that slaves were so abundant on the Saint Louis market that they sold for one piece of *guinée*, or bolt of Indian dyed cloth. The same document reported that the raid on Waalo was encouraged by English advances of cloth and guns to the Trarza Moors.[86] But the subjugation of Waalo posed serious problems for Saint Louis and contributed to the *habitants'* decision to drive Governor O'Hara from the island in 1775. O'Hara's decision to use warfare as part of his trade diplomacy was described by a later British governor as an effort to subdue "the inhabitants of Walo, then exceedingly powerful," because they "threatened to prevent communication with the upper part of the river." There is little doubt that O'Hara played a personal role in the destruction of Waalo in 1775.

> General O'Hara, then governor, entered into a treaty with the Trarsar Moors and King Damel, to assist him in attacking that nation, which they did most effectually, and the Walo country received a blow from which it has never since recovered; its villages on the river's banks are yet deserted and abandoned, its people have been carried into captivity, and those who remain are constantly subjected to the plunder of the Moors, who treat them as a dependent and tributary state. O'Hara's name is still used by the Walo mothers to frighten their crying children.[87]

Governor O'Hara's use of war to weaken an adversary and to expand slave exports was the most spectacular example of a strategy that appealed to many Atlantic merchants. Brasseur, the French governor of Gorée, fantasized about using the Moors to weaken his enemies and expand slave exports, just as he contemplated forcing the *habitants* of Gorée to sell their slaves.[88] A French memoir of 1783 which reported on O'Hara's activities advocated fomenting war "between the Moors and the black kingdoms" as a way of increasing slave exports. According to the authors of this memoir the Wolof kingdoms failed to export sufficient numbers of slaves even though "there are among the Yaloffs and in the kingdom of Kayor as many negroes as in the Gold Coast or in Angola."[89] The problem was that the Wolof kings were not warlike enough, because the king "of Kayor only carries out raids when he is in great need."[90] This complaint, like similar ones written in the 1760s and 1770s, reflected the declining slave trade from Senegambia. Even the advocates of promoting slaving wars between the Moors and the Wolof admitted that these could only create "momentary, convulsive" increases in slave exports, but slave-trading merchants saw no other advantages from the African trade.[91]

Atlantic merchants who saw increased warfare between desert societies and savanna societies as the answer to declining slave exports were waging a futile battle against the trends of economic specialization that designated the Lower Senegal as a grain-producing region, and the western Sahara as a gum-exporting region in the economy created by Atlantic commerce. In fact, the controversial memoir of 1783, which favored war between "the Moors and the black kingdoms" represented only the opinion of the slave traders of Le Havre and Nantes. The Compagnie de la Guyane offered a diametrically opposed view of how the Senegal trade should be managed, based on its desire to obtain exclusive rights to the gum trade. According to Company merchants "the principal product of Senegal is gum." The colony could also furnish some ivory, some slaves, and gold dust from the mines in Bambouck.[92] According to the Company gum exports under the British occupation had reached over 2 million pounds, or 1,000 tons, although the French had only managed to export 500 tons a year in the period from 1778 to 1783. The trade in slaves "could be brought to 2,000 a year, but to obtain this number of slaves, Europeans had to favor war between the Moors and the negroes, and such a war could only harm the work needed for the gum trade and for the production of the mines [in Bambouck]." This report concluded that the gum trade was "the only product of Senegal that is really profitable for France."[93] By granting the Compagnie de la Guyane a monopoly over the gum trade, the French government seemed to agree that the future of Senegal was in gum rather than slave exports.

The slaving wars which haunted the imaginations of some Atlantic merchants had little impact on the secular trends in Atlantic commerce in the late eighteenth century. Slave exports declined steadily, at least in part because of the growing demand for slave labor in Saint Louis, in the gum forests, and in the grain fields. The new power of desert warriors, used by O'Hara in 1775, was based on the wealth provided by gum exports, but it also reflected a long-term drive by desert warriors to secure control over grain from the savanna. The villages left in Waalo after 1775 paid a tribute to the Moors, and the French in 1778 said that the Moors "left only as many inhabitants as was necessary for their annual pillages, which bring them as much as the saplings left in the forest to prepare for regular cuttings."[94] By the end of the century both Waalo and Kajoor were paying some tribute or protection money to the Trarza Moors as the desert-edge states gained in wealth and military strength with the profits of the gum trade.

The eruption of desert warriors in the Lower Senegal in 1775 was one symptom of the prolonged ecological crisis in the desert edge which resulted from the dry climatic patterns of the eighteenth century. The destruction of Waalo, once a prosperous and powerful state on the borders of the desert and the savanna, began during the drought of the 1750s when Waalo intervened repeatedly in Kajoor's civil wars, sometimes with the aid of Trarza warriors. Makodu Kumba Jaring, the Geej king who restored

Kajoor to a position of military and economic strength, conquered Kajoor from Bawol after it had been laid to waste by warriors from Waalo and the desert. When he became Dammel-Teeñ one of his first acts was to encourage a rebellion in Waalo that led to the definitive annexation of the provinces of Ganjool and Tuube, long disputed between the two kingdoms. This event, which occurred sometime after 1766, left a weakened Waalo between Kajoor and the Trarza. When the Trarza destroyed Waalo in 1775, they did so with the complicity of Kajoor. According to Yoro Jaw, Waalo fought almost continuous wars with Trarza between 1763 and 1800. "In the course of these wars the Moors destroyed 337 villages, the majority of whose inhabitants became their slaves, while the others took refuge in Cayor where they founded quarters in villages and even entire villages."[95] Massive enslavement in Waalo by Trarza warriors was more akin to conquest than slave raiding, and amounted to a dramatic shift in the border between the desert and the savanna.

The dramatic events that transformed Waalo into a weak buffer state dependent on Saint Louis made Kajoor-Bawol the dominant power in the Lower Senegal. The conflicts that erupted into violence in the 1770s were the culmination of frontier tensions that spanned much of the eighteenth century. But the conquest of Waalo in 1775 was a crisis in desert–savanna relations, not a shift in the political economy of the slave trade. The slave-raiding role which some European traders wished to confer on the Moors remained unrealized. In the early 1780s Europeans reported that victims of the slave raids of the 1770s who were carried into the desert continued to flee back into the Lower Senegal, sometimes with the aid of raiding parties from Waalo.[96] And by the 1780s French merchants in Senegal had opted for the gum trade and saw warfare between the desert and the savanna as counterproductive because it harmed the development of the gum trade.[97]

The new Geej regime that restabilized itself in the 1770s devoted new attention to agriculture in an effort to rebuild Kajoor-Bawol from the ruins left by famine and civil war. The state reemerged as a military force, and the *ceddo* army formed between 1770 and 1809 rivaled the military state originally formed by Latsukaabe. An infantry corps of about 500 trained riflemen, recruited from the ranks of the royal slaves, became the backbone of the Dammel's army. But this new military strength did not result in expanded slave exports. Instead, the restoration of Geej power was carried out by a king who personally directed the labor of 300 naked slaves at the first breaking of ground after the beginning of the rains.[98]

Islam and revolution

In the second half of the eighteenth century Senegambia was swept by a movement of Islamic reform and revival. In different forms the renewal of Islamic learning and Islamic political activism continued for over a century,

155

and the movements of the late eighteenth century were directly linked with the wave of reform that reached its peak in the mid-nineteenth century.[99] The geographical core of Islamic renewal was located at the congruence of the Atlantic and the desert-edge economies, in western Fuuta Tooro and northern Kajoor, in grain-exporting regions tied to the Atlantic and the desert trades.[100] In both regions peasants and slaves who produced grain surpluses were exposed to the violence of competing warrior aristocracies, and lived suspended between the reign of tribute and protection and the reign of theft and arbitrary violence. Like many warrior regimes the Wolof kingdoms attempted to create relations of protection and tribute between aristocratic warriors and agricultural producers and to keep predation within bounds. During periods of crisis these efforts failed and peasant communities and slaves bore the full brunt of aristocratic competition, interstate warfare, and ecological crisis.

Islamic scholars and merchants, caught between their own constituencies and the warrior elite, were directly implicated in the logic of tribute and protection. In western Fuuta Tooro and northern Kajoor they benefited most directly from the commercialization of grain surpluses in times of relative peace and stability. In times of warfare and ecological crisis they inhabited frontier zones exposed to warfare, famine, and commercial crisis. Ecological crisis and civil war overlapped with conflict in the Atlantic world, creating a succession of crises in the second half of the eighteenth century. This was the historic context in which Islam entered politics, first in Fuuta Tooro and then in Kajoor.

In Fuuta Tooro drought, famine, and warfare along the frontier with the desert dominated much of the eighteenth century. The revolutionaries who emerged in the 1760s began their careers by establishing communities under their own protection. The goal of the *toorobbe* ("reformers") was to protect their people from the Brakna Moors and the Saatigi regime, centered in eastern Fuuta. The leaders shared an education obtained at Pir in Kajoor and the determination to free at least part of Fuuta from the oppression of the Moors and the Saatigi. During the period of drought and ecological crisis that began in 1771 the movement gained strength, expanding its following by absorbing refugees, and Muslim armies succeeded in seizing power from the Saatigi in 1776.

The same period of drought was accompanied by important tensions throughout Senegambia, and Kajoor was no exception. In 1773 the French commander on Gorée took note of a spirit of rebellion in Kajoor, particularly on Cap Vert, and he reported to Paris that "several villages have asked me for aid against the Damel since my arrival on Gorée." He also reported a slave revolt on a British ship that had purchased "two hundred natives of Damel [Kajoor]," all of whom had perished when they set fire to the ship's gunpowder in the Gambia river.[101] These reports of unrest in Kajoor in the 1770s are suggestive, because Cap Vert was to play a major role in the movement of rebellion that swept Kajoor in the 1790s.

156

They also indicated that the stability achieved by the restored Geej dynasty was only partial. In the 1770s Kajoor appeared stable when compared to Waalo or Fuuta Tooro, but the crisis brewing between Muslim leaders and the old regime was only postponed for another two decades.

In spite of Kajoor's reputation in the early nineteenth century as the prototypical *ceddo* regime, recalcitrant to Islam and a stronghold of "paganism," there is little evidence from the period from 1766 to 1790 of a rupture between the monarchy and Islam,[102] European sources suggest that marabouts in Kajoor held an honored position at court in the late 1760s. "Their priests or marabouts are the educated class and they are the only ones who read and write Arabic. They are also the only ones who do not greet the king [by prostrating themselves] when they approach him. Instead they say a prayer and spit saliva on his head. These marabouts are at peace with everyone, they travel freely through the kingdom, and carry messages for the king. They can only be punished for the crime of treason."[103] Another European source described the Dammel Makodu Kumba Jaring (1766–78) as "constantly surrounded by marabouts who advised him on the future" and who constituted his inner circle of advisors.[104]

Dynastic traditions and oral traditions from Muslim villages portray Makodu Kumba Jaring and his successor Biraam Fatim Penda (1778–90) as pious Muslims. Biraam Fatim in particular was said to have "become a marabout" and conferred honors on Islam during his reign.[105] One of the reasons for this reputation was the positive reception given to the messengers sent by the Almaami Abdul of Fuuta Tooro, who urged neighboring kingdoms to adopt Islam.[106] The prestige and importance of Pir and Kokki as centers of Islamic learning also contribute to the impression that Islam had an established place in Kajoor in the late eighteenth century.

The reasons for the violent rupture between the court of Kajoor and the marabouts which occurred in 1790 remain somewhat unclear. One reading of the evidence suggests that reformist marabouts, encouraged by the status they enjoyed and inspired by the example of Fuuta Tooro, initiated the conflict. The movement in Kajoor was led by titled marabouts (Wolof, *seriñu lamb*), warrior clerics with arms and military experience. Dynastic traditions say that a general rising of Njambur province greeted the enthronement of Amari Ngoone Ndella, called back from years of exile in Waalo to assume the throne after the death of Biraam Fatim. The new king, supported by his army of *ceddo* defeated the marabouts twice, once outside of Kokki in Njambur, and again at Pir, driving the remnants of the marabout army into Cap Vert, where they sought refuge with the Lebu.[107] In these two confrontations between the marabouts and the monarchy the rebels were soundly defeated and many of their leaders were killed or taken prisoner and sold into slavery. French sources confirm that at least the first confrontation occurred in 1790 at the beginning of Amari Ngoone's reign. In August 1790 Boucher, the French commander at Saint Louis reported that no millet could be purchased in Kajoor "where there was widespread warfare."[108]

Sources from Muslim villages and families explain that the insurrection of Njambur was preceded by a series of confrontations between the marabouts and the royal slaves. Royal slaves attacked the village of a marabout named Malamin Saar, selling some of his relatives and students into slavery. In retaliation the marabout killed or captured several royal slaves, leading to a raid on his village. It was only after these events that the marabouts of Njambur organized a full-scale rebellion against the monarchy.[109] The confrontation betwen the monarchy and the marabouts developed in several stages. Dynastic traditions recall one battle in Njambur and another outside of Pir in the central provinces. The marabouts, who had formed an army, were defeated by the *ceddo* and killed or enslaved. The survivors took refuge in Cap Vert. This bloody conflict between the monarchy and Islam forms the root of the evil reputation of the Kajoor monarchy in the eyes of Senegambian Muslims. The defeated marabouts represented the most important Muslim villages of northern Kajoor: Luuga, Kokki, and Ñomre. Malamin Saar was Seriñ Luuga and his allies included most of the prominent Muslim families of Njambur, who were killed or sold into slavery.[110]

The insurrection of Njambur in 1790–1 was the first phase of the conflict between the monarchy and Islam. The revolt began in northern Kajoor, where the memory of the War of the Marabouts had taken hold.[111] The second phase of the Islamic movement took place in Cap Vert, another Atlantic province, but historically quite distinct from Njambur. The Lebu villages of Cap Vert had developed important trade ties with Gorée over the course of the eighteenth century. When the Lebu received refugees from Njambur in the 1790s, this proved to be the spark for the movement which led to the independence of Cap Vert.[112]

Cap Vert shared an Atlantic orientation with Njambur, but it was also the destination of an important caravan traffic organized by desert traders. European visitors to the coast from the mid-eighteenth to the early nineteenth century described the Moor caravans that purchased dried fish at Cap Vert and carried on an important trade in millet and other provisions, selling Indian cloth, animals, and European trade goods.[113] Europeans believed that the same Moor caravans brought Islam, which gained strength in the region throughout the eighteenth century.[114] In spite of the differences between Njambur and Cap Vert, they were the two provinces of the Lower Senegal which participated most actively in both the Atlantic and the desert trades, and the growth of commerce provided a fertile ground for the cultivation of Islam.

Several distinct perspectives inform oral traditions and early written accounts of the independence of Cap Vert. Some sources stress the leadership of Jall Joob, a marabout from Kajoor.[115] Jall Joob was one of the refugees from Njambur who arrived in Cap Vert after 1790. He played an important role in the decision to resist the Dammel and in organizing the defense of the peninsula. Other oral traditions present the conflict between Kajoor and the Lebu villages as a result of Kajoor's tyranny and collection of tribute. These sources do not mention the role of Islam or the leadership of the marabouts, but stress the military engagements between the Lebu and the army of the Dammel and the strategies which led to victory.[116] Rather than seeing one of these perspectives as more legitimate, they reflect different elements in the Lebu struggle against Kajoor, in which both Lebu villages and refugees from Kajoor played a key role. The alliance brought together committed Muslims and fellow travelers who supported the rebellion for their own reasons.

Lebu secession from Kajoor was the result of a protracted process of struggle. According to a British source from 1811, the first confrontations between the monarchy and the rebels occurred in 1791, almost immediately after the defeat of the marabouts of Njambur.[117] Armed conflict continued at least until 1811 or later, when the successor of Amari Ngoone Ndella made his peace with the Lebu.[118] The military success of the rebellion depended on the gradual creation of a series of fortifications across the peninsula. The Lebu first built a walled redoubt on Cap Manuel, at the extremity of the cape, and then gradually extended a series of stone walls or fences across strategic sites on the peninsula. The extension of the walls was a response to the blockade imposed by the Dammel, who tried to starve the Lebu into submission by denying them access to their fields.[119] In addition to their roles as fortified barriers, which could slow the cavalry and serve as shelters for rebels armed with guns, the walls were enchanted. In the alliance of Lebu and marabouts, the marabouts proposed the construction of the walls, which they then fortified with their prayers, promising that the *ceddo* of the Dammel would never cross them. This dual role of the walls appears in the account of Lebu independence by Maxwell in 1811.

> The peninsula of Cap Verd was included in the dominions of that prince [Dammel], but in consequence of the heavy contributions levied on them, and differing in their religious opinions from their fellow-subjects, the inhabitants of the peninsula, headed by an able chief, threw off their allegiance and erected themselves into an independent republic. They built a wall and fenced it with superstition. Damel assembled a large army to attack them; but such was the superstitious terror of this sacred wall, and perhaps the more rational dread of the brave and desperate men that were behind it, that though he remained in the vicinity several weeks, he never ventured a serious attack, and from famine and desertion amongst his ill-combined army, was obliged to return discomfited.[120]

The use of fortifications, even of a rudimentary kind, attracted the attention of Europeans in the early nineteenth century, who speculated that the inspiration came from the *habitants* of Gorée, who were familiar with European fortifications.[121] But the earliest written sources attribute the construction and enchantment of the wall to marabouts from Kajoor who took refuge in Cap Vert.[122] In reality, both marabouts from Njambur and the Lebu would have had ample opportunity to familiarize themselves with European techniques of fortification through their contacts with Saint Louis and Gorée, even without the direct intervention of the *habitants*. The *habitants* of Gorée did actively aid the Lebu during their rebellion by supplying them with guns and millet, as noted by Maxwell. "During the period that their independence was doubtful, they received much assistance from Gorée, and when Damel blockaded them, and obliged them to abandon their farther villages and provisions, and retreat behind their wall, they were supplied with corn from thence."[123] The French, on the other hand did not play an active role in spite of their previous efforts to purchase Cap Vert from Kajoor. In the 1790s, with revolution at home, and almost no maritime contact with France, French officials concentrated on maintaining a fragile hold on Saint Louis.[124]

The "enchanted wall" played the most critical role in the defense of the village of Dakar, near the extreme end of the peninsula. The protracted conflicts which eventually led to the independence of Cap Vert were fought on a series of fronts. In more outlying villages like Waakam and Yoof, the walls played a lesser role. Oral traditions from those villages stress the use of firearms, and more traditional defensive techniques, such as sending swarms of bees against the Dammel and his cavalry.[125] The commerce of Cap Vert with Gorée played a critical role in supplying the Lebu with muskets, as part of a more general exchange of provisions for European trade goods described by Maxwell. "They subsist on the produce of their agricultural labour, the cattle and poultry which they rear, their fishing, but above all, on the commerce they carry on with Gorée in fish, stock, vegetables, and many other necessaries of life; for this they receive in return, iron, tobacco, gunpowder, beads and muskets. With Gorée their connection is great and constant; to many of its inhabitants they are allied, and have been always considered as nearly the same people."[126]

In the conflict with Kajoor the Lebu enjoyed periods of success in which they took the war to Kajoor, because Maxwell related how "they, for a considerable time, made incursions into his territories, and made large pillages of Slaves and cattle." But Maxwell noted also that they had abandoned this practice in 1811, because of "two severe defeats" and the example of a village "destroyed by Damel."[127] By 1811 Maxwell estimated the population of Cap Vert to be 8,000, its independence secure, with the population "much increased by refugees from Cayor, maraboos from different parts of the neighborhood, and others, who found there greater security than they could elsewhere obtain." He also confirmed the Islamic character of the new state. "They are in general strict maraboos, conforming with regularity to the ordinances of their religion, and in particular, refraining from the use of vinous or spirituous liquors."[128] Like Njambur, Cap Vert was integrated into the Atlantic economy, and this integration had favored the progress of Islam.

The historic context of Lebu independence was also important for explaining its success. Lebu secession was the one exception to the success of Kajoor in defeating the forces of Islam in the 1790s. In 1795–6 Kajoor fought a major war with the Islamic state of Fuuta Tooro. The decisive defeat of the Almaami Abdul at Buukoy in 1796, when an army from Fuuta with allies from Jolof was destroyed and the Almaami taken prisoner, marked the turning point in confrontations between the old regime and Islam. The Almaami Abdul decided to invade Kajoor in the name of Islam to avenge the defeat and enslavement of the marabouts of Njambur in 1790–1. Many of the defeated marabouts had been fellow students of the Almaami at Pir, and the pleas of the survivors for aid provoked the intervention of Fuuta. By filling wells and destroying food supplies on the edge of the desert that separated northern Kajoor and Jolof, the Dammel was able to attack an exhausted, hungry, disorganized army with fresh troops. Many of the Almaami's *taalibe* were slaughtered, and many others were sold to the slave merchants.[129]

Mungo Park related the story of the battle as told by "singing men" in the Gambia in 1797, who focused on the victorious Dammel's treatment of his prisoner.

> When his royal prisoner was brought before him in irons, and thrown upon the ground, the magnanimous Damel, instead of setting his foot upon his neck, and stabbing him with his spear, according to custom in such cases, addressed him as follows. "Abdulkader, answer me this question. If the change of war had placed me in your situation, and you in mine, how would you have treated me?" "I would have thrust my spear into your heart," returned Abdulkader with great firmness; "and I know that a similar fate awaits me." "Not so, (said Damel) my spear is indeed red with the blood of your subjects killed in battle, and I could now give it a deeper stain by dipping it in your own; but this would not build up my towns, nor bring to life the thousands who fell in the woods. I will not therefore kill you in cold blood, but I will retain you as my slave, until I perceive that your presence in your own kingdom will no longer be dangerous to your neighbors; and then I will consider of the proper way of disposing of you." Abdulkader was accordingly retained, and worked as a slave, for three months; at the end of which period, Damel listened to the solicitations of the inhabitants of Foota Torra, and restored to them their king.[130]

Amari Ngoone Ndella also listened to the councils of his court, who feared the consequences of shedding the blood of such a prominent marabout. The Almaami was returned to Fuuta with an armed escort from Kajoor, with gifts of horses from the Dammel and other presents. But the Almaami Abdul was never again a threat to Kajoor, or any other state in the region.[131]

Several elements of the religious conflicts of the 1790s prefigured the much more extensive confrontation between the old regime and militant Islam that occurred in the mid-nineteenth century. First, there was a striking congruency between centers of dissidence and the regions linked most closely to the commercial networks of the Atlantic and the desert. This was true of Njambur and Cap Vert in the 1790s, and it would be true of Njambur and the Saalum valley in the mid-nineteenth century.[132] More ominously, the warriors of Islam had a strong tendency to assimilate the warrior culture of the old regime, even if it took a new Islamic form. The *taalibe* of the Almaami, as eager for war booty as anything else, prefigured the armies of *taalibe* and *sofa* ("slave warriors") who ravaged much of the middle Niger valley under the leadership of al Hajj Umar.[133] According to oral traditions the insurgents of Njambur even imitated the ritual drinking bouts of the *ceddo* before battle, but the Muslim warriors replaced the cursed alcoholic libations of the *ceddo* with tamarind juice.[134] In the nineteenth century Muslim warrior-scholars attempted to create a new political order in Senegambia. But by adopting the ways of the warrior their efforts often led to massive enslavement, famine, and destruction. It is probable that the religious wars of the 1790s provided more captives from the Lower Senegal to the slave traders than any other crisis since the famine of the 1750s.

The religious revolts in Kajoor in the 1790s were the precursors of the greater upheavals that occurred in the nineteenth century. In the eighteenth century, as in the nineteenth century, the centers of rebellion and secessionist sentiment were regions that had been most deeply affected by the development of maritime commerce and the grain trade. Northern Kajoor exported salt from coastal deposits, and was the center of important commercial exchanges with Saint Louis. Riverboats purchasing salt, grain, cattle, and other provisions stopped regularly at Ganjool, where the *habitants* of Saint Louis maintained permanent trading posts. Northern Kajoor was also the center of a camel- and donkey-based caravan trade carrying salt and European trade goods into the interior. The Lebu villages of Cap Vert sold fresh fish to Atlantic merchants, produced dried fish for export inland, and controlled the major trade routes linking Kajoor to Gorée. Lebu vessels competed with craft owned by the *habitants* in ferrying grain, fish, cattle, and other provisions from the mainland to Gorée. Atlantic maritime trade animated the commerce of all these regions, and provided an important stimulus to the spirit of rebellion that was articulated by the scholars of Islam.

6

From river empire to colony: Saint Louis and Senegal, 1800–1860

Colonialism emerged first in the Lower Senegal on the island of Saint Louis, where the eighteenth-century system of interlocking merchant networks was replaced by a colonial system based on European dominance and African dependency. The transformation of French interests in Senegal was a result of the new international order that began to emerge after the British victory over Napoleon. In West Africa the new order signaled the ending of the slave trade, channeling European ambitions in new directions. This change was only a project in 1817, but the French who reoccupied Senegal regarded the territory as a colony in a way that the merchant directors and royal officials of the eighteenth century never had. The change in attitudes was immediately recognized by the *habitants*. François Valentin, who represented a prosperous *métis* family wrote in 1819: "They [the *habitants*] see that their country no longer belongs to them, that the Europeans are the masters, that soon they will no longer form the majority, that the Europeans will become more numerous than them, that they will control all of the commerce, and that the government, like Saturn, will devour its own children."[1]

The most important change after 1817 was the nature of the French commercial presence in Senegal. Resident French merchants, mainly from Bordeaux, representing small commercial firms replaced the merchant directors and employees of trade monopolies. Resident merchants had profoundly different attitudes toward Senegal and the *habitants* than their predecessors. They had a long-term commitment to the colony, where they lived for decades at a time, unlike Company officials who had appointments that lasted for a few years. They also had a different attitude toward the firms they worked for. Owners or part-owners of small commercial firms, the resident merchants identified their personal interests with the profitability of their firms. While Company directors filled their own pockets at the expense of the Company, they viewed their employer as a secure, monopoly enterprise, controlled by Parisian bankers, supported by royal subsidies, and politically powerful. If the Company failed to show profits or went into bankruptcy, the men on the spot could be

163

confident that a new Company would be formed by financial interests and royal officials eager to secure a supply of slaves and gum arabic for the French empire.

The change in business organization and attitudes meant a change in the relations between Atlantic merchants and *habitants*. The intermediary role of the *habitants* represented a needless loss of profits to the resident merchants. Because they worked for small firms in competition with one another, they were unwilling or unable to fix the relationship between the purchase price of gum in the river ports and its resale value in Saint Louis. This price differential had guaranteed *habitant* profits in the past. Resident merchants lent Indian guinea cloth at one price and sold their own *guinées* for a lower price in the river ports, contributing to the financial ruin of the *habitants*.

The end of monopoly undermined the system of smuggling for personal profit which had formed the basis for the economic alliances between European merchants and *signares*. Even when nineteenth-century resident merchants married *signares*, as some of them did, the meaning of the relationship changed completely. Resident merchants had no interest in concealing their private trade operations by forming a liaison with a local woman and her family. Eventually, the old system of "marriages according to the customs of the country" broke down. After 1830, when the French civil code was introduced in Senegal, merchants either married *signares* under French law or kept concubines who were now nothing more than courtesans. This legal change was reinforced by a missionary assault on the lax Catholicism and morals of the *habitants*. In 1822 the first missionary sent by the Holy Ghost fathers, Fournier, arrived in Saint Louis and began a campaign against the superstition, moral corruption, and ignorance of the *habitant* Catholic community. His prime targets were the influence of Islam on so-called Catholics, and the immorality of customary marriage.[2]

The changes in commerce were paralleled by changes in government. After 1818 Senegal was ruled as a colony by a governor sent from Paris and supported by a colonial budget. Although the early colonial government was weak and dependent on the cooperation of the *habitants*, the governors after 1818 regarded themselves as the heads of a sovereign colonial state. The colonial government inherited the diplomatic and military responsibilities that had been managed by Company officials. The colonial government had to pay the customs duties demanded by African states, to protect French traders, to police the islands and forts under French command, and to manage the internal diplomacy required to maintain peace between the *habitants* and the French community. With the separation of political and commercial power, the new colonial government was empowered to collect customs duties on the import–export trade of the colony, and to tax and license merchants.

The period between 1818 and 1848 was a transition between the Atlantic commerce of the eighteenth century and the period of colonial expansion

Table 2: *Population of Saint Louis*[a]

1786	5,460
1798	8,000
1811	7,000
1819	9,000
1832	9,030
1838	12,081
1844	13,523

[a] Sources for estimates are Philip Curtin,
*Economic Change in Precolonial Africa:
Senegambia in the Era of the Slave Trade*
(Madison, 1975), II, 41; C 6 20, Blanchot à
Ministre, April 18, 1798; *British Parliamentary
Papers, Colonies, Africa* (Shannon, 1967), I, 151;
Michael David Marcson, "European–African
Interaction in the Precolonial Period: Saint Louis,
Senegal, 1758–1854," unpublished Ph.D.
dissertation, Princeton University, 1976, 38; 13 G
22, "Mémoire Laissé par M. Thomas," Dec. 11,
1845, and 3 G 2/124. These estimates
underestimate the population, because a large
floating population of free Africans was not
counted.

which began with the abolition of slavery on Saint Louis and Gorée in 1848 and continued in the 1850s and 1860s with military campaigns intended to secure French hegemony over strategic regions in the Senegal River valley. Gum exports dominated international trade, but the export trade in gum had a wide impact on the societies of the Senegal River valley.[3] The most obvious outgrowth of the gum trade was the expanding population of Saint Louis as shown in table 2. While the island's population had stagnated near 3,000 for most of the eighteenth century, the urban population grew much more rapidly after 1780 when gum exports began to rival slave exports in importance.

The population of Saint Louis, which depended entirely on food imports from the mainland, created an expanding urban market which was supplied by Kajoor, Fuuta Tooro, and Gajaaga. Although the transatlantic slave trade no longer played a significant role in commerce, the expansion of gum exports fueled a strong demand for slave labor in the desert, Saint Louis, and grain-producing regions. In all these ways there were striking continuities with the exchange patterns of the eighteenth century.

In the first half of the nineteenth century Saint Louis became the center of an expanding commercial empire. The commerce of Saint Louis made it one of the most important ports of trade in West Africa. While many other Atlantic ports went into decline because of the gradual abolition of the Atlantic slave trade, Saint Louis was transformed into a bustling urban center by the export trade in gum arabic.[4] During the gum boom of the 1830s and 1840s much of the city was rebuilt and to this day the architecture of Saint Louis attests to the commercial prosperity of the early nineteenth century. The gum trade was the lifeblood of Saint Louis, but it was also the source of growing tensions between *habitants* and Atlantic merchants. Conflicts between *habitants* and French merchants dominated the political and economic history of the islands.[5]

Saint Louis du Sénégal gave its name to the colony that gradually emerged after 1818 and the city of Saint Louis provided an economic and demographic base for the imperial expansion that began in earnest after 1850. Nevertheless, it would be a mistake to see the Senegal of the early nineteenth century as simply a smaller version of the colonial territory that was conquered in the late nineteenth century. Saint Louis was the commercial hub of a system whose trade hinterland encompassed much of the western Sahara and extended into the upper and middle Niger valleys, as well as the Senegal River valley. This river empire linked together the desert and the savanna, and early nineteenth-century descriptions of Senegal gave equal weight to the "Moors" of the right bank of the river, and the "Negroes" of the left bank.[6] Until well after 1850 exports from the desert outweighed savanna exports in importance. A commercial empire of this kind required no territorial conquests, and none were made in the period up until 1850. French policy focused on establishing favorable conditions for trade with the riverine states, and building forts along the river to protect French trade. In the trade hinterland the nineteenth-century river empire was an extension of the concessionary trade empire of the eighteenth century.

The slave society that emerged in Saint Louis in the eighteenth century was gradually transformed by an unprecedented wave of free migration from Waalo, Kajoor, Fuuta Tooro, and Gajaaga. Long before the abolition of slavery on the islands *habitant* merchants faced new competition from an expanding class of free African traders. These traders became the allies of Atlantic merchants in their drive to open up the river trade, which had virtually become the monopoly of the *habitants* at the end of the eighteenth century. Newcomers to Saint Louis, free African traders received goods on credit from French merchants and were often willing to serve as the direct agents of French commercial firms. This new threat to the commercial position of the *habitants* led to a dramatic change in *habitant* attitudes toward free trade. The *habitants* tried to protect their position by supporting restrictions which regulated the access of European and African traders to the gum markets. Throughout the 1830s and 1840s French colonial officials experimented with various ways of organizing commerce to reconcile the conflicting interests of French merchants, *habitants*, and free African traders. Since the French depended on the military and political support of the *habitants* and their slaves, French officials were not yet prepared to support the drive of Atlantic merchants to take over the river trade.[7]

The commercial economy of Saint Louis, built on the foundations laid down by the monopoly companies and *habitants*, underwrote the imperial visions of French naval officers and financed the expeditions of explorers who retraced the routes taken by Company officials in the seventeenth and eighteenth centuries. The nineteenth-century era of the river trade strongly influenced the goals and character of French colonialism as it emerged in the 1850s. French commercial and colonial interests were concentrated in a string of forts and *escales* along the Senegal River. Long before the French staked out any real claims to sovereign authority on the mainland, they pursued a forward policy in river towns like Richard Toll, Dagana, and Bakel, where forts were constructed in 1818–20. This chain of river forts was completed in the 1850s with the addition of forts at Podor and Medine.[8]

The river empire of the nineteenth century was based on the gum trade and the expansion of Saint Louis, but it rested as well on the imperial visions of Europeans who believed that the voyage upriver would lead them to the sources of the wealth from the east that had animated Atlantic commerce throughout the eighteenth century. The river held sway over the imagination because it had carried slaves, gold, and ivory to Atlantic ports for centuries. While French soldiers pursued these historical phantoms to the east and founded a vast inland empire after 1850, French commerce transformed the economic geography of Senegambia, turning the peanut fields of the Lower Senegal into the base of a new export economy. This process would eventually undermine the importance of the Senegal River as a commercial system. But the new export economy, like the gum economy which preceded it, was linked to the history of eighteenth-century Atlantic commerce. Peanut cultivation began in the grain-exporting regions of the eighteenth-century trade system.

Structural adjustment: the gum cycle in Atlantic commerce

Atlantic merchants saw Africa only as a source of exports to the Atlantic world. When economic and social development in the Atlantic world rendered one set of African exports obsolete, West Africa was faced with a period of structural adjustment if it wished to maintain its economic links with the Atlantic world. The classic case of structural adjustment was the economic transition between the period of the Atlantic slave trade and the period of so-called "legitimate" commerce which followed. In West Africa the history of structural adjustment depended on a number of factors, and took quite different forms in different regions. If the same merchant networks and labor systems that had supplied the Atlantic slave trade could supply the "new" export or exports, as was true of gum arabic in Senegambia, peanuts in the lower Gambia, and palm oil in the Bights

167

of Benin and Biafra, structural adjustment could be a relatively rapid process, essentially completed in 1850, and often providing the catalyst for early colonial expansion.[9]

In Senegambia the structural adjustment to the post-slave-trade era was rapid and successful from the point of view of Atlantic merchants. It nevertheless had a deep impact on the economic geography of Senegambia, and affected various regions in profoundly different ways. In the broadest sense this transition occurred between 1800 and 1850, in two phases. The first, from 1800 to 1840, was a gum cycle based on the river trade, and the second, from 1840 on, saw the emergence of a second export, peanuts, cultivated by peasants and slaves in the Atlantic coastal region and the Senegal River valley. The first cycle was an extension of trade patterns of the seventeenth and eighteenth centuries. There was no revolution in gum extraction, but there were fundamental changes in commercial organization, as the *habitant* commercial network was destroyed and replaced by a colonial one dominated by French merchants.

The gum cycle of the export economy tied colonial commerce to the complex economic ties that linked the desert and the savanna. This aspect of the gum economy was poorly understood, but it had a powerful impact on the growing struggle between French merchants, *habitants*, and free African traders, and pulled the emerging French colonial state into the political conflicts between desert and savanna states. Gum exports were extracted from stands of *acacia Senegal* on the desert edge. Gum arabic was extruded from the trees in the natural conditions of the desert-edge climate, but the extrusion of gum could be increased by scoring the bark of the trees shortly before the harvest.[10] In the nineteenth century gum was gathered by groups of up to fifty slaves working under the supervision of a marabout. The slave gangs included the slaves of the marabout and those of his kinsmen and allies. The marabout who served as overseer received the product of one day's labor per week from the slaves he did not own. Each slave could gather only about six pounds of gum per day, because gum-bearing trees were dispersed over a wide area.[11] Herds that accompanied the work teams supplied them with milk during the gum harvest, but work conditions were harsh, and gum extraction depended on the continuous import of slaves from savanna societies.

The gum extracted from the desert provided desert merchants with a product that could be exchanged for imported Indian cloth and millet.[12] During conditions of drought, when the subsistence base of desert society contracted, gum exports helped even out desert patterns of grain consumption, as imported savanna grain replaced reduced or lost desert-edge harvests. Economic need and the ecological factors promoting gum extraction coincided because conditions of drought following years of higher rainfall increased the natural extrusion of gum from the *acacia Senegal*.[13] The most dramatic expansion of gum exports occurred in the cycle of drought from 1828 to 1839. But the benefits of gum exports were unevenly distributed in the desert. Because the merchants organized the extraction of gum, they profited most from the gum trade. Hassani warriors taxed the trade, and they received food known as the "king's supper" from *habitant* merchants during the trading season, but their subsistence needs were met primarily by tribute collected from their clients and dependants.[14] As their subsistence base shrank during periods of drought, desert warriors often tried to extend the territorial base of their tribute extraction south into the savanna.

The social and ecological conditions of gum extraction strongly influenced gum exports, contributing to the boom and bust cycles typical of extractive economies.[15] The gradual destruction of gum trees by overexploitation and climatic stress led to a steady retreat of the gum-exporting regions to the south over the course of the eighteenth and nineteenth centuries. In the 1830s and 1840s, at the height of the gum boom in the Lower Senegal, the erratic export patterns intensified competition and conflict between merchant groups. Although none of these groups understood or could control the social and ecological factors that influenced the size of the gum harvests, they used their political influence with the French colonial government and with gum suppliers to influence conditions at gum markets. French merchants, who controlled supplies of imported cloth and credit, lobbied for free trade and free access to gum markets. *Habitants*, who had privileged relationships with gum merchants and desert political authorities, tried to restrict the access of both French merchants and free African traders to the gum markets. Free African traders, mainly recent immigrants to Saint Louis from neighboring states, tried to use their important position in the millet trade to obtain access to gum markets, where millet was one of the staples used to purchase gum arabic.

The struggle over merchant profits developed gradually, due to the unsettled conditions of trade in Senegambia early in the nineteenth century. French policy was partly responsible for the political turmoil that disrupted commerce. French colonial officials attempted to create a plantation economy on the lower river in the period from 1818 to 1828. Senegal was seen as a potential replacement for the loss of Saint Domingue. As an economic experiment the plantation economy was a total failure, historically more important for the wars it provoked than for its economic results.[16] In 1819 the Trarza Moors raided the plantations that had been established in the kingdom of Waalo. By 1820 the colony of Senegal was at war with the Trarza and with Fuuta Tooro, leading to a boycott of the gum trade and the collapse of commerce. Warfare continued in 1821, when the Trarza threatened French commerce by boycotting river markets and selling their gum to the British at Portendick, located to the north of the Senegal River on the Mauritanian coast.[17]

Waalo's alliance with the French was a calculated effort by the aristocracy to shore up its position in the face of multiple threats.[18] Since 1775,

169

following Kajoor's annexation of the provinces of Tuube and Ganjool and the devastating invasion by the Trarza Moors, Waalo was the weakest state in the Lower Senegal. The provinces north of the river had been lost to the Moors, and the eastern provinces which bordered Fuuta Tooro were threatened by conquest and internal revolt. Much of Waalo's population sympathized with the Islamic state of Fuuta Tooro, and whole villages had migrated across the border. Other groups sought refuge in Kajoor, where a stronger monarchy provided protection against Trarza raids and exactions by provincial warlords. Factional struggles between aristocratic families further weakened the monarchy, unleashing the chaotic violence of armed retainers, and making the Waalo peasantry easy prey to warrior bands from the desert and the savanna. In this context Waalo promised to provide land and workers to the French in exchange for over 10,000 francs in extra customs payments from the French.

At first the French hoped to model their plantation economy on the Dutch example in Indonesia. Local elites were to furnish "free laborers" in exchange for increased customs payments and a fixed fee per laborer to village headmen who provided workers. The kingdom of Waalo provided lands for the project, but the promised laborers never appeared.[19] By 1822 free labor had failed. A French official argued that the aristocracy of Waalo did not have the power to compel free persons to work.[20] He concluded that only slave labor under European control could supply the plantations with workers. The war of 1819–20 and the difficulties experienced in Waalo from 1819 to 1822 convinced the French that they would have to make far-reaching changes to ensure the success of the plantation project. In 1823 the French decided to legalize the slave trade from Gajaaga to supply indentured servants to the French colony.

Beginning in 1823 French merchants were allowed to purchase slaves in Gajaaga for shipment to Saint Louis, but in theory slaves introduced to the island were sold as indentured servants with fourteen-year contracts.[21] This decision appeared to conform with the anti-slavery principles proclaimed by the French beginning in 1818, but its real purpose was to solve the labor crisis in the plantation project. The use of indentured servants disguised the failure of free labor. At the same time it awarded the slave trade to the Compagnie de Galam, which supported the plantation project in exchange for a monopoly on the trade from Gajaaga.[22] From 1823 to 1830 the Galam Company provided the indentured servants required by the French plantations. Since the laws regulating the import of indentured servants were rarely enforced and easily subverted, the distinction between slaves and indentured servants lost almost all meaning.

The creation of a monopoly company in Galam was part of a complex compromise introduced in 1823 to stabilize the commerce in gum, provide workers to the plantations, and ensure the peace. Governor Roger made peace with the Trarza Moors by guaranteeing that Waalo would continue its tribute payments to the Moors, and by restricting the gum trade to official river ports where the trade could be easily taxed by Trarza political authorities. The *habitants*, who had played a key role in the diplomacy that led to the reconciliation of the Moors and the end of their boycott of French commerce, were rewarded by restrictions on the gum trade that gave them a monopoly on the trade in the river *escales*.[23]

For Atlantic merchants and *habitants* the plantation project was a pretext for the division of the river into exclusive spheres of commerce, in which the *habitants* received a monopoly over trade in the gum *escales* in exchange for a monopoly given to French merchants in the Gajaaga trade.[24] The losers in this deal were the free African traders of Saint Louis, who could only participate in the Gajaaga trade during the high water season, and French merchants who did not belong to the exclusive Galam Company.[25] This compromise brought stability to the gum trade in the period from 1823 to 1825 and reopened an interregional slave trade under the control of French merchants. Apart from supplying the plantations, the trade in indentured servants provided the French colonial army and navy with a source of recruits which supplied soldiers to Senegal and other French colonies in the 1830s and the 1840s.[26]

Before 1835, frequent warfare between Waalo, the French, and the Trarza Moors provided a strong rationale for the colonial government to continue policies which gave the *habitants* a privileged position in the gum trade. Throughout the period from 1824 to 1827 the *habitants* played a key role in the annual diplomacy which established the terms of trade. Tensions remained high between the colony and the Trarza, and brief wars occurred in 1827 and 1831. The conflict in 1827 was provoked by Trarza incursions in Waalo, where a succession struggle broke out following the death of the Barak. Because the French had no military forces that could be used in the interior, the French relied on the *habitants* to provide their *laptots* for retaliatory raids into Trarza territory.[27] The war of 1827 was the beginning of a long crisis at the desert edge.

The crisis in Waalo was the product of long-term factors and could not be resolved by French diplomacy and military intervention. The crisis of aristocratic rule, which encouraged Trarza military conquest and Muslim rebellion, was rooted in ecological crisis at the desert edge. The period of most acute crisis at the desert–savanna border (1827–35) occurred during one of then most intense periods of drought in West Africa (1828–39) in the last four centuries.[28] Although this drought cycle did not repeat the disasters of the great famine of the 1750s, it caused severe famine in the Cape Verde Islands and created intense pressures in the desert borderlands of the western Sahara.[29] In the desert societies of the western Sahara, the consequences of the drought were cushioned by food imports from the savanna, which could be paid for by gum exports. But this form of famine relief was most important for desert merchants and their clients.

The structure of desert society meant that the warrior groups were most affected by drought. They themselves maintained no permanent wells, and

171

had fewer slaves and less livestock than desert marabouts. During a prolonged period of drought it was imperative for them to extract tribute from populations with surplus grain. The movement of desert warriors into the savanna during periods of drought was a logical extension of their predatory way of life. Waalo was the weakest link in the chain of states along the desert edge, and each successive period of drought intensified the ecological pressures that blurred the transition between the desert and the savanna. The collapse of Waalo reflected changes in the environment and shifts in the human ecology of the lower Senegal valley. These changes resulted from the overexploitation of the fragile ecology of the northern savanna during the unusually dry climatic conditions of the eighteenth century.

Deforestation is the most easily documented change in the savanna and riverine environment near Saint Louis. Eighteenth-century observers like Adanson (1750s) described the estuary of the lower Senegal as an ecology of dense mangrove at the river edge, with stands of forest further inland, filled with birds and wildlife. Dense mangrove growth began just north of Saint Louis, and the islands near Saint Louis (Sor, Biseche) were heavily wooded.[30] A domesticated landscape of cleared fields and open pasture-land existed side by side with undeveloped woodland and mangrove. The demands of Saint Louis and the Atlantic economy for fuel and wood for shipbuilding contributed to the transformation of the environment over the course of the eighteenth century. Grain production and livestock herding in the vicinity of Saint Louis led to extensive clearing and the destruction of woodlands and mangrove.[31] Although none of these changes had dramatic effects on the human ecology of the river valley in times of normal rainfall, during the frequent periods of drought that punctuated the eighteenth century, they contributed to the crisis in desert–savanna relations.

The failure of the French plantation project, where crops withered under the desert wind, or died in soils ruined by erosion and salt, had its roots in the ecological changes which resulted from deforestation and the destruction of the mangrove borderlands.[32] By the 1840s the French described much of Waalo and the regions near Saint Louis as near desert, devastated by the harmattan, with their farmlands reduced by salt erosion, so that extensive pastoralism and intensive cultivation of fertile river floodplains became the primary resources of a relatively small population.[33]

Environmental changes in the lower river valley were most important for the way they contributed to a cycle of decline in Waalo that under-mined its viability as a savanna state. The inability of Waalo's warrior aristocracy to provide protection to village communities led to depopulation through emigration, and this depopulation further weakened the tributary base of aristocratic power, leading to further military defeats and emigrations.[34] On a voyage downriver from Podor to Saint Louis in the early 1750s Adanson counted "nine or ten villages on the north bank, and forty-seven on the south." By the mid-nineteenth century there were at most a few dozen villages on the same stretch of the river. The French estimated the total population of Waalo to be only 16,000, and believed that 150 Wolof villages had disappeared from the lower river valley between Lake Cayar [Kajaar] and Saint Louis in less than 100 years.[35]

The decline of the aristocracy in Waalo was balanced by the rising power of the marabouts. In 1824 when René Caillié visited the village of Mpaal, he described it as "entirely independent" and "governed by a marabout who is its sovereign master." Unlike many other villages in Waalo, Mpaal flourished on the basis of its trade with Saint Louis. "The inhabitants harvest in abundance everything that they require for their needs. Accustomed to live a very sober life, they often have a surplus, which they sell at Saint Louis. In exchange they receive arms for their defense, amber, coral, and glass beads to adorn their women. This village is reputed to be the richest in the vicinity of Saint Louis, with a population that can be estimated at two thousand, all of them marabouts."[36] The Muslims of the village protected themselves with guns purchased in Saint Louis, with prayers, and with a "magic stone," the abode of Maam Kantaar, the protecting spirit of the village. According to Caillié and village traditions, in times of danger the stone circled the village, produced rain out of season, and showered Mpaal's enemies with burning coals and flames. The stone was powerful in protection because the Moors participated in the cult which surrounded it, and left offerings just as the villagers did.[37] The story of Mpaal is a parable of sorts about life and social order at the desert edge in the early nineteenth century. Desert warriors replaced the *ceddo* as warrior predator-protectors, and the charismatic and economic power of Islam provided the new base for the social order.

The social crisis at the desert edge during the decade of drought conditions from 1828 to 1838 culminated in events that led to the destruction of the eighteenth-century commercial system. A civil war in Waalo from 1828 to 1830 led to the intervention of the Moors, Fuuta Tooro, and the French colony. Just when a compromise was reached Waalo was swept by a Muslim revolt. In the aftermath of these wars, the aristocracy of Waalo saw an alliance with the Trarza as the only way to preserve their power, and in 1833 the princess and *lingeer* Njumbott married the Trarza emir, Muhammad al-Habib.[38] This marriage alliance led the French to fear the emergence of a powerful Trarza state which would dominate both banks of the lower Senegal valley, and extend its power south into Kajoor.[39] In 1833 the French colony went to war with the Trarza to annul the marriage and end Trarza dominance in Waalo. Warfare accelerated the collapse of Waalo because French forces torched millet fields and raided granaries, leading to further emigration to Kajoor and Fuuta.[40]

During the French–Trarza war of 1833–5, underlying tensions in the

173

commercial community of Saint Louis were fully revealed. The *habitants* had profited from their *de facto* monopoly of the river *escales* since 1823 and refused to fight for the French or allow their *laptots* to serve with the French military forces.[41] In desperation, the French turned to the free African traders, promised them protection from prosecution for debt, and enrolled them as volunteers. Although they were used in French raids in 1833, the *traitant* ("trader") volunteers could not defeat the Trarza. French–*habitant* relations reached a low point in 1834, when the French blockaded the river to prevent the *habitants* from continuing their "disloyal" trade in gum with the Trarza. In the last year of the war the French decided to bring the *habitants* back into the picture by promising them a new monopoly on the gum trade, and allowing them to negotiate a new peace treaty in 1835. This decision helped end the war, but it in turn enraged French merchants, who now demanded free access to the gum *escales*.[42]

The tensions in Saint Louis were fueled by the boom in gum exports. When peace returned in 1835, Saint Louis was on the eve of a commercial revolution. The real structural adjustment that occurred during the gum cycle was a struggle between Atlantic merchants, *habitants*, and free African traders over the division of profits in the river trade. The gum trade revealed its potential to the French when they compared its success to the failure of the plantation economy. The total value of Senegalese exports and imports rose rapidly after 1823, based on the expansion of gum exports. The colony's commerce, worth 3.6 million francs in 1824, reached the value of 5 million francs in 1832, 7.7 million francs in 1835, 12 million francs in 1837, and 17 million francs in 1838. The dramatic expansion of Senegalese trade created unbounded enthusiasm in French colonial circles, where Senegal was compared to the Dutch East Indies and Australia.[43] Gum exports expanded rapidly in the decade from 1828 to 1838. In 1828 gum exports from Senegal reached 1,759 metric tons, which just surpassed the highest exports of the eighteenth century. In 1838 Senegal exported 4,200 metric tons, as exports more than doubled in the course of a decade.[44]

After 1836 French merchants began to trade upriver in the river markets, either directly or through free African traders who worked for salaries and commissions. The competition of French merchants in the gum trade precipitated a crisis which undermined the economic power of the *habitants*. The crisis was exacerbated by a sharp drop in the price of imported Indian cotton cloth. The *guinée* inflation gave a psychological edge to French merchants, who flooded the market with cheap *guinées* after lending cloth to *habitants* at higher prices. The fluctuation in *guinée* prices intensified the instability of markets in the critical years between 1836 and 1840, when French merchants made their bid to control the gum markets under the banner of free trade. Although strictly speaking trading conditions varied from year to year, and "free trade" was applied only in 1836, 1838, and

1840, the years from 1836 to 1840 were disastrous for the *habitants*.[45] Rather than relinquish market control to the French merchants, the *habitants* sold *guinées* at less than cost to preserve their privileged relations with desert merchants. By 1841 the *habitants* and free black merchants of Saint Louis owed the French commercial firms 2,250,000 francs.[46]

The gum boom collapsed rapidly as exports dropped in 1842–4 to the levels of the early 1820s. French colonial officials and *habitants* blamed the collapse on "free trade" and "excessive competition" in the gum markets, while French merchants blamed the "restrictions" on trade that were reintroduced to protect the *habitants* in 1842. In reality, the decline in gum exports was linked to the changing conditions of gum extraction in the desert. With the return of normal rainfall in the early 1840s, the ecological and economic conditions which had favored expanding gum exports disappeared. Desert markets were saturated with imported cloth and local grain supplies increased, with the result that less labor was devoted to collecting gum. This drop in gum extraction, combined with the crushing debt of the *habitants* and free African traders, led to the end of "free trade" and the reimposition of market controls designed to allow the *habitants* to recover some of their market share and repay their debts. But these market controls could only guarantee the *habitants* a share of the profits generated by the gum trade. The illusion of an expanding colonial economy based on gum exports was destroyed by the erratic and essentially static character of gum supply in the period from 1840 to 1850.

The gum crisis revealed clearly the underlying tensions in the merchant community of Saint Louis. French merchants wanted to use their economic strength to eliminate the remnants of monopoly that protected the *habitants* from open competition. But the French merchants found that the colonial state was compelled to protect the *habitants* so long as they held the keys to the diplomacy and military strength of the colony. At first the crisis reinforced the position of the *habitants*, who had many of their privileges restored after 1842. But their position depended on the graces of the colonial state. The dependency of the *habitants* was a sign of their weakness and would prove fatal when slavery was ended in the French empire in 1848. The merchant conflicts of the 1840s were prolonged by French weakness in the Lower Senegal. French efforts to reduce Trarza military strength in Waalo were a total failure, and by the mid-1840s the Trarza dominated the whole lower river valley from Saint Louis to Dimar in Fuuta Tooro, and collected tribute from every village in the region. "Free trade" would remain a dead letter as long as the Trarza dominated the lower river valley.

Slavery and emancipation on the islands: the formation of a colonial society

Ironically, Atlantic merchants triumphed over the *habitants* when a revolutionary government in France proclaimed the abolition of slavery in the French colonies. The *habitants*, who had emerged in the shadows of the Atlantic trade, fell victim to the crisis of slavery in the Atlantic world. Emancipation resulted from the colonial status of Saint Louis and Gorée in 1848. Because the *habitants* had failed to resist the imposition of colonial rule from 1818 to 1848, they were unable to oppose the laws which freed their slaves and undermined their social power. The passivity of the *habitants* in 1848, which contrasted sharply with their resistance to trade monopolies and seizures of their slave property in the eighteenth century, reflected the new colonial dependency which defined relationships between Frenchmen and Africans on the islands in 1848. Deeply in debt to European merchants and trading firms, faced with new competition from resident European merchants and their African employees, their activities restricted and regulated by laws enforced by the colonial government the *habitants* no longer controlled their own destinies and could not negotiate as equals with the European occupying power.

Emancipation undermined the maritime slave society that developed in the eighteenth century and reached its peak in the early nineteenth century. From 1800 to 1848 Saint Louis and Gorée remained slave societies linked to Atlantic commerce and the river trade on the Senegal. The majority of the slaves were women who pounded millet, prepared food for the island inhabitants, washed clothes and kept house. When not otherwise occupied women slaves spun cotton fiber into thread, which was woven into cloth by male slaves whose employment as weavers was justified primarily by the need to keep women slaves busy.[47] Male slaves were employed as sailors on the river and in the coasting trade, and worked as craftsmen and artisans with the specialized skills needed to construct and maintain a fleet of ships. *Habitants* continued to own the vast majority of slaves, particularly the skilled sailors and craftsmen who were rented to the French administration and French merchants.

Habitant control over skilled slave labor and the specialized fleet of vessels used on the Senegal River reached its peak during the gum boom, in the decades preceding emancipation. In 1825 the *habitants* controlled a fleet of 109 coasting vessels and river craft, with a capacity of 1,886 tons, and 164 small craft of various kinds (pirogues, sloops, and flat boats) with a combined capacity of 349 tons.[48] The riverboats and coasting vessels which made up the bulk of the fleet ranged from 5 tons to 50 tons. The entire fleet had been constructed at Saint Louis or Gorée. Local wood was used in ship construction, although most of the other construction materials, such as fittings, nails, and pitch, were imported from France or the United States.[49] Skilled slaves built the ships, and slave *laptots* formed the vast majority of the crews who worked in the river trade.

In the 1820s the French administration made several surveys of the labor force employed in maritime and river commerce. The data collected revealed the dependency of the economy on slave labor. In 1821 the merchant vessels of Saint Louis and Gorée employed a labor force of

Table 3

	Vessel captains[a]	Pirogue pilots	Sailors	Total
Europeans	5	–	–	5
Free blacks[b]	8	30	200	238
Freed slaves	4	–	6	10
Slaves	44	200	1,447	1,691

[a] The terms used in the source are *maîtres de cabotage, patron de pirogues*, and *marins*: 0 3, Navigation et Marin, Table 1821.
[b] This survey, like others in this series (0), was compiled by the navy, and uses terminology that differs from that of most other administrative documents. The term translated as "free black" here is *aborigène*, or "native" of the islands, and it included both *habitants* and free black traders or *traitants*.

1,944, including 1,691 slaves, as shown in table 3. Slaves dominated all categories of seamen, from commanders of medium-sized craft to ordinary sailors.

Other surveys of the labor force confirmed the overwhelming predominance of slaves in the merchant marine. The only substantial change between 1821 and 1826 was a decline in the number of free black sailors and commanders to 51, and a rise in the number of freed slaves to 151. Slaves still formed the vast majority in all categories of employment.[50]

Slave sailors were the only group of skilled seamen in the 1830s and 1840s. This dependence on slave labor presented legal problems for the French merchant fleet and the French navy. Ocean-going vessels frequently lost part of their European crews to disease on the African coast. When this occurred in Senegal, it was almost impossible to hire free African sailors to replace the Europeans for the return voyage to France. Slave sailors were available, but French law did not protect slave property once a slave had reached French soil. French ships were sometimes forced to purchase slaves and free them before they could hire them as sailors. The slave rental system which served the French within Senegambia could not be extended to ocean-going vessels returning to Europe.[51] The French navy also found the slave rental system inconvenient. Slave sailors rented for thirty francs a month in 1839, but the navy was forced to pay more than this or experience labor shortages because slaves rented out by merchants received trade goods and opportunities to trade in addition to their wages and they preferred commercial employment to work on French naval vessels.[52] Because the *habitants* owned most of the slave sailors, they could withhold their labor when there were conflicts between their interests and those pursued by the French administration.

The French saw indentured servants imported from Gajaaga as the only real alternative to slave labor in spite of the important wave of free emigration to Saint Louis from the mainland. The free blacks who came to Saint Louis aspired to become merchants rather than laborers. During the struggle between French merchants and *habitants* for control over the commerce of Saint Louis it was easy for free blacks with no capital to become petty traders working as agents for French commerce. This undermined the eighteenth-century pattern in which new immigrants started their careers as *laptots* and gradually acquired the capital needed to enter commerce.[53] The decline in the number of free black sailors reflected this trend. In the nineteenth century free black traders with little capital began in the. millet trade, and tried to move on to the more lucrative and prestigious trade in gum.[54] The main constraint on poor traders was the cost of acquiring a boat that could be used in the millet trade. Once a trader owned a small boat capable of making the voyage to Gajaaga, the highly profitable exchange of salt for millet at Bakel could serve as the base for accumulation.[55]

In the 1830s and 1840s slaves formed the absolute majority of the population on Saint Louis and Gorée. In 1836 a preliminary census of the slave population on Saint Louis and Gorée counted 9,849 slaves, including 3,353 children fourteen or younger, 5,568 adults from the ages of fourteen to forty years, and 928 slaves over forty years of age.[56] The most detailed census of slavery was undertaken in 1845, three years before developments in France would lead to emancipation. The census data was gathered on orders from the French government, which complained that Senegal had been exempted from all the reforms which had affected slavery in the other French colonies and had still not provided the French government with a complete census of the slave population.[57] The census of 1845 counted 10,196 slaves out of a total population of 18,753 on Saint Louis and Gorée.[58] According to another document from the same year (which counted 10,096 slaves), the distribution of the slave population was 6,061 on Saint Louis, 236 on the adjacent fishing village at Guet Ndar, and 3,799 on Gorée.[59]

The census data was returned to Paris with a defense of slavery in the colony of Senegal. The report argued that slavery in Senegal differed fundamentally from slavery in the other colonies. Specific points supported this claim: (1) there were no field slaves in Senegal; (2) many slaves were domestic servants; (3) slaves owned property and even other slaves; and (4) slaves received wages. The report concluded with the ludicrous claim that slaves in Senegal were "a thousand times happier than the free inhabitants of the mainland." Because Africa "was the original homeland of slavery" and because "Saint Louis and Gorée were surrounded by peoples who accepted and practiced slavery" it was impossible to expect Senegal to follow the same policies as other French colonies.[60]

The surveys of slavery undertaken in the 1830s and 1840s provide important information on the slave populations of Saint Louis and Gorée. This documentation provides a reasonably accurate census of the slave population, providing information on the occupations, age and sex composition, origins, and fertility of the slave population. The most detailed

178

records come from Gorée, where the influence of Catholicism among the *habitants* contributed to their more rigorous compliance with French laws requiring them to record births and deaths and comply with administrative surveys.[61] In 1847 a survey of the slave population on Gorée provided a complete occupational profile of the "active" slave population, between the ages of fourteen and sixty. This group consisted of 983 men and 1,407 women. In descending order, male slaves were sailors (312),[62] masons (118), weavers (107), laborers (92), joiners (90), ship's carpenters (73), cooks (59), servants (28), blacksmiths (15), coopers (10), bakers (7), traders (5), stokers (4), tailors (4), with a scattering of individuals in lesser trades, and 44 slaves with no particular skill (*sans profession*).[63] Women slaves were employed as millet pounders (965), laundresses (274), seamstresses (51), cooks (40), servants (24), and traders (5), plus 1 day laborer, and 51 women slaves with no particular skills.[64]

The slave populations of Saint Louis and Gorée were highly skilled, and held a virtual monopoly over many trades. Male slaves more frequently received special training in their crafts. On Gorée seventy-nine slave boys under the age of fourteen were apprenticed in trades, while all of the girls, and the remaining 479 boy slaves, were described as having no particular skills.[65] The education of girl slaves was informal, since most were employed as domestic laborers requiring skills and knowledge shared by slaves and free women on the mainland. Nevertheless, women working as seamstresses and cooks were skilled workers, as these terms referred to special knowledge of European tailoring and European cuisine that gave these slaves special value and permitted them to produce marketable commodities or rent out their labor. The slave labor force on Saint Louis was similar in composition to Gorée. The main difference was that a higher proportion of male slaves in Saint Louis were employed on merchant vessels. While sailors formed about a third of the male slave population on Gorée, on Saint Louis more than half of the male slaves worked as *laptots*.[66]

Slave holdings on Gorée and Saint Louis ranged in size from one slave to more than 100. Based on a survey of 120 slave-owning households on Gorée, about 40 percent owned from one to five slaves, while 25 percent of the households owned six to ten slaves. The remaining 35 percent of slave owners were equally divided between households with eleven to twenty slaves and households owning more than twenty slaves.[67] In this last category (households with more than twenty slaves), an important difference can be seen between Gorée and Saint Louis. Very few of the large slave owners on Gorée owned more than thirty slaves, and only ten households owned more than fifty slaves. A much less complete survey of individual slave holdings on Saint Louis shows seventeen owners with more than fifty slaves. But many of the largest slave owners on Saint Louis were closely related to one another.[68] The larger size of slave holdings on Saint Louis reflected the greater wealth of Saint Louis.

Another characteristic of slave holdings was their diversity, which echoed the sexual and occupation profile of the entire slave population. Most slave owners, large and small, owned men and women with a variety of skills, although women tended to predominate. One slave owner on Gorée with twenty-five slaves owned nine men (four sailors, two weavers, one mason, one ship's carpenter, one joiner) and twelve women (all described as millet pounders), plus four children.[69] This lack of occupational specialization was the norm. Its economic logic was based on the common practice of renting out slaves. Even a small slave owner with only a few slaves might wish to own a slave with specialised skills as a sailor, because such slaves could be rented out to European merchants or *habitants* in the peak trade season. More rarely in large slave holdings there were concentrations of occupational skills that suggest that skilled slaves worked together in a kind of workshop system. The Aubon family of Gorée, with seventy-two slaves, owned ten seamstresses.[70]

Data on slave fertility, slave mortality, and slave origins are fragmentary, but far more detailed than data from the eighteenth century. The 1847 census of Gorée permits a comparison of the fertility and death rates of slaves and free blacks. The crude birth rate of the slave population was thirty-seven per 1,000, compared to thirty-one per 1,000 for free blacks.[71] The death rate of slaves was slightly lower than that of free blacks, forty-one per 1,000 compared to forty-five per 1,000. Nevertheless, the gap between the two groups was not great, and the most important aspect of the data is the fact that deaths exceeded births in both groups in 1847 (154 slave deaths and 134 births, 52 deaths among free blacks and 32 births).[72]

This data on mortality and fertility can be supplemented by the information provided by a detailed list of slave deaths on Gorée in 1835 and 1836. The list, in the most complete entries, gives the name of each slave, his or her age, the slave owner, and the cause of death. Although some of the information should be treated with skepticism, the sample can be used to reconstruct the most dangerous times of life in the slave life cycle. The "ages" recorded for adult slaves tend to cluster around decades. Adult slaves are described as twenty, thirty, or forty, categories which suggest "young adulthood," "mature adults," and "old age" rather than real ages in years. In a sample of 100 slave deaths, 17 percent of deaths were of infants from birth to one year, 21 percent were small children between one and five years, 27 percent of deaths were children and teenagers under twenty years, 12 percent of deaths were in the group of young adults from twenty to thirty years of age, 12 percent were over thirty years of age, and 4 percent were slaves over fifty years of age.[73] The most striking fact is that 65 percent of recorded deaths occurred in the population under twenty years of age, suggesting that infant mortality and childhood diseases were the most important limiting factors on natural population growth in the slave population. This helps explain why census data divided the population into three age groups, children under fourteen, an active population from fourteen to sixty years of age, and slaves over sixty. Children under fourteen were the group most at risk to early death from disease.

Fertility and death rates for the slave population would lead to a demographic projection of a population declining at a modest rate of about 1 percent per year. In reality the slave populations of Gorée and Saint Louis did decline in the period betwen 1832 and 1845. The rate of decline on Gorée was very close to 1 percent per year between 1832 and 1847, two years with good census data, as the slave population declined from 4,355 to 3,645.[74] In the period between 1832 and 1845 the slave population of Saint Louis declined at nearly the same rate, from 6,966 to 6,061.[75] However, in the same period the free black population on Gorée grew by slightly more than 1 percent a year, from 906 in 1832 to 1,116 in 1847, in spite of slightly lower birth rates in the years in which data are available.

The ratio of births to deaths in the slave population forms only part of the explanation for the 1 percent annual decline in the number of slaves in this period. During the economic crisis caused by declining gum exports and growing *habitant* debt, the *habitants* sold off some of their slaves on the mainland in order to pay off their debts.[76] Selling off slaves was only one source of slave losses on Saint Louis and Gorée. In October, 1848 the census on Gorée reported an abrupt drop in the slave population of 827 slaves. The causes were "unreported deaths, runaways, voluntary manumissions" and the fact that "slaves who have resided for a long period in the Gambia have not been considered as part of the population of Gorée, because they are in fact free."[77] This reevaluation of the slave population was motivated by the approach of emancipation and the refusal of the French to pay compensation for slaves who could not be physically produced by their masters. Runaways who fled prior to the debate on emancipation in 1848 constituted a significant drain on the slave population.[78] "Voluntary manumissions" is a misleading description of the process by which slaves purchased their own freedom. Between 1830 and 1841 261 slaves purchased their own freedom for an average of 750 francs.[79] The cumulative number of these liberations cannot be quantified, but they help to explain why the free black population on Gorée expanded in spite of fertility and death rates that differed little from those of slaves.[80]

The rate of decline in the slave population was less than might have been expected, given birth and death rates, individual manumissions, slave runaways, and the occasional sale of slaves. The most likely explanation of this discrepancy is the continuation of slave imports to the islands, at least on a small scale. Further evidence for this can be found in the sex ratios of male and female slaves. If slave imports had ended in 1823, this would have led to a gradual decline in the slave population, and the gradual emergence of equal sex ratios, first among slave children born on the islands and then among the adult slave population. Any labor deficit

181

would have been filled by an expansion of the numbers of indentured servants. There is evidence of this occurring on Saint Louis in the 1830s, because in the census of 1832 the ratio of male to female slaves was 987 per 1,000.[81] On Gorée, by contrast, the ratio of male to female slaves ranged from 690 to 750 per 1,000 in the 1830s and 1840s and the predominance of females remained notable among slave children under fourteen.[82] This contrast correlated with the much larger numbers of indentured servants on Saint Louis than on Gorée.

The census data from Gorée suggests a very age-specific and sex-specific slave trade. A survey of the population of slaves and indentured servants in 1847 reveals two complementary trends. First, there was a preponderance of adult men in the population of "illegally" imported slaves (eighteen of twenty-one illegal slaves) and indentured servants (seventy-one of ninety-one indentured servants). Secondly, there was an important excess of girls in the population of slave children under fourteen years of age (671 girls and 574 boys).[83] The simplest explanation is a clandestine slave trade in young girls. This was precisely the pattern which emerged on Saint Louis after 1848, involving girls from the ages of seven to ten years of age.[84] The legal import of adult male indentured servants and the illegal trade in slave girls reflected labor demands and the relative difficulties of concealing illegal slave imports in these two groups. While the demand for male slave labor was for adult males, the group most difficult to smuggle onto the islands without being detected, girls performed many of the same domestic tasks assigned to women slaves, and could more easily be smuggled onto the islands and concealed until they could be passed off as part of the native-born slave population. The *habitants* filled the shortages in the male labor market by purchasing indentured servants, while an illegal slave trade from the mainland supplied young girls.

The need for a small-scale slave trade to sustain a diminishing slave population would seem to support interpretations which stress the inability of African slave populations to sustain themselves through natural increase.[85] For example, if one adjusts the census figures from Gorée in 1847 to get a closer approximation of the number of women of child-bearing age, the result is that there were 1,241 children under fourteen for 1,171 fertile women, or only slightly more than one child per woman.[86] This kind of calculation needs to be qualified in two important ways. The high rates of infant and child mortality on Gorée suggest that the actual number of live births would have been much higher than the number of living children. Secondly, without detailed information on the age composition of the population any estimate of this kind underestimates the birth rate. Census data which distinguishes only children and adults (in this case with adults being defined as anyone over fourteen) will inevitably list mothers and daughters, and mothers and sons in the same "adult" category.[87] For these reasons the crude birth and death rates are much more reliable guides to the demographic profile of the population. On

182

Gorée the birth and death rates, and the overall rate of population decline, suggest that the slave population came very close to sustaining itself by natural reproduction. The excess of deaths to births had more to do with the disease environment of a dense urban center than with slavery.[88]

The data on slave origins in census records suggests an important shift in the sources of slave supply for the islands in the nineteenth century. In the eighteenth century most of the islands' slaves had come from the same upriver sources that supplied the export slave trade. Both Saint Louis and Gorée had slave neighborhoods known as "Bambara" quarters in the eighteenth century. Nineteenth-century census records that list birthplaces show a different pattern. In the mid-nineteenth century most slaves were born on the islands, and the rest were from the immediate hinterland of Saint Louis and Gorée. One slave list which provided seventy-one slave birthplaces listed twenty-eight slaves born on Gorée, one on Saint Louis, one in "Joal," five in "Galam," one in "Walo," nineteen in "Sine," six in "Baol," three in "Cayor," two in "Salum," and five were described as "mandingues."[89] Another slaveholding listed sixty-four slaves born on Gorée, six in "Sine," two in "Baol," two in "Cayor," and one "Nones."[90] When an effort is made to correlate the information on origins with data on age structure, the resulting pattern suggests that the shift to more local slaves occurred at the end of the eighteenth century rather than as a direct response to French efforts to outlaw or regulate slave imports after 1817.[91]

The occupational and demographic profile of the slave population on the islands of Saint Louis and Gorée helps to explain the course of emancipation on the islands, once it was decided by events in the wider Atlantic world. The urban slave population contained a high proportion of skilled laborers, and a high proportion of native-born slaves. While comparative data suggests that such slaves were unlikely to revolt (they had too much to lose), they were also well prepared to understand and to take advantage of emancipation. The French, who deluded themselves with clichés about the catastrophic consequences of emancipation, argued that the slaves of Senegal were incapable of understanding freedom, that they would refuse to work if they were freed, and that they would quickly return to the security of their masters' households and virtual servitude.

The inability of the colonial administration to even contemplate emancipation before 1848 is hardly surprising.[92] For French officials slavery was a fact of life, a "natural" part of the African social order. Even when they defended the practice of slavery in Senegal, it was purely a matter of convenience that aroused little passion. Few of the reports on slavery showed any real understanding of the institution or of the conditions under which slaves lived and labored. French officials seemed unaware that the principal victims of emancipation would be the *habitants*, whose wealth was heavily invested in slavery. Even French resident merchants, who had struggled for over twenty years to reduce the influence of the *habitants*, showed no prescience of the fact that slave emancipation was the perfect weapon to employ against a slave-owning class that had thus far been able to frustrate their drive for hegemony.

On the issue of slavery, the *habitants* were doubly disarmed. Two decades of efforts by the colonial administration to persuade the French government that slavery in Senegal differed fundamentally from slavery in the other French colonies and should be exempted from colonial emancipation lulled the *habitants* into complacency. Local colonial officials gave them little reason to fear that anti-slavery would ever be used as an arm in the struggle between French officials, French merchants, and *habitants* for control over the commerce of Saint Louis. In addition, when the crisis came, colonial officials could count on the desire of slaves for their freedom to undercut any resistance by the *habitants*. In previous crises with the French and British, the *habitants* had relied on the military force of their slaves or on the economic disruption they could cause by withdrawing their slaves from the labor market. Neither of these options was open in 1848. Because the autonomy of the *habitants* depended to a large degree on their position as slave owners in a slave society, that autonomy was effectively destroyed by slave emancipation.[93]

For colonial officials emancipation was an administrative problem that could be approached with detachment, once emancipation was decided. The slave owners with the most to lose were the *habitants* and their interests did not provoke passionate concern. For similar reasons, the French were not deeply concerned with the fate of the slaves they liberated. Almost every action taken by the colonial state was a countermove to African initiatives that threatened to disrupt the implementation of the emancipation decree. One of the first problems that arose was the need carefully to circumscribe the scope and limitations of the decree, which in theory made French soil in Senegal an island of liberty in a sea of slavery.[94] In 1848 two immediate problems arose. When the *habitants* threatened to sell their slaves in the interior, the French contacted the principal political leaders and traders along the Senegal River, warning them that if they purchased slaves from the *habitants* the French would welcome runaway slaves from their territories.[95] At the same time French officials reassured neighboring states that under normal conditions the emancipation decree would have no effect on slavery outside of French territory and received authority from Paris to expel unwanted runaway slaves from the colony.[96]

Within the colony of Senegal the emancipation decree provoked important tensions between masters and slaves, particularly in Saint Louis. Bloody conflict was narrowly averted, but Saint Louis lived through several tense months between April and August of 1848. Slaves greeted the decree with joy, while masters were filled with fear and apprehension. With slaves and masters mobilized to resist or defend the emancipation law, new conflicts broke out within *habitant* households. By June masters complained to the governor that their slaves no longer obeyed them and pleaded for French help.[97] A twenty-year-old male slave beat his mistress and threatened to kill her. He was immediately arrested, and Governor Du Chateau warned slaves to respect their masters until their emancipation. Three masters were accused of inflicting corporal punishments of severe brutality, in defiance of the emancipation decree. They were charged and tried in French courts.[98]

Tensions reached their peak in July and August, when the French reported rumors that the *habitants* and free African traders had formed an alliance and planned to massacre the French and flee to the mainland with their slaves. Other rumors predicted mass demonstrations against emancipation and an alliance between the *habitants* and the Trarza.[99] In response to these threats, the French governor contacted the slave population and encouraged them to form an emancipation club which eventually attracted 500 members.[100] The governor's report on his contact with the slaves makes it clear that they were already organized, because he was able to use their organization to inform himself about events in Saint Louis. The slaves also promised their aid against internal or external enemies.[101] In this tense climate conflicts reached their head when Samba Agui, one of the masters arrested for brutality, was found guilty by a court. Charged with beating a slave, and declaring his intention to defy the emancipation law, he was sentenced to five days in jail. When the news of this sentence reached the *habitants*, the case of Samba Agui became a *cause célèbre*, and the *habitants* vowed to resist if he was found guilty on appeal.[102]

Samba Agui was a particularly interesting symbol for tensions between masters and slaves. A former slave himself, he had become one of the wealthiest and most respected merchants of Saint Louis and a substantial slave owner with eighty-seven slaves.[103] As a self-made man who rose under the old order, Agui particularly resented a law which threatened to erase the distance he had placed between himself and his former slave status. The result of the case was paradoxical. The French governor called out the troops to protect public order, and publicly received the support of over 400 slaves who gathered outside the court house to show their support for the governor and the French. But the appeal itself was a victory for Samba Agui and the *habitants*, as he was acquitted and left the court to the acclaim of the *habitants*. Nevertheless, in spite of the slaves' disappointment at the acquittal, the overall impression left behind was that the slaves were stronger than their masters, if it came to a show of force. The acquittal of Samba Agui was the last serious attempt by the *habitants* to defy the emancipation decree.[104]

The most important long-term effect of emancipation was that it completed the impoverishment of the *habitants* that began with the crisis of the gum economy. This occurred in spite of the indemnity that was paid by the French government to slave owners, which in Senegal averaged 330 francs. Although the indemnity compared favorably to the purchase price of a new slave on the river (300 francs), it represented only twice the annual return to a master for a skilled slave who rented out his or her labor for twelve months.[105] Furthermore, the French used their powers to verify slave ownership to reduce the number of slaves from 10,075 to 6,703.[106] The way in which the indemnity was paid reduced its value for most *habitants*. The French government paid almost 95 percent of the indemnity in the form of certificates which could be converted into interest-bearing bonds.[107] The *habitants* sold at least one-third of the certificates for cash or trade goods for two-thirds of their face value. When the certificates were exchanged for trade goods, as was frequently the case in Saint Louis, the real value was further reduced by the normal mark-up on trade goods. French merchant firms acquired the lion's share of the certificates. They circulated as a kind of paper currency among French merchants and were used to settle debts with France. Eventually the certificates formed part of the capital that was subscribed when the Banque du Sénégal was founded in 1855.[108] The less wealthy and well connected of the *habitant* slave owners were most likely to sell their certificates to French merchants.

Emancipation was the ruin of the *habitants* as a distinct social group. The blow seems to have fallen particularly heavily on the *métis* Catholic population. When Frederic Carrère and Paul Holle wrote about their society in the early 1850s they lamented the passing of slavery and the extinction of "the intermediary race," once influential and wealthy, now ruined, and blamed emancipation for the rise of Muslim fanaticism and the decline of French civilization in Saint Louis.[109] Abbé Boilat, describing Saint Louis in the same period, wrote: "The beginning of the trading season is no longer a cause of joy for families, but of chagrin and sadness: it means the sale of their homes or their land on the order of the courts and the mortgaging of what little remains to them."[110] On the other hand, Boilat described the freed slaves "as the class of people . . . most happy at present." Trained as skilled workers from their youth, slaves continued to practice their trades, and they were now able to keep all of their wages for themselves.[111] The leveling of society by emancipation was far from complete. Some merchant families were able to reestablish their fortunes by trading on the margins of the expanding colonial economy in the second half of the nineteenth century. They were joined by some former slaves, who became merchants and followed their masters to the remoter outposts of the French commercial empire. But successful independent African merchants were a minority, and most of Saint Louis' traders became the agents of European firms.

The era of the *habitants* was over. Never again would the *habitants* see themselves as the masters of Saint Louis and Gorée, a merchant slave-owning elite that exercised real control over river commerce and the slave laborers who had provided the backbone of its labor force. To regain some of their former influence, the *habitants*, led by the *métis* elite, turned to politics and to administrative service. Most importantly, they began to appropriate for themselves their identity as French citizens, which was one of the legacies of the revolutionary events of 1848. That appropriation would eventually lead them to play a leading role in the emergence of a modern politics of protest in the colony of Senegal.

The river empire at mid-century

In the 1850s the trade of Senegal recovered dramatically from the gum crisis. The new phase of expansion was made possible by the rapid expansion of peanut cultivation in the Senegal River valley after 1840, particularly in Kajoor. The expansion of peanut exports gave the colonial economy an economic base independent of the gum trade and river convoy traffic, which could be disrupted in time of conflict.[112] Kajoor supplied three-quarters of peanut exports. Most of the peanut crop came on boats from Ganjool or overland through territories outside Trarza control. During the late 1840s the collapse of the gum boom had provoked widespread economic suffering in Saint Louis and pessimism about the future of the French colony. Although few realized it at the time, the solution to Saint Louis' problems was already at hand. During the gum crisis of the 1840s French merchants began accepting peanuts in payment for debts owed by *habitants* and African traders.[113]

The gum boom had blinded French merchants to the possibilites of the peanut trade, which began in the Lower Gambia and spread from there to Gorée and its trade hinterland. This transfer was facilitated by the close connections between Gorée and the Gambia in the early nineteenth century. When the British left Gorée in 1817 to establish themselves first on Saint Mary's and then on MacCarthy Island, they were followed by an important group of *habitant* merchants, artisans, freed slaves, and *laptots* from Gorée whose skills were needed to establish a river fleet trade system to replace the trade between ocean vessels and caravans that had dominated the Gambia in the eighteenth century.[114] Migrations back and forth between the Gambia and Gorée were frequent in the early nineteenth century and help explain the rapid expansion of peanut cultivation and peanut trade in the Lower Senegal after 1840.

The regions that took up peanut cultivation before 1850 shared a number of features. They were too distant from the Senegal River to profit directly from the gum trade and the associated expansion of trade in millet, cattle, and other provisions. At the same time they were regions which had played an important role as transit points for the slave trade, having once supplied millet, cattle, cattle hides, and other products with little or no value as exports. Commerce with the Atlantic world had depended on the export traffic in slaves. Such regions were hard hit by the ending of the British and French slave trade. Peanut cultivation provided a solution to the commercial crisis of the early nineteenth century. It was taken up most rapidly in regions that had previously sold grain to Atlantic merchants in substantial quantities.[115] In the Gambia Soninke merchants played a key role in establishing peanut cultivation on rented land. The new pattern substituted peanuts for the millet which had been grown by Soninke merchants on rented land to feed slaves in transit and to provision slave ships in the eighteenth century.[116] In the Lower Senegal, where peasants and slaves had cultivated millet for commercial sale, the same pattern continued when peanuts were adopted as an export crop.

After 1850 peanut exports were the most important new element in the revitalization of the river trade. In the mid-1850s peanuts were exported in significant quantities to the river from Kajoor, Fuuta Tooro, and Gajaaga. But most of the trade on the river continued patterns of commerce established in the eighteenth century. Apart from peanuts, gum and millet were the most important commodities. Kajoor, Fuuta Tooro, and Gajaaga supplied the bulk of the millet which was consumed in Saint Louis and traded along the river as a "reexport" important in the gum trade with the western Sahara.[117] Gum remained the most important export. The only new development in the gum trade was the emergence of Bakel as a major center of the gum trade in the upper river valley, which had supplied little gum in the eighteenth century.[118] There were significant differences between the major trading regions. Kajoor supplied large quantities of millet and most of the peanuts purchased. Fuuta Tooro was an important source of millet, but supplied relatively few peanuts. Fuuta also exported cattle hides and Podor was the site of the important gum trade from the Brakna Moors. The trade from Bakel and Gajaaga was most diverse. The region supplied gum, millet, and peanuts to the river trade. All three regions had also been major suppliers of millet in the eighteenth century.

In many ways millet was the key commodity in the river trade. Commercial production of millet was the best indication of a region's integration into the river trade system. In the trading season for 1857–8, it is possible to give a detailed breakdown of the trade in millet on the Senegal River. Saint Louis' millet imports have been calculated for the year between March 1857 and February 1858 and are shown in table 4. Although this is the year for which the best data is available, it was not a typical year. Trade patterns were affected by the conditions of war that existed between the Trarza and the French, which depressed gum exports in the lower river valley. In the upper river valley trade was disrupted by the state of war between the French and al-Hajj Umar from 1857 to 1860. Gum exports from Bakel seem to have been little influenced, but millet and peanut exports from Bakel were far smaller than in normal years. Nevertheless, the trade figures provide important information on the regional distribution of Saint Louis' trade, especially for the lower and middle river valley.

Some interesting patterns appear from these figures on the origins of Saint Louis' millet imports. The predominant role of Kajoor contradicts

Table 4: *Millet imports (in metric tons)*[a]

	Kajoor	Podor	Bakel
March 1857	152.9	10.2	20.0
April 1857	161.4	62.4	26.0
May 1857	144.1	131.3	–
June 1857	81.7	217.9	–
July 1857	49.1	211.2	–
August 1857	35.3	64.0	12.5
September 1857	70.4	9.6	–
October 1857	86.8	19.8	–
November 1857	92.2	29.0	–
December 1857	96.8	18.0	–
January 1858	95.7	–	–
February 1858	100.0	2.2	–
Total	1,166.4	775.6	58.5

[a] Sources are *Moniteur du Sénégal et Dépendances*, April 7, 1857; May 12, 1857; June 9, 1857; July 7, 1857; August 18, 1857; September 15, 1857; October 13, 1857; November 17, 1857; December 15, 1857; January 12, 1858; February 9, 1858; March 9, 1858.

many prior assumptions about the critical role of Fuuta Tooro in the millet trade to Saint Louis.[119] Secondly, Saint Louis' millet imports closely reflected the city's consumption needs. The total millet imported in the twelve months studied was 2,068.8 metric tons, a figure which corresponds closely to the estimated minimum needs of a population of 14,000.[120] However, rather than indicating a city living on the margin of hunger, the millet imports of Saint Louis were supplemented by significant quantities of rice and wheat flour in the 1850s, and these grains were increasingly consumed by all elements of the population.[121] In normal years, when 300 to 400 metric tons of millet were exported from Bakel, Saint Louis had access to a surplus of 400 to 500 tons above consumption needs from the three major exporting regions along the river.[122] Thirdly, the monthly distribution of millet purchases indicates that Africans spaced out their sales of millet over the course of the year, conserving significant surpluses well into the "hungry period" of the rainy season. The reduced commercial activity of July and August in Kajoor reflected the most intense period of farm labor. Millet exports from Fuuta followed a different pattern, influenced by two grain harvests and the seasonal movement of trade on the river.

Saint Louis probably imported from 2,100 to 2,400 metric tons of millet in the late 1850s, but this represented only a fraction of the commercial trade in millet. Three major trades do not appear in the statistics discussed so far. One was the overland trade in millet from Kajoor, which entered Saint Louis from the island of Sor. In the late 1850s a bridge was completed across the *marigot* ("creek") of Leybar, which was one of the two most important entry points for products from Kajoor to Saint Louis. If the peanut trade is any indication, more millet entered Saint Louis by this route than by riverboat from Ganjool.[123] Secondly, the millet imports of Saint Louis do not include the millet that passed through the hands of French and African merchants as part of the transactions leading to the purchase of gum and other exports. In the late 1860s, when French merchants protested against efforts to regulate the millet trade, they placed millet sales to the desert above the consumption needs of Saint Louis in importance: "After the harvest, the cultivators who have a surplus sell to the merchants, who furnish it to those who need it throughout the year, principally to the Moors in exchange for gum, and also to the inhabitants of Saint Louis and its suburbs."[124] Finally, there was a direct trade between the desert and the savanna, in which animals were traded for grain and other products. The real size of the commercialized millet crop along the river was probably closer to 10,000 metric tons.

Exports of peanuts and gum on the river in 1857–8 were adversely affected by the hostilities between the French and the Trarza and by the Umarian jihad. Kajoor sold 2,787.7 metric tons of peanuts through the river trade in 1857–8. Kajoor's total peanut exports in 1857–8 were 7,936 tons, which indicated that only about a third of Kajoor's peanut crop reached Saint Louis by riverboat.[125] Peanut exports from Bakel were relatively insignificant in 1857–8, only 66.3 metric tons from a region which had exported 1,007 tons in 1852–3.[126] The poor trade in peanuts and millet from Bakel reflected the massive disruption of agriculture production by the Umarian jihad. Warfare, the seizure of harvests and grain reserves by foraging armies, and abandoned fields led to famine in the upper river valley in 1859.[127] By contrast, Bakel exported 880.3 metric tons of gum in the high-water season of 1857.[128] Gum exports from Podor, where the Brakna Moors traded, totaled 323.8 metric tons. Although trade on the river in 1857–8 suffered from the state of war between the French and the Trarza on the one hand, and the French and Umar on the other, the vitality of the river trade was remarkable. The warfare signaled the beginning of a new imperial era of French trade.

French expansion in the 1850s consolidated the river empire and transformed it by completing the destruction of the eighteenth-century commercial system that was begun by slave emancipation in 1848. In the 1850s a series of French military campaigns imposed "free trade" along the Senegal River, abolishing the *escales* and the system of customs payments to African states which had defined commercial relations between the Atlantic world and Senegambia throughout the period from 1700 to 1850. French political and economic goals were a logical extension of the policies which had eliminated the *habitants* as privileged intermediaries in the river trade. The new policy reflected an alliance between colonial military officers, led by Governor Faidherbe, and French merchants who wanted the right to trade freely along the Senegal River. Both groups regarded the customs payments and the traditional diplomacy of trade as a humiliating anachronism.[129]

The military confrontations on the Senegal River took place in two phases and in two theatres. To consolidate their "sovereignty" over the river the French had to defeat the Trarza, who dominated the lower river valley and much of western Fuuta Tooro. More unexpectedly the French had to confront the challenge presented by the emergence of al-Hajj Umar's jihad in the upper river after 1854.[130] French success depended on their limited military goals: commercial rather than territorial empire, sovereignty over the river markets, rather than conquest and annexations. The policy was shaped by the commercial lobby of Saint Louis, colonial merchants in France, and colonial officials sympathetic to their demands and goals.[131]

The wars of the 1850s were a turning point in the history of river commerce because the French defeated two expanding powers who threatened their control of river commerce. One of their advantages in these wars was the inability of French opponents to impose effective boycotts. The Trarza declared a boycott of the gum trade, but the boycott exacerbated tensions within desert society. By 1857 desert merchants began to resume trade on a small scale and named the year of Trarza capitulation "the year of justice."[132] The Umarian trade boycott was ineffective even in Bakel, which exported near record amounts of gum in 1857. There was a sharp decline in peanut and millet exports from Bakel, but the decline resulted from war rather than a refusal to trade.[133] The river campaigns of the 1850s, in addition to defeating military threats to French power on the Senegal, completed the processes which gave French merchants control of trade, eliminating the *habitants* as serious rivals.

French goals in the French–Trarza war of 1854–8, which abolished the river *escales* and established the right of French traders to trade freely along the river, clearly reflected the demands of French merchants. French commercial interests had petitioned the French minister in charge of colonies for precisely these changes in 1853. In 1855 Faidherbe announced the new principles followed by the government in Saint Louis: "Today there is no longer a privileged class: Europeans, mulattoes, blacks, all have the same rights, and no favors will be accorded to one group and refused another."[134]

The French–Trarza war ended Trarza power in Waalo and established the Senegal River as the colonial border between desert and savanna societies. The Trarza defeat led to the annexation of Waalo in 1855 and the continuation of the war on the north bank of the river. In February 1856 Faidherbe occupied the area surrounding Lake Rkiz (Lake Kajaar), cutting the Trarza off from their dry-season watering sites and pasture. Losses of livestock were important, and the coalition of warriors and marabouts gradually fell apart. By 1857 the desert merchants were eager to return to the gum markets, and in 1858 Faidherbe was able to sign a treaty with the Trarza emir that met French demands.[135]

The French confrontation with Umar in the upper Senegal had similar consequences for the riverine states of that region. The French consolidated their control over a series of fortified trade towns, from Podor and Matam in Fuuta, to Bakel and Medine in the upper river valley. By the end of the 1850s commercial treaties with the riverine states had been revised to recognize the principle of French sovereignty over these enclaves, and customs payments to the riverine states had been abolished and replaced with a new system of market taxes collected by the French. But neither the war in the lower river nor the war in the upper river had added significant new territories to the colony of Senegal. Up until 1859 French expansion followed the course charted by French merchants and followed by Faidherbe. Its goal was to consolidate French commercial hegemony, while avoiding the costs and problems created by territorial conquest.[136]

By 1858 French military actions had achieved most of the goals which had been set in 1854. Just as emancipation had destroyed the remnants of the eighteenth-century commercial system within the colony, the military campaigns of 1854–9 had destroyed the "tributes, humiliations, and concessions" based on the traditions of the eighteenth century. By 1860 the eighteenth-century commercial system had been destroyed and the foundations of a new commercial empire had been laid. Saint Louis was still the center of French economic and military power. The city expanded in the 1850s, incorporating runaway slaves and free migrants from the states of the Senegal River valley. Fifteen hundred new migrants to the city were counted by the French in 1857. Their origins reflected the recent history of French war and economic expansion: there were 250 "Bambara," mainly former slaves from Segu and Kaarta seized during French campaigns in the upper Senegal; 200 Soninke, mainly free migrants who worked as *laptots*; 150 free migrants from Kajoor who worked as common laborers; and 500 "Pourognes" (Wolof, *puuroñ*), slaves of the Moors who had fled from their masters or been seized by the French during the French-Trarza war.[137]

As the 1850s drew to a close, it became clear that French military successes had generated their own momentum. By 1859 Faidherbe was pleading with the French government for the resources to intervene in Kajoor, in spite of peaceful relations and a prosperous commerce. Faidherbe now wanted a change of government in Kajoor, because he believed that the depredations and violence of the *ceddo* reduced French commerce to less than what it could have been. "There is much to do in Cayor. The majority of the population, composed of peaceful cultivators, aspires to peace, and there is no doubt today that our successes against the Moors and the other peoples of the river have proved to all our strength, which was previously denied in the country, and that we will receive vigorous support if we try to repress the brigandage of the tiedos [*ceddo*] of the Damel, and create a regular system of government."[138] Faidherbe's words contained the seeds of the shift to territorial empire that began in the 1860s, plunging the Lower Senegal into a period of civil war, religious revolt, and colonial conquest that would culminate in 1865 in the worst famine since the mid-eighteenth century.

Conclusion

When Faidherbe published his "Note on the History of Cayor" in 1883, he invoked the eighteenth-century cliché of the king who raided his own people, recast to suit the Victorian and imperial tastes of the period. When the Dammel of Kajoor was offered a magnificent horse by a marabout from the desert, he desired it at any price. The marabout asked for "one hundred virgins." Immediately the *ceddo* in the king's entourage mounted on horseback and pillaged a dozen villages.[1] The cliché, first used by slave traders to justify the slave trade as the only possible commerce with Africans, later served as a justification for colonial conquest. In the late 1850s, when Faidherbe sought official approval for his plans to conquer Kajoor, he combined the European stereotype of the king who raided his own people with an emphasis on the tyranny of drunken warriors that echoed one of the main themes of Muslim resistance to the Wolof old regime. In the reports he sent back to Paris Faidherbe promised that French military action would liberate the hard-working Muslim peasantry of the Wolof kingdoms from brutal tyranny and allow a dramatic expansion of French commerce. But there was a deep cynicism embedded in the ideology of conquest. The first French military "expedition" in Kajoor was an unprovoked attack on three large Muslim villages in Njambur in 1858. The villages were burned to the ground.[2] A year later the French raised false hopes that they would aid Muslims who rebelled against the monarchy. When the slaughter between Muslims and partisans of the old regime ended, the French began their first attempt to assert colonial sovereignty over the Lower Senegal.

The period of civil war and colonial conquest that began in Kajoor in 1858 and continued for three decades forms the opening phase in the colonial history of Senegal. But the tensions that Faidherbe attempted to manipulate were the direct product of a century and a half of Atlantic commerce. In the first phases of colonial expansion the French found ready allies in the provinces whose trade linked them closely to Saint Louis. As early as 1835 a letter from Seriñ Ñomre, one of the most powerful marabout chiefs of northern Kajoor, concluded a request for arms with an aside on French disputes with the Dammel. "We have not visibly separated ourselves from the Damel; that could not be because we live in his country, but our ideas are those of Senegal."[3] Another letter from the marabouts of Njambur requested an advance of arms, powder and shot for self-defense, to be repaid with millet after the next harvest.[4] The close ties between northern Kajoor and Saint Louis, based on the trade in millet and other foodstuffs, were reinforced by the new trade in peanuts after 1840. The secessionist spirit that culminated in open revolt in 1859 swept over the same provinces that rebelled against the monarchy in the 1790s.

The regional divisions that threatened the integrity of Kajoor and Bawol in the 1850s took a variety a forms, but the rebellious provinces were all avatars of the eighteenth-century Atlantic world. In northern Kajoor Muslim leaders led the rebellion, depicting themselves as pious Muslims and defenders of ancient Wolof freedoms against the pagan, slave power of the monarchy. By the mid-nineteenth century the power of the slave warriors of Kajoor had reached the height of its development. In the 1850s slave officials screened all visitors to the court and spoke for the king. A delegation of Catholic missionaries who tried to contact the Dammel in 1851 met the Fara-Kaba, whose residence was guarded by nine huts protected by slave warriors. The missionaries found the dreaded slave official stretched out on his bed, with his elbows resting on one of his slaves. "At his feet his slaves and his guards sat in the dust, and all of them seemed filled with a sentiment of joy and pride to find themselves in the service of such a great master."[5] Although Muslims regarded the royal slaves as the embodiment of pagan corruption, the Fara-Kaba employed a distinguished marabout "to write precious talismans for him and to teach his son all the precepts of the religion of Mahomet."[6]

In the nineteenth century even oral traditions about Kocc Barma, the seventeenth-century *jambur* leader and Wolof folk hero, became vehicles for criticizing the overweening power of the royal slaves. In a tradition recorded by Boilat, Kocc Barma expressed outrage at the atrocities committed by the Dammel's slave warriors. Kocc met a group of refugees fleeing a pillaged village and addressed himself to a corpse being carried away for burial.

> Go tell our ancestors that today death is preferable to life. Go tell our ancestors that in their days power was in the hands of free men who understood honesty and duty . . . today it is slaves who rule, who execute the unjust desires of their masters in order to enjoy their favor.[7]

The goal of Muslim rebels was not to create a new Islamic state but to restore powers to village communities that had been usurped by the monarchy. That is why they turned to Saint Louis and to royal pretenders from dynasties long out of power for aid in the struggle against the Geej regime and its slave warriors.

195

In southern Kajoor and Bawol the Sereer minorities took advantage of their trade ties with Gorée and the expanding city of Dakar to form special alliances with the French, while at the same time they refused to pay tribute to the dual monarchy of Kajoor-Bawol.[8] As non-Muslims the Sereer minorities had been the most frequent targets of slave raiding and pillage throughout the eighteenth and nineteenth centuries. Although no unified movement of resistance to the monarchy emerged in the 1850s, large coastal villages like Mbuur sought the protection of the French and smaller rural communities took advantage of any weakness at the center to assert their autonomy and independence. The independence of the Lebu villages of Cap Vert encouraged rebellion in the southern provinces of Kajoor, particularly in Jander, where the French began military probes in 1861 in response to the situation of "anarchy" that they believed was developing.[9]

The regional, religious, and ethnic conflicts that swept across Kajoor-Bawol in the 1850s were products of the three great historical transformations that had emerged after a century and a half of Atlantic commerce. Interlinked and in many ways inseparable, these were (1) the development of important urban centers and an urban Wolof culture founded on Atlantic trade, (2) the commercialization of agricultural production, particularly in the Senegal River valley and near the Atlantic coast, and (3) the emergence of slavery as the primary means of organizing economic production and political control. All three had their historical roots in eighteenth-century Atlantic commerce, rather than in the better-known colonial export cycle based on peanuts which predominated in the second half of the nineteenth century.[10]

By the late eighteenth century Saint Louis and Gorée were important urban centers, with a distinctive population of *habitant* merchants and slave laborers. Historically, they were Wolof cities. Their cultural identity was a function of the geography of Atlantic trade. The core cities that emerged in the late eighteenth century and flourished in the first half of the nineteenth century were new settlements founded by migrants of free and slave origins. Slaves played a critical role in maintaining the population and providing labor throughout the eighteenth century. By the early nineteenth century the core cities had begun to expand from the islands to the mainland, creating satellite settlements in what became the suburbs of Saint Louis and a new city in Dakar, adjacent to the Lebu village which gave the city its name.

The eighteenth-century island cities were the most fully developed slave societies in the Lower Senegal. Their population of merchants and slaves reproduced the values and institutions of the wider Atlantic world, while remaining firmly anchored in the cultural and demographic realities of Senegambia. The interpenetration of the two systems transformed the Atlantic islands into the cultural interface between two worlds, opening a door of no return for the societies of the Lower Senegal. The passageway they opened for ideas, technologies and commodities from the Atlantic world could no more be closed than slaves could be recalled to Africa unchanged from the cargoes of the middle passage. By the mid-nineteenth century, the maritime societies of the islands had become a base for further colonial expansion into the Senegal River valley. During the Wolof civil wars of the 1860s the Atlantic islands identified with the French colonial state.

The trade in grain and other provisions was the crucial link between the island cities, the economy of the Lower Senegal, and the expansion of slavery. The commercialization of agriculture had greater effects on the political economy of the Lower Senegal than did the modest volume of slave exports. In addition, food supplies had a measurable impact on the overall performance of the export sector in the Senegal River valley. The availability of surplus grain put a cap on the volume of slave exports that could pass through the Senegal River valley, with its long line of supply. This influence can be discerned in the periodic "subsistence crises" which threatened the slave trade in the first half of the eighteenth century, marked by a relatively high volume of slave exports.

Food supplies also played an important role in determining the geographic origins of slaves sold to Atlantic merchants. Commercial trade in grain encouraged a long-distance trade in slaves from the Niger River valley, while societies in the Senegal River valley and the Atlantic coastal plain exported fewer slaves than they retained for grain production. When ecological crisis and warfare created true famine conditions, as occurred in the 1750s, slave exports from the Atlantic coastal region increased dramatically, while long-distance trade withered during the crisis. Although neglected by historians, the rhythms of agricultural production and ecological crisis exerted a strong influence over the export economy.

Perhaps most importantly the trade in grain helps to explain why slave exports through the Senegal River valley declined in the second half of the eighteenth century. Because the gradual creation of a regional market in grain increased the demand for slave labor, grain production had a dynamic impact on the supply of slaves available for export. If grain production was neglected or disorganized, periodic "subsistence crises" disrupted trade, as in the first half of the eighteenth century. As grain markets became better organized, they came to depend on the use of slave labor for the commercial production of grain. Therefore grain production cut into the available supply of slaves. This influence, probably modest in itself, was compounded by the expansion of gum exports. Gum extraction required the import of slave labor by desert merchants. The increased desert population and the use of slave labor for gum extraction translated into an expanded demand for savanna grain in the desert. The gum export trade thus increased the demand for slave labor in the desert and in the savanna as well.

The commercialization of agriculture had an equally important impact

197

on the internal development of the societies of the Lower Senegal. Islam was reinforced in grain-producing regions, both as an ideology of protest and as a principle of social organization. The political fragmentation of the Wolof states into rebellious borderlands and central strongholds of aristocratic power reflected the corrosive influence of Atlantic commerce on the state structures of the Wolof old regime. Economically, commercial grain production laid the groundwork for the subsequent development of the export trade in peanuts, which took hold first in regions that had been integrated into the eighteenth-century Atlantic economy.

Slavery played a critical role in the construction of the eighteenth-century economy. In the grain fields, in the maritime economy of the islands and in the political structures of the Wolof states, slaves provided the labor and services that embodied the adaptations and innovations of the eighteenth century. The dramatic expansion of slavery in the eighteenth century was a direct result of the Atlantic slave trade. If approximately 150,000–200,000 Africans were exported through the Senegal River system to the New World, at least that many were enslaved and stayed within the region.[11] There is no census data on slavery for the mid-nineteenth century. In 1904 the French colonial administration counted over 150,000 slaves (in round numbers) in the societies of the Senegal River valley and the Atlantic coast.[12] That count was certainly an under-estimate, but the real question is: how many slaves were there in 1860?

Some historians have argued that there was a dramatic increase in the number of slaves in the late nineteenth century, due to extensive warfare in the western Sudan and the demand for labor in the peanut export economy.[13] The evidence for this is French colonial reports suggesting that at least 10,000 slaves passed downriver through Medine in 1889, and another estimate that "60,000 slaves per year" were exported from Kaarta to the Senegal River valley.[14] However, there are good reasons to be skeptical about these reports. The estimate of 60,000 slaves a year came from a political report on slavery infused with conquest rhetoric about the barbarity of African slave raiding. The estimate exceeded eighteenth-century slave exports from Senegambia as a whole by a factor of ten or twenty to one. Although there is little reason to doubt that French officials observed a huge slave trade on the river in 1889, it is less clear that they actually counted slaves. Colonial sources from the *cercles* of the peanut basin do not provide supporting evidence for an influx of slaves of this magnitude.[15] Neither does the behavior of slaves in the early colonial period. If there had been a massive influx of newly enslaved persons in the Lower Senegal in the 1880s and 1890s, involving some 100,000 people, the early colonial period would have been marked by a massive slave exodus and the formation of numerous liberty villages, as occurred elsewhere in the western Sudan under similar conditions.[16] In fact there was only one liberty village in the peanut basin and most slave runaways fled to the city or joined Muslim communities. Little evidence supports the view that there were nearly 100,000 new slaves from the Niger valley in the Lower Senegal in 1900, still traumatized by their recent incorporation in Wolof society.

The alternative is to argue that the slave trade of the late ninteenth century replenished slave populations and contributed to a slight overall increase, compared to the situation at mid-century. In this case, the colonial census of slavery provides a rough estimate of the number of slaves in 1860. If there were approximately 150,000 slaves in the Senegal River valley and the Lower Senegal in 1860, the inescapable conclusion is that more slaves were retained in West Africa from 1700 to 1860 than were exported across the Atlantic. Even assuming favorable conditions of slave reproduction, it is reasonable to suggest that the same regions would have been required to import at least 150,000–200,000 slaves over the same time period to establish a slave population of that size, not including slave imports into the western Sahara.[17] If so, the societies of northern Senegambia absorbed more slaves than were exported across the Atlantic during the era of the slave trade.

Slavery expanded in the Lower Senegal as a result of historical developments in the Atlantic world. The eighteenth century was the time of slavery on both sides of the Atlantic. Just as the American edifice of slavery was unimaginable without the keystone provided by African slave labor, slavery in Africa would never have developed to the extent and in the way that it did without the stimulus of Atlantic commerce. This is true in spite of the fact that slavery in the Senegal River valley had ancient foundations in the production of surplus grain in the borderlands of the desert and the savanna. Patterns of trade between the desert and the savanna were annexed to the Atlantic world as the export of slaves and gum arabic reconfigured local economies and interregional trade. The human meaning of that reconfiguration was experienced by slaves in the savanna, in the desert, and in the wider Atlantic world. Traces of their experience remind us that the time of slavery was the watershed of modern history in the Lower Senegal.

Notes

Guide to archival sources

Archives Nationales Françaises (ANF), Paris
Series C 6 – Senegal, eighteenth century
Archives Nationales du Sénégal (ANS), Dakar
Series D – Military affairs
Series E – Councils, assemblies
Series B – Correspondence
Series O – Navigation, naval affairs
Series Q – Commercial affairs
Series G – Administrative affairs
Series K – Slavery

1 Cosaan: "the origins"

1 Philip Curtin, *Economic Change in Precolonial Africa: Senegambia in the Era of the Slave Trade* (Madison, 1975), remains the standard study of this period. For a critique of Curtin see Boubacar Barry, *La Sénégambie du XVe au XIXe Siècle: Traite Négrière, Islam et Conquête Coloniale* (Paris, 1988).
2 Although it focuses primarily on the Sereer, Henri Gravrand, *La Civilisation Sereer: Cosaan, Les Origines* (Dakar, 1983), 25–104, gives the most complete discussion of the origin myths of the major ethnic groups of the Lower Senegal, based on a critical analysis of oral traditions.
3 The most detailed presentation of Lebu origin myths is the fictional, epic account of Abdoulaye Sadji, *Tounka* (Paris, 1965). Sadji, born in Rufisque in 1910, used Lebu oral traditions as the source for this work. For an early version of Lebu traditions see Abbé David Boilat, *Esquisses Sénégalaises* (Paris, 1853), 57–9. More recent collections of Lebu traditions, but in a more traditional form than Sadji's narrative, include "Cosaanu Tengeej," and "Lu-tax am jigeeni Ngor nu dul am Jekker," in Lilyan Kesteloot and Cherif Mbodj, (eds.) *Contes et Mythes Wolof* (Dakar, 1983).
4 Sadji, *Tounka*, for a discussion of the origins of the Lebu *ndep*, a technique of healing through ritual possession characteristic of the Lebu.
5 Boilat, *Esquisses*, 59–60. Boilat uses the term "None" (Wolof, *noon*, "enemy") to describe not only the group described by ethnographers as Noon, living near Thies, but also other Cangin groups, Joobas, and Saafen. The Cangin linguistic group is used to describe those languages identified as "Sereer," but forming a separate group from Sereer-Siin.

200

6 Boilat, *Esquisses*, 90.

7 Gravrand, *Civilisation Sereer*, 29–30.

8 For a good theoretical discussion of the ecological and economic foundations of the desert–savanna trade see Paul Lovejoy and Steven Baier, "The Desert-Side Economy of the Central Sudan," *International Journal of African Historical Studies*, 8, 4, (1975). For various estimates of the importance of the desert-side economy in the western Sudan see Curtin, *Economic Change*, 156; Paul E. Lovejoy, *Transformations in Slavery: A History of Slavery in Africa* (Cambridge, 1983), 24–6; Richard L. Roberts, *Warriors, Merchants, and Slaves: The State and Economy in the Middle Niger Valley, 1700–1914* (Stanford, 1987), 46–58; and James L. A. Webb, "Shifting Sands: An Economic History of the Mauritanian Sahara, 1500–1850," unpublished PhD thesis, Johns Hopkins University, 1984, 160–3.

9 Paul Pelissier, *Les Paysans du Sénégal, Les Civilisations Agraires du Cayor à la Casamance* (St Yrieux, 1966) is the best introduction to the geography and agriculture of the region.

10 Jean Boulègue, *Le Grand Jolof (XIIIe–XVIe Siécle)* (Paris, 1987) 18–21 examines Portuguese sources and finds a striking continuity between ethno-linguistic borders of the fifteenth century and those of more recent periods. The one exception would be the reduction of the Sereer space in Kajoor and Bawol.

11 I have used an eighteenth-century English translation of Adanson: Michael Adanson, "A Voyage to Senegal, the Isle of Gorée, and the River Gambia," in John Pinkerton, *A General Collection of the Best and Most Interesting Voyages and Travels . . .* XVI, (London, 1814) 598–674. For Adanson's descriptions of elephants, ibid., 629; a walk through the forests of Cap Vert, 640–3.

12 Ibid., 622.

13 This map is reproduced in Felix Brigaud and Jean Vast, *Saint-Louis du Sénégal, Ville aux Mille Visages* (Dakar, 1987), 18, and the forest is described in Adanson, "Voyage," 641–3.

14 Boilat, *Esquisses*, 58, 67–78.

15 See George E. Brooks, *Western Africa to c. 1860 AD: A Provisional Historical Schema based on Climate Periods* (Bloomington, 1985), 1–22, for a summary of the data and its interpretation.

16 See Henri Gravrand, *Civilisation Sereer*, 59–158. *Cosaan* means "ancestors," "origins," "traditions," in Wolof, Sereer, and Pulaar, the languages of the three main ethnic groups who claim the Senegal River valley as their homeland.

17 The forests described in oral traditions may have been "relic forests," remnants of stands which developed in a period of more rainfall. Once cut down or burned for use as farmland or fuel and then used as grazing land for domesticated animals, such forest stands could not regenerate themselves in the drier climate of more recent centuries.

18 Brooks, *Western Africa*, 63–4, 99–100. See also Bruno A. Chavane, *Villages de l'Ancien Tekrour: Recherches Archéologiques dans la Moyenne Vallée du Fleuve Sénégal* (Paris, 1985).

19 Brooks, *Western Africa*, 99–100.

20 The process of ecological change was independent of climatic change, which exerted more long-term influences. There is no ecological history of the western Sudan or its sub-regions comparable to the work of William Cronon, *Changes in the Land: Indians, Colonists, and the Ecology of New England* (New York, 1983). The rapid ecological transformation of the landscape in the "new lands" in the region around Tambacounda suggests patterns for understanding the past.

21 For discussions of this system and the *laman* see Abodoulaye-Bara Diop, *La Société*

Notes

Wolof: Tradition et Changement. Les Systèmes d'Inégalité et de Domination (Paris, 1981), 120–7; Pelissier, *Paysans du Sénégal*, 124–9.

22 "Cosaanu Nguur ci Bawol," in Aram Diop, Oumar Ben Khatab Dia, Jean-Claude Galdin, *Jukib Tanneefu Baat-Yu-Sax/ Recueil de Textes Choisis* (Dakar, Centre de Linguistique Appliqué de Dakar, 1975), 10.

23 *Booba Tengeej gol lawoon gu lendem keriis, diy xeer ag i garab gu nit masul jam tankam*, or "Tengeej was a forest so dark nothing could be seen, with rocks and trees, where no human had ever set foot," in "Cosaanu Tengeej," in Lilyan Kesteloot, Cherif Mbodj, *Contes et Mythes Wolofs*, 155.

24 Diop, Dia and Galdin, *Jukib Tanneefu*, 10.

25 "Cosaanu Tengeej," in Kesteloot and Mbodj, *Contes et Mythes Wolof*, 157–9; "Cosaanu Nguur ci Bawol," in Diop, Dia and Galdin, *Jukib Tanneefu*, 10, and the dynastic traditions discussed below.

26 The technology of these wells impressed Gaspard Mollien, who described them in some detail in Hubert Deschamps (ed.), *L'Afrique Occidentale en 1818* (Paris, 1967), 57. Wells ranging anywhere from 150 feet to 300 feet in depth provided permanent supplies of water to Wolof villages.

27 "Questions posed to Lt-Col. Maxwell, Island of St Louis, Senegal, 1 January, 1811," in *British Parliamentary Papers, Colonies, Africa* (Shannon, 1967), I, 149.

28 For the oral traditions of Tuube, see R. Rousseau, "Le Sénégal d'Autrefois. Etude sur le Toube. Papiers de Rawane Boy," *Bulletin du Comité d'Etudes Historiques et Scientifiques sur l'Afrique Occidentale Française*, 3, (1931) 1–31. See also Philip D. Curtin, "Jihad in West Africa: Early Phases and Interactions in Mauritania and Senegal," *Journal of African History*, 7, 1 (1971).

29 On maroon societies see Richard Price (ed.), *Maroon Societies: Rebel Slave Communities in the Americas* (New York, 1973). For a discussion of some of the defensive techniques of the Sereer of Bawol, see Adama Ndiaye, "Le Bawol Occidentale: Mbadaan, Sandok, Jegem, Joobas, du Milieu du XIXe Siècle à 1907," mémoire de maitrîse, Université Cheikh Anta Diop, Département d'Histoire, Décembre 1988, 22–7.

30 See Boubacar Barry, "Emiettement Politique et Dépendance Economique dans l'Espace Géopolitique Séngambien du XVe au XVIIe Siècle," *Revue Française d'Histoire d'Outre-Mer*, 68 (1981).

31 For a general study see Nehemiah Levtzion, *Ancient Ghana and Mali* (New York, 1973).

32 It is quite possible that the migrants fused with populations already in the region. Wolof and Sereer traditions mention a prior presence by the *Soos*, sometimes identified with a Mande people (Soce, Sousou). The term may simply refer to the original inhabitants with no precise ethnic reference.

33 Gravrand, *Civilisation Sereer*, 107–27.

34 The most important version of the legend of Njaajaan Njaay is that of Yoro Jaw: Henri Gaden, "Légendes et Coutumes Sénégalaises, Cahiers de Yoro Dyao," *Revue d'Ethnographie et de Sociologie*, 3–4 (1912).

35 The best study of this period is Jean Boulègue, *Le Grand Jolof*.

36 The Cangin group of Sereer has not been studied systematically, so controversies remain about its status and relationship to other Sereer groupings in Senegal. Some studies emphasize its unique characteristics and the particularities of the Cangin language group: Gravrand, *Civilisation Sereer*, 144–6; Walter J. Pichl, *The Cangin Group: A Language Group in Northern Senegal* (Pittsburg, 1966). At the same time linguists have classified Sereer-Cangin languages as part of the northern group of the West Atlantic languages, along with Wolof, Sereer-Siin, and Pulaar: Brooks, *Western Africa*, 56–61.

37 Interview, Bandia elders, March 28, 1989. Foundation myth of Bandia: Principal informant, Farba Siis.

202

38 In recent times this process has been accelerated by massive Wolof settlement under the aegis of the Murid brotherhood. But the Murids have continued a process begun by the Wolof aristocracy of Bawcl. For a study of this process, Rokhaya Fall, "Le Royaume du Bawol du XVIe au XIXe Siècle. Pouvoir Wolof et Rapports avec les Populations Sereer", thèse de 3e cycle, Université de Paris-I, Décembre 1983.

39 For some myths see "Cosaanu Tengeej," in Kesteloot and Mbodj, *Contes et Mythes Wolof*, 57, 155, "Njalbeenu Diine Lislam Ci Wakaam," in Lilyan Kesteloot and Bassirou Dieng, *Du Tieddo au Talibe* (Paris, 1989), 172; Gravrand *Civilisation Sereer* 27–30, for the founding myth of Fatick. These myths resemble the founding myth of Bandia (interview Bandia elders) which recounts the arrival of the three founding figures of the three sections of the village, in a forested land free from political rule.

40 Here I differ from Boulègue, *Le Grand Jolof*, 25–6, 34–6, who hesitates to make this identification. However, the reasons given, such as aristocratic consumption of alcohol, imply standards which are inappropriate in assessing a culture's religion. Historians have been much too influenced by the Islamic critique of the Wolof old regime, which describes the aristocratic class as "pagan."

41 On the Mande epic see David C. Conrad, *A State of Intrigue: The Epic of Bamana Segu according to Tayiru Banbera* (Oxford, 1990) and John William Johnson, *The Epic of Son-Jara: A West African Tradition* (Bloomington, 1986). The Mande form places greater emphasis on the music and the performer as artist. Wolof dynastic traditions are recited by a senior *gewel*, and musical accompaniment and interludes are provided by younger associates.

42 Yoro Jaw in Henry Gaden, "Légendes et Coutumes."

43 The most recent critical discussion is in Boulègue, *Le Grand Jolof*, especially 24–48. Boulègue's discussion is limited to French texts. He argues for the historical accuracy of the traditions, based on comparisons with other written sources. But this "accuracy" mainly refers to Yoro Jaw's reworking and rationalization of the traditions. Yoro Jaw was educated at the *école des hotages*, opened by Faidherbe in 1856.

44 "Histoire des Damels du Cayor," in *Moniteur de Sénégal*, 1864.

45 These levels are interpretive. My reading is structuralist in the sense that it is based on features common to different versions of the tradition. For a good discussion of the problems involved in interpreting myths of this kind see Steven Feierman, *The Shambaa Kingdom: A History* (Madison, 1974), 40–5. On the problem of revision see Benjamin C. Ray, *Myth, Ritual and Kingship in Buganda* (Oxford, 1991), 55–63.

46 There are several important versions of the myth of Njaajaan Njaay: in the eighteenth century Brasseur recorded the earliest version, Charles Becker and Victor Martin, "Détails Historiques et Politiques, Mémoire Inédit (1778) de J. A. Le Brasseur," *Bulletin de l'IFAN*, 39, B, 1 (1977), 94–5; the most important is that of Yoro Jaw in Gaden, "Légendes et Coutumes." Other traditionalists have recorded versions more recently: the text of Morokaya Samb, a Kajoor *gewel* is conveniently available in Kesteloot and Dieng, *Du Tieddo au Talibe*, 184–7.

47 "Njaajaan" is explained as meaning "marvelous" or "extraordinary" in Sereer. This recognition prefigures the expansion of the Jolof empire. Many of the details of the myth have specific meanings, which are ignored here.

48 This is noted by Boulègue, *Le Grand Jolof*, 26, 60–1, but little is made of it.

49 Brasseur, "Détails Historiques," 98, described the enthronement ritual as practiced in Kajoor in the eighteenth century. Mansour Bouna Ndiaye, *Panorama Politique du Sénégal ou les Mémoires d'un Enfant du Siècle* (Dakar, 1986), 56–7, describes the rituals in Jolof as remembered by his father Bouna Ndiaye, the last Burba.

50 In most versions of the myth Njaajaan Njaay settles disputes over land between quarreling *laman*.

203

51 For a full study of the period of the Jolof empire, see Boulègue, *Le Grand Jolof*.
52 Boulègue, *Le Grand Jolof*, 165–74.
53 All the dynastic traditions mention the payment of tribute, but Yoro Jaw and Assan Marokaya Samb focus almost exclusively on the tribute in white sand, which is given symbolic importance: R. Rousseau, "Le Sénégal d'Autrefois. Etude sur le Cayor. Cahiers de Yoro Dyao," *Bulletin du Comité des Etudes Historiques et Scientifiques sur l'Afrique Occidentale Française*, 16 (1933), 254–5; Assan Marokaya Samb, *Cadior Demb. Essai sur l'Histoire du Cayor* (Dakar, 1964), 7. The list quoted above is based on Charles Becker and Victor Martin (eds.), "Recueil sur la Vie des Damel par Tanor Latsoukabe Fall," *Bulletin de l'IFAN*, 36, B, 1 (1974), 99.
54 Cadamosto in Gerald Roe Crone, ed., *The Voyages of Cadomosto and Other Documents on Western Africa in the Second Half of the Fifteenth Century* (London, 1937) 29.
55 Ibid., 38. This calls into question the traditional etymology of Dammel, explained by Yoro Jaw and other traditional historians as being derived from the verb *dam*, "to break", and meaning the "breaker" of the empire. Portuguese sources use the title Budomel or Budamel (Buur Dammel) before Kajoor's war for independence.
56 Curtin, *Economic Change*, 12–13. The samples used are from the Spanish empire, Mexico and Peru.
57 Yoro Jaw in Rousseau, "Etude sur le Cayor," 255, which lists the principal villages where iron weapons were manufactured (seven in all). There is a likelihood that the weapons were made with European iron, as iron quickly became one of the principal Senegambian imports from Europe.
58 For this aspect of the movement for independence, Boulègue, *Le Grand Jolof*, 101–43.
59 Ibid., 166–7.
60 See the discussion of the expansion of the kingdom in Mamadou Diouf, *Le Kajoor au XIXe Siècle: Pouvoir Ceddo et Conquête Coloniale* (Paris, 1990), 39–41. The same process occurred in Bawol, where the seventeenth century formed an important step in the expansion of Wolof power.
61 Diop, *Société Wolof*, 162–9, gives an essentially structural explanation of the emergence of royal matrilineages. I have not followed his terminology, but rephrased the argument.
62 Fall, "Recueil," 103.
63 Yoro Jaw, "Etude sur le Cayor," 264–5.
64 "Biram Njeeme Koo-Njaay," in Kesteloot, Dieng, *Du Tieddo au Talibe*, 107–12. Although this story uses the name of a king of the Jolof empire, it has the form of a folktale rather than dynastic history.
65 "Biram Njeeme," 108. This same story is told in the version of the dynastic traditions of Kajoor given by Assan Marokaya Samb, *Cadior Demb*. The most detailed version of this story, used to explain Latsukaabe's rise to power is given by Frederic Carrère and Paul Holle, *De la Sénégambie Française* (Paris, 1855), 42–6.
66 This point is mentioned several times by Yoro Jaw in R. Rousseau, "Le Sénégal d'Autrefois. Etude sur le Oualo. Cahiers de Yoro Dyao," *Bulletin du Comité des Etudes Historiques et Scientifiques sur l'Afrique Occidentale Française*, 12 (1929), 133–211, and explained by the fact that property held by the paternal family was divided between the children, while property belonging to the maternal family was kept together. As a result, noble families kept their slave holdings intact by owning them through the maternal family.
67 Yoro Jaw, "Etude sur le Oualo,' 158.
68 Ibid., 172–3.
69 Yoro Jaw, "Etude sur le Cayor," 263–4; Diouf, *Le Kajoor*, 63–4. The council of electors was an assembly of *laman*, who as the descendants of the founders of communities, represented the free population. The power of the council was limited by

the military power of the matrilineal royal clans, and by the fact that the families who inherited the position of *laman* were often forced into client roles vis-à-vis the monarchy, limiting their independence. The electors inherited their position in the council.

70 Yoro Jaw, "Etude sur le Cayor," 258–60.

71 *Jambur* has several meanings in Wolof. On the one hand it describes the entire class of free persons who were neither slaves nor members of caste groups. But when used to describe an individual in the past it referred to the much smaller group of free, non-aristocrats who had special positions of authority, like the *laman* and village heads. *Jambur* can also describe moral qualities of honor, honesty, and good fortune, usually including respectable wealth.

72 Circumcised youths (Wolof, "circumcise", *xaraaf*; "the circumcised", *njulli yi*) spent time in seclusion together (Wolof, *lel*), after which they were considered blood relations (Wolof, *mbokk benn deret*), so Daawda Demba's attempt to have Kocc Barm put to death was a direct violation of Wolof codes of honor. My understanding of Wolof circumcision owes much to my informant, Ibou Sarr.

73 The most detailed account is given by Yoro Jaw, "Etude sur le Cayor," 269–73. The figure of Kocc Barma appears in numerous Wolof folk tales. In the nineteenth century a version of these traditions was recorded by Boilat, *Esquisses*, 343–7. More recent versions of the Kocc Barma traditions appear in Kesteloot and Mbodj, *Contes et Mythes Wolof*, 143–51.

74 This summary of the events in based on Yoro Jaw, "Etude sur le Cayor," 276–8.

75 I am here reformulating arguments first presented in James F. Searing, "Aristocrats, Salves, and Peasants: Power and Dependency in the Wolof States, 1700–1850," *The International Journal of African Historical Studies*, 21, 3 (1988), 475–503.

76 For a more detailed discussion of this period, Rokhaya Fall, "Le Royaume de Bawol," 74–104.

77 Ibid., 104–44.

78 Abdoulaye-Bara Diop, *Société Wolof*, 167.

79 The Wolof verb is *sukootu*, describing the limping walk of someone supporting themselves on crutches. See Tanor Latsoukabe Fall, "Recueil," 112. This explanation is common to all versions of the dynastic traditions. See also the version recorded in Diop, Dia, and Galdin, *Jukib Tanneefu*, 18–28, "Nguurug Lat Sukaabe."

80 This stay with the Fulbe shepherds and the maternal uncle explains why his name Latsukaabe is more closely derived from the Pulaar verb related to the Wolof verb *sukootu*, Tanor Latsoukabe Fall, "Recueil," 112; Diop, Dia, and Galdin, *Jukib Taneefu*, 18.

81 Fall, "Recueil," 112. The visit to Mbuur also appears in Diop, Dia, and Galdin, *Jukib Taneefu*, 18.

82 Fall, "Recueil," 113; Diop, Dia, and Galdin, *Jukib Taneefu*, 20.

83 The traditions about Latsukaabe resemble the story of "Biram Njeeme Koo-Njaay," in Kesteloot, Dieng, *Du Tieddo au Talibe*.

84 Diop, Dia, and Galdin, *Jukib Taneefu*, 20–5; Fall, "Recueil," 113.

85 Diop, Dia, and Galdin, *Jukib Taneefu*, 24.

86 Wolof, *Nguur doole la, nanu xare ku rey sa moroom doon buur*, cited by Diop, *Société Wolof*, 167.

87 For the chronology of Bawol, Victor Martin and Charles Becker, "Les Teeñ du Baol: Essai de Chronologie," *Bulletin de l'IFAN* 38 (1976), 480–1.

88 "Premier Voyage de Brüe (1697)," in C. A. Walckenaer, *Histoire Générale des Voyages* (Paris, 1826), II, 416. The text or notes of André Brüe also appear, with other materials, in Jean Baptise Labat, *Nouvelle Relation de l'Afrique Occidentale* (Paris, 1728).

89 Brüe, "Premier Voyage," 416, 421–2.

90 Fall, "Recueil," 114. See also informants cited by Rokhaya Fall, "Royaume de Bawol," 136–7. It is likely that earlier kings purchased some arms, but Latsukaabe was the first to purchase hundreds of guns and make systematic use of them in his armies.
91 Fall, 'Recueil," 114, Brüe, "Premier Voyage," 381. Brüe lent Latsukaabe two *laptots* (sailors).
92 Brüe describes the infantry brigade of 200. Other eighteenth-century sources and oral traditions confirm this same pattern. See Charles Becker and Victor Martin (eds), "Mémoire Inédit de Doumet (1769). Le Kayor et les Pays Voisins au Cours de la Seconde Moitié du XVIIIe Siècle," *Bulletin de l'IFAN*, 36, B, (1974), 39. Oral traditions describe the royal guard of the Dammel Birima Fatma Cubb in the early nineteenth century: Fall, "Recueil," 126, 127.
93 Brüe, "Premier Voyage," 383, 404. The general is described as the *condi* or *kondi* (387, 404), a word which does not conform with Wolof titles. It may be related to *conndi* (Pulaar, "gunpowder"). If so the title probably made reference to the recent introduction of firearms.
94 Barry treats the eighteenth century as a period of *ceddo* power in *Sénégambie*, 97–184. Mamadou Diouf uses *ceddo* in the title of his study of nineteenth-century Kajoor, and attributes the practice to Latsukaabe, *Kajoor*, 92–6. The word *ceddo* has several meanings in Wolof. Its primary meaning is "unbeliever," "pagan," or "traditionalist." In the early nineteenth century Muslim critics of the old regime labeled the monarchy and its warrior henchmen as *ceddo*, with the result that "warrior" became a secondary meaning of the word.
95 Cadamosto, *Voyages*, 29–30.
96 Valentim Fernandes, *Description de la Côte d'Afrique de Ceuta au Sénégal (1505–1507)*, (eds.) P. de Cenival and Theodore Monod (Paris, 1938), 11.
97 Cadomosto, *Voyages*, 17–18. I have changed the punctuation in Crone's translation and eliminated some of his bracketed additions to the text.
98 Here I differ from the interpretation of Jean Boulègue, *Le Grand Jolof*, 73–5, who argues from the same oral traditions that military slavery was a more or less perennial feature in the Senegambian states.
99 For an account of this conflict, Brüe, "Premier Voyage," 429–34.
100 Ibid., 380.
101 For a different interpretation of these events see Jean Boulègue, "Lat-Sukaabe Fall ou l'Opiniatrété d'un Roi contre les Echanges Inegaux au Sénéngal," in *Les Africains* (Paris, 1977), IX, 171–93.
102 See the important article of Lucie G. Colvin, "Islam and the state of Kajoor: A Case of Successful Resistance to Jihad," *Journal of African History*, 15, 4 (1974), 587–606, which criticizes the view that there was a conflict between a Muslim and a Pagan party in Kajoor in the nineteenth century as a partisan Muslim distortion of the conflict between rulers and clerics.
103 Carson I. A. Richie (ed.), "Deux Textes sur le Sénégal (1673–77)," [Louis Moreau de Chambonneau], *Bulletin de l'IFAN*, B, 30, 1, (1968) 338.
104 Ritchie, "Deux Textes," 33–9.
105 This factor in the jihad was first emphasized by Boubacar Barry, "La Guerre des Marabouts dans le Région du Fleuve Sénégal de 1673 à 1677," *Bulletin de l'IFAN*, B, 23, 3, (1971), 564–89. The same interpretation was elaborated in more detail in Boubacar Barry, *Le Royaume du Waalo, Sénégal avant la Conquête* (Paris, 1972).
106 Boubacar Barry was the first to combine these two themes in his interpretation of this period. Other scholars, such as Curtin, "Jihad in West Africa," place more emphasis on religious reform; or like H. T. Norris, "Znaga Islam during the Seventeenth and

Eighteenth Centuries," *Bulletin of the School of Oriental and African Studies*, 33, (1969) 496–526, on tensions in Mauritanian society.

107 Ritchie, "Deux Textes," 351–3.

108 Jean Boulègue, "La Participation Possible des Centres de Pir et de Ndogal à la Revolution Islamique Sénégambienne de 1673," in Jean Boulègue (ed.), *Contributions à l'Histoire du Sénégal* (Paris, 1987), 119–25.

109 See sources cited in Colvin, "Islam and Kajoor," 597–8; Boulègue, "Participation," 121.

110 Brüe, "Premier Voyage," 400.

111 Ibid., 415.

112 Boulègue, "Participation," 121, on the restoration of Pir, whose marabouts now trace the foundation of their village to the reign of Latsukaabe.

2 Slavery and the slave trade in the Lower Senegal

1 See Stuart B. Schwartz, *Sugar Plantations in the Formation of Brazilian Society: Bahia, 1550–1835* (Cambridge, 1985) and Richard S. Dunn, *Sugar and Slaves: The Rise of the English Planter Class in the English West Indies, 1624–1713* (Chapel Hill, 1972).

2 Philip Curtin, *Economic Change in Precolonial Africa: Senegambia in the Era of the Slave Trade* (Madison, 1975).

3 In particular see Paul E. Lovejoy, *Transformations in Slavery: A History of Slavery in Africa* (Cambridge, 1983).

4 "Premier voyage de Brüe (1697)", in C. A. Walckenaer, *Histoire Générale des Voyages* (Paris, 1826), II, 383.

5 Ibid., 427.

6 Boubacar Barry, *La Sénégambie du XVe au XIXe Siècle: Traite Négrière, Islam et Conquête Coloniale* (Paris, 1988), is a recent and important example for all of Senegambia. Abdoulaye Bathily, "Guerriers, Tributaires, et Marchands. Le Gajaaga (ou Galam) le 'Pays de l'Or'. Le Développement et la Régression d'une Formation Economique et Sociale Sénégalaise (*c*. 8e–19e Siècle)," thèse pour le Doctorat des Lettres, Université de Dakar, 1985, 3 volumes, offers a similar analysis, in greater detail, of the kingdom of Gajaaga. A similar interpretation is presented in many of the essays of Martin Klein, for example, "Slavery, the Slave Trade, and Legitimate Commerce", *Etudes d'Histoire Africaine*, 2 (1970), 19–20.

7 Barry, *Sénégambie*, 127.

8 French National Archives, Paris: C 6 6, Charpentier, Mémoire sur le Galam, 1725.

9 Philip Curtin, "The Abolition of the Slave Trade from Senegambia", in David Eltis and James Walvin (eds.), *The Abolition of the Atlantic Slave Trade: Origins and Effects in Europe, Africa, and the Americas* (Madison, 1981), 89.

10 *House of Commons Sessional Papers of the Eighteenth Century* (ed. Sheila Lambert) (Wilmington, 1975), LXXIII, 292.

11 Curtin, "Abolition", 89–91, presents a convincing case for this analysis of the distribution of profits, but does not mention the trade in grain. Richard L. Roberts, *Warriors, Merchants, and Slaves: The State and Economy in the Middle Niger Valley, 1700–1914* (Stamford, 1987), whose work focuses on the nineteenth century, does not specifically discuss the numbers and profitability of the Bambara slave trade. See Curtin, *Economic Change*, 177–82.

12 The economic geography of the Lower Senegal and its trade hinterland are discussed in more detail below, in chapter 3 "The Atlantic Kingdom."

13 It is sometimes assumed, particularly by non-Africanist scholars, that this data gives relatively precise figures on regional and ethnic origins. However, the terms used were

Notes

often vague, and referred to ports of trade, "Gambia" or "Senegal." Ethnic or linguistic data reported in the New World colonies is also suspect, because there is little reason to believe that precise identification was made. The existence of ethnic preferences in some slave-purchasing regions may have encouraged slave traders to present slaves as members of well-known and desirable ethnic groups. Ports of export were associated with particular ethnic labels, even if they drew on a fairly large hinterland. This is the main reason why most estimates, beginning with the pioneering study of Philip Curtin, *The Atlantic Slave Trade: A Census* (Madison, 1969) aggregate the data into large supply regions: 221.

14 Two efforts to estimate the trade from the Lower Senegal have been made: Curtin, *Economic Change*, I, 184, presents a table which indicates "Slave Exports from Wolof and Sereer Coastal States" in different years. A more detailed presentation of the same kind is given by Charles Becker and Victor Martin, "Kayor et Baol: Royaumes Sénégalaises et Traite des Esclaves au XVIIIe Siècle," *Revue Française d'Histoire d'Outre-Mer*, 52 (1975), Table 2, 279–81, but the subsequent analysis of the data presented in this table is quite summary.

15 C 6 3, Mémoire: La Courbe, September 14, 1705.

16 This can be deduced from the table of Becker and Martin, who describe the debt system as characteristic of the early eighteenth century.

17 The context indicates that he does not include the upriver trade here. I have used the text edited by Charles Becker: Joseph Pruneau, *Mémoire sur le Commerce de la Concession de Sénégal* (Kaolack, 1983).

18 Pruneau, *Mémoire*, 19–20.

19 Ibid., 50.

20 C 6 13, June 30, 1751.

21 C 6 13, February 24, 1752.

22 Pruneau, *Mémoire*, gives the price of a slave in Kajoor, Bawol, or Siin as five guns, 53.

23 C 6 14, June 20, 1753; ibid., July 11, 1754; ibid., July 31 1755. The figures given by Becker and Martin for 1755 indicate 600 slaves at Saint Louis and 500 at Gorée. The totals are the same.

24 C 6 15, Mémoire sur la Coste d'Affrique, 1765.

25 C 6 15, Gorée, May 12, 1766.

26 The French were at least partially aware of this and commented on it: C 6 16, Observations sur l'Isle de Gorée par M. le Rocheblave, 1773. Another document, ibid., March 22, 1773, suggests that part of Kajoor and Bawol's trade was also attracted south to the Gambia.

27 This data is summarized by David Richardson, "Slave Exports from West and West-Central Africa, 1700–1810: New Estimates of Volume and Distribution," *Journal of African History*, 30 (1989), 1–22, especially Table 6, 14.

28 C 6 15, Mémoire sur la Coste d'Affrique, 1765.

29 C 6 17, Mémoire sur l'Isle de Gorée, Mess. de Bellecoube et Chevreux, April 19, 1776.

30 C 6 16, Mémoire, May 1771.

31 Comment in C 6 16, Observations sur l'Isle de Gorée par M. le Rocheblave, 1773.

32 For a discussion of the famine and its effects on slave exports see chapter 5 below.

33 C 6 14, Lettres, June 20, 1753; June 20, 1754; July 11, 1754; July 31, 1755.

34 Pruneau, *Mémoire*, 88; Richardson, "New Estimates", 14.

35 C 6 19, Résultat de la Traite des Nègres, 1786; C 6 19, Tableau d'Exportation, 1788; Richardson, ibid.

36 Pruneau, *Mémoire*, 51, 53.

37 Ibid., 52–3, gives a list of goods needed to trade in Kajoor, Bawol, and Siin.

38 Charles Becker and Victor Martin (eds.), "Mémoire Inédit de Doumet (1769). Le Kayor

et les Pays Voisins au Cours de la Seconde Moitié du XVIIIe Siècle", *Bulletin de l'IFAN*, 36, B, (1974), 39, 41.

39 Ibid., 39–40.

40 Ibid., 40.

41 *House of Commons Sessional Papers*, LXXIII, 292–3, 295.

42 Doumet, "Le Kayor," 43.

43 For a discussion of early sources on the Sereer minorities of Kajoor and Bawol see Jean Boulègue, *Le Grand Jolof (XIIe–XVIe Siècle)* (Paris, 1987) 19–21. The Sereer of the north-west or Sereer-Cangin are linguistically distinct from Sereer-Siin speakers, but are conventionally referred to as Sereer in Senegal. There were also Sereer-Siin speakers in south-west Bawol (Jegem, Sandok, Mbadaan) who were independent of the kingdom of Siin and who resisted incorporation in Bawol. Their social structure resembled the small-scale, stateless communities of the Sereer-Cangin.

44 Michael Adanson, "A Voyage to Senegal, the Isle of Gorée, and the River Gambia," in John Pinkerton, *A General Collection of the Best and Most Interesting Voyages and Travels . . .* (London, 1814), XVI., 641, 643.

45 For a general introduction to the problem of maroonage in the Americas see Richard Price (ed.), *Maroon Societies: Rebel Slave Communities in the Americas* (New York, 1973). See also his *First-Time: The Historical Vision of an Afro-American People* (Baltimore, 1983) for a discussion of Saramaka collective identity, based on the opposition between freedom and slavery and impregnated with distrust of outsiders and fear of betrayal, 11–12. Joseph Miller, *The Way of Death: Merchant Capitalism and the Angolan Slave Trade, 1730–1830* (Madison, 1988), 38, 129. 134, 161, discusses the formation of maroon communities and territories of refuge during the Angolan slave trade.

46 Cadamosto, as quoted by Boulègue, *Le Grand Jolof*, 20.

47 C 6 5, Lettre: Brüe, October 3, 1719.

48 C 6 15, Mémoire sur la Coste d'Affrique, 1765.

49 No village of this name currently exists. However, Guereau can probably be identified with Nguekokh, located just south of the Cap de Naze, and about five kilometres inland from the coast.

50 Interview, Bandia elders, March 28, 1989. Principal informant: Farba Siis.

51 Rokhaya Fall describes the Sereer revolt and the land policy of Ceendela in "Teeñ Ce Ndela ou la d'Autorité Politique des Faal dans le Bawol" in Jean Boulègue, ed., *Contributions à l'Histoire du Sénégal* (Paris, 1987) 109–117, and in more detail in "Le Royaume du Bawol du XVIe au XIXe Siècle," thèse de 3e cycle, Université Paris–I, 1983.

52 Adanson, "Voyage," 643–4.

53 Abbé David Boilat, *Esquisses Sénégalaises* (Paris, 1853), 174.

54 *House of Commons Sessional Papers*, LXVIII, 7, testimony of John Barnes.

55 Abdoulaye-Bara Diop, *La Société Wolof: Tradition et Changement. Les Systèmes d'Inégalité et de Domination* (Paris, 1981). Diop uses the caste model and describes the *geer* (free persons not belonging to a "caste" group) as the superior caste, and slaves as a pseudo-caste in an effort to analyze all Wolof society in terms of caste, 35–6.

56 Diop, *Société Wolof*, discusses all these points in detail, 27–107.

57 On the role of blacksmiths in circumcision, Diop, *Société Wolof*, 63. In the Wolof folktale, "The Woodcutter's Son," *Doomu Lawbe*, the *fara tegg* ("head blacksmith") is described as a keeper of the dead in all the country, Lilyan Kesteloot and Cherif Mbodj (eds.), *Contes et Mythes Wolof* (Dakar, 1983), 109.

58 See the discussion of the *nyamakala* in Patrick R. McNaughton, *The Mande Blacksmiths: Knowledge, Power and Art in West Africa* (Bloomington, 1988).

Notes

59 Diop, *Société Wolof*, 92.
60 Ibid., 52–3, 93.
61 Yoro Jaw in R. Rousseau, "Le Sénégal d'Autrefois. Etude sur le Oualo. Cahiers de Yoro Dyao," *Bulletin du Comité des Etudes Historiques et Scientifiques sur l'Afrique Occidentale Françaises*, 12 (1929), 180–1, gives the titles and functions of these leaders in the Wolof kingdoms.
62 Sometimes the *sabb-lekk* are subdivided into groups who specialize in the verbal arts and others who specialize in music. A separate group of courtiers, the *ñoole*, can also be distinguished, primarily because of their different origins and their practice of endogamy. See Diop, *Société Wolof*, 61.
63 Yoro Jaw, "Etude sur le Oualo," 177–9, recounts the myth of *ñoole* origins, described as the descendants of a *cadavre* and a woman. For the Wolof text of this myth, Lilyan Kesteloot and Bassirou Dieng, *Du Tiedo au Talibe* (Paris, 1989), 179–80. Abdoulaye-Bara Diop gives a similar myth which explains the origins of the *gewel*. When two brothers were lost in the desert, the eldest cut off a piece of his own flesh to save his younger brother who, when he discovered this extraordinary act, began singing his praises: Diop, *Société Wolof*, 43.
64 Yoro Jaw, "Etude sur le Oualo," 185–8, 203–5, for a general discussion of the *gewel*. European merchants have left numerous descriptions of their meetings with Wolof kings and nobles, always accompanied by their *gewel*: Prosper Cultru (ed.), *Premier Voyage du Sieur de la Courbe Fait à la Coste d'Afrique en 1685* (Paris, 1913), 40–4, 71–3, 139, 144.
65 Yoro Jaw describes these performances, "Etude sur le Oualo," 204–5.
66 Kesteloot and Dieng, "Cossanu Noole," *Du Tiedo au Talibe*, 179; *Booba noo doon liggeyal boroom alal yi di leen taxawal ci seen buntu ker yi walla di nekk seen jotalikat, walla itam seen laman*, "They used to work for the nobles [literally, "masters of wealth"], standing for them in the doors of their houses, serving as their tax collectors, or as those who received rents on land." In this passage *laman* refers to those who collected taxes on agriculture.
67 Yoro Jaw, "Etude sur le Oualo," 200.
68 Yoro Jaw, "Etude sur le Oualo," makes this distinction, noting that the slaves of the king were divided into ranked orders, 191.
69 Ibid. The distinction between these crown slaves and the larger group of royal slaves (*jaami-burr*) is not often made. Yoro Jaw divides this latter group into slaves owned by the maternal family (*jaami-ndey*), and slaves owned by the paternal family (*jaami-baay*). The former were more numerous and more important, ibid., 190, 193.
70 Ibid., 166.
71 Ibid., 193.
72 Yoro Jaw defined *dag* as a "noble courtier-soldier attached to a chief" in "Etude sur le Oualo," 194.
73 Ibid., 166–7.
74 Personal communication, Ibou Sarr.
75 Doumet, "La Kayor," 39.
76 In Kajoor and Bawol, the political chief of the royal slaves, called the Jawrin Mbul Gallo in Kajoor, and the Fara Lambaay in Bawol, was one of the most important royal officials, chief of the police and one of the army commanders. The Fara Sef was responsible for collecting royal taxes, for providing the army with provisions, weapons, and horses, and was the chief of staff and first general of the royal army. The Fara Biir Ker, or House Intendant, and the Jaraaf Bunt Ker, were responsible for the management of the royal household. For a discussion of these officials, Diop, *Société Wolof*, 139–40; Aram Diop, Oumar Ben Khatab Dia, Jean-Claude Galdi, *Jukib Tanneefu Baat-Yu-Sax/ Recueil de Textes Choisis* (Dakar, 1975), 42–4.

210

77 Yoro Jaw, "Etude sur le Oualo," 173.
78 Charles Becker and Victor Martin (eds.), "Recueil sur la Vie des Damel par Tanor Latsoukabe Fall," *Bulletin de l'IFAN*, 36, B, 1 (1974), 117–18.
79 Charles Becker and Victor Martin (eds.), "Details Historiques et Politiques Inédit (1778) de J. A. Le Brasseur," *Bulletin de l'IFAN*, 39, B, 1 (1977), 98. Although not directly identified as slaves in the text, nakedness was often symbolic of slavery in Senegambia, and in this case 300 naked field workers leaves little doubt as to their slave status.
80 Fall, "Recueil," 122.
81 Curtin, *Economic Change*, 156–68, discusses economic and political enslavement as pure types, and then presents data which shows that Senegambia tended more to the political model, because of the relative inelasticity of supply in relation to price increases. No strong argument is made for a political model, except implicitly, in the overall emphasis on merchant activities. Curtin's later essay on abolition restates his views in stronger terms, based on an analysis of the distribution of profits from slave trading: Curtin, "Abolition of the Slave Trade," 89–91.
82 This is particularly true in the historiography of Dahomey. For a recent review of the literature stressing these points see Robin Law, "Slave-Raiders and Middlemen, Monopolists and Free-Traders: The Supply of Slaves for the Atlantic Trade in Dahomey c. 1715–1850," *Journal of African History*, 30 (1989), 45–68.
83 This idea appears in Martin Klein's early essay on slavery in Senegambia: Martin A. Klein, "Servitude among the Wolof and Sereer of Senegambia," in Suzanne Miers and Igor Kopytoff, *Slavery in Africa* (Madison, 1977), 351.
84 Barry, *La Sénégambie*; Klein, "Slavery, the Slave Trade, and Legitimate Commerce"; Martin A. Klein, "The Impact of the Atlantic Slave Trade on the Societies of the Western Sudan," *Social Science History*, 14: 2 (1990), 233–6; Roberts, *Warriors, Merchants, and Slaves*.
85 This interpretation is expressed most clearly and comprehensively by Lovejoy, *Transformations*.
86 For theoretical discussions of the conditions that favor slavery and forced labor see Evsey D. Domar, "The Causes of Slavery or Serfdom: A Hypothesis," *Journal of Economic History*, 30 (1970), 18–32; and Ester Boserup, *The Conditions of Agricultural Growth: The Economics of Agrarian Change under Population Pressure* (Chicago, 1965). Moses I. Finley has related these factors to the creation of slave systems in the ancient and modern worlds, *Ancient Slavery and Modern Ideology* (New York, 1980), 85–6. For a detailed case study which relates demographic and labor supply factors to the development of slavery see Allan Kulikoff, *Tobacco and Slaves: The Development of Southern Cultures in the Chesapeake, 1680–1800* (Chapel Hill, 1986).
87 This factor has been recognized in some studies of the eighteenth century. There is a brief discussion of the millet trade in the Gambia in Curtin, *Economic Change*, 230–1, who noted that *juula* traders employed some of their slaves in producing millet which they then sold to Europeans to provision ships, or to feed slaves awaiting shipment. Millet was sold to obtain salt and European manufactures which could be resold inland. See François Manchuelle, "Slavery, Emancipation and Labour Migration in West Africa: The Case of the Soninke," *Journal of African History*, 30 (1989), 93, who further develops Curtin's analysis. However, in both cases the focus is on the strategies of long-distance merchants, not on the structure of the regional economies.
88 Fall, "Recueil," 114. According to oral tradition, this innovation would have occurred about 1707. Each family owed one animal from each of its herds and a granary of millet.
89 Ibid., 115.

Notes

90 Yoro Jaw, "Etude sur le Oualo," 189, makes this distinction. See also Diop, *Société Wolof*, 119.

91 For a discussion of the factors that reduced the value of the locally enslaved, see Curtin, *Economic Change*, 155.

92 In the early colonial period *jaam sayoor* was defined as follows. "The condition of those called *saiors* is different. They are entirely supported by those who own them, and they owe all their time, all their labor in exchange for this support. They can be sold or traded and cannot marry or dispose of their children without the consent of the master, who has the absolute right to give them in inheritance to their children or to other members of their family as they wish." ANS, K 18, Pièce 5, Thies, January, 1904.

93 Martin Klein and Paul Lovejoy, "Slavery in West Africa," in Henry A. Gemery and Jan S. Hogendorn (eds.), *The Uncommon Market: Essays in the Economic History of the Atlantic Slave Trade* (New York, 1979), 181–212; David Northrup, "Nineteenth-Century Patterns of Slavery and Economic Growth in Southwestern Nigeria," *International Journal of African Historical Studies*, 12 (1979), 1–16. Northrup's argument is particularly interesting because he notes the development of slavery in three regional sectors: the coastal maritime sector, oil production, and food production.

94 Paul E. Lovejoy, "Plantations in the Economy of the Sokoto Caliphate," *Journal of African History*, 19, 3 (1978), 341–68; Paul E. Lovejoy, "The Characteristics of Plantations in the Nineteenth Century Sokoto Caliphate (Islamic West Africa)," *American Historical Review*, 4 (1979), 1267–92; Jan Hogendorn, "The Economics of Slave Use on Two 'Plantations' in the Zaria Emirate of the Sokoto Caliphate," *International Journal of African Historical Studies*, 10, 3 (1977), 369–84. For comments on this interpretation, James F. Searing, "Aristocrats, Slaves, and Peasants: Power and Dependency in the Wolof States, 1700–1850," *The International Journal of African Historical Studies*, 21, 3 (1988), 475–503.

95 By this last criterion the plantations of East Africa, studied by Fred Cooper, *Plantation Slavery in East Africa* (New Haven, 1977), provide much closer parallels to plantations in the Americas than those in nineteenth-century West Africa. But Cooper argues that slavery in East Africa "leaned more in the precapitalist direction," ibid., 111. Any discussion of this issue has to come to terms with the controversy generated by Eugene D. Genovese, *The Political Economy of Slavery: Studies in the Economy and Society of the Slave South* (New York, 1965), who argued that Southern slavery was essentially precapitalist and aristocratic. I agree with Genovese's critics, and therefore prefer to reserve the term "plantation" for the capitalist slave economies of the Americas.

96 The alternate phrase for the *jaam juddu* in Wolof is *jaami neeg*, "slaves of the house." Diop, *Société Wolof*, 200. *Jaamu neeg* (sing.) was translated into French as *esclave de case*.

97 Yoro Jaw, "Etude sur le Oualo," 195. This system of defining slave obligations, and the changes that occurred over a slave's life, particularly after marriage and the birth of children, have often been neglected by scholars, who refer only to the two legal status groups. However, they are discussed in colonial sources which have been used by many historians of slavery: K 18, Pièce 7, Baol Oriental, Thies, February 4, 1904, describes in some detail the work regime of slave children. On slave marriage see Diop, *Société Wolof*, 200–1.

98 This is true of Yoro Jaw, who describes court slaves, the forms of slave property and, very generally, the use of slave labor in agriculture.

99 C 6 15, Mémoire, September 14, 1765.

100 In the 1750s Adanson noted the slaves owned by the village chief at Sor, Adanson, "Voyage," 612. A French Company document from the 1780s, which described a voyage from Ganjool to Galam, noted that the travellers were received at every stop by *maîtres*

de village and *notables*, who placed them in the care of slave women: C 6 19, Voyage du Sénégal à Galam Par Terre, M. Durand, September 12, 1786. The same pattern was noted by Mollien in the early nineteenth century, who described the slaves of the headman of Niakra and Kokki; Gaspard Mollien in Hubert Deschamps (ed.) *L'Afrique Occidentale en 1818* (Paris, 1967), 52, 61.

101 *House of Commons Sessional Papers*, LXXIII, 14.

102 Ibid., 296.

103 Ibid., 299. Dalrymple described slave punishments on Grenada in detail.

104 Doumet, "Le Kayor", 43.

105 This survey data is summarized in K 16, Pièce 45, Tableau: Etat Synoptique des Renseignments Fournis par les Commandants de Cercle sur le Régime de la Captivité dans l'AOF. According to this survey there were 26,045 slaves in Bawol and southern Kajoor (cercle de Thies), 25,000 slaves in Kajoor and Jolof (cercle de Tivaoune and cercle de Louga), 26,000 slaves in Waalo (cercle de Dagana). Further concentrations of slaves were in Podor (18,600), Kaedi (18,600), Matam (20,000), and Bakel (35,000).

106 Pruneau, *Mémoire*, 51.

107 Ibid., 50–1.

108 For a more complete analysis of the problem of estimating grain sales, including more detailed discussion of this data, see chapter 3 and chapter 5 below.

109 Doumet, "Le Kayor," 37–8.

110 For examples and discussion from Brazil, see Stuart B. Schwartz, *Sugar Plantations in the Formation of Brazilian Society: Bahia, 1550–1835* (Cambridge, 1985), 155–9.

111 Mungo Park, *Travels in the Interior Districts of Africa . . . in the Years 1795, 1796 and 1797* (London, 1800), 432. In the same chapter Park also affirmed that most war captives were "re-enslaved" slaves, because free persons were less likely to be captured in times of war, and more likely to be ransomed, 431.

112 Park, *Travels*, 439.

113 *Voyages to the Coast of Africa by Mess. Saugnier and Brisson* (London, 1792), 275, an English translation of M. Saugnier, *Relations de Plusieurs Voyages à la Côte d'Afrique* (Paris, 1791).

114 For a good discussion of this problem see Martin A. Klein, "Women and Slavery in the Western Sudan," in Claire C. Robertson and Martin A. Klein (eds.), *Women and Slavery in Africa* (Madison, 1983), 67–92. Some of the other essays in this volume show the general importance of this trend in the slave trade (Herbert S. Klein, "African Women in the Atlantic Slave Trade") and discuss its demographic implications (John Thornton, "Sexual Demography: The Impact of the Slave Trade on Family Structure"). See also Patrick Manning, "The Enslavement of Africans: A Demographic Model," *Canadian Journal of African Studies*, 15 (1981), 499–526. Recent research has revised the sex ratios in the export trade from Senegambia downwards, from earlier estimates, particularly from regions near the coast, like the Lower Senegal: see David Geggus, "Sex Ratio, Age and Ethnicity in the Atlantic Slave Trade: Data from French Shipping and Plantation Records," *Journal of African History*, 30 (1989), 23–44.

115 For a counter-view see Claude Meillasoux, "Female Slavery," in Robertson and Klein, *Women and Slavery in Africa*. Meillasoux speaks of "laws of slave reproduction" in this essay, referring to his belief that no slave population could reproduce itself biologically, so all slave systems depended on purchase and raiding. The low fertility of slave women shown by much African data does not prove that masters took no interest in female slaves' capacity for reproduction. Second generation slaves had special characteristics which made them valuable, even if low fertility reduced their numbers.

116 For a good discussion of the special position of women slaves, see Martin Klein, "Women and Slavery," 67–92. For a recent discussion of the export data see David

Geggus, "Sex ratio." Philip Curtin, *Economic Change*, 175–7, gives sample data with much higher sex ratios than this average, from 8 : 1 to 4 : 1.

117 This point is stressed by Paul E. Lovejoy, "Concubinage in the Sokoto Caliphate (1804–1903)," *Slavery and Abolition*, 11 (1990), 158–89.

118 Park, *Travels*, 430.

119 Saugnier, *Voyages*, 336.

120 Ibid., 332, 335.

121 André Delcourt, *La France et les Establissements Français au Sénégal entre 1713 et 1763* (Dakar, 1952), 130; James L. A. Webb, "Shifting Sands: An Economic History of the Mauritanian Sahara, 1500–1850," unpublished Ph.D. thesis, Johns Hopkins University, 1984, 157–63. Adanson, "Voyage," 609, noted the different ethnic origins of slave and free populations in Saint Louis and the kingdom of Waalo. There are many references to "Bambara" slaves, a term which probably referred to a number of peoples from the upper Senegal and middle Niger.

122 Francis Moore, *Travels into the Inland Parts of Africa* (London, 1738), 43. Saugnier, *Voyages*, 275–8, stressed the dangers for European slave traders of violating the provision against the sale of household slaves.

123 *House of Commons Sessional Papers*, LXXIII, 18.

124 Testimony of Charles Wadstrom, ibid., LXXIII, 35.

125 Many of the debates center around Suzanne Miers and Igor Kopytoff, "African 'Slavery' as an Institution of Marginality," in Miers and Kopytoff, *Slavery in Africa*, 3–81, which focuses on the absorbtive dynamic of African slave systems and gives a systematic and quasi-normative status to the kinship idiom used to describe rights and status in many African slave systems. Critics of their interpretation notably Lovejoy in *Transformations* and elsewhere, have reinterpreted the "norms" as ideology and emphasized the cases in which they were violated.

126 For a nineteenth-century description of this labor system see Frederic Carrère and Paul Holle, *De la Sénégambie Française* (Paris, 1855), 53, 55. In the earliest Portuguese descriptions of slavery in Senegambia travelers described a six-day work week for the master, and one day where the slave was free to labor for him/herself: Valentim Fernandes, *Description de la Côte d'Afrique de Ceuta au Sénégal (1505–1507)*, (eds.) P. de Cenival and Theodore Monod (Paris, 1938), 11. Early colonial sources describe the same labor regime: K 18, Captivité, 1904.

127 There were a number of common elements to the stories. Europeans were said to purchase slaves as food for consumption in their homelands. The European homeland was depicted as a watery kingdom with no solid land. Europeans like Mungo Park reassured Africans by telling them slaves who "had crossed the salt water . . . were employed in cultivating the land." Park, *Travels*, 475.

128 La Courbe, *Premier Voyage*, 51–2.

129 Adanson, "Voyage," 656.

130 In his summation of early French colonial surveys of slavery in West Africa, Georges Deherme arued that the difference between "household slaves" and "trade slaves" was less a matter of birth than the result of the master's decision to grant a plot of land and permit marriage: Georges Deherme, *L'Afrique Occidentale Française: Action Politique, Action Economique, Action Sociale* (Paris, 1908), 384–5.

131 Ibid.

132 According to Carrère and Holle slaves dispersed when labor in the fields was finished and supported themselves during the dry season from their labor as weavers: *Sénégambie Française*, 54–5. Other sources suggest that slaves paid their master half their wages when they were hired out, as frequently occurred in Saint Louis and Gorée: Curtin, *Economic Change*, 120–1. The difference may be related to whether or not the master

was responsible for slave subsistence during the agricultural off season. If Carrère and Holle are correct, the only motivation for slaves to return to their masters would have been landlessness and fear of reenslavement and sale.

133 This is recognized by Lovejoy, *Transformations*, 206, but his overall emphasis is on the emergence of a "highly developed plantation economy," 191.

134 Tenancy labor systems evolved in Latin America as one way of extracting labor from Indian villages and dispossessed Indian tenants. The so-called "second serfdom" in Eastern Europe enserfed peasant communities in a period marked by world demand for grain exports. For general discussions of these labor systems, see Magnus Morner, "The Spanish American Hacienda: A Survey of Recent Literature," *Hispanic American Historical Review, (HAHR)* 53, 2 (1973), 13–216; James Lockhart, "Encomienda and Hacienda: The Evolution of the Great Estate in the Spanish Indies," *HAHR* 49, 3, (1969), 411–29; Arnold J. Bauer, "Rural Workers in Spanish America: Problems of Peonage and Oppression," *HAHR*, 59, 1 (1979), 34–63; Jerome Blum, "Rise of Serfdom in Eastern Europe," *American Historical Review*, 62, 4 (1957), 807–36; Withold Kula, *An Economic Theory of the Feudal System: Towards a Model of the Polish Economy* (London, 1976); and Peter Kolchin, *Unfree Labor: American Slavery and Russian Serfdom* (Cambridge, 1987), 3–5, 58–78, 104, for definitions and discussions of labor management in Russian serfdom. Serfs under *barshchina* owed three full days of labor, from sunrise to sundown, to their masters. Serfs under *obrok* management paid an annual rent in grain or cash.

135 Yoro Jaw, "Etude sur le Oualo," 194; Diop, *Société Wolof*, 200–1.

136 Yoro Jaw, "Etude sur le Oualo," 189, 197.

137 Boilat, *Esquisses*, commentary on plate 6 of illustrated atlas.

138 Yoro Jaw, "Etude sur le Oualo," 167.

3 The Atlantic kingdom: maritime commerce and social change

1 Mungo Park, *Travels in the Interior Districts of Africa . . .in the Years 1795, 1796 and 1797* (London, 1800) gives a first-hand account of a slave caravan traveling the alternate route to the upper Gambia, and Park noted the deaths, runaways, and slave sales that occurred on the way. For estimates of slave mortality in the Gajaaga trade, Abdoulaye Bathily, "Guerriers, Tributaires et Marchands. Le Gajaaga (ou Galam) le 'Pays d'Or.' Le Développement et la Régression d'une formation Economique et Sociale Sénégalaise (*c.* 8e–19e Siècle)," thèse pour le Doctorat ès Lettres, Université de Dakar, 1985, II, 400–3.

2 Joseph Pruneau, *Mémoire sur le Commerce de la Concession de Sénégal* (Kaolack, 1983) 35.

3 Ibid., 34–5.

4 According to Pruneau, ibid., 36–8.

5 On the grain trade from Gajaaga in the eighteenth century, Bathily, "Guerriers, Tributaires et Marchands," II, 414–18, who stresses its links with the slave trade.

6 For a more detailed discussion of the development of slavery on Saint Louis and Gorée, see chapter 4. Both islands had Bambara quarters in the eighteenth century, where the slaves lived.

7 M. Saugnier, *Relations de Plusieurs Voyages à la Côte d'Afrique* (Paris, 1791), 246.

8 Ibid., 247. The reference to pistachio nuts probably refers to peanuts.

9 According to Pruneau, the French purchased about 130 to 150 slaves on the lower and middle river from Waalo, Kajoor, and Fuuta Tooro. One-third were brought to the fort on Saint Louis, and the other two-thirds were purchased by ships trading on the river: Pruneau, *Mémoire*, 18.

Notes

10 The grain trade has been neglected in most studies of the slave trade. Philip Curtin, *Economic Change in Precolonial Africa: Senegambia in the Era of the Slave Trade* (Madison, 1975), set the pattern by classifying millet as a minor product by default. It was important, but not much is known about it, 229. There are important exceptions to this neglect. One of the earliest discussions of millet was written by André Delcourt (ed.), *Pierre David: Journal d'un Voiage Fait en Bambouc en 1744* (Paris, 1974), Appendix VIII, "Le Mil: Un Problème d'Alimentation Africaine," 247–53.

11 See also Bathily, "Guerriers, Tributaires et Marchands," II, 414–18; Oumar Kane, "Le Fuuta Tooro des Satigi aux Almaami (1512–1807)," thèse pour le Doctorat d'Etat, Université de Dakar, 1986, 3 volumes. I, 362–4; Boubacar Barry, *Le Royaume du Waalo: Sénégal avant la Conquête* (Paris, 1972), 125–7.

12 Recent research has emphasized in particular the role of drought, epidemics, and famine as symptoms of the social and economic crisis provoked by the slave trade. Charles Becker argues that, rather than being natural disasters, these crises were often precipitated by warfare, and form part of the broader impact of the slave trade: Charles Becker, "Conditions Ecologiques, Crises de Subsistance et Histoire de la Population à l'Epoque de la Traite des Esclaves en Sénégambie," *Canadian Journal of African Studies*, 20, 3 (1986), 357–76; and Charles Becker, "Notes sure les Conditions Ecologiques en Sénégambie aux 17e et 18e siècles," *African Economic History*, 14 (1985), 167–216.

13 Ocean fishing and the exploitation of coastal salt deposits were important economic activities before the expansion of the Atlantic maritime trade. See Jean-Pierre Chauveau, "Une Histoire Maritime Africaine Est-Elle Possible? Historiographie et Histoire de la Navigation et de la Pêche Africains à la Côte Occidentale Depuis le XVe Siècle," *Cahiers d'Etudes Africaines*, 26 (1986), 173–235.

14 On the purchase of fish from neighboring villages to feed slaves in transit on Saint Louis and Gorée, C 6 14, Repose du Conseil Supérieur au Mémoire et Observations, February, 1754.

15 On the importance of salt and the salt trade in the western Sahara and the western Sudan, E. Ann McDougall, "Salts of the Western Sahara: Myths, Mysteries, and Historical Significance," *International Journal of African Historical Studies*, 23, 2 (1990), 231–57.

16 On the trade in footstuffs, Pruneau, *Mémoire*, 23–4, 29.

17 On the trade in manufactured goods, *House of Commons Sessional Papers of the Eighteenth Century*, (ed. Sheila Lambert) (Wilmington, 1975) LXXIII 32–5.

18 George E. Brooks, *Western Africa to c. 1850 AD: A Provisional Historical Schema based on Climate Periods* (Bloomington, 1985) 197–213, for this general theme.

19 For a general discussion of this theme, Joseph C. Miller, "The Significance of Drought, Disease, and Famine in the Agriculturally Marginal Zones of West-Central Africa," *Journal of African History*, 23, 1 (1982), 17–61.

20 Sekene Mody Cissoko, "Famines et Epidémies à Tombouctou et dans le Boucle du Niger du XVIe au XVIIIe Siècles," *Bulletin de l'IFAN*, B, 30, 3 (1968), 806–21, suggests that drought and famine were the underlying causes for the decline of the civilizations of the Niger in this period. This view is supported indirectly by recent archaeological research (particularly by the McIntoshes on Jenne), which suggests high population densities for the inland delta of the Niger c.500–1500. See summary in Graham Connah, *African Civilizations: Precolonial Cities and States in Tropical Africa* (Cambridge, 1987), 103–20.

21 *House of Commons Sessional Papers*, LXVIII, 205–6.

22 For a discussion of the Segu Bambara warrior state see Richard L. Roberts, *Warriors, Merchants, and Slaves: The State and Economy in the Middle Niger Valley, 1700–1914*

(Stanford, 1987), and "Production and Reproduction of Warrior States: Segu Bambara and Segu Tokolor," *International Journal of African Historical Studies*, 13, 4 (1980).

23 Gerald Roe Crone, ed., *The Voyages of Cadamosto and Other Documents on Western Africa in the Second Half of the Fifteenth Century* (London, 1937) 29.

24 Quoted in Oumar Kane, "Le Fuuta Tooro," I, 393–4.

25 For a good study of the commerce of this earlier period see Jean Boulègue, *Les Luso-Africains de Sénégambie, XVIe–XIXe Siècle* (Dakar, Université de Dakar, 1972) and Boulègue, *Le Grand Jolof (XIIIe–XVIe Siècle)* (Paris, 1987).

26 Early examples of this form of address to Atlantic merchants are Carson I. A. Ritchie (ed.) "Deux Textes sur le Sénégal (1673–77)," [Louis Moreau de Chambonneau], *Bulletin de l'IFAN*, B, 30, 1, (1968), 328; Prosper Cultru (ed.), *Premier Voyage du Sieur de la Courbe fait à la Coste d'Afrique en 1685* (Paris, 1913) 73.

27 For the history of the Compagnie du Sénégal in this period see André Delcourt, *La France et les Establissements Français au Sénégal entre 1713 et 1763* (Dakar, 1952).

28 For a discussion of the enormous importance of sugar in the world economy of this period, Sindey W. Mintz, *Sweetness and Power: The Place of Sugar in Modern History* (New York, 1985). There is no comparable history of tobacco, that "stinking weed," except through more general studies of colonial Virginia and the Chesapeake.

29 Robert Louis Stein, *The French Slave Trade in the Eighteenth Century: An Old Regime Business* (Madison, 1979) 18–21, 28, 148.

30 T. Bentley Duncan, *Atlantic Islands: Madeira, the Azores and the Cape Verdes in Seventeenth Century Navigation* (Chicago, 1972).

31 Bathily, "Guerriers, Tributaires et Marchands," II, 420–30.

32 Delcourt, *Pierre David*, 255–64, discusses the interrelations of the directors, related by family ties and friendship.

33 La Courbe, who replaced Chambonneau as director, and was later relieved of duty by Chambonneau on his return to Senegal, denounced the corruption that flourished under his predecessor, and left Senegal convinced that Chambonneau had blackened his name in Paris. On these events *Premier Voyage*, 4, 39, 65–7, 187–8.

34 Most of what is known about corruption and smuggling in the Company appears in the forms of accusations and counter-accusations, few of which can be verified. Pierre David, director of the Company in the 1740s, was denounced by one of his subordinates, Golberry, for smuggling gold out of Galam (Gajaaga) for his own profit: see Delcourt, *Pierre David*, 36–40.

35 Michael Adanson, "A Voyage to Senegal, the Isle of Gorée and the River Gambia," in John Pinkerton, *A General Collection of the Best and Most Interesting Voyages and Travels . . .*, (London, 1814) XVI, 599, 607.

36 Ibid., 611.

37 Adanson's analysis of the famine of the 1750s is discussed in chapter 5.

38 For a good discussion of the labor conditions in the eighteenth-century maritime world see Marcus Rediker, *Between the Devil and the Deep Blue Sea: Merchant Seamen, Pirates, and the Anglo-American Maritime World, 1700–1750* (Cambridge, 1987), 45–50, on the African trade. My comments on Senegal are based on Company archives.

39 C 6 5, Livres de Comptes: Bissaux, Juillet 1718.

40 C 6 5, Lettre: Brüe, October 3, 1719; December 31, 1719.

41 The focus on firearms has produced detailed studies such as Joseph E. Inikori, "The Import of Firearms into West Africa, 1750–1807: A Quantitative Analysis," *Journal of African History*, 18, 3, (1977), 339–68. For discussion of some of the assumptions underlying the debate on firearms see George Metcalf, "A Microcosm of Why Africans Sold Slaves: Akan Consumption Patterns in the 1770s," *Journal of African History*, 2 (1987), 377–94.

Notes

42 For a good discussion of the importance of African demand for foreign imports, Joseph C. Miller, *The Way of Death: Merchant Capitalism and the Angolan Slave Trade, 1730–1830* (Madison, 1988), 71–104; David Richardson, "West African Consumption Patterns and Their Influence in the Eighteenth-Century English Slave Trade," in Henry A. Gemery and Jan S. Hogendorn (eds.), *The Uncommon Market: Essays in the Economic History of the Atlantic Slave Trade* (New York, 1979).

43 Pruneau, *Mémoire*, 51 on the trade of millet for iron in Kajoor and Bawol, 22 on the trade for gum.

44 Ibid., 22–4, 51–3.

45 For a Company assessment of its costs see C 6 13, Mémoire, 1751. In the early eighteenth century the cost of imported African slaves in the sugar islands was so low that high mortality, much of it preventable, was accepted as part of operating costs. After 1763 the costs of slaves and imported food rose, causing changes in slave management, but even in this period it was the high price of food, rather than the high price of slaves from Africa, which encouraged reform. For a discussion which treats these issues see J. R. Ward, *British West Indian Slavery, 1750–1834: The Process of Amelioration* (Oxford, 1988), 1–61. It is instructive that in the 1770s a newly imported slave cost about 60 pounds, but that the same slave could cost 550 pounds a year in imported food, ibid., 45, 65.

46 David Robinson, for example, in his work has stressed Fuutanke perceptions of their superiority to the "people of the water," David Robinson, *The Holy War of Umar Tal: The Western Sudan in the Mid-Nineteenth Century* (Oxford, 1985), 140–1.

47 La Courbe, *Premier Voyage,* 78–9.

48 For a discussion of the form of Wolof folktales, Lilyan Kesteloot and Cherif Mbodj (eds.), *Contes et Mythes Wolof*, (Dakar 1983) 9–22.

49 Curtin, *Economic Change*, 289–93, interprets the payment of customs in the tradition of a mutal exchange of gifts, but he also notes that these payments paralleled similar taxes and tolls paid by African merchants.

50 These taxes were justified according to African market practice: one bar went to the person who had lodged the merchant selling the slave, a half-bar to the merchant who sold. In royal ports like Rufisque and Portudal, the fee for lodging costs went to a state official whom Europeans referred to as the Alquier. Usually a royal slave, the Alquier supervised and taxed the market. On these taxes see Pruneau, *Mémoire*, 51, 55.

51 Ibid., 38.

52 *House of Commons Sessional Papers*, LXXIII, 8–9.

53 Ibid., 180.

54 Ibid., 10.

55 Ibid., 17.

56 La Courbe, *Premier Voyage,* left Saint Louis on March 7, 1686, paid customs to the Barak of Waalo, opened a market on March 20, and began to trade in early April: 128–51.

57 Pruneau, *Mémoire*, 19, 38.

58 Pruneau recommended abandoning the French *escale* ("port of call") at Podor, where trade was insignificant, ibid., 31. Gum sold by Moor merchants at Terrier Rouge and Coq, two river *escales*, were the most important trade sites in Fuuta Tooro.

59 There the transit trade had a very important impact, as is shown in Boubacar Barry, *Le Royaume du Waalo: Sénégal avant la Conquête* (Paris, 1972). That, along with the relative weak position of Waalo as an agricultural state, set its history apart from that of Kajoor-Bawol.

60 Curtin, *Economic Change*, 290, points out that market taxes generated far more revenue.

61 C 6 15, Gorée, May 12, 1766.

62 Ibid.
63 The identification of the Dammel is not difficult, because the French described him as a young man of eighteen, C 6 15, Gorée, May 12, 1766. This could only be Majoor, who ruled from 1763 to 1766: Charles Becker and Victor Martin (eds.), "Recueil sur la Vie des Damel par Tanor Latsoukabe Fall," *Bulletin de l'IFAN*, 36, B, 1 (1974), 121.
64 Ibid.
65 Ibid.
66 C 6 17, Etat des Présents et Coutumes, 1775–6, November 30, 1776.
67 C 6 17, Mémoire sur l'Isle de Gorée, Mes. de Bellecoube et Chevreux, April 19, 1776. According to this memoir the bar prices were the equivalent of 380 to 400 livres. This price increase was mainly a reflection of the end of the monopoly, however inefficient, exercised by the Compagnie des Indes until 1758. Before that date French prices were notably lower than what the British paid in the neighboring Gambia.
68 The list from which this figure is taken is C 6 19, Coutumes, 1786. The highest payment by far went to "Alicoury, chef Maure des Trarzas," (11,299) livres), the second highest payment to Hamet Moctar, "chef Maure Bracnas," (5,584 livres). The Moors controlled a real resource, the gum trade. The other riverine states received less: Fuuta-Tooro 5,013, Waalo 4,568, and the various "princes of Galam" 3,574. It is interesting that essentially transit areas (Fuuta-Tooro, Waalo) received higher payments than Gajaaga, which held the major slave market for the export trade.
69 ANS: 13 G 13, Etat Général des Coutumes, Chemise 3, 1785, Coutumes du Cayor.
70 The best introduction to the merchant networks of Senegambia is Curtin, *Economic Change*, 59–152, which contains extended discussions of *juula* trade networks, and of Atlantic merchants. Curtin's fascination with the *juula* gives his work a strong focus on the middle Niger, upper Senegal, and upper Gambia trade routes. He pays much less attention to the desert trade.
71 For a discussion of the importance of grain imports in the desert see James L. A. Webb, "Shifting Sands: An Economic History of the Mauritanian Sahara, 1500–1850," unpublished Ph.D. thesis, Johns Hopkins University, 1984, 153–7.
72 Ibid., 62–6.
73 Both of these *escales* were controlled, from the desert side, by the Trarza emirs, who taxed the trade carried on by the marabout-merchants of the Idaw al Hajj (or Darmancour). Nevertheless, the *escale* of the Desert was more firmly controlled by the Barak of Waalo than Serinpate, as can be seen in La Courbe, *Premier Voyage*, 137–45.
74 Roberts, *Warriors, Merchants, and Slaves*, 46–50, discusses the desert-side trade of the Maraka, and the yearly arrival of salt caravans from the western Sahara. See also Webb, "Shifting Sands," whose Mauritanian informants also insisted on the Malian origin of most of their slaves, 159–63.
75 This system was in place as early as 1686, when La Courbe met the "Chamchy" (Shems) and set aside one-eighth of the gum for his profit; *Premier Voyage*, 127, 152. Pruneau described this tax in the 1750s, *Mémoire*, 22.
76 La Courbe, *Premier Voyage*, 152.
77 On the position of the Shems see Webb, "Shifting Sands," 68–9, 81.
78 La Courbe, *Premier Voyage*, 151–2. Pruneau, *Mémoire*, 22, said that the French actually fed a whole group of Moors with no gum to sell, and proposed reforms which would have created a ration of two pounds of meat and two pounds of millet for each quintal of gum.
79 La Courbe, *Premier Voyage*, 158.
80 C 6 11, Rolle Générale des Blancs et Nègres au Service de la Compagnie des Indes, May 1, 1736.

Notes

81 For a more detailed discussion of this labor system, see below, chapter 4, "Merchants and slaves."

82 The Wolof word is still used today to mean "interpreter." I thank my Wolof teacher Ibou Saar for his aid in interpreting this word, which is not as commonly used now as it once was.

83 The best guide to European frustrations is the accounts left by the merchants. See for example Delcourt, *Pierre David*.

84 This was true during the 1680s, when La Courbe defined *laptots* as "free negroes who hire themselves to us to work as sailors in our boats for the salary of one bar a month," La Courbe, *Premier Voyage*, 35.

85 C 6 11, Lettre du Conseil Supérieur, January 28, 1738.

86 I borrow the phrase from Winthrop Jordan, *White over Black: American Attitudes toward the Negro* (New York, 1968).

87 The development of slavery on the coastal islands, and the conflicts it caused, are discussed in more detail in chapter 4.

88 For these events, La Courbe, *Premier Voyage*, 100–1, 107–8.

89 La Courbe, who describes these Christians, ibid., 107, 109, does not give any details about them. If they were not slaves, they may have been members of the Luso-African community of Senegambia. See Jean Boulègue, *Les Luso-Africains*, 77–83.

90 Pruneau, *Mémoire*, writing in the 1750s often uses "Bambara" to mean slave: 29, 82.

91 Pruneau, *Mémoire*, 21.

92 This village no longer exists, although its people now live in the village of Gaaya, not far from Dagana. Their seriñ or marabout is still called Seriñ Kajaar, in memory of their previous settlement. The movement of the village occurred during the late eighteenth century when the villagers sided with the Islamic state of Fuuta Tooro in the war with Waalo. See "Cosaanu Gaaya" in Aram Diop, Oumar Ben Khatab Dia, Jean-Claude Galdin, *Jukib Taneefu Baat-Yu-Sax/Recueil de Textes Choisis* (Dakar, Centre de Linguistique Appliqué de Dakar, 1975) 12–16.

93 La Courbe, *Premier Voyage*, 99.

94 Cited by Oumar Kane, "Le Fuuta-Tooro," II, 562–3. In the early nineteenth century Mollien described a slave village which he visited, formed entirely by persons enslaved during a famine, when they accepted grain from their future master: Mollien in Hubert Deschamps, ed., *L'Afrique Occidentale en 1818* (Paris, 1967) 89–90.

95 David Northrup, "Nineteenth Century Patterns of Slavery and Economic Growth in Southeastern Nigeria," *International Journal of African Historical Studies*, 12 (1979) 1–16 and *Trade Without Rulers: Pre-Colonial Economic Development in South-Eastern Nigeria* (Oxford, 1978), 171–6, 178–82.

96 Robin Law, "Slave-Raiders and Middlemen, Monopolists and Free-Traders: the Supply of Slaves for the Atlantic Trade in Dahomey c. 1715–1850," *Journal of African History*, 30, (1989)

97 This is mentioned by Jan Vansina, *Paths in the Rainforests: Toward a History of Political Tradition in Equatorial Africa* (Madison, 1990), 139, 145.

98 Fred Cooper, *Plantation Slavery in East Africa* (New Haven, 1977) 80–113.

99 Miller, *Way of Death*, has argued for the fundamental role played by the introduction of new crops (manioc and maize) in western central Africa, agricultural revolutions which altered the demography of the region, and help explain the volume of slave exports, 19–20. These same crops provided most of the locally supplied provisions as well, 393-400. In Senegambia manioc and maize did not play an important role, except as famine foods.

100 For a detailed presentation of the archival evidence see Charles Becker, "Les Conditions Ecologiques et la Traite des Esclaves en Sénégambie: 'Climat', 'Sécheresse', 'Famines',

'Epidémies' au 17e et 18e Siècles," unpublished paper, Kaolack, 1982, 5–24; a shorter published version of this paper appeared as Charles Becker, "Notes sur les Conditions Ecologiques."

101 This can be seen repeatedly in the testimony given in the *House of Commons Sessional Papers*, where witnesses described how they purchased provisions on the coast, but then specifically denied the possibility that this commerce could expand and become the basis for a new system of international trade. See testimony of John Barnes, LXVIII, 5–10. Such a possibility was proposed by the abolitionists on the committee, with reference to cotton, rice, and other commodities, but witnesses constantly denied the possibility of Africans producing such crops for the international market.

102 On this chronology see Victor Martin and Charles Becker, "Les Teeñ de Baol: Essai de Chronologie," *Bulletin de l'IFAN*, 38 (1976) 481–2. The succession struggle was bitter. The defeated pretenders renewed their struggle for the throne of Kajoor periodically until they succeeded in seizing the throne. The conflict was fought between sons and grandsons of Latsukaabe, belonging to different matrilineages, who ruled Kajoor until 1777. The conflicts are discussed in oral tradition: see Yoro Jaw, "Histoire des Damels," in Amadou Duguay-Cledor, *La Bataille de Guile* (ed. Mbaye Gueye) (Paris, 1985), 157–62.

103 Document quoted in Oumar Kane, "Le Fuuta Tooro," II, 551–2. On this crisis see Becker, "Les Conditions Ecologiques," 8–9.

104 C 6 5, Rapport: Brüe, February 13, 1716.

105 C 6 11, Lettre, June 1, 1736.

106 C 6 11, Lettre: Galam, September 2, 1736; Lettre: Senegal, September 7, 1736.

107 For an estimation which places great importance on Gajaaga as an eighteenth-century source see Xavier Guillard, "Un Commerce Introuvable: l'Or dans les transactions du XVe au XVIIIe Siècle," in Jean Boulègue, *Contributions à l'Histoire du Sénégal* (Paris, 1987) 61–3, where he argues that the importance placed on the slave trade and millet trade prevented French traders from capturing the gold trade.

108 See Roger Pasquier, "Un Aspect de l'Histoire des Villes du Sénégal: les Problèmes de Ravitaillement au XIXe Siècle," in Boulègue, *Contributions*, 177–214, particularly 185–7, where he quotes typical judgments on the importance of the trade from Fuuta Tooro. But he offers no quantitative evidence, and suggests there is none.

109 Delcourt, *Pierre David*, 209, 210. Delcourt's work contains one of the earliest discussions of the importance of the millet trade, 247–52.

110 Adanson, "Voyage," 645–6, described Moor donkey caravans purchasing dried fish in Cap Vert, which they bought with millet, and noted their dominant role in the region.

111 C 6 12, Lettre: July 15, 1743.

112 Golberry's text, which can be read as a critique of David's policies, is cited at length in Bathily, "Guerriers, Tributaires et Marchands," II, 417–18, in Charles Becker, "Les Conditions Ecologiques," 13, and by Delcourt, *Pierre David*, 368.

113 C 6 12, Lettre: Senegal, July 28, 1744.

114 C 6 12, Lettre, December, 1744.

115 Delcourt, *Pierre David*, 95–6, 98.

116 Quote from David; Delcourt, *Pierre David*, 107. The mortality figures for 1742 are taken from C 6 12, Lettre, January 14, 1741.

117 See Golberry, in Delcourt, *Pierre David*, 36–8.

118 Document cited in Oumar Kane, "Le Fuuta Tooro," I, 364.

119 C 6 11, Lettre, June 1, 1736.

120 C 6 11, Rolle Générale des Blancs et Nègres au Service de la Compagnie, May 1, 1736.

121 There is little complete census data for Saint Louis until the 1750s. Curtin, *Economic Change*, II, 39, offers no global figures before 1755.

122 Company grain rations were high, but they were based on imports of raw grain, and included allowances for losses due to spoilage and rats. The figures for slave exports come from Company records, Pruneau, *Mémoire*, 88, and include the slaves purchased in the Gambia at Albreda, including the slaves supplied by the British in exchange for gum. Mettas' figures from shipping records suggest a lower figure, an average of 1,250 slaves per year, see David Richardson, "Slave Exports from West and West-Central Africa, 1700–1810: New Estimates of Volume and Distribution," *Journal of African History*, 30 (1989) 14.

123 Pruneau, *Mémoire*, 45–6.

124 Ibid., 29–31. The structure of the accounting used by Pruneau suggests that he included only grain purchased within each department to compile these figures. The large population of Saint Louis, estimated by Pruneau at 4,000 in 1752, ibid., 18, plus the important export slave trade would have created an important grain deficit within the "department of Saint Louis," from Saint Louis to Podor. This deficit was met by imports from upriver and from Gorée.

125 Ibid., 82–4.

126 The total purchases were converted into tons by using the figure of 500 pounds per hogshead. Pruneau estimated that Gorée could purchase the grain required to feed 2,000 negroes for a year (ibid., 50) and all his estimates are based on the ration of two pounds a day per person (82), a relatively high figure, because it represented the consumption of an adult worker, but probably reasonable, because of the problems of spoilage.

127 Adanson, "Voyage," 609, said Saint Louis had "upwards of three thousand negroes" in 1749 and he repeated this estimate in Charles Becker and Victor Martin (eds.), "Mémoire d'Adanson sur le Sénégal et l'Ile de Gorée," *Bulletin de l'IFAN*, B, 42, 4 (1980), 736–7. Pruneau gave an even higher estimate of the population of Saint Louis in 1752, saying that the island "could have 4,000 inhabitants" in *Mémoire*, 18.

128 Adanson, "Mémoire," 737.

129 The development of slave-owning merchant societies on the islands is discussed more fully in chapter 4.

130 C 6 13, Lettre, February 24, 1752.

131 This quote is taken from the archival sources published by Charles Becker, "Notes sur les Conditions Ecologiques," 195–6.

132 This document does not even mention Fuuta Tooro, normally one of the three sources of grain supplies for Saint Louis. From 1776 to 1800 grain exports from Fuuta were erratic, because of the trade policies of the Islamic state which ruled the region after seizing power in 1776. For much of this period, Fuuta was an unreliable source of grain exports.

133 Particularly the works of Boubacar Barry, *Le Royaume du Waalo*, and *La Sénégambie du XVe au XIXe Siècle: Traite Négrière, Islam et Conquête Coloniale* (Paris, 1988). For a case study of Islam in Fuuta Tooro, see Oumar Kane, "Le Fuuta Tooro," who discusses the background to the revolution of 1776 primarily in terms of resistance to the regime of the Saatigi and to the domination of the Moors. Bathily, "Guerriers, Tributaires et Marchands," centres his discussion of the nineteenth century around the emergence of Islam as the expression of resistance to the old order.

134 The best example is Barry, *La Sénégambie*, who avoids the tendency to hagiography which detracts from the otherwise fine study of Robinson, *The Holy War of Umar Tal*. For a similar interpretation of these Muslim revolutions see Martin Klein, "Slavery and the Social Order in the Muslim States of the Western Sudan," paper presented at the annual meeting of the Canadian African Association, Kingston, Ontario, May, 1988.

135 Kajoor, in this perspective, becomes the preeminent example of the failure of jihad:

Lucie Colvin, "Islam and the state of Kajoor: A case of Successful Resistance to Jihad," *Journal of African History*, 15, 4 (1974), 587–606.

136 The main exceptions to this are the studies of *juula* merchants, starting with Curtin's pioneering discussion of the *juula* of the Gambia and upper Senegal in *Economic Change*. A recent example of this kind of study is Roberts, *Warriors, Merchants, and Slaves*. In those parts of Senegambia where *juula* influence and presence was less important, Islamic revolution and jihad is linked directly to the emergence of "legitimate commerce" in the nineteenth century. For the classic statement of this interpretation see Martin A. Klein, "Social and Economic Factors in the Muslim Revolution in Senegambia," *Journal of African History*, 13 (1972) 419–41.

137 La Courbe, *Premier Voyage*, 90.

138 Ibid., 91–3.

139 Ritchie (ed.), "Deux textes," 316.

140 Ibid.

141 Philip Curtin, *Economic Change*, 59–91, for an excellent discussion of the *juula* trade diaspora. For Curtin's further exploration of the trade diaspora concept, see Philip Curtin, *Cross-Cultural Trade in World History* (Cambridge, 1984).

142 Webb, "Shifting Sands," sees this as a gradual transformation of ethnic identity on the part of the Idaw al Hajj who settled in Kajoor and became Wolof, 65–6.

143 Ibid., 59–60.

144 See the discussion of Nehemia Levtzion, "Islam and West African Politics: Accommodation and Tension Between the Ulama and the Political Authorities," *Cahiers d'Etudes Africaines*, 18, 3 (1977).

145 Fall, "Recueil," 117, from a passage describing the royal capital of Maka in the early eighteenth century.

146 For an early description of marabouts teaching students by firelight, see Ritchie, "Deux Textes," 323.

147 For a mid-nineteenth-century description of this system, Frederic Carrère and Paul Holle, *De la Sénégambie Française* (Paris, 1855), 60.

148 In older marabout villages like Pir in Kajoor and Ndogal in Bawol, even marabout families with distant Moor origins adopted Wolof patronyms. See Jean Boulègue's discussion of the Faal marabouts of Pir and the Jeng of Ndogal in "Pir et Ndogala et la Révolution Sénégambienne," *Contributions*.

149 Nehemia Levtzion, "The Eighteenth Century Background to the Islamic Revolutions in West Africa," in N. Levtzion and J.O. Voll (eds.), *Eighteenth-Century Renewal and Reform in Islam* (Syracuse, 1987).

150 Louis Brenner, "Concepts of Tariqa in West Africa: the Case of the Qadiriyya," in Donal B. Cruise O'Brien and Christian Coulon (eds.), *Charisma and Brotherhood in African Islam* (Oxford, 1988), 38–40.

151 The threat of Moor political and commercial domination appeared real to Europeans throughout the period from 1720 to 1750. See Curtin, *Economic Change*, 49–54, for an overview of desert–savanna relations in this period. In 1744 Pierre David, the director of the French Company, equated Muslim influence with Moor domination: Delcourt, *Pierre David*, 95–6, 100, 153–4.

152 See Charles C. Stewart, "Southern Saharan Scholarship and the Bilad al-Sudan," *Journal of African History*, 17, 4 (1976), 73–93, who links the development of jihad to regions supplying grain to the desert.

153 See Moustapha Kane and David Robinson, *The Islamic Regime of Fuuta Tooro: An Anthology of Oral Tradition Transcribed in Pulaar and Translated into English* (East Lansing, 1984), 19–21. For a discussion of the importance of the school at Pir in the

preparation of the revolution in Fuuta Tooro see Oumar Kane, "Fuuta Tooro," II, 653–8.

154 For the struggle of the new Islamic regime against the Moors, see Oumar Kane, "Fuuta Tooro," II, 666–9, 703.

155 The tendency to separate the history of Saint Louis from the mainland has led to a neglect of these relationships. But for an excellent discussion of the relations of Njambur and Saint Louis in the nineteenth century, see Mamadou Diouf, *Le Kajoor an XIXe Siècle: Pouvoir Ceddo et Conquête Coloniale* (Paris, 1990) 141–95. The same factors were already at work in the eighteenth century.

156 Adanson, "Voyage," 643. Such burial customs are now far rarer, but they existed until quite recently among the independent Sereer of Bawol.

4 Merchants and slaves: slavery on Saint Louis and Gorée

1 One of the best discussions of the history of the islands is in Philip Curtin, *Economic Change in Precolonial Africa: Senegambia in the Era of the Slave Trade* (Madison, 1975), 92–152. However Curtin's trade diaspora concept imposes a particular perspective. The *habitant* population was not a European or Afro-European trade diaspora from overseas, so much as a local merchant society based on slave labor.

2 Many works and articles on Saint Louis and Gorée focus almost entirely on French life and activities on the islands, and on French relations with the *signares*: P. Alquier, "Saint-Louis du Sénégal pendant la Révolution et l'Empire," *Bulletin du Comité d'Etudes Historiques et Scientifiques de l'Afrique Occidentale Française*, 5 (1929), 277–320, 411–63; Marie-Hélène Knight-Baylac, "La Vie Quotidienne à Gorée de 1677 à 1789," *Revue Française d'Histoire d'Outre-Mer*, 17 (1970), 377–420; Françoise Deroure, "La Vie Quotidienne à Saint Louis par ses Archives (1779–1809)," *Bulletin de l'IFAN*, 26 (1964), B, 397–439. These works are full of descriptions of the charm and fecundity of the *signares* and the libertine life of European traders. They simply reproduce the popular colonial image of the islands, as in Jean Pierre Biondi, *Saint-Louis du Sénégal: Mémoires d'un Métissage* (Paris, 1987).

3 Michael Adanson "A Voyage to Senegal, the Isle of Gorée and the River Gambia," in John Pinkerton, *A General Collection of the Best and Most Interesting Voyages and Travels . . .* (London, 1814) XVI, 608.

4 Ibid., 611–12.

5 On the Niger delta see G. I. Jones, *The Trading States of the Oil Rivers: A Study of Political Development in Eastern Nigeria* (London, 1963).

6 Robert W. Harms, *River of Wealth, River of Sorrow: The Central Zaire Basin in the Era of the Slave and Ivory Trade, 1500–1891* (New Haven, 1981), 1, 30–2, 71–5.

7 On the use of slaves as "canoeboys" in the Gambia: testimony of Henry Ellison, 1790, in *House of Commons Sessional Papers of the Eighteenth Century* (ed. Sheila Lambert) (Wilmington, 1975) LXXIII, 376.

8 *House of Commons Sessional Papers*, LXVIII, 262.

9 See Robin Law, "Between the Sea and the Lagoons: The Interaction of Maritime and Inland Navigation on the Precolonial Slave Coast," *Cahiers d'Etudes Africains*, 29, 114 (1989), 209–37; Peter C. W. Gutkind, "The Canoemen of the Gold Coast (Ghana)," *Cahiers d'Etudes Africaines*, 29, 115–16 (1989), 339–75.

10 See Jones, *Trading States*, 51–62, 162–76.

11 *House of Commons Sessional Papers*, LXVIII, 113.

12 For this epidemic, C 6 17, Gorée, Mémoire sur l'Epidemie qui a Affligée l'Isle de Gorée, July 1778. Although this document does not give a census, we have data from

1776, C 6 17, Recensement Général, Brasseur, April 18, 1776, listing a total of 139 Europeans on Gorée.

13 See sources cited by Natalie Reyss, "Saint-Louis du Sénégal a L'Epoque Précoloniale. L'Emergence d'une Société Métisse Originale, 1650–1854," thèse de 3e cycle, Université de Paris-I, 2 vols., 1982–3, 69.

14 [Joseph] Pruneau de Pommegorge, *Description de la Nigritie* (Paris 1789), 3.

15 C 6 19, Tableau des Maladies du Sénégal et de leur Traitement: Crespin, August 17, 1786.

16 For a discussion of the role of biology, disease history, and ecology in the history of European expansion see Alfred W. Crosby, *Ecological Imperialism: The Biological Expansion of Europe, 900–1900* (Cambridge, 1986). The importance of these factors in African history is discussed in Kenneth F. Kiple (ed.), *The African Exchange: Toward a Biological History of Black People* (Durham, 1987).

17 Prosper Cultru (ed.) *Premier Voyage du Sieur De La Courbe Fait à la Coste d'Afrique en 1685* (Paris, 1913) 36–7.

18 Ibid., 153.

19 Ibid.

20 "Relation du Sieur Mathelot," 1687, quoted in La Courbe, *Premier Voyage*, 26.

21 Ibid., 28.

22 See "Voyage de Le Maire (1682)," in C. A. Walckenaer, *Histoire Générale des Voyages*, (Paris, 1826) II, 359. "After six days of tiring travel we arrived at the port of Bieurt, at the mouth of the Senegal. Le Maire observed that in this place all trade is under the control of women, and that, under the pretext of bringing their trade goods, they come and amuse themselves with the sailors." Bieurt was one of the villages in the immediate vicinity of Saint Louis.

23 La Courbe, *Premier Voyage*, 28.

24 "Premier voyage de Brüe (1697)," in Walckenaer, *Histoire Générale*, 391, 396.

25 C. A. Walckenaer, notes and additions to Brüe, "Premier Voyage," 390, citing Villaut, *Voyage de Guinée* (1666).

26 C 6 11, Lettre: Gorée, June 14, 1736.

27 C 6 11, Mémoire sur la Concession du Sénégal, October 8, 1734.

28 This calculation is based on the prices for labor and millet given by La Courbe, *Premier Voyage*, 35, 99, compared with the estimates of millet production given by Claude Meillassoux, "Etat et Conditions des Esclaves à Gumbu (Mali) au XIXe Siècle," in Claude Meillassoux (ed.), *L'Esclavage en Afrique Précoloniale* (Paris, 1975), 249. However, the value of salaries declined later in the century, measured against the price of millet.

29 *Lappato bi.*

30 C 6 11, Mémoire sur la Concession du Sénégal, October 8, 1734.

31 Ibid.

32 Ibid.

33 C 6 11, Rolle Générale des Blancs et Nègres au Service de la Compagnie des Indes (Sénégal), May 1, 1736. For a discussion of the European presence in Gajaaga (Galam) see Abdoulaye Bathily, "Guerriers, Tributaires, et Marchands Le Gajaaga (ou Galam) le 'Pas de l'Or'. Le Développement et la régression d'une Formation Economique et Sociale Sénégalaise (*c*. 8e–19e Siècle)," thèse pour le Doctorat ès Lettres, Université de Dakar, 1985, II, 389–95.

34 C 6 11.

35 C 6 14, Réponse du Conseil Supérieur du Sénégal au Mémoire et Observations, February 1754.

36 Ibid.
37 C 6 12, Lettre: Gorée, July 9, 1744.
38 For the high value placed on slaves born on the islands see M. Saugnier, *Relations de Plusieurs Voyages à la Côte d'Afrique* (Paris, 1791) 275.
39 For the decision to train Africans, C 6 11, Lettre du Conseil Supérieur, January 28, 1738.
40 Adanson, "Voyage," 609.
41 Ibid., 662–3.
42 See document cited by Reyss, "Saint Louis," 66. "We had to confess the women through interpreters because they did not understand French."
43 Abbé David Boilat, *Esquisses Sénégalaises*, (Paris, 1853), 115–57, 224. See also Dominique Harcourt Lamiral, *L'Affrique et le Peuple Afriquain* (Paris, 1789) 43.
44 Frederic Carrère and Paul Holle, *De la Sénégambie Française* (Paris, 1855) 8.
45 Ibid.
46 This stereotype has been perpetuated by colonialist historiography, which sees Saint Louis as a French and Catholic island in the eighteenth century. See for example Brigaud and Jean Vast, *Saint-Louis du Sénégal, Ville aux Mille Visages* (Dakar, 1987), heavily influenced by missionary interpretations.
47 See the discussion of the British occupation in Michael David Marcson, "European-African Interaction in the Precolonial Period: Saint Louis, Senegal, 1758–1854," unpublished Ph.D. dissertation. Princeton University, 1976, 39, 57, citing British documents.
48 This appears most clearly in British efforts to win the loyalty of the *habitants* by granting them a mayor and agreeing to rent their slaves for political reasons. British policy was determined by *habitant* influence with mainland states. See Marcson, "European-African Interaction," 56–9.
49 See Ousmane Sane, "Urbanisation, Urbanisme et Architecture dans l'Ile de Gorée aux XVIIIe et XIXe Siècles," Mémoire de maîtrise, Universite de Dakar, 1972, 50.
50 C 6 14, Lettre, October 20, 1754.
51 C 6 15, Mémoire d'Adanson, May–June, 1763.
52 C 6 17, Recensement General des Habitants de Gorée, Brasseur, April 18, 1776.
53 C 6 15, Lettre, Poncet de la Rivière, May 25, 1764.
54 Ibid., Mémoire d'Adanson.
55 Ibid.
56 C 6 15, Règlements pour le Corps de *Laptots*, 1765.
57 The population figures are taken from C 6 15, Mémoire d'Adanson, 1763; C 6 16, Mémoire de Doumet sur l'Isle de Gorée, 1773; and C 6 17, Recensement Général des Habitants de Gorée, April 18, 1776. In the last document the term "creole" slave seems to be used to refer to the slaves who lived permanently on the island, as opposed to the slaves destined for export. It could not refer to slaves born on the island; the growth of the slave population was far too rapid to be accounted for by natural demographic growth.
58 C 6 16, Mémoire de Doumet, 1773.
59 For a discussion of the politics of the French slave trade in this period see Robert Louis Stein, *The French Slave Trade in the Eighteenth Century: An Old Regime Business* (Madison, 1979) 33–9.
60 For a contemporary analysis of the trade of Gorée, favoring the abandonment of the island, which was written by French slaving interests at Nantes: C 6 15, Mémoire sur la Coste d'Affrique, Nantes, May 10, 1766. In the 1760s French exports from Gorée averaged only about 350 a year (1765–70), increasing to an average of 820 a year in the 1770s. See David Richardson, "Slave Exports from West and West-Central Africa,

1700–1810: New Estimates of Volume and Distribution," *Journal of African History*, 30 (1989) 14.

61 C 6 17, Lettre-mémoire de Brasseur, April 14, 1776.

62 C 6 17, Mémoire sur l'Isle de Gorée, MM de Bellecoube et Chevreux, April 19, 1776.

63 C 6 17, ibid.

64 C 6 16, Mémoire: Doumet, 1773, sur l'Isle de Gorée.

65 "En piastres" in the French document: C 6 15, Lettre du Poncet de la Rivière, May 15, 1764.

66 C 6 17, Mémoire sur L'Isle de Gorée, April 19, 1776.

67 C 6 17, Lettre-mémoire de Brasseur, April 14, 1776.

68 Ibid.

69 C 6 17, Recensement Générale des Habitants de Gorée, April 18, 1776.

70 C 6 17, Correspondance: Gorée, April 29, 1777, and May 19, 1777.

71 C 6 17, Gorée, August 4, 1777.

72 Brasseur gave a detailed account of this revolt in C 6 17, Lettre, August 4, 1777.

73 Ibid.

74 C 6 17, Correspondance: Gorée, March 5, 1778.

75 C 6 16, Mémoire des Habitants de Gorée à Ministre de la Marine, December 26, 1772.

76 C 6 16, Mémoire des Habitants, December 26, 1772.

77 This is the explanation given by Adanson in his memoir on Gorée, C 6 15.

78 See for example, Pruneau, *Description*, 3–6; Lamiral, *L'Affrique*, 44–8.

79 C 6 15, Lettre: Gorée, Poncet de la Rivière, May 1765.

80 See documents cited by Marcson, "European-African Interaction," 58–60. The full range of O'Hara's activities remain obscure, because he filed very few official reports during a nine-year tenure as governor from 1766 to 1775.

81 C 6 17, Gorée, Mémoire sur l'Epidémie qui a Affligé l'Isle de Gorée, July 1778; Reyss, "Saint-Louis," 69.

82 C 6 17, Gorée, Mémoire sur l'Etat Actuel du Sénégal et les Moyens que la France peut Employer pour le Conquérir au Premier Signal de Guerre, June 23, 1778. See also the discussion of Marcson, "European-African Interaction," 57–61.

83 *House of Commons Sessional Papers*, LXXIII, 6.

84 Ibid., 8.

85 C 6 17, Recensement, Saint Louis, Juillet 1779.

86 In the eighteenth century the demographic growth of Saint Louis was sharply limited by disease. The census of 1779 was taken after the yellow fever epidemic of 1778, which reduced the island's population. The population of slightly over 3,000 in 1779 did not exceed population estimates at mid-century. Adanson, writing about Saint Louis in 1750, estimated the population at "upwards of three thousand negroes"; Adanson, "Voyage," 607. The growth in Saint Louis' population in the eighteenth century thus required a constant influx of free and slave migrants to replace the victims of disease.

87 There are few detailed comparative studies of urban slavery, but there are a number of case studies: Gary B. Nash, *Forging Freedom: The Formation of Philadelphia's Black Community, 1720–1840* (Cambridge, 1988); Arthur Zilversmit, *The First Emancipation: The Abolition of Slavery in the North* (Chicago, 1967). Demographic data on colonial slave populations is given in Winthrop Jordan, *White Over Black: American Attitudes towards the Negro* (New York, 1968) 102–3. On colonial Charleston see Peter Wood, *Black Majority: Negroes in Colonial South Carolina from 1670 through the Stono Rebellion* (New York, 1974) 147, 150. For a study of urban slavery in the nineteenth-century American South see Richard C. Wade, *Slavery in the Cities: The South 1820–1860* (New York, 1964).

88 The sexual balance among slave children in 1779 is very similar to what one would expect from a population experiencing natural demographic growth.
89 ANS, K 7, Notes . . . sur l'Affranchissement, June 29, 1836.
90 Pommegorge, *Description*, 3–6. It is clear from his description of this practice by *signares* owning "between thirty and forty slaves," that he is referring to only the very wealthiest families.
91 On the labor demands for the Galam voyage see C 6 19, Paris, January 21, 1789. For the use of the *laptots* to guard herds see Jean Baptiste Labat, *Nouvelle Relation de l'Afrique Occidentale* (Paris, 1728), II, 142.
92 C 6 18, Inventaire des Biens Achetés par les Habitants.
93 C 6 18, Inventaire des Biens Achetés par les Habitants, December, 1784.
94 C 6 19, Résultat de la Traite des Nègres, 1786.
95 C 6 19, Voyage de Galam: Résultat, 1788.
96 Saugnier, *Voyages*, 326. Saugnier was an independent merchant who sailed to Galam in 1785. Because he lacked capital, he modeled his trade on that of the *habitants*.
97 Lamiral, *L'Affrique*, 2, 21–2. There has been some dispute over the authorship of this work, particularly whether it reflects the views of the *habitants* or Lamiral. In my view, the first section of the work, the *cahier*, should be accepted as reflecting *habitant* views. For a discussion of the controversy see Marcson, "European-African Interaction," 67–76.
98 Lamiral, *L'Affrique*, 11–13, 24–5.
99 French relations with Fuuta Tooro are discussed in C 6 20, Senegal, July 31, 1790. For a discussion of the historic developments in Fuuta see David Robinson, *The Holy War of Umar Tal: The Western Sudan in the Mid-Nineteenth Century* (Oxford, 1985) 60–5.
100 On the Kajoor boycott and the subsistence crisis: C 6 19, Lettre: Gorée, Jan. 10, 1788; ibid., Paris, February 14, 1789.
101 C 6 19, Mémoire à Monseigneur le Compte de la Luzerne par la Compagnie du Sénégal, 1788; ibid;, Lettre, Paris, January 21, 1789.
102 C 6 20, Rapport de Boucher, August 21, 1791. This report summarizes the conflicts between the Company and the *habitants*. For the dispute over the millet trade: C 6 19, Extrait: Greffes de Gorée, July 25, 1789.
103 C 6 20, Lettre, July 31, 1790; Rapport de Boucher, August 21, 1790.
104 Ibid., Rapport de Boucher, August 21, 1790.
105 The best example of this trend is the work of Marcson, "European-African Interaction." Recent Senegalese research has focused on the role of the *habitants* in commerce, stimulated by debates about the decline of African economic enterprise during the colonial period: Mamadou Diouf, "Traitants ou Négotiants? Les Commercants Saint-Louisiens (2e Moitié XIXe, Début XXe Siècle) Hamet Gora Diop (1846–1910): Etude de Cas," unpublished paper, 1988; Mamadou Fall, "Des Marchés du Cayor aux Marchés du Fleuve: le Fait Marchand entre l'Epee et le Croissant, XVIIIe – Debut XXe Siècles," unpublished paper, 1988.
106 This tradition is still alive, if not well: Biondi, *Saint-Louis du Sénégal*.
107 See for example Reyss, "Saint-Louis," who restates the thesis of "happy slaves," 103–4, even though evidence she herself presents contradicts this view.
108 *British Parliamentary Papers, Colonies, Africa* (Shannon, 1967). I, 150.
109 Labat, *Nouvelle Relation*, II, 301.
110 For the presence of women slaves in the crews see Saugnier, *Voyages*, 186–7, where he describes the crew of the *Furet* which sailed upriver in 1785.
111 On the wages paid the *laptots* at the end of the seventeenth century La Courbe, *Premier Voyage*, 35; on their wages at the end of the eighteenth century Lamiral, *L'Affrique*,

339, and Saugnier, *Voyages*, 186–7. Although figures for wages and their value vary somewhat from source to source, the principle of wage sharing between the slave and the master is noted in all the sources.

112 La Courbe, *Premier Voyage*.
113 Lamiral, *L'Affrique*, 68.
114 These figures are taken from Saugnier, *Voyages*, 308–9, based on his experience in 1785.
115 Joseph Pruneau, *Mémoire sur le Commerce de la Concession de Sénégal* (Kaolack 1983) 27, 81.
116 This is the number listed in C 6 19, Voyage de Galam: Résultat, 1788.
117 ARS, 0 3, Navigation et Marine 1819–39, Pièce 8, 1825.
118 0 3, Pièce 1, May 1, 1809.
119 Saugnier, *Voyages*, 307–8.
120 Ibid., 300–3.
121 Ibid., 243.
122 Ibid., 242.
123 C 6 18, Lettre des Habitants au Maréchal de Castries, October 2, 1784; C 6 20, July 31, 1790.
124 K 7, Notes . . . sur l'Affranchissement, January 29, 1836. This document dates before the creation of the *tirailleurs* and could only refer to the *laptots*.
125 Saugnier, *Voyages*, 187–8.
126 Boilat, *Esquisses*, 148.
127 C 6 18, Inventaire des Biens . . . December 1784.
128 Saugnier, *Voyages*, 185–6.
129 Ibid., 275, 277–8.
130 *British Parliamentary Papers*, I, 150.
131 Reyss, "Saint-Louis," 164, quotes the document detailing this case in full.
132 *House of Commons Sessional Papers*, LXXXII, 239.

5 Famine, civil war, and secession, 1750–1800

1 Three thousand five hundred was the average for the decade 1740–9, according to David Richardson, "Slave Exports from West and West-Central Africa, 1700–1810: New Estimates of Volume and Distribution," *Journal of African History*, 30 (1989). This represented a decline from the peak decades of the century, 1720–9, with 5,250 per year, and 1730–9, with 5,700: Richardson, "New Estimates," Table 7.
2 For general discussions of this period see Robert Louis Stein, *The French Slave Trade in the Eighteenth Century: An Old Regime Business* (Madison, 1979); Robin Blackburn, *The Overthrow of Colonial Slavery, 1776–1848* (London, 1988), 1–31.
3 Even such an event as the Stamp Act crisis affected the British sugar colonies by cutting off their usual sources of imported food and disrupting trade. See the discussion in J. R. Ward, *British West Indian Slavery 1750–1834: The Process of Amelioration* (Oxford, 1988), 61–118. The importance of the American revolution in the British West Indies is discussed in Eric Williams, *Capitalism and Slavery* (New York, 1966), 108–25. On the relation of debt and revolution in Virginia see T. H. Breen, *Tobacco Culture: The Mentality of the Great Tidewater Planters on the Eve of Revolution* (Princeton, 1985).
4 The development of anti-slavery in the Western world, and its relation to economic developments and ideology has spawned an immense literature. Blackburn, *The Overthrow of Slavery*, surveys recent studies. For a study which discusses the development of British anti-slavery in relation to economic issues see the recent book by David Eltis, *Economic Growth and the Ending of the Transatlantic Slave Trade* (Oxford, 1987),

Notes

and the collection of essays edited by David Eltis and James Walvin. *The Abolition of the Atlantic Slave Trade: Origins and Effects in Europe, Africa, and the Americas* (Madison, 1981).

5 K. David Patterson, "Epidemics, Famines, and Population in the Cape Verde Islands, 1580–1900," *International Journal of African Historical Studies*, 21, 2 (1988), 304–6.

6 Sekene Mody Cissoko, 'Famines et Epidémies à Tombouctou et dans le Boucle du Niger du XVIe au XVIIIe Siècles," *Bulletin de l'IFAN*, B, 30, 3 (1968), 806–21.

7 Philip Curtin, *Economic Change in Precolonial Africa: Senegambia in the Era of the Slave Trade*, I, (Madison, 1975), 109–12, discusses the famine, and he presents data on climate in II, 3–7. Charles Becker, "Les Conditions Ecologiques et la Traite des Esclaves en Sénégambie: 'Climat', 'Sécheresse', 'Famines', 'Epidémies' au 17e et 18e Siècles," unpublished paper, Kaolack, 1982, presents evidence about famines, food shortages, drought and other factors, which are summarized in a table, 35–6.

8 Much of Curtin's evidence for a prolonged period of low rainfall from 1705 to 1720 is based on data from the Cape Verde Islands: Curtin, II, 3, and Patterson, "Epidemics, Famines," 306. However, I have no data confirming these drought conditions for the Lower Senegal, except for one letter dated 1721 which describes a drought that had lasted for ten years from 1710 to 1720: C 6 6, Lettre, Saint Robert, March 28, 1721. The letter claimed that the drought which followed a famine in 1710 had led to a ten-year decline in the trade in cattle hides and local cotton cloth.

9 Curtin's interpretation of the climatic data seems to be influenced by his view of this eruption of desert peoples in the savanna, which culminated in the 1720s. It may be that the climatic crisis in the desert (and in the Cape Verde Islands) was more severe than in the savanna. This was true of the drought of 1771–5, which forcibly struck the Niger bend, the western Sahara, and the Cape Verde Islands, but had a lesser impact in Senegambia. See Curtin, I, 53–4, II, 3–5; Patterson, "Epidemics, Famines," 304, 306–7; and James L. A. Webb, "Shifting Sands: An Economic History of the Mauritanian Sahara, 1500–1850," unpublished Ph. D. thesis, Johns Hopkins University, 1984, 109.

10 These famines and periods of shortage are discussed above, chapter 3.

11 Sekene Mody Cissoko, "Famines et Epidémies à Timbouctou"; Patterson, "Epidemics, Famines," 306–7; Webb, "Shifting Sands," 109.

12 Document quoted by Charles Becker, "Les Conditions Ecologiques," 23.

13 Saint Louis' problems with food supply are discussed in Dominique Harcourt Lamiral, *L'Affrique et le Peuple Afriquain* (Paris, 1789) 11–13, 24–5. In 1788 and 1789 Kajoor boycotted the grain trade with Saint Louis and Gorée, partly because of poor harvests: C 6 19, Lettre, Gorée, January 10, 1788; and Paris, February 14, 1789. Mungo Park reported on an extensive famine that culminated in 1793–5, Mungo Park, *Travels in the Interior Districts of Africa . . . in the years 1795, 1976 and 1797* (London, 1800).

14 On these crises: Curtin, *Economic Change*, 51–4, 125; Webb, "Shifting Sands," 62–5, 109.

15 C 6 13, Lettre: Saint Louis, November 24, 1751.

16 C 6 13, Lettre, June 30, 1751.

17 C 6 13, Lettre, November 16, 1751; Lettre, November 24, 1751. For the extraordinary food purchases in Galam in 1751 see Abdoulaye Bathily, "Guerriers, Marchands, et Tributaires. Le Gajaaga (ou Galam) le 'pays de l'or'. Le Développement et la Régression d'une Formation Economique et Sociale Sénégalaise (c. 8e–19e siècle)," thèse pour le Doctorat ès Lettres, Université de Dakar, 1985, II, 415.

18 For contemporary French evaluations of their relations with Kajoor and Waalo see C 6 13, Lettre, June 30, 1751; Lettre, November 24, 1751; Lettre, February 24, 1752.

19 C 6 13, Lettre, June 31, 1751.

20 C 6 13, Lettre, February 24, 1752.

21 C 6 14, Lettre, Gorée, February 11, 1753.
22 C 6 14, Lettre, June 20, 1753.
23 C 6 14, Mémoire, April 25, 1754.
24 C 6 14, Lettre, Gorée, August 14, 1753.
25 C 6 14, Lettre, Saint-Louis, October 25, 1753.
26 C 6 14, Lettre, Saint-Louis, June 3, 1754.
27 C 6 14, Mémoire, April 25, 1754.
28 C 6 14, Lettre: Galam, June 20, 1754; Lettre, Saint Louis, July 11, 1754.
29 For this period in Waalo, see Boubacar Barry, *Le Royaume du Waalo: Sénégal avant la Conquête* (Paris, 1972). Dynastic oral traditions treat this as a great period of power and expansion.
30 For a more detailed discussion of desert–savanna relations, and the develoment of the crisis in Waalo, see chapter 6, "The gum cycle in Atlantic commerce."
31 C 6 14, Lettre, October 20, 1754.
32 C 6 14, Lettre: Saint-Louis, August 23, 1754.
33 C 6 14, Lettre, October 20, 1754.
34 C 6 14, Lettre, July 7, 1755, July 31, 1755.
35 This model provides a global estimate which can be related to the fragmentary data. The assumptions are constructed to overestimate, rather than to underestimate, grain consumption. The grain ration used is 500 pounds of millet per person per year. The assumptions used to estimate the grain consumed by slaves in transit assumes six months as the standard time between purchase by the Company and arrival in the Americas. For many slaves the time would have been four months or less. The figure of 1,600 slaves is an estimate of the French trade from Saint Louis and Gorée.
36 The testimony gathered in the *House of Commons Sessional Papers of the Eighteenth Century* (ed. Sheila Lambert) (Wilmington, 1975) provides important evidence. This topic has not received treatment by historians who have studied the shipping records of the slave trade. In Jean Mettas, *Répertoire des Expéditions Negrières Françaises au XVIIIe Siècle* (ed. Serge Daget), (Paris, 1978), the topic of ship provisions receives almost no attention. There are only scattered comments such as the statement that *La Gentille* "took no provisions in Senegal" in 1752 (*Répertoire*, I, 362), a sign that famine conditions disrupted normal patterns of trade.
37 *House of Commons Sessional Papers*, LXVIII, 213. "Guinea corn" was another term for millet.
38 *House of Commons Sessional Papers*, LXXXII, 239.
39 This contrasts with other regions in Africa. The testimony of ship captains before the House of Commons noted that ships going to Angola almost always carried full supplies, because of the uncertainty of local food supplies. In most parts of Africa some local food supplies were purchased, but the coastal areas selling millet and rice were considered more self-sufficient than areas where only yams or cassava flour could be purchased.
40 C 6 14, Réponse du Conseil Supérieur au Mémoire et Observations, February 1754. This was the most important effort by the Company to analyze the famine of the 1750s.
41 C 6 14, Réponse du Conseil, February 1754.
42 C 6 14, Réponse du Conseil, February 1754. The phrase "captifs à la chaîne" was often used to describe slaves waiting to be shipped out.
43 C 6 14, Réponse du Conseil, February 1754.
44 Charles Becker and Victor Martin (eds.), "Mémoire d'Adanson sur le Sénégal et l'Ile de Gorée," *Bulletin de l'IFAN*, B, 42, 4 (1980), 736–7.
45 Ibid., 737.
46 For a good discussion of millet consumption in Senegalese coastal cities in the nineteenth

century, and the archival sources which permit a calculation of per capita consumption see Roger Pasquier, "Un Aspect de l'Histoire des Villes du Senegal: les problèmes de Ravitaillement au XIXe Siècle," in Jean Boulègue (ed.), *Contributions à l'Histoire du Sénégal* (Paris, 1987), 181.

47 Charles Becker and Victor Martin (eds.) "Recueil sur la Vie des Damels par Tanor Latsoukabe Fall," *Bulletin de l'IFAN* 36, B, 1 117–18.

48 Few historians have proposed such a model in a pure form, although Curtin regarded "economic" enslavement and "political" enslavement as two ideal types defining possible explanations: Curtin, *Economic Change*, I, 156–7. In the literature on Senegambia, the "economic" interpretation in one form or another is fairly common. It can be found in Boubacar Barry, *La Sénégambie du XVe au XIXe Siècle: Traite Négrière, Islam et Conquête Coloniale* (Paris, 1988). 127; in Charles Becker, "Conditions Ecologiques," and in Richard L. Roberts, *Warriors, Merchants, and Slaves: The State and Economy in the Middle Niger Valley, 1700–1914* (Stanford, 1987).

49 Warrior interpretations of slavery have played a predominant role in recent literature. See Claude Meillassoux, *Anthropologie de l'Esclavage: Le Ventre de Fer et d'Argent* (Paris, 1986). His interpretation turns the economy of production on its head, with predation rather than economic production driving the system. He pays little attention to the role of the middle Niger valley as a center of intensive grain production, strategically located between the desert and the forest belt.

50 Park, *Travels*, 435–41, listed warfare and famine as the most productive causes of enslavement, while noting these other factors.

51 This is one of the questions that provoked contradictory testimony before the House of Commons investigating committee: see the testimony of John Barnes, *House of Commons Sessional Papers*, LXVIII, 7, who denied that Africans went to "war for the express purpose of making Slaves"; and of Charles Wadstrom, ibid., LXXIII, 22–3, who testified that kings went to war "when excited by the French officer and the Mulattoes that accompanied the embassy." Such examples could be multiplied many times over from the testimony gathered.

52 See, for example, Fall, "Recueil," 111–18.

53 On the chronology of the succession crisis, see Victor Martin and Charles Becker, "Les Teeñs de Baol: Essai de Chronologie," *Bulletin d l'IFAN*, 38 (1976) 481–2. For dynastic traditions which treat these conflicts see Yoro Jaw, "Histoire des Damels," in Amadou Duguay-Cledor, *La Bataille de Guile*, (ed. Mbaye Gueye) (Paris, 1985) 157–62.

54 Eventually the military slaves of the Geej dynasty, the *jaami geej*, became a distinct faction capable of influencing the course of events. They are first explicitly described in this way in oral traditions in the reign of Mayssa Tend (1832–55) in Yoro Jaw, "Histoire des Damels," 166.

55 Yoro Jaw, "Histoire des Damels," 158.

56 Ibid., 159–60.

57 Joseph Pruneau, *Mémoire sur le Commerce de la Concession de Sénégal* (Kaolack, 1983) 49.

58 Ibid., 50.

59 Ibid., 49.

60 C 6 14, Lettre, October 16, 1756.

61 See the discussion of his career in Charles Becker, "Le Témoignage de Joseph Pruneau de Pommegorge sur la Traite au 18e Siècle," Communication au Colloque International pour le Tricentenaire du Code Noir, Dakar, July, 1986.

62 [Joseph] Pruneau de Pommegorge, *Description de la Nigritie* (Paris, 1989) 102–3.

63 Ibid., 109.

64 Ibid., 114–17.
65 Brasseur reported that the Alquier of Portudal was "a son of the Damel's slave" and his title Faracaba (Fara-Kaba) was the title of a slave dignitary of Bawol, Charles Becker and Victor Martin, "Détails Historiques et Politiques, Mémoire Inédit (1778) de J. A. Le Brasseur," *Bulletin de l'IFAN*, 39, B, 1 (1977) 97.
66 C 6 14, Lettre, October 16, 1756.
67 C 6 15, Lettre, Gorée, Poncet de la Rivière, May 29, 1764.
68 C 6 15, Gorée, May 8, 1765.
69 C 6 15, Instructions pour le Sieur Pierre De La Courbe, Envoyé à Roi Damel en Cayor, September 21, 1766; Lettre, October 23, 1766.
70 Brasseur, "Détails," 95.
71 Ibid., 95, 97.
72 Ibid., 97.
73 Dynastic traditions suggest that relative stability returned under the reign of Makodu Kumba Jaring (1766–77), the king whose reign coincided with Brasseur's term as Governor of Gorée. See Fall, "Recueil," 122.
74 The most detailed dynastic traditions are Fall, "Recueil," 121–2. For the chronology of the reign see Martin and Becker, "Les Teeñ," 483–5. Written sources on his reign include Doumet in Charles Becker and Victor Martin (eds.) 'Mémoire Inédit de Doumet (1769). Le Kayor et les Pays Voisins au Cours de la Seconde Moitié du XVIIIe Siècle," *Bulletin de l'IFAN*, 36, B (1974) and Brasseur, "Détails." The texts of both Doumet and Brasseur complain of what they perceive as the "mediocrity" of the slave trade in this period, compared to the years of Company rule.
75 Amari Ngone Ndella, elected Dammel-Teeñ in 1790, had been driven into exile by his predecessor and maternal uncle, the Dammel-Teeñ Biram Fatim Penda (1778–90). Amari Ngoone Ndella (1790–1809) in turn exiled his own nephew, Birima Fatma Cubb, but in spite of his efforts to favor his own son the electors chose the exiled nephew as Dammel. Birima Fatma Cubb (1809–32) was in turn replaced by his nephew, Mayssa Tend Joor (1832–55). See dynastic traditions in Fall, "Recueil," 123–7, Yoro Jaw, "Histoire des Damels," 162–7. The systematic preference for nephews suggests a revival of the influence of the council of electors.
76 This is true of the reign of Mayssa Tend Joor (1832–55): Yoro Jaw, "Histoire des Damels," 166.
77 This payment was ten livres per slave to compensate the Company for the cost of maintaining its forts and trading posts in Senegal. See Abdoulaye Ly, *La Compagnie du Sénegal* (Paris, 1958). The Senegal Company changed hands several times, while keeping intact its closely knit board of directors. The Company often combined with larger companies, beginning with the Compagnie des Indes Orientales. See also Stein, *French Slave Trade*, 18–21, 27–9.
78 C 6 13, Mémoire, 1751.
79 Ibid.
80 Curtin, *Economic Change*, 216–17; Webb, "Shifting Sands," 193–4. Gum was also used in the manufacture of paints, glues, and ink, but by far its most important use was in the textile industry.
81 For the text of this treaty see Pruneau, *Mémoire*, 67–9.
82 See Richardson, "New Estimates," Table 7. The one exception was in the decade from 1790 to 1799, when slave exports increased relative to 1780–9. However the increase was modest, from 15,240 slaves (1.9 per cent of total slave exports from Africa) to 18,320 slaves (2.4 per cent of total slave exports).
83 C 6 15, Mémoire sur la Coste d'Affrique, Nantes, May 10, 1766. In fact the Bight of

Benin was by far the most important area of the French slave trade in the first half of the eighteenth century, and in the second half of the century it shared this position with West Central Africa: Richardson, "New Estimates", Table 6, 14.

84 For the decision to downgrade Gorée, C 6 17, Brasseur: Lettre-Mémoire, April 14, 1776, and ibid., Mémoire, December 24, 1776. The war plan to seize Saint Louis is outlined in C 6 17, Mémoire sur la Concession du Sénégal, 1777.

85 This idea is expressed by Pruneau, *Mémoire*, 50, reflecting on the lessons of the civil wars in Kajoor and Bawol.

86 C 6 18, Remarques: Etat en Aperçu des Esclaves, 1783. This document has generated a controversy between Barry, who accepts the evidence, and Curtin, who disputes it. See Barry, *Royaume de Waalo*, 208–11, and his restatement, with new evidence, *Sénégambie*, 111-113, and Curtin, *Economic Change* 126-7. Curtin's main objection seems to be the late date of the most detailed report of these events, but he himself cites evidence that shows that the French believed that the British had instigated the Moor attack on Waalo as early as 1777–8. For a French document which refers to this raid on Waalo see C 6 17, Correspondance: Gorée, April 29, 1777. Barry cites a report by O'Hara that describes Moor military domination of the river on both banks in 1775, *Sénégambie*, 112.

87 "Answers to questions posed to Lt. Col. Maxwell, January 1, 1811," in *British Parliamentary Papers, Colonies, Africa* (Shannon, 1967) I, 152.

88 Brasseur's conflicts with the *habitants* of Gorée are discussed above, chapter 4. For his plans to use the Moors to devastate Kajoor see C 6 17, Correspondance: Gorée, Lettre April 29, 1777, Lettre October 20, 1777. These fantasies tormented Brasseur during the eleven-month trade boycott by Kajoor in 1777–8.

89 C 6 18, Remarques: Etat en Aperçu des Esclaves, 1783.

90 Ibid.

91 Ibid.

92 C 6 18, Sénégal: Mémoire No. 74, February 1783.

93 Ibid.

94 C 6 17, Lettre, Armeny, March 5, 1778.

95 Yoro Jaw, in R. Rousseau, "Le Sénégal d'Autrefois. Etude sur le Oualo. Cahiers de Yoro Dyao," *Bulletin du Comité des Etudes Historiques et Scientifiques sur l'Afrique Occidentale Française*, 12 (1929) 147–8. Yoro Jaw dates the annexation of Tuube and Ganjool earlier, in 1763, but this date is doubtful, because Makodu Kumba Jaring did not come to power in Kajool until 1766, and even after that date he had to fight for his throne on several occasions. On the role of Waalo in Kajoor's civil wars, Yoro Jaw, "Histoire des Damels," 161–2. Yoro Jaw was from Waalo. Kajoor's own dynastic traditions, as presented by Fall, "Recueil," 121–2, minimize the importance of these foreign interventions in Kajoor, but they are confirmed by European sources. James Webb has argued, on the basis of these events, and ascendant Trarza military power in the late eighteenth century, that the Trarza exercised hegemony in Waalo and Kajoor after 1758, where their warriors "were free to pillage at will"; Webb, "Shifting Sands," 106, 107–111.

96 See document cited by Webb, "Shifting Sands," 111–12.

97 See for example C 6 15, Mémoire sur le Sénégal, 1758, which already expresses this position; and C 6 18, Mémoire sur le Commerce du Sénégal, 1783, which argues clearly against the policy of encouraging war between the Moors and the blacks, because of the need to develop the gum trade.

98 Brasseur, "Détails," 98. The development of the royal guard can be traced in dynastic traditions: Fall "Recueil," 122–7.

Notes

99 The most detailed published study of this period, focusing on Fuuta, is David Robinson, "The Islamic Revolution of Futa Toro, *The International Journal of African Historical Studies*, 8, 2 (1975), 185–221. For a slightly different interpretation see Oumar Kane, "Le Fuuta Tooro des Satigi aux Almaani (1512–1807)," thèse par le doctorat d'Etat, Université de Dakar, 1986, II, especially 653–8, 707–8. Kane makes broader use of archival sources, and places the movement in the context of the old regime and Atlantic commerce.

100 This region included the two major ports of Fuuta Tooro in the eighteenth century, Podor and Salde. For a discussion of the geography of the region see Moustapha Kane and David Robinson, *The Islamic Regime of Fuuta Tooro: An Anthology of Oral Tradition Transcribed in Pulaar and Translated into English* (East Lansing, 1984) 1–7. In Kajoor Njambur province and Ganjool were most affected by these developments.

101 C 6 16, Gorée, Lettre, Boniface, March 22, 1773.

102 The reputation of Kajool's monarchy for resistance to Islam, based on the rupture that occurred between 1790 and 1796, has been projected backwards in time. See Lucie Colvin's revisionist essay, "Islam and the state of Kajoor: A Case of Successful Resistance to Jihad," *Journal of African History*, 15, 4 (1974) and Oumar Kane's discussion of Islam in the early monarchy: Oumar Kane, "Fuuta Tooro," I, 369.

103 Doumet, "Le Kayor," 41.

104 Brasseur. "Détails," 97. Brasseur's account of his conflict with Makodu, during the grain boycott of 1777–8, (discussed above, chapter 4), also confirmed the role of marabouts at court, because they were among the hostages seized by the French on Gorée in 1777.

105 See Oumar Kane, "Fuuta Tooro," II, 707–8. The best discussion of Islam in Kajoor in this period is Lucie Colvin, "Kajor and its Diplomatic Relations with Saint-Louis du Sénégal, 1763–1861," unpublished Ph.D. dissertation, Columbia University, 1972, 53–70. Much of this material is discussed in her article, "Islam and the state of Kajoor."

106 For the positive reception of the envoy of Fuuta, see Lucie Colvin, "Islam and the State of Kajoor," 599. On the conflict between Kajoor and Fuuta see Amadou Bamba Diop, "Lat Dior et le Problème Musulman," *Bulletin de l'IFAN*, 28, B (1966), 503–4; Oumar Kane, " Fuuta Tooro," II, 707–8. David Robinson, "The Islamic Revolution of Futa Toro," 204–5, interprets this data to mean that Kajoor, Waalo, and Jolof "submitted" to the Almaami and paid some kind of tribute, on the theory that Fuuta exercised some kind·of regional hegemony after 1786.

107 See Yoro Jaw, "Histoire des Damels," 163; Fall, "Recueil," does not discuss the uprising in Kajoor at all, mentioning only the later war (1795–6) with Fuuta.

108 C 6 20, Lettre: Boucher, August 21, 1790.

109 See Lucie Colvin, "Kajor," 53–70, "Islam and the State of Kajoor," 599. There are slightly different versions of these same traditions in Oumar Kane, "Fuuta Tooro," II, 707–8; Amadou Bamba Diop, 'Lat Dior," 504. These versions differ somewhat in details, but agree on most essentials.

110 Yoro Jaw, "Histoire des Damels," 163, gives a list of the most important marabouts who were captured or killed. For a recent analysis of this conflict see Mamadou Diouf, *Le Kajoor au XIXe Siècle: Pouvoir Ceddo et Conquête Coloniale* (Paris, 1990).

111 The links between the War of the Marabouts and the eighteenth-century Islamic movement in Fuuta Tooro are stressed both by Oumar Kane, "Le Fuuta Tooro," II, 653–8, and David Robinson, "The Islamic Revolution," 190–2, 207. The memory of the War of the Marabouts was conserved in religious schools, the most prominent of which was Pir.

112 The best discussion of Lebu independence is Diouf, *Le Kajoor*, 99–103.

113 Michael Adanson, "A Voyage to Senegal, the Isle of Gorée, and the River Gambia," in

Notes

John Pinkerton, *A General Collection of the Best and Most Interesting Voyages and Travels* . . ., (London, 1814) XVI, 645–6; Doumet, "Le Kayor," 43; Gaspard Mollien in Hubert Deschamps (ed.) *L'Afrique Occidentale en 1818* (Paris, 1967) 64–5.

114 Mollien, ibid.; Diouf, *Le Kajoor*, 99.

115 These sources include the early French colonial investigations of Cap Vert's history. The most important, particularly for its influence on French perceptions of the Lebu is ARS 13 G 304, Gorée: Correspondance au Gouverneur, February 18, 1862, "Note sur la Presqu'île de Cap Vert et les Mesures Prises Jusqu'à ce Jour par le Gouvernement Français à l'Egard de la Presqu'île." This report was prepared by Pinet Laprade. Earlier sources like "Answers to questions Proposed to Lt.-Col. Maxwell (1811)", *British Parliamentary Papers*, I, 154, also stress the importance of leadership, the role of marabouts from Kajoor, and the emergence of the Seriñ Ndakaaru.

116 A good example is "Ndimmalu Njare ci xeexu Yoof ak Kajoor," in Lilyan Kesteloot and Bassirou Dieng, *Du Tieddo au Talibe*, (Paris, 1989) 157–8. This source, which focuses on Yoof, mentions only Lebu elders as playing a leadership role, and stresses not the aid given by Islam, but by Njare, the "spirit" whose cult is practiced in Yoof.

117 "Answers to Questions proposed to Lt.-Col. Maxwell," *British Parliamentary Papers*, 154. Diouf, *Le Kajoor*, 101, dates the beginning of the conflict to 1798, which seems too late.

118 Oral and written sources attribute the end of the conflict to the recognition of Cap Vert's independence by Birama Fatma Cubb (1809–32), but the precise date remains unclear. See the account in 13 G 304, "Note sur la Presqu'île." Diouf, *Le Kajoor*, 103, suggests 1815 on the basis on the visible ruins of villages that remained in 1822.

119 13 G 304, "Note sur la Presqu'île.".

120 "Answers to Questions proposed to Lt.-Col. Maxwell," *British Parliamentary Papers*, 154.

121 Mollien in Deschamps, *L'Afrique Occidentale*, 66–7.

122 See the text of Corry (1807), cited by Raymond Mauny, "Du Nouveau sur les Murs *Tata* de Dakar," *Notes Africaines*, 17 (1943), 14–15 and the discussion of Diouf, *Le Kajoor*, 101–2.

123 "Answers to Questions," *British Parliamentary Papers*, 154.

124 This was the conclusion of Pinet Laprade in 1862: "We were completely unimplicated in the events which led to the separation of Cap Vert from Cayor, and it was by their energy alone that this country freed itself from the Damel." 13 G 304, "Note sur la Presqu'île."

125 "Ndimmalu Njare ci xeexu Yoof ak Kajoor," 158. The use of bees in defense was also a technique used by Sereer villages in the Lower Senegal.

126 "Answers to Questions," *British Parliamentary Papers*, 154.

127 Ibid.

128 Ibid.

129 There are a number of nearly contemporaneous accounts of this conflict. The most detailed is Baron Roger, *Keledor: Histoire Africaine* (Paris, 1829), 32–55. Roger was governor of Senegal when he gathered materials for this book, which he based mainly of the accounts given by Pulaar informants, who were among those enslaved in 1796. His account is highly colored by his sources, and his own "abolitionist" leanings. Mungo Park, *Travels*, gives a nearly contemporary account, since he heard a version from "the singing men" or *griots* of the upper Senegal in 1797. His version is much more favorable to Kajoor, stressing the aggression of the Almaami, and the magnanimous behavior of the Dammel toward his prisoner.

130 Park, *Travels*, 511–13.

131 Amadou Bamba Diop, "Lat Dior," 504. See also the discussion of David Robinson, "The Islamic Revolution," 206–8, Lucie Colvin, "Islam and the State of Kajoor," 600–1.

132 I refer here to the regions most clearly linked to the Lower Senegal. The connection between nineteenth-century jihads and the peanut trade is discussed for the Lower Senegal and Saalum by Martin Klein, "Social and Economic Factors in the Muslim Revolution in Senegambia," *Journal of African History*, 13 (1972) 419–41. The same was true in a different way of the jihad of al Hajj Umar, although his links were mainly to the slave trading and desert-side economy of the middle Niger valley, rather than to the Atlantic trade. See Roberts, *Warriors, Merchants, and Slaves.*

133 The *sofa* of al Hajj Umar were in majority Bambara military slaves who switched allegiance to the new warlord of the region. For a contemporary account of the middle Niger valley in the 1860s see Eugene Mage, *Voyage au Soudan Occidental (1863–66)* (Paris, 1872).

134 The drinking ritual, *xas* in Wolof, and its adaptation by the rebels of Njambur are discussed in Amadou Bamba Diop, "Lat Dior," 504.

6 From river empire to colony: Saint Louis and Senegal, 1800–1860

1 François Valentin, Mémoire sur la Colonie du Sénégal, 1819, quoted in Natalie Reyss, "Saint Louis du Sénégal à l'Epoque Précoloniale. L'Emergence d'une Société Métisse Originale, 1650–1854," thèse de 3e cycle, Université de Paris – I, 2 vols., 1982–3, 159.

2 This story is told from the inside by Abbé Boilat, a *métis* priest trained to carry on the work of Fournier, in Boilat, *Esquisses Sénégalaises* (Paris, 1853) 212–22.

3 This impact has been underestimated by historians who focus exclusively on the import–export trade. In "The Abolition of the Slave Trade from Senegambia," in David Eltis and James Wolvin (eds.) *The Abolition of the Atlantic Slave Trade: Origins and Effects in Europe, Africa, and the Americas* (Madison, 1981), Curtin assumes that the gum trade affected only gum-producing regions. He ignores the millet trade and the urban growth of Saint Louis, both linked to the gum export trade.

4 For an overview of the decline of the slave trade from Senegambia and the rise of a new economy based on "legitimate" exports see Curtin, "The Abolition of the Slave Trade." On the gum trade, James L. A. Webb, Jr., "The Trade in Gum Arabic: Prelude to French Conquest in Senegal," *Journal of African History*, 26 (1985), 149–68.

5 The best history of Saint Louis in this period is Michael David Marcson, "European-African Interaction in the Precolonial Period: Saint Louis, Senegal, 1758–1854," unpublished Ph.D. dissertation, Princeton University, 1976.

6 See for example M. le Baron Roger, *Keledor, Histoire Africaine* (Paris, 1828), "Introduction," vii–x.

7 For a detailed account of the swings in French commercial policy see Marcson, "European-African Interaction," 154–91. Marcson analyzes the tripartite division between French merchants, *habitants*, and free African traders and its relation to the trade crises of the period. Other authors, like Roger Pasquier, "Les Traitants des Comptoirs du Sénégal au Milieu du XIXe Siècle," in *Entreprise et Entrepreneurs en Afrique, XIXe, et XXe Siècles* (Paris, 1983), I, 141–63, stress the conflict between French *négotiants* and African *traitants*. His analysis is based on the terminology used by the French administration in establishing taxes and fees, but these categories are of little use for historical analysis.

8 For discussions of the role of these towns in mid-nineteenth century Senegambia see Monique Chastanet, "Les Crises du Subsistances dans les Villages Soninke du Cercle de Bakel, de 1858 à 1945," *Cahiers d'Etudes Africaines*, 89–90, 23 (1983), 6–9; David

Robinson, *The Holy War of Umar Tal: The Western Sudan in the Mid-Nineteenth Century* (Oxford, 1985) 165–72, 205–14.

9 On the Bight of Biafra see David Northrup, "Nineteenth-century Patterns of Slavery and Economic Growth in South-Eastern Nigeria," *International Journal of African Historical Studies*, 12, 1 (1979), 1–16, where slave exports and palm oil exports overlapped for much of the first half of the century, and where this export trade was linked to the commercialization of food production. On the Bight of Benin see A. G. Hopkins, "Economic Imperialism in West Africa: Lagos, 1890–92," *Economic History Review*, 21, 3 (1968), 580–606; and Patrick Manning, "Slave Trade 'Legitimate' Trade, and Imperialism Revisited: the Control of Wealth in the Bights of Benin and Biafra," in Lovejoy (ed.) *Africans in Bondage: Studies in Slavery and the Slave Trade* (Madison, 1986), 203–33. On the lower Gambia the classic study of transition in exports and labor systems is George E. Brooks, "Peanuts and Colonialism: Consequences of the Commercialization of Peanuts in West Africa, 1830–70," *Journal of African History*, 16, 1 (1975), 29–54. See also, Joyle L. Bowman, ' "Legitimate Commerce' and Peanut production in Portuguese Guinea, 1840s–1880s," *Journal of African History*, 28 (1987), 87–106.

10 James L. A. Webb, "Shifting Sands: An Economic History of the Mauritanian Sahara, 1500–1850," unpublished Ph.D. thesis, Johns Hopkins University, 1974.

11 René Caillié, *Journal d'un Voyage à Temboctou et à Jenne dans l'Afrique Centrale* (Paris, 1829), I, 133–5. Caillié pointed out that although eighteenth-century merchants believed that gum was produced in forests north of the Senegal, the trees were scattered over a wide area. The names Europeans gave to the different forests were the names of the wells that permitted slaves and overseers to live in the desert during the harvest.

12 The conventional description of the gum trade as a one-currency trade based on imported cloth is misleading. Regulations enacted in the 1830s and 1840s established "conversion" rations for gum and millet, and for millet and imported cloth. See Q 18, Compromis pour les Trois Escales pendant 1839, and *Sénégal, Bulletin Administratif des Actes du Gouvernement, 1819–42* (Paris, 1844), No. 13, 1826, Règlement sur les Poids et Mesures.

13 Webb, "Shifting Sands," 204–5.

14 Caillie, *Journal d'un Voyage*, I, 200–6, for a good description of the gum trade in the early nineteenth century.

15 For a valuable discussion of the characteristics of extractive economics, see Stephen G. Bunker, *Underdeveloping the Amazon: Extraction, Unequal Exchange, and the Failure of the Modern State* (Chicago, 1985), 1–76.

16 The first full study of this period was by Georges Hardy, *La Mise en Valeur du Sénégal de 1817 à 1854* (Paris, 1921). See also Marcson, "European-African Interaction," 96–153.

17 See Paul Marty, *L'Emirat des Trarzas* (Paris, 1919), 100–2, for French–Trarza relations. For estimates of the gum trade at Portendick see Webb, "Shifting Sands," 223.

18 On Waalo see Boubacar Barry, *Le Royaume de Waalo. Sénégal avant la Conquête* (Paris, 1972), 237–87. See also Boubacar Barry (ed.), "Mémoire Inédit de Monserat sur l'Histoire du Nord du Sénégal de 1819 à 1839," *Bulletin de l'IFAN*, 32, B, 1 (1970), 1–43.

19 For the agreement that governed this first phase of the plantation project, see ANS 13 G 2, Traité avec Brack et les Principaux Chefs du Royaume du Walo pour la Formation d'Establissements de Culture Libre dans Leurs Pays, May 8, 1819. Although the treaty provided substantial customs to the king and twenty-four members of the court, including some *griots*, the village chiefs only received four bars of iron per laborer, at the completion of the contract.

20 See analysis in Q 16, Rapport de M. Huzard, Fils, sur la Colonie de Sénégal, April 13, 1822.
21 *Sénégal: Bulletin Administratif des Actes du Gouvernement, 1819–1842* (Paris, 1844), 67–9, No. 6, Arrête sur le Régime des Engagés à Temps, September 28, 1823. This text allowed slaves to be imported into the island, on the condition that they were declared and registered.
22 On the Gajaaga trade under the Company see Abdoulaye Bathily, "Guerriers, Tributaires et Marchands, Le Gajaaga (ou Galam) le 'pays de l'or'. Le Développement et la Régression d'une Formation Economique et Sociale Sénégalaise (*c*. 8e–19e siècle)," thèse pour le Doctorat ès Lettres, Université de Dakar, 1985, II, 523–30.
23 The regulations excluded small craft, of the type used by free African traders, from the river ports, and forbade the trade to merchants trading directly with France, which excluded most of the French merchants. Marcson, "European-African Interaction," 128–35.
24 Marcson, 135–7.
25 This company, which existed in varying forms from 1824 to 1848, was dominated by Bordeaux merchants residing in Senegal, sometimes with the participation of the *habitants*. See Eugène Saulnier, *La Compagnie de Galam au Sénégal* (Paris, 1921). For a discussion of the conflicts between French resident merchants, mainly from Bordeaux, and French merchants from Marseilles, who generally favored free trade and free access to the *escales* see Margaret O. McLane, "Commercial Rivalries and French Policy on the Senegal River, 1831–1858," *African Economic History*, 15 (1986), 39–67. The upriver trade brought together diverse merchant groups, Soninke, Moor, French, and *habitant*. Much of the trade was centered at Bakel. See Bathily, "Guerriers, Tributaires et Marchands," II, 517–47.
26 For a discussion of French military recruitment in this period see Claude Faure, "La Garnison Européenne du Sénégal et le Recrutement des Premières Troupes Noires (1779–1858)," *Revue de l'Histoire des Colonies Françaises*, 8 (1920), 5–108.
27 Marty, *L'Emirat des Trarzas*, 104, Marcson, "European-African Interaction," 164–7.
28 S. E. Nicolson, "The Methodology of Historical Climate Reconstruction and its Application to Africa," *Journal of African History*, 20 (1979), 31–50, distinguishes three periods of intense drought in the entire West African region, 1681–7, 1738–56, and 1828–39. Her periodization of climatic trends is useful, but at times the climate is used to explain phenomena (changes in flora and fauna) that resulted as much from human use of the environment as from climate. For a good historical discussion of the relationship of climate, famine, and environment in the central Sudan see Michael Watts, *Silent Violence: Food, Famine and Peasantry in Northern Nigeria* (Berkeley, 1983), 92–147.
29 On the famine in the Cape Verde Islands see K. David Patterson, "Epidemics, Famines, and Population in the Cape Verde Islands, 1580–1900," *International Journal of African Historical Studies*, 21, 2 (1988), 305. Philip Curtin, *Economic Change in Precolonial Africa: Senegambia in the Era of the Slave Trade* (Madison, 1975), II, 4, reports a period of drought and famine in Fuuta Tooro from 1833–7.
30 Michael Adanson, "A Voyage to Senegal the Isle of Gorée, and the River Gambia," in John Pinkerton, *A General Collection of the Best and Most Interesting Voyages and Travels . . .* (London, 1814) XVI, 613.
31 Anne Raffenel described the course of the river between Saint Louis and Richard Toll in 1846–7 as dominated by sand dunes, grasslands, mangrove scrub, and mangrove trees, and noted that the riverbanks were so imbedded with salt that they could not be cultivated until just before Richard Toll. See Anne Raffenel, *Voyage dans l'Afrique*

Occidentale (Paris, 1846), 12–13, and Anne Raffenel, *Nouveau Voyage dans le Pays des Nègres* (Paris, 1856), I, 15.

32 French analyses of the failure of the plantation project always cited a number of ecological factors, in addition to labor problems, and political instability. See 13 G 22, Instructions du Ministre à M. Renault de St. Germain, Gouverneur du Sénégal, April 15, 1831, p. 16.

33 See for example Charles Cottu, "Le Sénégal: Histoire et Situation Actuelle de la Colonie," *Revue des deux mondes* (1845) 270, who described Waalo as being made up of "large flat sterile plains," apart from the rich floodplains. "Everywhere the vegetation struggles vainly against the sea, which devours the soil, and the desert wind, which passes over the plants."

34 On the flight of refugees from Waalo to Saint Louis, see ANF-OM, Sénégal VII, 26, Conseil Privé, December 11, 1832. The movement of entire villages into Kajoor is noted by Yoro Jaw, in R. Rousseau, "Le Sénégal d'Autrefois, Etudo sur le Oualo. Cahiers de Yoro Dyao," *Bulletin du Comité des Etudes Historiques et Scientifiques sur l'Afrique Occidentale Française*, 12 (1929), 148. The ancient village of Kajaar moved into Fuuta at the end of the eighteenth century, Aram Diop, Oumar Ben Khatab Dia, Jean-Claude Galdin, "Cossanu Gaya," in *Jukib Tanneefu Baat-Yu-Sax/Recueil de Textes Choisis* (Dakar, 1975).

35 On the population of Waalo in the 1840s, see E. Bouet-Willaumez, *Commerce et Traite des Noirs aux Côtes Occidentales d'Afrique* (Paris, 1848), 32. The estimate of the number of abandoned villages in the lower valley is made in "Voyages et Expeditions au Sénégal et dans les Contrées Voisines. Le Sénégal, 1447–1860," in *Le Tour de Monde*, 3 (1861), 23. Yoro Jaw's history of Waalo sugests the destruction of many more villages in this period: Yoro Jaw, "Etude sur le Oualo," 148.

36 Caillié, *Voyage à Temboctou*, I, 34–7. Caillié calls the village N'pal, but the identification with Mpaal is clear, based on its location, and on Caillié's account of the protecting "spirit" of the village, 37. This "spirit" manifested itself in a magic rock which protected the village from raids by Moors and *ceddo*: "Maam Kantaar: doju Mpaal," in Lilyan Kesteloot and Cherif Mbodj, *Contes et Mythes Wolof* (Dakar, 1983) 181–3.

37 Caillié, *Voyage à Temboctou*, I, 37–8, "Maam Kantaar," 181.

38 For an analysis of French policy in this period see Marcson, "European-African Interaction," 166–75.

39 Monserat, "Mémoire Inédit," 6, 30, 33, saw the Trarza interst in Kajoor as motivated by their search for grain supplies.

40 Monserat, 'Mémoire Inédit," 22, 24, 30, 32, for accounts of French raids on Waalo villages, destruction of crops, and raids on livestock, followed by massive emigration.

41 Marcson, "European-African Interaction," 167–8.

42 Ibid., 168–75.

43 Cottu, "Le Sénégal," 259.

44 Cottu, "Le Sénégal," 275, 282. In the eighteenth century peak exports reached about 1,500 English tons.

45 For discussions of the crisis see Webb, "Trade in Gum Arabic," 164–7, who stresses the inflation in *guinée* prices and European control of supply, and Pasquier, "Les Traitants des Comptoirs," 142–7, who emphasizes free trade and merchant competition.

46 Cottu, "Le Sénégal," 282–3. See also Bouet-Willaumez, *Commerce et Traite*, 14–15, Webb, "Trade in Gum Arabic," and Marcson, "European-African Interaction," 175–85.

47 There were 107 male slaves on Gorée in 1847 employed as weavers. Given the abundance of imported and local cloth, this specialization was required only to make use of the thread produced by 1,407 women slaves. 3 G 2/124, Gorée: Etat Civil Pièce 2, 1847.

48 ANS, 0 3, Navigation et Marine, 1819–39, Pièce 8, 1825.

49 Ibid.

50 0 3, Navigation et Marine, Gorée: marine Locale, 1826, and ibid., Pièce 8.

51 This problem was analyzed by J. Dagorne, a French naval officer, in 0 3, Navigation et Marine, Projet d'Amélioration pour la Marine Coloniale, Gorée, July 10, 1839.

52 Ibid.

53 By the middle of the nineteenth century commerce was the only occupation regarded as suitable for a free black from Saint Louis. For a discussion of the identity of Saint Louisians as merchants see Frederic Carrère and Paul Holle, *De la Sénégambie Française* (Paris, 1855) 11–13.

54 This pattern appears in the various regulations governing the gum trade, particularly in the measures taken to prevent millet traders from purchasing gum. These restrictions supported the position of the *habitants*: Q 18, Compromis pour les Trois Escales pendant 1839, 1840. A decree of December 23, 1840 required millet traders to sell their millet to gum traders to prevent them from trading directly for gum.

55 These millet traders were often called *marigotiers*, because they worked the smaller tributaries of the Senegal, where they purchased grain.

56 K 7, Notes sur l'Affranchissement des Captifs, Guillet, January 29, 1836.

57 K 8, Letter No 149, Ministre de la Marine à Gouverneur, Paris, June 17, 1844.

58 13 G 22, Mémoire Laissée par M. Thomas, December 11, 1845. The data in this census dates from 1844.

59 Cottu, "Le Sénégal," 262–3.

60 K 8, Rapport: Esclavage et Engagements à Temps, January 22, 1846.

61 Many of the records of the *état civil* on Gorée were maintained by missionaries and priests. By contrast the *habitants* of Saint Louis were notorious for their non-compliance with European efforts to keep records. This resistance was based on the council of the marabouts of Saint Louis and its immediate vicinity.

62 The document distinguishes 286 *marins* and 26 *laptots*. The distinction between *marins* and *laptots* appeared in the 1840s. This latest shift in the meaning of *laptot* reserved the term for skilled boatmen, such as pilots and boat captains, as opposed to ordinary sailors.

63 3 G 2/124, Gorée: Etat Civil, Pièce 2, 1847.

64 Ibid.

65 Ibid.

66 This was determined by comparing the data provided by the surveys of the maritime labor force in 0 3, Navigation et Marine, 1819–39 with the census data on Saint Louis in 13 G 22, Mémoire Laissée par M. Thomas, December 11, 1845. It is striking that almost all the detailed information on slave holdings in K 9, Emancipation: 1849, and other files in the K series relates to Gorée.

67 This data is based on the records in K 9, Emancipation: 1849, July 10, 1849, and K 10, Emancipation: 1849.

68 A list of the most important slave owners on Saint Louis in 1842 includes Elisa Pellegrin (fifteen slaves), Charlotte Pellegrin (seventy-four slaves), Charles Pellegrin (ten slaves), Madame Jerome Pellegrin (forty-nine slaves), the "widow" Pellegrin (forty-three slaves), and Betty Pellegrin (twenty-six slaves). See the data presented by Natalie Reyss, "Saint-Louis," 144–50, based on a study of marriage contracts and wills.

69 K 9, Emancipation: 1849, Dominga Panet.

70 Ibid., Aubon.

71 The census data are recorded in a different form: one birth for every twenty-seven slaves, one birth for every thirty-two free blacks.

72 3 G 2/124, Goree: Etat Civil, Pièce 2, Etat des Naissances, Décès et Marriages pendant l'Année 1847. This data relates to a total population of 3,645 slaves: 574 boys under

fourteen, 671 girls under fourteen, 967 men between the ages of fourteen and sixty, 1,394 women between the ages of fourteen and sixty, 7 male slaves over the age of sixty, and 32 women over the age of sixty.

73 3 G 2/66 Gorée: Etat Civil, Naissances et Décès des Captifs de Gorée de 1835 à 1839. The sample of 100 was taken from the years 1835 and 1836, where the data was most complete. The sample of 100 included 7 percent where age could not be determined. These are not included in the percentages given, but form part of the complete sample used.

74 The data for 1832 is given in Curtin, *Economic Change*, II, 42, that for 1847 is from 3 G 2/124, Gorée: Etat Civil, Pièce 2.

75 Curtin, *Economic Change*, II, 41; Cottu, "Le Sénégal," 262–3.

76 See the letter from the "chiefs of Gandiole" (Ganjool) to Saint Louis, written in 1848. "We inform you that our slaves are revolting to run to Saint Louis and demand their liberty. We bought them from the *habitants* of Saint Louis at the time when they were pursued for debts." In 13 G 256, Cayor: Correspondance, Chemise 1848.

77 3 G 2/124, Tableau de la Population du 31 Decembre 1849, Recensement de la Population Captive au 15 Juillet 1848, Pièce 3, Note October 16, 1848.

78 Runaways appear on individual lists of slave holdings submitted by the *habitants* in hopes of receiving compensation. The list of Frances de Saint John, one of the largest slave owners, with 111 slaves, included 17 runaways, slightly more than 16 percent of all slaves: K 9, Emancipation: 1849, July 10, 1849, Frances de Saint John.

79 According to Ousmane Sane, "La Vie Economique et Sociale des Goréens entre 1817 et 1848," Université de Dakar, thèse de 3e cycle, 1978, 197–8.

80 On Gorée immigration was insignificant compared to Saint Louis, so the movement of former slaves into the free population must have accounted for a significant portion of the expansion of the latter group. All census material on Saint Louis and Gorée from the 1830s and 1840s notes the presence of freed slaves.

81 Curtin, *Economic Change*, II, 41.

82 Ibid., 42, (for 1832), 3 G 2/124, with census data on 1845, 1847, and 1848.

83 The "illegally imported slaves" were listed separately in the census data for 1847. 3 G 2/124, Gorée: Tableau de la Population au 31 Decembre 1847.

84 This "illegal slave trade" was discussed at length in an article in the *Moniteur du Sénégal et Dépendances*, II, No. 90, December 15, 1857.

85 This is one of the main topics of discussion in the collection of essays edited by Claire C. Robertson and Martin A. Klein, *Women and Slavery in Africa* (Madison, 1983).

86 I have calculated this figure by estimating the proportion of slaves over "thirty" by using the information on slave mortality for the years 1835–7.

87 Put simply an adult female slave in her mid-thirties could easily have one or more children counted as "adults" as well as offspring counted as "children."

88 The birth and death rates of Gorée conform closely to data for preindustrial cities in Europe. For example in seventeenth-century London the death rate exceeded the birth rate by ten per 1,000 (1 percent), and the crude birth rate was thirty-four per 1,000. On Gorée the death rate exceeded the birth rate by roughly the same proportion and the crude birth rate was thirty-seven per 1,000. See Roger Finlay, *Population and Metropolis: The Demography of London, 1580–1650* (Cambridge, 1981), 8–9, and Jan de Vries, "The Population and Economy of the Preindustrial Netherlands," in Robert I. Rotberg and Theodore K. Rabb (eds.) *Population and Economy: Population and History from the Traditional to the Modern World* (Cambridge, 1986), 109. In preindustrial cities disease was the main factor behind the excess of deaths over births.

89 K 9, Emancipation: 1849, Etat Nominatif.

90 K 10, Etat Nominatif, Pécarrère Frères.

91 For Gorée, the information of age structure is from 3 G2/66, Gorée: Etat Civil. Naissances et Décès des Captifs de Gorée de 1836 a 1839.

92 This is particularly clear in the last major study of slavery by the administration before 1848: K 8, Esclavage et Engagments à Temps, Rapport, January 22, 1846.

93 There are a number of studies of slave emancipation on Saint Louis and Gorée: M'Baye Gueye, "La Fin de l'Esclavage à Saint-Louis et à Gorée en 1848," *Bulletin de l'IFAN*, 28, B (1968), 637–56; Roger Pasquier, "A Propos de l'Emancipation des Esclaves au Sénégal en 1848," *Revue Française d'Histoire d'Outre-Mer*, 54 (1967), 188–208; Marcson, "European-African Interaction," 219–41. The interest in this topic contrasts with the neglect of slavery itself on the islands in the first half of the nineteenth century.

94 This was the result of Article 7 of the emancipation decree: "The principle that the soil of France frees the slave who touches it, is applied to the colonies and possessions of the Republic." This principle of law had developed in the eighteenth century to prevent the extension of colonial slavery to metropolitan France. For a discussion of its effects in Senegal, see François Renault, "L'Abolition de l'Esclavage au Sénégal: L'Attitude de l'Administration Française (1848–1905)," *Revue Française d'Histoire d'Outre-Mer*, 59 (1971), 5–12.

95 K 8, Correspondance: Avril–Mai 1848, Lettre, Saint Louis, April 25, 1848.

96 K 8, Correspondance: Avril–Mai 1848, Lettre No. 115, Paris, Ministre à Sénégal, April 18, 1849.

97 2 B 27, Folio 120, Du Chateau à Ministre, June 10, 1848.

98 For a good discussion of these incidents, M'Baye Gueye, "La Fin de l'Esclavage," 642–3.

99 Marcson, "European-African Interaction," 229.

100 2 B 27, Folio 132, Du Chateau à Ministre, July 25, 1848.

101 Ibid.

102 The best discussion of this affair is M'Baye Gueye, "La Fin de l'Esclavage," 643; see also Marcson, "European-African Interaction," 230.

103 M'Baye Gueye, "La Fin de l'Esclavage," 643; Pasquier, "A Propos de l'Emancipation," 193.

104 M'Baye Gueye, "La Fin de l'Esclavage," 644; Marcson, "European-African Interaction," 230–2.

105 Skilled slaves, such as *laptots*, rented their labor for thirty francs a month, half of which was paid to the master. Although most slaves so employed were not employed throughout the year, the indemnity was only a fraction of a skilled slave's value.

106 2 B 31, Lettre No. 287, Protêt, June 8, 1852. Although some of this reduction was legitimate, much of it was more dubious. *Habitants* out of favor found it more difficult to prove their claims, as did Muslims with no documentation. The French claimed that many slaves were really indentured servants, or were illegally imported after 1823, and refused to pay compensation. There was often little proof one way or another of these various claims.

107 The best study of the financial aspects of emancipation is Pasquier, "A Propos de l'Emancipation," 199–205.

108 Pasquier, ibid., 203–7.

109 Carrère and Holle, *De La Sénégambie*, 14–16.

110 Boilat, *Esquisses,* 211.

111 Ibid., 213.

112 By the late 1850s peanut exports formed a significant portion of total exports in value: for example in 1859 peanut exports were 8,629 metric tons, with a value of 2,243,712 francs out of total exports valued at 4,005,000 francs. The proportion of peanuts in overall trade during the period of war from 1854 to 1860 averaged over 50 percent. For

these figures see *Revue Algérienne et Coloniale*, 2 (1860), 94–6, and Oskar Lenz, *Timbuktu: Reise durch Morokko die Sahara und den Sudan* (Leipzig, 1884), II, 348. Lenz got his figures from Governor Brière de l'Isle.

113 Marcson, "European-African Interaction," 194.

114 See Mohamed Mbodj, "D'une Frontière à l'Autre, ou l'Histoire de la Marginalisation des Commerçants Sénégambiens sur la Longue Durée: La Gambie de 1816 à 1979," 12–15, paper presented at "Colloque: Les Grands Commerçants Africains," April 30–May 4, 1990, Dakar, Senegal.

115 The standard accounts of the beginnings of peanut cultivation are Brooks, "Peanuts and Colonialism," and Ken Swindell, "Serawoollies, Tillibunkas and Strange Farmers: The Development of Migrant Groundnut Farming Along the Gambia River, 1848–95," *Journal of African History*, 21, 1 (1980), 93–104. Brooks emphasizes the role of Atlantic merchants, while Swindell focuses on the role of migrant merchants and laborers from the upper Gambia and upper Senegal. Swindell seems unaware that this pattern continued eighteenth-century practices which supplied millet to the slave trade.

116 For a discussion of this practice see Curtin, *Economic Change*, I, 230–1, and Manchuelle, "Slavery, Emancipation, and Labour Migration," 92–4.

117 This general analysis of the patterns of trade is based on the detailed month-by-month data on the river trade published in the *Moniteur du Sénégal et Dépendances* in 1857 and 1858. These reports are discontinued thereafter. The interest of these sources is that they give a month by month breakdown of the trade between Saint Louis and the major regions of the river.

118 The gum was supplied by the Idaw Aish Moors (*Dowiche* in French sources). On the trade at Bakel see Bathily, "Guerriers, Tributaires, et Marchands," II, 523–30; Saulnier, *Compagne de Galam*. After the mid-1860s some of this trade shifted to Medine. For a discussion of the trade in the 1860s and 1870s see John H. Hanson, "Generational Conflict in the Umarian Movement after the Jihad: Perspective from the Futanke Grain Trade at Medine," *Journal of African History*, 31, 2 (1990), 203–5.

119 This has been a common assumption, based on the idea that Fuuta had the advantage of two millet crops, one from rainfall agriculture, and another from the floodplain of the riverbanks (called the *waalo* in both Wolof and Pulaar). Pasquier, "Le Ravitaillement des Villes du Sénégal," 185, reaches the same conclusion, but supports his judgement by quoting French officials.

120 The figures tabulated in the text do not include the imports from Dagana, which supplied an additional 68.3 tons, bringing total imports to 2,068.8 metric tons. Pasquier, "Le Ravitaillement des Villes," 181, calculated annual consumption of millet at 127.75 kilograms per person, based on a ration of 350 grams a day. By this figure the recorded imports of Saint Louis in these twelve months exceeded the estimated consumption of a population of 14,000 (1,787.8 tons) by about 80 metric tons. Census data from 1858 indicated a population of 14,048 for Saint Louis, including the "suburbs" of Guet Ndar, Ndar Toute, and Bouet-Ville (on the island of Sor). See M. Courtet, *Etude sur le Sénégal* (Paris, 1903), 138.

121 Pasquier's study shows that about 450 tons of rice and approximately the same amount of wheat flour were imported into Saint Louis and Gorée in the 1850s, and that the consumption of these grains far exceeded the needs of the European population: Pasquier, "Le Ravitaillement des Villes," 182.

122 For a sampling of Bakel's millet exports to Saint Louis in the 1850s and 1860s, see Pasquier, "Le Ravitaillement des Villes," 185.

123 This overland trade still had to cross the river from Sor. But there were many small craft to ferry traders and producers selling their own goods, and French commercial statistics did not include the traffic between Sor and Saint Louis as part of the river traffic.

124 Q 24, Lettre, March 23, 1869, signed Deves, Chaumet, Delmas, Maurel et Prom, etc.
125 I have used the figures on Kajoor's exports for 1858 given in 3 E 29, Procès-verbaux du Conseil d'Administration du Sénégal, February 28, 1861, which indicates 7,936 tons in 1858 and 6,179 tons in 1859. This probably included Kajoor's exports from Rufisque, which averaged about 1,500 metric tons in this period: Jean Adam, *L'Arachide: Culture, Produits, Commerce, Amélioration de la Production* (Paris, 1908), 124.
126 For peanut exports from Bakel from 1840 to 1853, see Saulnier, *La Compagnie de Galam*, 187.
127 Robinson, *Holy War*, 233–40, documents the serious nature of this famine and its toll in lives. Curiously, he attributes the decline of French trade "in gum and other products" from 1854 to 1858 to Umar's boycott. There is no evidence for this. The decline in French trade was mainly caused by the war with the Trarza from 1854 to 1858, and the decline in gum exports from the lower river.
128 The only years when Bakel's gum trade exceeded this figure were 1850, 1851, and 1852: see Saulnier, *Compagnie de Galam*, 187. The rapid expansion of gum exports from Bakel from 1848 to 1853 occurred during a period of drought and failing rains in the upper valley, from 1846 to 1853: Curtin, *Economic Change*, II, 4. This suggests that desert demand for grain in this period increased the rate of gum extraction, as occurred in the desert borderlands of the lower river valley in the 1830s.
129 The best study of this alliance is Leland Barrows, "The Merchants and General Faidherbe: Aspects of French Expansion in Senegal in the 1850s," *Revue Française d'Histoire d'Outre-Mer*, 61 (1974) 236–83.
130 The domination of the Trarza in the lower river in this period was documented by Raffenel, *Voyage*, 5–30, who noted that every village between Maka (in Waalo) and Fanaye (in Dimar, western Fuuta) paid tribute to the Trarza. For a discussion of the emergence of the Umarian jihad in the upper river, see Robinson, *Holy War*, 138–60.
131 This is the major argument of Barrows, "The Merchants and General Faidherbe."
132 Webb, "Shifting Sands," 116, quoting from an oral informant from one of the major *zawaya* groupings.
133 Although he discusses a later period, Hanson, "Generational Conflict," documents the tensions generated by Umarian recruitment drives in areas with important commercial links with Medine.
134 Faidherbe to Minister, quoted in Pasquier, "Les Traitants des Comptoirs," 161.
135 Marty, *L'Emirat des Trarzas*, 116–19.
136 Barrows, "The Merchants and Faidherbe," makes it clear that the model which the merchants wanted to avoid was represented by the French conquest of Algeria.
137 *Montieur du Sénégal et Dépendances*, No. 49, March 5, 1857.
138 2 B 32, Folio 154, Lettre No. 471, Gouverneur au Ministre, October 13, 1859.

Conclusion

1 Faidherbe, "Notice Historique sur le Cayor," *Bulletin de la Société de Géographie de Paris* (1883), 528–9.
2 1 D 11, Expédition du N'Diambour (Affaires de N'Guick, M'Birama et Niomre), 1858.
3 13 G 255, Cayor: Correspondance avec les Chefs Indigènes, Lettre: Serigne Gnomeray, Chef du Ghiambour (arabic original with French translation), February 26, 1835.
4 Ibid., Lettre 1840, n.d.
5 Abbé David Boilat, *Esquisses Sénégalaises* (Paris, 1853) 171.
6 Ibid., 170.
7 Ibid., 346.
8 On the dispute over Mbuur see 13 G 256, Cayor: Correspondance, Chemise 1850. On

the early organization of what became the *cercle* of Gorée-Dakar, see 13 G 304, Gorée Correspondance, 1862.

9 On Jander province see 1 D 11, Compte Rendu des Diverses Excursions Faites dans le Diander, Capitaine Millet, March 9, 1861,

10 One reason for the neglect of the eighteenth century and the overemphasis on the new and revolutionary conditions created by the peanut trade is the false assumption that the monarchy was able to monopolize the benefits of eighteenth-century Atlantic commerce. See Lucie Colvin, "Kajor and its Diplomatic Relations with Saint-Louis du Sénégal, 1763–1861," unpublished Ph.D. dissertation, Columbia University, 1972, 293–5; Martin A. Klein, "Social and Economic Factors in the Muslim Revolution in Senegambia," *Journal of African History*, 13 (1972), 419–41. The difference was one of degree, not of kind.

11 Richardson's estimate of the total Senegambian slave trade for the eighteenth century is 336,880, but less than half of that number passed through the Senegal River valley. Since my research suggests an upward revision of estimates based on shipping date, I have allowed for a substantial undercount in making this rough estimate of the trade.

12 K 16, Pièce 45, Tableau: Etat Synoptique des Renseignments Farnis par les Commandants de Cercle sur le Régime de la Captivité dans l'AOF. This data is discussed in more detail in chapter 2.

13 See Bernard Moitt, "Slavery and Emancipation in Senegal's Peanut Basin: The Nineteenth and Twentieth Centuries," *International Journal of African Historical Studies*, 22 (1989), 32–6; Bernard Moitt, "Peanut Production and Social Change in the Dakar Hinterland: Kajoor and Bawol, 1840–1940," Ph.D. dissertation, University of Toronto, 1985, 218–26; Martin A. Klein, "Emancipation of Slaves, Agricultural Colonization and Labor Migration in 20th Century Senegal," Paper presented at the school of Advanced International Studies, Johns Hopkins University, April, 1987, 3–7.

14 Moitt, "Peanut Production," 218, 226, citing Martin Klein's summary of colonial reports from Bakel and Medine in 1888–9, and quoting Deherme, K 25, L'Esclavage en AOF, 208.

15 Slave caravans were active in the peanut basin in this period, but the formation of the colonial state already impeded their movement, for a number of reasons. See K 13, Captifs: Affaire de Traite, Sénégal, 1893–4. This topic is too complex to be discussed fully here. I am presenting the conclusions of research that will be discussed more fully elsewhere.

16 See Martin A. Klein and Richard Roberts, "The Banamba Slave Exodus of 1905 and the Decline of Slavery in the Western Sudan," *Journal of African History*, 21 (1980).

17 Any estimate of this kind depends on the assumptions that one makes about the demography of slave populations, including the importance of runaways and manumissions. Comparative quantitative data for slave societies in the Americas is summarized by David Eltis, "Free and Coerced Transatlantic Migrations: Some Comparisons," *American Historical Review*, 88, 2 (1983), 278. A model like the British West Indies would suggest a 2 : 1 ratio between slave imports and slave populations; the French, Dutch, and Danish West Indies a nearly 3 : 1 ratio; Brazil approximately 1 : 1; while the US is alone with a ratio close to 1 : 3. What scanty evidence exists suggests that West Africa's slave populations did not reproduce themselves and required new slave imports to sustain their numbers.

Index

Abdul Qaadir, Almaami, 119, 157, 161
Adanson, Michel, 4, 56, 66–7, 93, 105, 107, 108, 140, 142, 143, 172
agriculture, 3
  centrality of, 43, 150, 155
Agui, Samba, 185
Amari Ngoone Ndella, Dammel-Teeñ (1790–1809), 157, 159, 161
Amari Ngoone Sobel, 12–16, 149

Bakel, 188, 189, 191, 192
Bambara, 29, 61, 183
Bandia, 26–7
Barry, Boubacar, 29
Bawol, 6, 7, 9
  independence of, 12–13
  and Wolof old regime, 18–19
Biraam Fatim Penda, Dammel (1778–1790), 157
Boilat, David (Abbé), 2, 57, 105, 126, 195
Bordeaux, 163
Boulègue, Jean, 14, 25
Brakna, 72, 190
Brasseur, 109, 110, 111, 149
Brüe, André, 23, 28, 66, 68, 100

Cadamosto, 36, 63
Callié, René, 173
Cape Verde Islands, 132, 133, 171
Cap Vert peninsula (see also Lebu), 4, 7, 73, 93
  French attempts to purchase, 148
  independence of, 131
  Islamic reform in, 158
  and trade with Atlantic world, 162
Casamance, 111
"caste" (ñeeño), 8, 16, 38–41
cattle, 4, 15, 19, 30, 33, 62, 67, 69, 137
ceddo ("slave warriors"), 24, 29, 123, 147, 157, 158, 159, 162, 192, 193, 194

Chambonneau, Louis Moreau de, 25, 89
climate, 3, 5
Compagnie de Galam, 170, 171
Compagnie de la Guyane, 112, 154
Compagnie des Indes Occidentales, 23, 64, 65, 95, 151
credit, role of, 28
Curtin, Philip, 29, 44, 132
customs (tax), 71–4
  abolished by French, 192

Dalrymple, Henry, 35, 50, 71
deforestation, 5, 172
disease (see also yellow fever), 67, 97–8, 180, 183
Doumet, 34, 35, 50
drought, 80, 131, 132–3, 134, 136, 156, 168, 171
  and gum extraction, 168

ecology
  changes in, 4–6
  and commerce, 4
  crises in, 131–3
  and ethnicity, 1–3
  emancipation in Saint Louis and Gorée (see also slavery), 183–7
    compensation for, 185–6
    French attitudes to, 184
    ruin of habitants caused by, 186–7
    tensions between masters and slaves caused by, 185
environmental change, 172

Faal patrilineage and monarchy, 14, 16
Faidherbe, 10, 190, 191, 192, 193, 194
famine, 79–80, 81, 83, 136–9
  and slave exports, 31, 33, 81, 136, 137–8
  of 1750–6, 132–9
  and Kajoor civil wars, 141, 143

247

Index

248

Index

Sereer, 2–3, 14, 196
  in Bawol, 18–19
  independence of, 36, 37
  origin myths of, 2
  Saafen, 9, 36–7
  in slave trade, 35–9
  social order, 9
Seven Years War, 106, 112, 129
signares, 77, 93, 96, 97, 98–101, 107, 108,
    117, 142
Siin, 8, 11, 12, 119
  slave exports from, 31, 32
slave caravans, 30, 59
slave exports (*see also* famine), 30–4, 135,
    136, 152
  decline of, 129, 130, 152
  from Gajaaga (nineteenth century), 170
  from Lower Senegal, 30–3
  from Senegambia, 34
  sex ratios in, 53
slave prices, in Lower Senegal, 33, 68
  rise in, 110
slave raids, 33–5
  European perceptions of, 28–9, 38
  and independent Sereer, 35–8
  Kajoor monarchy, role in, 34, 38
slave revolts (*see also* Gorée), 147–8, 156
slavery (*see also* Saint Louis and Gorée), 28
  census data (Senegal) for, 50, 198–9
  differentiation in slave population, 52–3
  and grain production, 50–1
  master–slave relations, 54
  as labor system, 47–8, 54–8
  resistance to, 2–3
  royal slaves, 16, 17, 20, 21, 23, 42–3,
    146–7, 148, 149, 195
  on Saint Louis and Gorée, 94, 95
  and slave trade, 45–6, 198–9
  slave warriors, 21–2, 145
  women slaves, 53–4
Soninke (*see also* Gajaaga), 59

laptots, 192
merchants, 188
sugar production
  and slave exports, 27, 65, 129

Takrur, 7, 8, 11
Thevenot, Charles, 106, 114, 124
traders, free African (*see also* Saint Louis),
    166, 169, 171, 178
Trarza, 72, 75, 76, 134, 153, 155, 170, 171,
    172, 173, 191
  boycott of gum trade by, 191
  domination of lower river valley by, 175
  invasion of Wallo by, 153
  French–Trarza War (1833–5), 173–4
  French–Trarza War (1854–8), 191–2

Umar, al-Hajj, 88, 162, 188, 191, 192
Umarian jihad, 190, 191

Valentin, François, 163
Valentin, Pierre, 128

Waalo, 11, 72, 153, 154, 155, 165, 169–70,
    171, 172, 173
  alliance wth Trarza, 173
  depopulation of, 173
  destruction of, 155
  and plantation experiment, 169–70
warfare, 22, 29, 144–5, 152, 153
  European encouragement of, 154
  and slave trade, 152–3
Wolof
  and arid savanna ecology, 6
  dynastic traditions, 9–10
  folktales, 15
  founding myths, 6
  kingship, 10–11
  in slave exports, 31
  social order, 8
  village communities,7

yellow fever, 97, 115

250

OTHER BOOKS IN THE SERIES